M000026019

Death Before Glory

Death Before Glory

*The British Soldier in the West Indies in the
French Revolutionary and Napoleonic Wars
1793–1815*

MARTIN R. HOWARD

Pen & Sword
MILITARY

First published in Great Britain in 2015 by
PEN AND SWORD MILITARY
an imprint of
Pen and Sword Books Ltd
47 Church Street
Barnsley
South Yorkshire S70 2AS

Copyright © Martin R. Howard 2015

ISBN 978 1 78159 341 7

The right of Martin R. Howard to be identified
as the author of this work has been asserted by him
in accordance with the Copyright, Designs and Patents Act 1988.

A CIP record for this book is available from the British Library.

All rights reserved. No part of this book may be reproduced or transmitted
in any form or by any means, electronic or mechanical including
photocopying, recording or by any information storage and retrieval
system, without permission from the Publisher in writing.

Printed and bound in England by
CPI Group (UK) Ltd, Croydon, CR0 4YY

Typeset in Times by CHIC GRAPHICS

Pen & Sword Books Ltd incorporates the imprints of
Pen & Sword Books Ltd incorporates the imprints of Pen & Sword
Archaeology, Atlas, Aviation, Battleground, Discovery,
Family History, History, Maritime, Military, Naval, Politics,
Railways, Select, Social History, Transport, True Crime,
Claymore Press, Frontline Books, Leo Cooper, Praetorian Press,
Remember When, Seaforth Publishing and Wharncliffe.

For a complete list of Pen and Sword titles please contact
Pen and Sword Books Limited
47 Church Street, Barnsley, South Yorkshire, S70 2AS, England
E-mail: enquiries@pen-and-sword.co.uk
Website: www.pen-and-sword.co.uk

Contents

Acknowledgements

The staffs at the British Library, London, and the National Army Museum, London, have given me valuable assistance. I am grateful to Rupert Harding, Ian Robertson and Jamie Wilson for their support and advice.

List of Illustrations

List of Maps

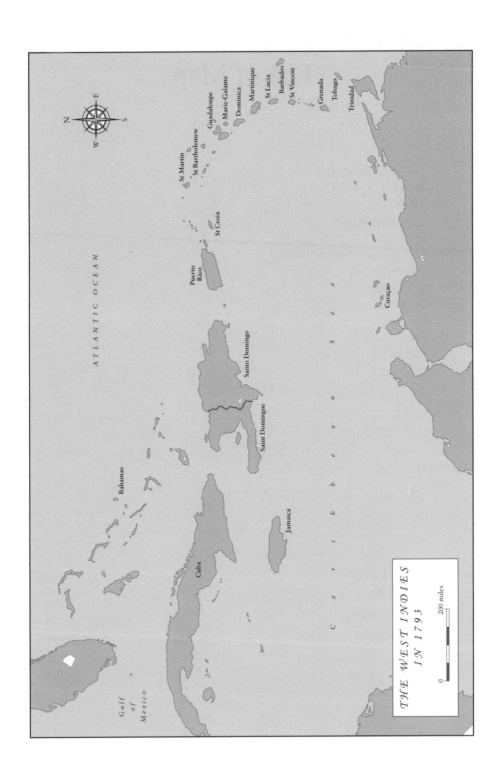

THE WEST INDIES
IN 1793

0   200 miles

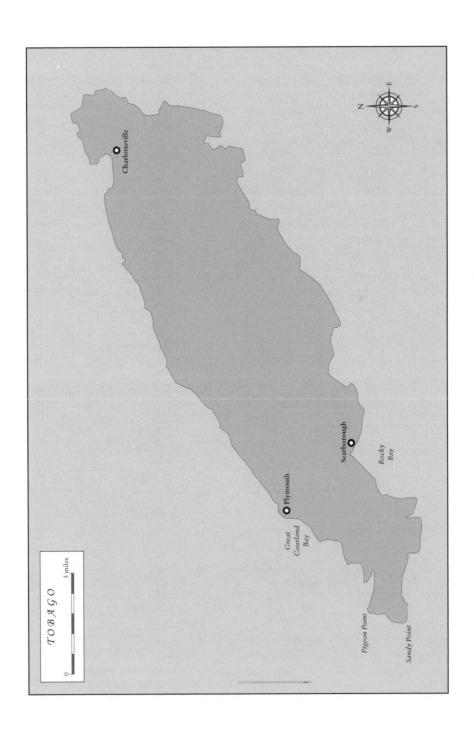

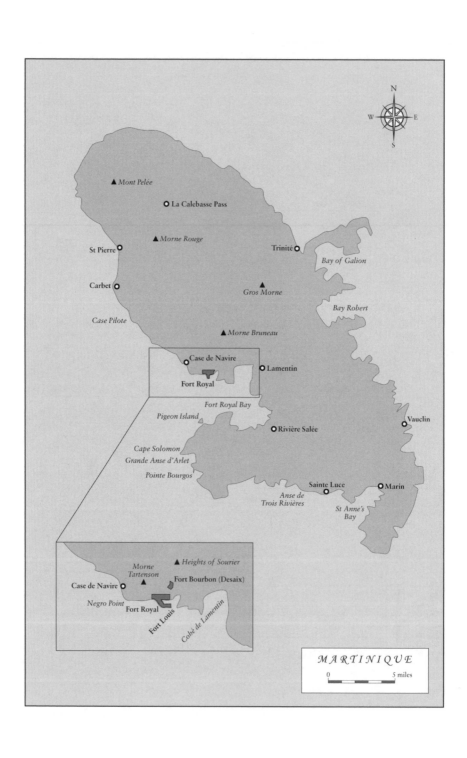

▲ Mont Pelée

○ La Calebasse Pass

▲ Morne Rouge

St Pierre ○

Trinité ○

Bay of Galion

Carbet ○

▲
Gros Morne

Bay Robert

Case Pilote

▲ Morne Bruneau

○ Case de Navire

○ Lamentin

Fort Royal

Fort Royal Bay

Pigeon Island

○ Rivière Salée

○ Vauclin

Cape Solomon
Grande Anse d'Arlet

Pointe Bourgos

Sainte Luce ○

○ Marin

*Anse de
Trois Rivières*

*St Anne's
Bay*

▲ *Heights of Sourier*

*Morne
Tartenson*
▲

Fort Bourbon (Desaix)

Case de Navire ○

Negro Point   Fort Royal

Fort Louis

Cohe de Lamentin

MARTINIQUE

0   5 miles

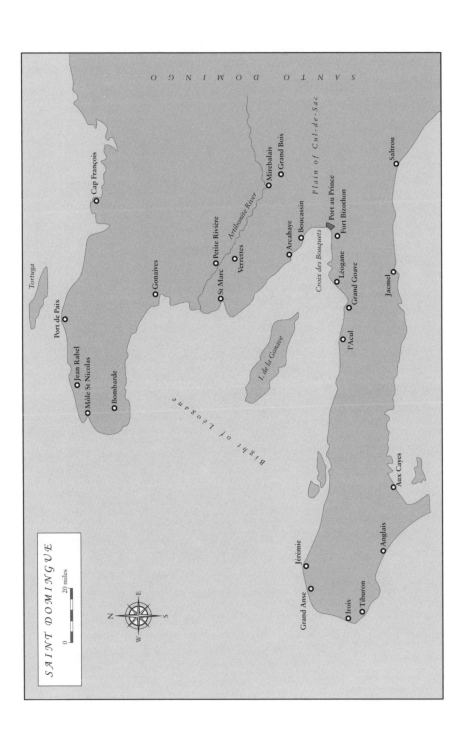

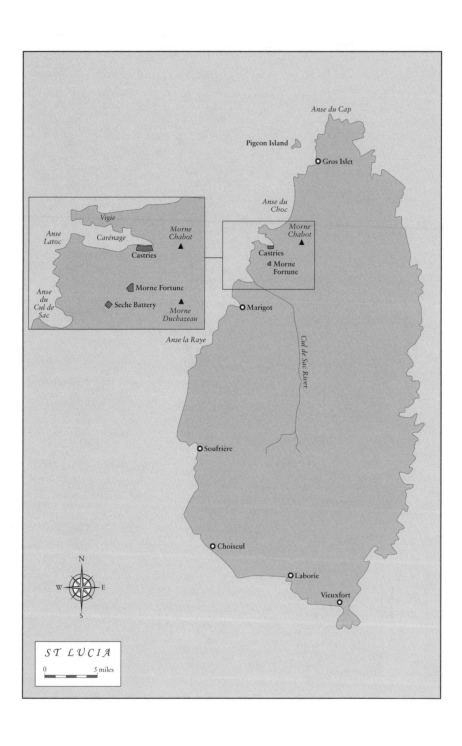

Anse du Cap

Pigeon Island

Gros Islet

Anse du Choc

Vigie

Anse Latoc

Carénage

Castries

Morne Chabot ▲

Morne Chabot ▲

Castries

◁ *Morne Fortune*

Anse du Cul de Sac

■ Morne Fortune

Seche Battery ◆

▲ *Morne Duchazeau*

Marigot

Anse la Raye

Cul de Sac River

Soufrière

Choiseul

Laborie

Vieuxfort

N
W ✦ E
S

ST LUCIA

0   5 miles

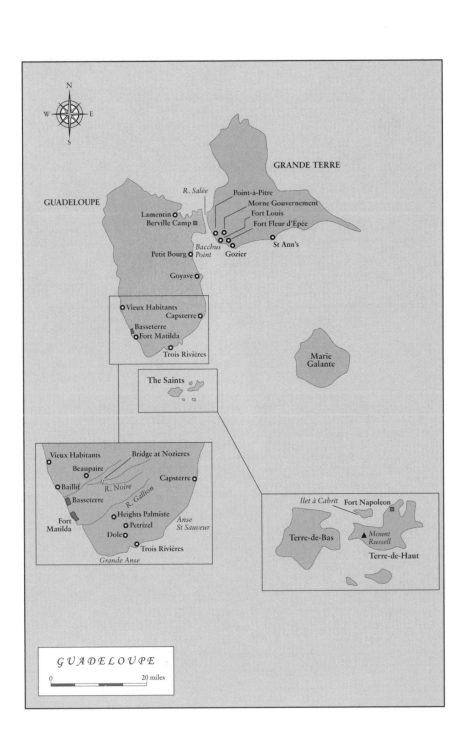

GRANDE TERRE

GUADELOUPE

R. Salée

Point-à-Pitre
Morne Gouvernement
Fort Louis
Fort Fleur d'Épée

Lamentin
Berville Camp

Bacchus
Point

Petit Bourg
Gozier
St Ann's

Goyave

Vieux Habitants
Capsterre

Basseterre
Fort Matilda

Trois Rivières

Marie
Galante

The Saints

Vieux Habitants
Bridge at Nozieres

Beaupaire
Capsterre

Baillif
R. Noire

Basseterre
R. Gallion

Heights Palmiste
Anse
St Sauveur

Fort
Matilda
Petrizel

Dole

Trois Rivières

Grande Anse

Ilet à Cabrit
Fort Napoleon

Terre-de-Bas
Mount
Russell

Terre-de-Haut

GUADELOUPE

0   20 miles

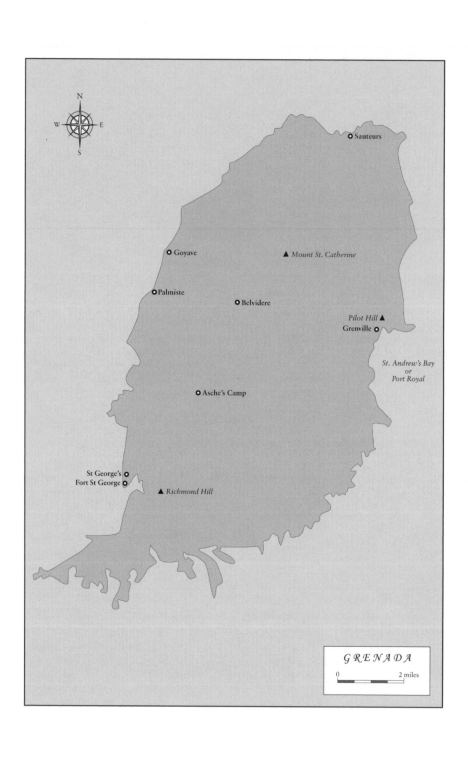

N
W E
S

Sauteurs

Goyave
Mount St. Catherine

Palmiste
Belvidere

Pilot Hill
Grenville

St. Andrew's Bay
or
Port Royal

Asche's Camp

St George's
Fort St George
Richmond Hill

GRENADA
0   2 miles

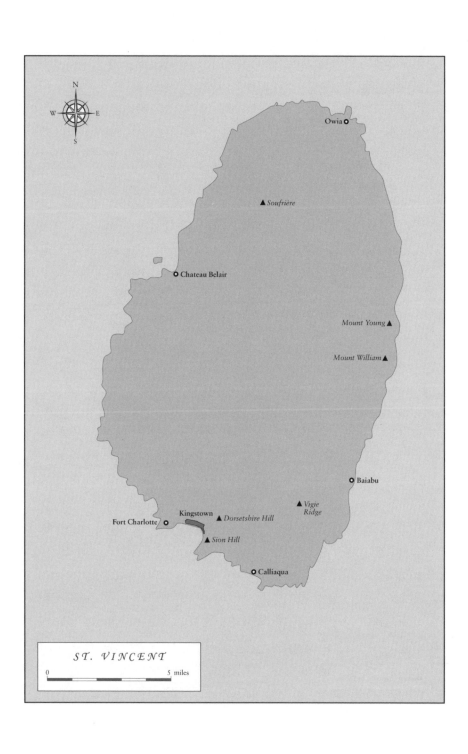

N
W E
S

Owia ○

▲ Soufrière

○ Chateau Belair

Mount Young ▲

Mount William ▲

○ Baiabu

▲ Vigie
Ridge

Kingstown ▲ Dorsetshire Hill

Fort Charlotte ○

▲ Sion Hill

○ Calliaqua

ST. VINCENT

0   5 miles

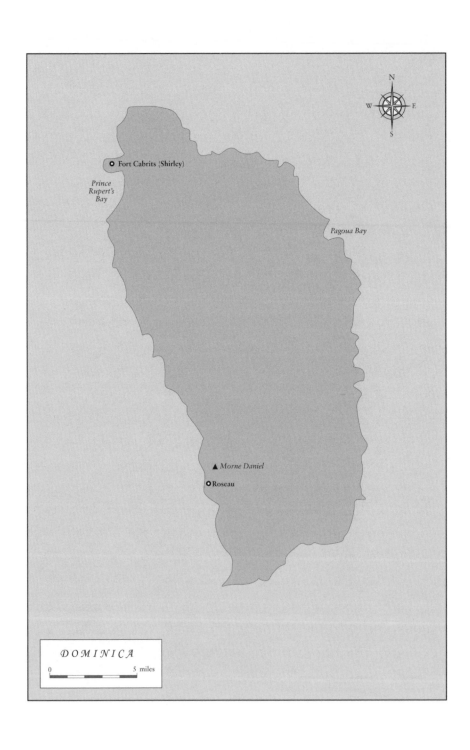

Fort Cabrits (Shirley)

Prince
Rupert's
Bay

Pagoua Bay

▲ Morne Daniel

O Roseau

DOMINICA

0   5 miles

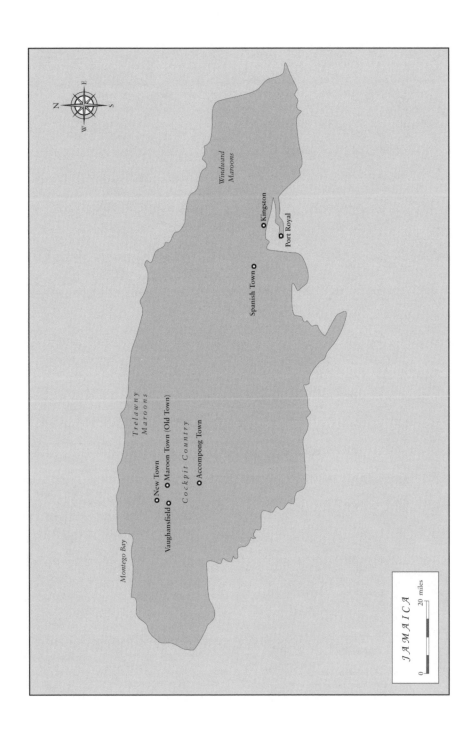

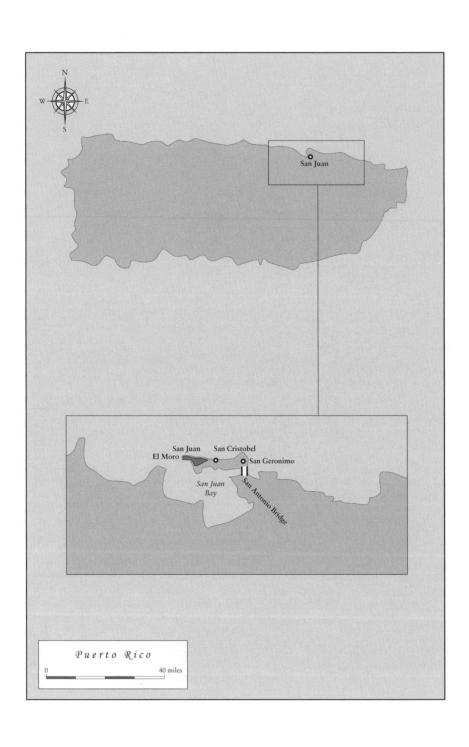

San Juan

San Juan   San Cristobel
El Moro
                                San Geronimo
        San Juan
        Bay
                        San Antonio Bridge

Puerto Rico

0   40 miles

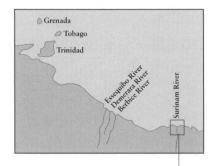

Grenada

Tobago

Trinidad

Essequibo River
Demerara River
Berbice River

Surinam River

N

W E

S

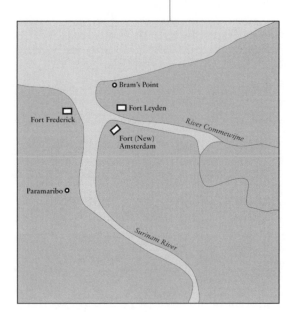

Bram's Point

Fort Leyden

Fort Frederick

River Commewijne

Fort (New)
Amsterdam

Paramaribo

Surinam River

S U R I N A M

0   10 miles

ARMIES

Chapter 1

Dangerous Battalions: The British Army in the West Indies

Britain's eighteenth-century army had three distinct functions. Beyond its obvious war role, it policed the population at home and garrisoned territories abroad. There were always regiments stationed in far flung places including the West Indies, which had British troops in attendance throughout the century. The absence of a national conscription system limited the size of the army and this impinged on the size of the Caribbean garrison which remained small for most of the period. Sporadic fighting might lead to reinforcements, but when peace intervened a 'paltry handful of all-but-forgotten and neglected regulars' was left to guard the islands. These troops were much criticised by their contemporaries. Indeed the British soldier was despised and distrusted by most of his countrymen and under-appreciated by his military and political masters. In 1761, Guadeloupe's governor, Campbell Dalrymple, anticipated Wellington's notorious verdict in describing his soldiers as 'the scum of every county, the refuse of mankind'. During periods of inactivity the wretched West Indian garrison was dissipated by a lethal combination of fever and boredom. Conversely, when there was fighting to be done the private soldier might suddenly rediscover his motivation and regimental pride. At the storming of Mount Tartenson on Martinique in 1762, the troops were commended for their gallantry which was such '... to do honour to their Country and ever distinguish them as Britons.'[1]

At the outset of the French Revolution in 1793 the British army was relatively weak, still feeling the effects of the reductions consequent on the peace of 1783. Britain was a wealthy and populous nation, but the Government was reluctant to spend money on an institution the power of which was resented and feared by Parliament. Only when the country lurched into a new war was the army suddenly expanded causing attendant problems in discipline, administration and recruiting. The army abroad numbered little more than 18,000 men, although by 1794 the demands of the new conflict, especially in the West Indies, led to its rapid growth to a force of 42,000. Many of these men were Scots and Irish; Scotland provided a fifth of the army's manpower and close to half of the regiments added to the line in 1794 were of Irish origin.

The destructive nature of campaigning in the Caribbean and elsewhere meant that during the 1790s it was difficult to maintain regiments at full strength. Of the 55 regiments at home in 1796 for which we have returns, only eighteen had more than half their establishment of 950 privates and only five were even close to their full contingent. In the latter years of the wars, from 1808 onwards, the army raised men through both regular enlistment and transfer from the militia, reaching its peak in early 1814 with a strength of 230,000 operatives. The weakness of the army at the onset of hostilities in 1793 is perhaps best understood by comparing it with the force available at the end of the Peninsular War. Whereas there were only seven battalions of Guards and 74 battalions of Foot in 1793, there were 186 battalions of infantry in 1814.

For much of the last decade of the eighteenth century Britain's aspirations to maintain peace at home and to fight a global war meant that her precious regiments were thinly spread. A return for October 1795 shows them scattered through Britain and Ireland, the West Indies, the East Indies, America, Gibraltar, the Cape of Good Hope, Corsica and the French coast. There is not space here to detail the mechanism of the nation's war machinery, but this infrastructure, 'intractable and ramshackle', was close to breaking point, military realities often subjugated to political convenience.

Whilst the navy was flexible and powerful enough to accommodate the Government's expansionist policies in the Caribbean and elsewhere, the army was placed under severe strain. It was not, however, at least at the start of the conflict, an institution which evoked great expectations. The period of peace prior to 1793 had, in the words of military historian J.A. Houlding, left both officers and men unprepared for action.

> ...it is clear that the majority of regiments found themselves, on the eve of war, to be quite without, or almost innocent of, experience of large-scale mock action or brigade manoeuvres, to have had inadequate opportunities to conduct the training of the field days and the 'excursions', and to be only just adequately prepared to perform on a parade ground the regulation firings and manoeuvres together with a selection of movements drawn from the army's store of customary practice.

It was widely accepted as late as 1800 that the British army was at best a clumsy weapon. Lady Holland's assertion that it was 'harmless against an enemy in battle array' was not much contested. Sir Henry Bunbury, a soldier of the 1790s, refers to lax discipline, the lack of system and weak numbers. 'Never', he declared, 'was a kingdom less prepared for a stern and arduous conflict'.[2]

There was undoubtedly some administrative corruption and neglect but the army of 1793 was not without hope. It has been argued that its shortcomings have been exaggerated to provide a convenient contrast to the later reforms of the Duke of York as commander-in-chief and the proficiency of Wellington's Peninsular army. Improvements had already begun and in some ways the army was better prepared for the West Indian and other campaigns than it had been for earlier less demanding conflicts.

One of the foundations of this recovery was the adoption of a new drill manual, Colonel David Dundas's *Principles of Military Movement*, published in 1788. Prior to Dundas's work the army lacked a uniform approach to tactical training. Regiments on colonial service were frequently divided into smaller units and they became inward-looking, all regimental affairs determined by the whim of the colonel. Soldiers at home were also widely dispersed in billets and distracted by their policing duties. This lack of a coherent approach was potentially exacerbated by the views of the 'American School' of officers who, heavily influenced by the American War, believed in a shallow two-deep line with an emphasis on skirmishing and light infantry tactics. Dundas had little faith in the American experience and his tactical manual espoused the methods of the 'Prussian School' with a three-deep line and well practised manoeuvres designed to resist cavalry and deliver shock. Wellington once commented that in the British army new regulations were read in the manner of an 'amusing novel', but the Duke of York overcame resistance and ensured the necessary uniformity. It must be understood that this took time and that, as will be discussed in a later chapter, the jungles and mountains of the Caribbean campaigns were more suited to the flexibility of the American system than the rigidity of the German approach. In the Peninsula, Wellington won his battles by combing the close-order battle drill of one system and the skirmishing light infantry of the other.

The army officers of the period are too easily stereotyped as underachievers who bought their rank; some two-thirds of the commissions held in the British army were purchased. They were, admittedly, drawn disproportionately from the aristocratic, professional and landed classes and would have had to be regarded as 'gentlemen'. However, significant numbers were of relatively modest origins and many had entered the service for life and had risen through steady and competent service. Some were ignorant of military matters but, as Bunbury points out, in the campaigns of the 1790s there was 'no lack of gallantry' among the officer class. The gentlemanly ideals of toughness, stoicism, fortitude and honour were well suited to the battlefield.[3]

The greatest challenge for the army was recruitment. The essential problem was that there were too few recruits to bring the force up to full strength and too many recruits in the serving army. By 'recruits' we mean soldiers with one year's service or less. Methods of recruitment included voluntary enlistment and coercion. The former accounted for the majority of recruits; often men were captured by the recruiting parties who toured likely areas 'beating up' for volunteers. The demand for new blood was relentless. Between the mid-eighteenth century and 1795, the erosive effect of deaths, discharges, drafts and desertion and the need for periodic top ups meant that foot regiments had to recruit 1.5% of their strength every month in peacetime and just over 2% in wartime.

The difficulties this posed are most clearly exposed at regimental level. Historian Roger Norman Buckley quotes the case of the 68th Regiment, which suffered heavy losses in the West Indies between 1794 and 1796. The few remaining fit men were drafted into another regiment and the beleaguered unit arrived back in England in September 1796 with only ten officers and twenty-seven other ranks. Despite the efforts of 13 beating up parties the regiment was still 955 men short of its establishment of 1,000 rank and file in March 1797 and it did not start to recover until 1800.

A poor harvest, such as occurred in the summer of 1795, might provide a fillip to the recruiting parties, the unemployed and starving driven into their hands, but more drastic means were sometimes employed to fill the ranks. Insolvent debtors and those guilty of more serious misdemeanours could escape prison and even the hangman's noose if they 'volunteered' for the army. Probably more numerous among those pressed into service were men who had committed no actual crime, but who fell into the disparate group of 'all such able bodied, idle, and disorderly persons who cannot upon examination prove themselves to exercise and industriously follow some lawful trade or employment'. Enlistment was generally for life, although from 1806 there was a scheme for limited service.

The use of duress was likely to be necessary to recruit directly to those parts of the world which were regarded as a death sentence. Strategies for recruitment to West Indian expeditionary forces included the use of foreign auxillary formations, the embodiment of regiments of black troops and the filling up of regiments with criminals and others judged not to be gainfully employed. The number of hardened criminals in British regular regiments was almost certainly fewer than is generally perceived. Most convicted men sent to the West Indies were only accepted into penal corps such as the Royal West India Rangers. The majority of men in the regular ranks were decent individuals forced into the army by economic circumstances.

Michael Durey has cogently argued that many of the 'culprits' despatched to the Caribbean were not Englishmen awaiting trial on common law charges, but Irishmen guilty of political offences. Following the collapse of the Rebellion of 1798, the Irish Government had to tackle the problem of dealing with thousands of Irish rebel prisoners. In Dublin, the military prisons and public buildings overflowed with them. A number of solutions were suggested, none of which were straightforward. In the words of a contemporary British officer, 'Our aversion to Blood, or putting to death a great number of people indiscriminately after they have surrendered themselves Prisoners leaves Government in a very embarrassed situation'. Drafting the rebels into the army and sending them to a deadly theatre such as the West Indies was a possible way forward, although this risked spreading disaffection in the ranks. Undersecretary John King expressed the view of many, alarmed at the prospect of a Caribbean army constituted of black soldiers '...and the Whites composed chiefly of prisoners and the worst of His Majesty's subjects!'

Despite the opposition, there was no viable alternative and between 1799 and 1804 five drafts of rebel prisoners were sent to the West Indies from Ireland, as many as 2,400 men. More may have reached the region by circuitous routes via the army depot at Chatham or Gibraltar. These were the most reluctant of all recruits, described as 'white slaves' by an Irish-American radical. Measures were taken to limit the deleterious effect on the wider forces in the West Indies. On the voyage out the drafts were accompanied by sizeable numbers of regular troops and on arrival they were spread thinly among as many regiments as possible. These efforts to turn the rebels into good soldiers were not entirely successful. Many of the first draft arriving at Jamaica deserted and fled into the mountains where they joined bands of natives and French and skirmished with British search parties.[4]

The West Indian garrison and expeditionary forces between 1793 and 1815 had a unique character, characterised by significant numbers of black and local colonial troops, foreign auxiliary units and the disproportionate influx of criminal and rebel elements into the ranks. It is, however, important to stress that the bulk of the force in the region throughout the Revolutionary and Napoleonic period was made up of regular British regiments. Between 1793 and 1801, 69 line regiments served in the West Indies and another 24 followed between 1803 and 1815. In 1795, half of all British regiments serving abroad (52 of 105) were either in the Caribbean or on their way to the islands. We can compare this show of force with the 65 line regiments who served in the Peninsula or the 28 at Waterloo. The numerical strength of the West Indian garrison underlines the scale of the British effort in the region. This varied considerably between 1793 and 1815, peaking at 22,000 in 1795. For much of the wars it remained around 17–18,000 falling to 13–15,000 between 1811 and 1815 when there was the decisive push in the Peninsula culminating in victory at Waterloo. Even during the final years of the conflict the manpower provided to support Britain's colonial wars in North America and the Caribbean was surprisingly large; between 1809 and 1813, the average annual manpower commitment was approximately 30,000 compared with 50,000 in the Peninsula. When the commitment to Spain and Portugal fell to nothing in 1815 the North American and West Indian forces remained little changed.

The weak state of the army at the onset of the conflict has been alluded to and the state of Britain's West Indian forces reflected the service's wider issues. It would be easy to over-generalise regarding the quality of an army which operated in the region for 22 years under numerous commanders and against an ever-changing enemy. We can, however, make some tentative judgements. In the early years, the British soldier fighting on West Indian soil was the target of much opprobrium. John Fortescue, in his magisterial *History of the British Army*, weighs in repeatedly against the poor-quality drafts sent out in 1795, soldiers who were 'raw and untrained', many sick and some only boys. The weaker units were not only ill-equipped, but were also decimated by disease before they even reached the Caribbean. Ministers such as Secretary of State Henry Dundas had to admit that the worst battalions were too undisciplined to fight and too unfit to 'encounter the fatigues of a West Indian campaign'. The men lacked the confidence of their own commanders. General John Graves Simcoe, in Saint Domingue in 1797, believed the state of his troops to be 'a great blow to English military honour' whilst John Moore, one of the pre-eminent British officers of the era, variously described his men on St Lucia in 1796 to be 'mere recruits', 'undependable' and 'very bad'.

Conversely, there is evidence that some British regiments fighting in the Caribbean were of high quality and that they performed well in the most difficult circumstances. Sir Charles Grey's army which attacked Martinique and Guadeloupe in 1794 was, in Fortescue's words, 'small and efficient', the troops performing admirably. The force included many veterans of the American War and the elite flank companies of all the regiments in Ireland. It was a superb strike force, possibly the best assembled in the whole war. Even where there was criticism of the bulk of the army, individual units might maintain higher standards. Saint Domingue often received poor-quality regiments, the better units reserved for the Windward Islands. They typically lacked cohesion and camaraderie and were, according to an army surgeon, 'men radically ill-calculated for soldiers'. In the midst of this mediocrity the Royals were the 'neatest looking men' in Port au Prince and the newly arrived 82nd Regiment, disembarking in August 1795, actually impressed the locals, the first reinforcement they had encountered which looked like a '*corps régle*'.

This mix was found in Sir Ralph Abercromby's army. It contained regiments which could be expected to be 'steady under arms', but others which were undermanned and underprepared. When the commander inspected his expeditionary force at Southampton in the summer of 1795 he was forced to remove many old men and boys from the ranks. George Beckwith's force which attacked Martinique in 1809 appears to have been of good quality, no doubt reflecting the wider regeneration of the army which had taken place since the start of the nineteenth century. Despite the fatigues of the campaign discipline was well maintained and deaths from disease were unusually few.

The officers who served in the West Indies have also polarised opinion. As has been noted, it is easy to stereotype this group of men. Just as for the ranks, the officer class of the early years of the Caribbean conflict received little praise from their contemporaries or later historians. It was difficult to induce men to serve in the region and many regiments were well short of their full complement of officers. Outspoken officers were exasperated by the incompetence of some of their fellows. John Moore is merciless in his criticism; the officers on St Lucia in 1796 were 'young, and without either zeal or experience'. Elsewhere in his journal, we find that, 'the officers and men are, unfortunately, so bad, that little dependence is to be put on them' and that 'I have hardly an officer capable of taking care of his corps...' Moore's words are widely quoted and used to vilify the whole officer cadre, but the reality was more complex. Moore was an example of an exceptional officer serving in the West Indies and men who fought with him, such as John Hope and John Knox, could also be trusted by Abercromby. The broader reforms of the British army, which improved the quality of the rank and file after 1800–1801, also brought benefits to its officers. The Duke of York's programme, including changes in the purchase and promotion system and better education, meant that the troops could expect to be better led.[2]

The quality of British regular regiments might have improved in the later stages of the Caribbean campaigns but they made up a smaller proportion of the total force in the region than was the case in the 1790s. The constant drain of men, largely attributable to disease, and the ongoing difficulties pertaining to recruitment, meant an increasing reliance on foreign mercenary corps to plug the gaps in home forces. The number of foreign troops in the whole British army increased by approximately 60% between 1808 and 1815 compared with the 25% growth in British troops. Some foreign units, notably the King's German Legion and some émigré regiments, were employed alongside British regiments in Europe, but there was a tendency to send the less trusted foreign corps to more peripheral theatres such as the West Indies. Their use in distant places was also encouraged by the suspicions of politicians at home; as late as 1812, Lord Palmerston, Secretary for War, had to remind the Commons that the 'employment of foreigners' was necessitated by Britain's limited population.

The foreign contingent was remarkably heterogeneous, including Corsicans, Swiss, Belgians, Russians, Albanians and Poles. The nationalities most commonly recruited for West Indian service were French Royalist émigrés, Germans and Dutch. The émigré corps were made up of refugees from the French Revolution and included old soldiers from the French Royalist army. The German troops were drawn from the German states, especially Hannover and Hesse-Cassel, and the Dutch mostly assimilated from captured Dutch colonies.

German corps were the most numerous and units which featured most prominently in the fighting included Hompesch's Hussars and Light Infantry, Lowenstein's Chasseurs, La Tour's Royal Étranger and the York Hussars. Hompesch's Corps was raised between 1794 and 1796. The Hussars were sent to Saint Domingue, where they were annihilated by disease, and the unit had dissolved by 1797. The Light Infantry arrived in Martinique in 1797 and participated in the capture of Trinidad before eventually being absorbed into the 60th Foot. Lowenstein's Chasseurs or Legion were raised in Germany in 1794, the officers being mostly French émigrés and the men mostly Prussian or Russian, or French deserters, or Germans who had previously served in German regiments in French service. The corps was sent to the West Indies in 1796 as part of Abercromby's force. La Tour's Royal Étranger or Royal Foreigners was over a thousand men strong and was sent to St Lucia and Grenada in the same year. The York Hussars was another predominantly German unit, although they were originally raised in Poland in 1793. Arriving in Saint Domingue in 1796, it was, like many of the foreign regiments, soon decimated by fever and it was eventually evacuated to Jamaica before being disbanded in 1802.

Among the Dutch units in British service was the York Light Infantry Volunteers, formed in Barbados in 1803 from the soldiers captured after the fall of the Dutch colonies of Demerara, Essequibo and Berbice. Many of the officers were British and the depleted ranks were later filled with French deserters from Spain. The regiment saw action in the attacks on Martinique and Guadeloupe in 1809 and 1810. We will finally mention Bouillé's Uhlans Britanniques, who typify the mixed nature of some of the foreign corps. Essentially an émigré cavalry unit, it was composed mostly of Germans and, after arriving at Saint Domingue, it was soon incorporated into a local colonial regiment.

A significant number of foreign units had either French émigré or British officers. Thus the Royal Foreign Artillery, formed from a number of independent artillery units in 1803, had many German and Dutch troops but the officers were mainly French émigrés. British officers were encouraged to lead foreign mercenary units with offers of double pay and rapid promotion. Thomas Phipps Howard, who has left one of the better accounts of the fighting in Saint Domingue, entered the York Hussars as a lieutenant in 1794 and remained in the regiment until 1802 when it was dissolved. Howard was promoted to captain whilst in the West Indies and the duration of his service suggests that he valued the rewards of being a British officer in a foreign corps.

The quality of the foreign troops sent to the Caribbean was very variable. Some signed up with the sole intent of seizing the bounty and deserting as soon as possible. British troops' attitude to West Indian service will be discussed in a later chapter. For German mercenaries, there was often little appetite for a posting in the tropics. Recruitment was difficult and the number of German troops actually arriving in the Caribbean was usually less than predicted; in a

German unit raised to support Abercromby's expedition in 1795, a third of the recruits deserted on the march from Hesse to the coast. Captain Lasalle de Louisenthal, a French officer in Lowenstein's Chasseurs, comments that the officers and men in foreign units viewed British West Indian service as thankless and dangerous, something to be avoided if at all possible. They complained of their treatment by the British Government, the climate, the lack of proper accommodation, the shortage of wine and the murderous nature of the war. Unsurprisingly, morale remained a problem on active service, Abercromby complaining of large-scale desertion from Hompesch's Hussars and the Uhlans Britanniques. The general wrote to Henry Dundas, expressing his exasperation; 'I clearly see that the German Regiments raised by adventurers will not answer. They are at best to be compared to the condottiers [Italian mercenaries] of the sixteenth and seventeenth centuries'.

The better foreign regiments, such as the York Hussars and Lowenstein's Chasseurs, gave good service during the campaigns. They were especially valued for their expertise as light infantry or cavalry, adept at skirmishing and irregular operations in the West Indian jungle and mountains. Abercromby, quick to criticise the foreign elements in his army, had respect for Lowenstein's Chasseurs and, as will be seen in the description of the campaigns, he entrusted the Germans with several key actions. Lasalle de Louisenthal was proud of his regiment. He blamed British officers for the poor state of the Uhlans Britanniques, who had to be ignominiously re-embarked from St Lucia and sent to Saint Domingue.

> These soldiers confirmed that they were rudely treated by their officers who stole their pay. The colonel and several officers were English little liked by the men. They were rude and brutal.

He says that he and his fellow officers were treated well by Abercromby and Moore. Other British officers offered them respect but little warmth; 'Most of them hated us when we were out of action and valued us in front of the enemy'. Relationships between British soldiers and foreign mercenaries appear to have been mostly amicable, although Norbert Landsheit of Hompesch's Hussars relates a fracas between German and British troops in Port au Prince in 1794 which was defused before there was bloodshed.[6]

The raising of the West India Regiments for regular service in the British army was one of the key developments of the war in the Caribbean during the Revolutionary and Napoleonic period. The main driver for this initiative was, as for the use of foreign mercenary corps, the ongoing problem of recruitment and manpower. It was obvious to ministers at home that black troops were better adapted to the climate and terrain. In 1799, Dundas informed the commander in the Leeward Islands, Thomas Trigge, that black corps 'are undoubtedly better calculated for those duties which are so apt to impair the health of European troops when engaged in active service in the West Indies'. British soldiers were soon exhausted by heavy physical work such as lifting and hauling ordnance. Many of those men shown as 'sick in quarters' in the returns were most likely simply debilitated. Black soldiers were more mobile in the heat, had intimate knowledge of the forest and mountain paths, and were hospitalised in much smaller numbers.

There were antecedents to the formal raising of the West India Regiments in 1795. Slaves had already been taken from the plantations, organised into units with European commanders and employed on several islands as what was effectively light infantry. These regiments, generally referred to as 'Rangers', did not appear on any official army list and were raised only for the duration of hostilities. Examples include Druault's Guadeloupe Rangers, Malcolm's Royal Rangers (raised on Martinique), the St Vincent Rangers, Loyal Black Rangers (Grenada), and the South American Rangers (Demerara). Another prototype body, the Black Carolina Corps, was formed in Saint Domingue. By October 1794, 3,600 blacks and mulattoes (of mixed black and white ancestry) were enrolled in British colonial corps of infantry, cavalry and artillery; we will further consider the various colonial mulatto and black corps later in the chapter. The number of black troops had risen to 2,630 by 1795.

The Rangers Regiments and black troops generally gave good service in the early campaigns. Rangers were frequently grouped into Legions of between 700 and 800 men. Major General Adam Williamson wrote to Dundas in August 1794 stressing their utility.

> Indeed, I may in great measure attribute our success to them. It is impossible that regular troops can ever follow the Brigands into the mountains: they must have people somewhat of their own description to engage them.[7]

The Rangers fought well but their operational capacity was limited. This was confined to the defence of their own islands, it only being possible to remove them from their homes by the sanction of both metropolitan and colonial governments. Sir John Vaughan, appointed commander in the West Indies in October 1794, was convinced that the rapid establishment of regular and permanent black and mulatto regiments in the British Army was vital to safeguard the nation's possessions in the region. The general informed the Duke of Portland, the Home Secretary, that he believed a new corps formed of a thousand blacks and mulattoes would be of more use 'than treble the number of Europeans who are unaccustomed to the climate'. He pointed out that the enemy, Republican France, had already adopted a similar plan. Vaughan proposed that the corps would be organised just as for traditional British line regiments, with the usual compliment of commissioned and non-commissioned officers. It would be on a permanent footing but intended specifically for service in the Caribbean. The soldiers would be mainly drawn from the 'ablest and most robust Negroes'.

There was much opposition to the new initiative, both in the West Indies and at home. Local planters and colonial assemblies regarded it at best a dangerous experiment, resenting both the extension of British Government power and the increased status of the black soldiers. The Jamaican Assembly warned that the men 'would entertain notions of equality' and would acquire habits pernicious to the welfare of the colony. It was accepted wisdom that a black soldier who had carried arms would never willingly return to plantation work. In Britain, a number of army officers railed against the idea, suggesting that these would be 'dangerous battalions' and that any black troops would be better dispersed through white regiments as pioneers. In the event the military imperative was such that Vaughan received government approval to raise what came to be known as the West India Regiments in April 1795.[8]

Vaughan was never to see the culmination of his considerable endeavours, dying of yellow fever later in the year. Eight West India Regiments were formed between April and September, each commanded by white officers and non-commissioned officers. In 1798, five more regiments were commissioned. The original plan had been to raise a sizeable force of almost 9,000 black soldiers, trained and equipped as for European regiments. Pre-existing Ranger corps were incorporated into the West India Regiments, but recruitment was slow and with reductions and disbandments the number of black troops in British service varied during the Napoleonic period. Nevertheless, by 1799 the proportion of black soldiers in the West Indian garrison was about one to every two white soldiers. Some posts in the Windward and Leeward Islands had a majority of black troops. In August 1807, the overall strength of the West India Regiments was just under 8,000 men; this had fallen to around 6,750 effectives at the end of 1810. This weakness of the force resulted from the attritional effects of fighting rather from any deliberate reduction. At the end of the conflict there were eight remaining regiments, the number reduced to a peacetime establishment of six in 1817.

The black units were organised along similar but not identical lines to British line regiments. They were initially made up of eight centre companies, each of 75 rank and file. In 1803/4, consistent with other British battalions of the period, they were increased to 1,000 rank and file (ten companies of 100 men), but the two additional companies had a centre company structure and were not formed as flank companies. The absence of the specially trained grenadier and light infantry flank companies probably reflected the West India Regiments' primary role as light infantry troops, destined to fight in mountain and forest rather than in close order on a more open battlefield. For short periods, two of the battalions were authorised an 800 rank and file structure.

All West India Regiments had a lieutenant colonel (two after 1808), and two lieutenants and one ensign per company regardless of size. At the heart of each regiment was a cadre of white European sergeants, corporals and drummers. At least in the early years, there were some white soldiers in the ranks; muster rolls for the First and Fourth Regiments show men 'enrolled in England', but it is likely that the majority were Irish.

Recruitment relied both on the purchase of slaves and the enlistment of free blacks. Each island was expected to contribute a specified quota of slaves. On the arrival of the slave ships, the men were lined up in the port and examined to establish whether they were fit to bear arms. They were required to be at least sixteen years of age and five feet three inches in stature. Those selected were led away to be given a regimental name and to be kitted out as a redcoat. Between 1795 and 1808 the British Government purchased more than 13,000 slaves for its West India Regiments at a cost of almost a million pounds. For an oppressed slave already on the islands the inducements to become a soldier included a full stomach and the prestige of the uniform. The army diet and the relative wealth were more than he could ever expect whilst working on a plantation.

Most of the recruits came from various West African countries, the number of mulattoes gradually diminishing. Many of the companies appear to have been formed from diverse nations, perhaps intentionally to reduce the likelihood of conspiracy and mutiny. African recruits were favoured as they were 'wholly unacquainted with and uncontaminated by the Vices which prevail among the Slaves in the Towns and Plantations, having no acquaintance or connection of any sort...' A commentator writing in 1801 believed that the typical newly arrived African recruit was able to adapt to military life as he had never had to suffer the 'debased state' of the slave.

The role of the West India Regiments in specific campaigns will be discussed in the next section but, as a generalisation, we can say that they performed creditably. The mutiny of the 8th Regiment on Dominica in 1802 was troubling, but apparently an isolated event. Their role in the period 1795 to 1797 was limited by poor recruitment, there still being reliance on the Ranger corps. In later years, for instance between 1804 and 1807, the reduction in white troops in the region was offset by the augmentation of black regiments. Actions in which the West India Regiments displayed particular gallantry included the 8th at St Martin in 1801, the 3rd at St Lucia in 1803, the 6th at Surinam in 1804, the 1st on Dominica in 1805, and the 3rd and 8th at The Saints in 1809. Open-minded British officers such as John Moore were quick to acknowledge the advantages of black troops over white Europeans.

In this country [St Lucia] much may be made of black corps. I have had occasion to observe them of late; they possess, I think, many excellent qualities as soldiers, and may with proper attention become equal to anything. Even as they are at present they are for the West Indies invaluable.

Lieutenant Colonel William Dyott, serving on Grenada in the same year, lamented the ineffectiveness of European soldiers in the climate and expressed the opinion that the garrison should be made up entirely of black troops. Not all were so approving. Captain Thomas Henry Browne witnessed the drill of the 1st, 3rd and 4th West India Regiments on Martinique in 1809. He admitted that the men were 'tall, well built fellows' but he judged them dirty and also clumsy in their movements.

It is not within the scope of this book to analyse the wider social and political repercussions of the Revolutionary and Napoleonic Wars in the West Indies, but it must be acknowledged that the establishment of the West India Regiments had non-military significance. Buckley, whose *Slaves in Red Coats* is the definitive work on the subject, believes that the policy of purchasing slaves as soldiers impacted both on the wider slave trade and the status of individuals. Although the legal status of the black soldiers was not explicit, it is clear that they regarded themselves as equal to their white comrades in arms. After all, they wore the same uniform, received the same pay and allowances, and were treated in the same hospitals. In 1807, all black troops in British service were declared free 'to all Intents and for all purposes whatever...'[9]

To conclude this review of troops in British service we must also briefly consider the local militias of the islands and the diverse auxiliary colonial corps. The militias were usually composed of able-bodied whites and free blacks. Wealthier whites would generally form cavalry units and free black units would usually have white officers. Local legislative assemblies often provided the arms and equipment and the men were expected to train regularly, but perhaps only once a month. The essential roles of what was effectively a policing body were to protect the island from invasion and to deter slave uprisings. The largest of all the militia forces was on Jamaica. Here, every free male between the ages of 16 and 60 was liable to service in the organisation. Each infantry regiment included one or two companies of free blacks and a company of mulattoes. Jews might also serve in separate units. In 1793, the total militia force was 8,000 strong of which approximately 3,000 were free blacks. Similar arrangements were made on other islands. The Tobago militia of 1803 was formed 'for the sole purpose of Defence against Internal Insurrection and Repelling the Attacks of Marauders'. On Grenada, the 1,200 men of the militia were prominent during the insurrections and in Saint Domingue there were 5,000 militiamen in 1795.

These were not proper troops and they were mostly of limited utility in action. There are many complaints of their uselessness in the contemporary records of the wars. They were inhibited by their purely defensive role and undermined by inadequate training, easy exemption from service and poor discipline. In Saint Domingue the militia was depicted as being 'bred up in ease and luxury and since worn down by anxiety and dismay'. Similarly, on Jamaica, the British commander, Lord Balcarres, complains in 1795 that his militia 'always go to the point of danger but never encounter it'. There was often reluctance to raise militia, there being concern that this might threaten security rather than ensure it.

Despite all this, there is patchy evidence that militia units could respond to good officers. Balcarres later contradicted himself, conceding that at least some militia had fought well with regular troops; 'They have encountered the extremity of danger and fatigue without a murmur'. In Saint Domingue, the militia were inept when acting in isolation but, according to a senior British officer, they did 'tolerably well' if joined to regular forces. When George Nugent gave up his governorship of Jamaica in 1808, he was thanked by the island's assembly for taking a personal interest in the militia. He had improved the esprit de corps and instituted good habits. That his successor, Sir Eyre Coote, immediately censured the militia perhaps tells us that even the best officers and administrators struggled to forge these men into a reliable weapon.[10]

When fighting erupted in Saint Domingue in 1793, there was a rush to create auxiliary colonial corps to support the British cause. The British commander, Sir Adam Williamson, supported this policy and many of the units were raised by French colonists with royalist sympathies. By the end of 1795, there were around forty different corps totalling some 7,000 men. Most of these units had both infantry and cavalry and some also had artillery companies attached.

We will mention a few which will make an appearance in the campaign chapters. Dillon's Regiment was derived from the disillusioned remnants of the 2nd Battalion of the 87th French line infantry regiment (formerly Dillon's Irish), which was in garrison at the Môle when the British arrived in September 1793. Antagonistic to French revolutionary politics, the rump of the unit remained loyal to the British until it disappeared in 1796. Jean Kina's Corps was raised in 1792 by the white planters of Tiburon and was made up of their best slaves. Captain Charles Colville reported its appearance in 1793 to be 'very grotesque', the men carrying the musical instruments of their homeland and a strange variety of arms including billhooks and plantation tools. The Légion de la Grand Anse was led by the Canadian-born Baron Jean Charles de Montalembert and numbered about a thousand men, including white colonists and free mulattoes. Dessource's Volunteers or Légion was raised by Claude Bruno Dessource, a former French colonial officer, and consisted of black slaves and white officers. The Légion d'York was commanded by a local mayor and commander of the National Guard, Jean-Baptiste Lapointe; it recruited from free blacks and mulattoes. Finally, the Légion Britannique de Saint Domingue well illustrates the complex nature of many of these units. Evolving from Montalembert's

Légion de la Grande Anse, it incorporated a number of other subsidiary forces and eventually absorbed Bouillé's Uhlans Britanniques, meaning that the corps was a mixture of colonial and European troops.

A number of these corps performed well in the desperate fighting for control of Saint Domingue. Kina's corps was renowned for its expertise in 'bush fighting' and Dessource's, Montalembert's and Lapointe's forces all had military success against the army of Toussaint Louverture. Their conduct was uneven and not all British officers were convinced of their value; Lieutenant Colonel John Whitelocke complained to a fellow French officer in 1794 that he had been 'tricked' by colonial troops and he vowed that he would never again expose British soldiers next to them. It was, of course, all too easy to highlight the frailties of colonial allies in explaining British failure. Ultimately, the colonial forces proved to be unwieldy and prohibitively expensive. Williamson had failed to control their proliferation and there was ample opportunity for corruption, some units listing fictitious men. They were often top-heavy with officers. When the British evacuated Saint Domingue in 1798, there were 6,000 colonial troops in British service, of which at least 3,000 were non-whites. A few got off the colony to reach Jamaica, the great majority being left to fend for themselves.

In 1796, on Grenada, William Dyott led a column of troops made up of the 8th, 9th and 25th 'British' regular line regiments, La Tour's Royal Étranger, Lowenstein's Chasseurs and local black militia. A year later in Saint Domingue, General John Graves Simcoe commanded an army composed of around 5,000 white troops, of which 40% were foreign, supported by 5,800 black chasseurs and 3–4,000 local militia. The war in the region was, with only a short interim, to last another 18 years. As British soldiers died in the heat, the need to close the ranks with local and foreign troops became ever more pressing. Britain's West Indian army was a remarkably diverse body of men.[11]

Chapter 2

Citizens and Warriors:
The French and Other Enemies

In his admirable study of Napoleon's overseas forces, René Chartrand observes that there is surprisingly little written on the Caribbean forces of Republican and Napoleonic France. There is, however, just enough information in the English and French literature to allow an overview of the soldiers of Britain's greatest enemy in the region. The army of Republican France between 1791 and 1794 was an army of 'citizen soldiers', men who fought out of a sense of duty and to retain their rights. They were, as John Lynn points out, quite different to the soldiers of the earlier eighteenth century who embraced military service only because society offered them little alternative. The army was now more socially representative of France, the number of peasants increasing and the average recruit becoming younger and shorter in stature. Two-thirds of the army's soldiers had served less than four years and more than a third less than one year.

As war approached, the army was effectively rebuilt. In early 1793, the line numbered 180,000, its regiments considered the central part of the nation's war effort. The organisation of this force was subject to ceaseless administrative change and political interference and cannot be detailed here. In addition to the regular units, young men willing to enlist could enter the 'Volunteers' where discipline was more lax, promotion quicker and pay higher. The National Assembly had decreed the levy of 100,000 'National Volunteers', the bulk of which were formed into line battalions which elected their own officers, non-commissioned officers and grenadiers. The army was a 'jumble of regular, volunteer, federal, legionary and free corps units'. Efforts were made to amalgamate regular and volunteer battalions to form a three-battalion *demi-brigade* which was classed as being either *ligne* (line infantry) or *légère* (light infantry). The volunteers were in excess – there were twice as many volunteer as regular battalions – and some brigades were volunteer only. The reorganisation was chaotic but it did give the army an improved basic structure that would be retained in the *Grande Armée* of 1805.

When war erupted in the West Indies, the garrison of the French islands was mostly made up of these line regiments and National Volunteers sent from France. For instance, in Saint Domingue in 1792, the Republican governor, Léger-Felicité Sonthonax, received a reinforcement of 6,000 men from an anxious government, 2,000 being regulars of the line and 4,000 National Volunteers. There was disaffection in these units, royalist officers rejected and men divided by the extreme political views of the period. Regular line regiments were despatched to the Caribbean throughout the wars, notably to fight Toussaint Louverture in Saint Domingue and to contest Martinique, Guadeloupe and other key islands with the British.

We will briefly review the nature and fate of four of these regular line battalions which saw action against British forces. We have only limited information from French sources. All the regiments experienced the devastating losses from disease which were the common lot of all European armies in the West Indies. The 37th *ligne* had a hundred men in the garrison of Fort Royal in Martinique in 1794. According to the French commander, the Vicomte de Rochambeau, the regiment deserved the highest praise for its conduct. By 1805, it had presumably been diminished by fighting and fever and the third battalion was absorbed into the reformed 82nd *ligne*. Battalions of the 26th *ligne* served both on Guadeloupe and Martinique forming part of the garrison of Fort Desaix in 1809. Its ranks included veterans of the Armies of Egypt and Italy and it was regarded as an excellent unit. The second and third battalions of the 66th *ligne* were in Guadeloupe in 1802. By 1807, the regiment had 1,300 men in the colony, but within the next two years it had been reduced to half strength by disease and at least a third of the 'fit' men could perform no useful duties. To salvage the unit, the French imported 1,500 black troops into the 15 centre companies, these new recruits armed with muskets which had been held in reserve. In late 1809 the regiment, 'hassled' by numerous changes in command, received another 320 recruits from France and, by now 2,500 strong including the black contingent, it performed well against the British on Guadeloupe in 1810.

Thanks to Paul Arvers's fine regimental history, we have a little more information pertaining to the experience of the 82nd *ligne* in the West Indies. Recruitment to regiments bound for the region was problematic. In 1802, General Henri-François Delaborde wrote to the Minister of War in Paris:

> It will be difficult to extract 600 men of the 82ᵉ and organise them for embarkation [to Martinique]. My fears are based on the pronounced repugnance of several officers and soldiers of the former 141ᵉ demi-brigade, incorporated into the 82ᵉ, the officers and soldiers of which have been almost four years in Saint Domingue. This repugnance has spread itself for some time in the 82ᵉ and it is manifested by a considerable desertion every time it receives the order to march to Brest, perhaps only

half the men destined to be embarked arriving in the town. Be this as it may, I have given the order that the senior officer of the 82^e demi-brigade form a battalion of 600 men.

The reluctant regiment was to see prolonged service in the Caribbean. It showed 'great bravery' at Castries on St Lucia in 1803. In May 1805, the 82nd was essentially reformed with the incorporation of a number of smaller units. Its greatest feat of valour was the capture of the British-held Diamond Rock off Martinique in the same year, the young officers praised for their military knowledge and intrepidity.

At the outset of 1809, the regiment's three battalions on Martinique were each formed of six companies, of which one was of grenadiers and one of *voltigeurs*. The grenadier company was weak due to recruitment problems. The 1,500 strong regiment apparently fought well in the subsequent campaign against the British although the 82nd was not regarded as an elite force, French historian and soldier Henry de Poyen comparing it adversely with the 26th *ligne* and describing it as containing '*beaucoup d'élements étrangers*'. After the capitulation of the island, the French commander Villaret de Joyeuse complained of large-scale desertions, mostly from the 82nd. 'These corps are unfortunately composed in large part of refractory conscripts, of prisoners and of poor quality individuals from the colonial depots.' The bulk of the men were captured and sent to the prison hulks in England.[1]

The French, just as the British, backed up their regular troops by the raising of a large number of local West Indian corps. The National Guards, sometimes referred to as 'Citizens Guards', were formed at the time of the Revolution. Despite the opposition of at least some whites, free blacks and mulattoes were commissioned as officers in a number of these units. Their uniform, consisting essentially of a dark blue coat, was virtually the same as that of the National Guard in France. Initially formed in a climate of revolutionary zeal, the tricolour cockade was widely displayed. In later years, National Guard units were created on Martinique and Guadeloupe. A decree of 1802 issued on Martinique instructed that all whites between the ages of 16 and 55 years were to report for service. The six battalions each had a company of grenadiers and one of chasseurs, the remaining companies being fusiliers. There were also six battalions on Guadeloupe, each battalion having black or mulatto chasseur companies, white fusilier companies and a company of dragoons. Similar arrangements were made on the neighbouring smaller islands.

In practice, the National Guard, sometimes present in significant numbers, were of limited help to the French regular forces. Three to four hundred were present in Fort Royal on Martinique in 1794, but Rochambeau explicitly excludes them from the praise he later gave to the French defenders. They performed little better at Fort Desaix 15 years later. Here there were an impressive 3,500 of them in the garrison. According to Admiral Louis Thomas Villaret, they started promisingly but soon melted away, led by the free blacks.

> Whilst the troops of the line gave such a good example the *gardes nationales* who had been brought together from various locations, disbanded entirely and returned to their homes. That of Saint-Pierre, which the day before had shown up so well, refused to cooperate in the defence of Fort-de-France and also disappeared abandoning their senior officer Després and two or three officers who remained.

In 1802, a number of corps of local Gendarmerie were raised. They were never particularly large, perhaps a hundred strong on Martinique. A return for the troops on Guadeloupe in 1807 includes the Gendarmerie Impériale, but this was composed of only 23 men. Other distinct local regular corps were raised in somewhat greater numbers. As early as May 1793, a body of Chasseurs de Martinique was formed. This was 400 strong and in the pay of the Republic. Similar local chasseur forces were formed during the conflict, especially on Martinique and Guadeloupe. Further initiatives included the creation of a corps of black Pioneers drawn from local slaves and the formation of companies of black Ouvriers who were generally under the direct orders of artillery and engineer officers.[2]

It was very quickly obvious that Republican France could not rely upon regular European forces to wage war in the Caribbean. The ruthless civil commissioner Victor Hugues responded by emancipating the slaves and calling them into his service. This, as will be detailed in a later chapter, fundamentally changed the nature of the war in the region, meaning that British soldiers would be facing a different sort of enemy. Hugues's success in driving this strategy and mobilising the blacks and mulattoes of the islands is clear from a return of Republican forces on Guadeloupe at the end of 1796 which shows that out of 4,600 'regulars' only a thousand were white soldiers (2,500 blacks, 1,000 whites, 1,000 mulattoes and other mixed race). More bodies of black and mulatto troops, described as being 'well disciplined', were in place on St Lucia and Grenada.

British troops, assembled at Barbados in 1794, were informed by General Adam Williamson that they would not be facing the elite troops of Republican France, '...the enemy being made up chiefly of negroes and mulattoes with a very small proportion of regular troops, to be beat by whom would be so disgraceful that he cannot entertain the most distant thought of it'. Eyewitness accounts confirm that the British were often facing a non-white and diverse foe. In Saint Domingue in 1794, Ensign Harry Ross-Lewin of the 32nd watched the enemy march out of a captured fort; '...they were men of all shades of complexion from white to black'. John Moore noted enemy casualties at Morne

Chabot on St Lucia in 1796; 'Among the killed were two whites, the rest blacks and men of colour, but chiefly the former'. We have seen that some black troops in French service, notably those raised as National Guard, were unreliable but it is important not to over-generalise regarding their fighting abilities. The French commander on St Lucia, Gaspard Goyrand, had to rely increasingly on his black soldiers at the subsequent stubborn defence of Morne Fortune where, he tells us, '...the [British] companies of grenadiers and several others were repelled three times over by African citizens who had never held a rifle...' After the capitulation to the British, Goyrand met his opponent, Sir Ralph Abercromby.

> He treated me with great estimation; he admitted that our prolonged defence was designed to humiliate a victor, since I [Goyrand] had not even 90 European soldiers. He then said to the English officers, 'These poor Africans that you have seen go past without stockings and shoes, have proved to us in the defence of this dump that they can distinguish good from bad when they are well led'.[3]

The most famous predominantly black army faced by the British in the Caribbean was that of Toussaint Louverture in Saint Domingue. Toussaint, born a slave in 1746, became the dominant black leader in the country, his sudden conversion to the Republican cause in the summer of 1794 being a major factor in Britain's eventual evacuation of the colony. By 1797, he was recognised as 'General in Chief' of the armies of Saint Domingue by the French. After the British departure in 1798, Toussaint was to fight a war against Napoleon's troops which culminated in his banishment to France and death in 1803. There is no doubt that he was an inspiring and capable military leader, his mere presence being enough to 'electrify' the men under his command.

Toussaint's regular army was substantial. During the struggle against the British, his increasingly disciplined force, in part reinforced and armed from France, was divided into twelve colonial infantry demi-brigades, these corps operating in the north, the centre and the south. At the height of his power in 1801, his total force, including infantry, cavalry and artillery, amounted to over 20,000 men. The great majority were blacks but there were around a thousand mulattoes and perhaps 5–600 French troops. These men were led by black or mulatto generals. Most regimental officers were also non-European, although there were a few white Republican officers.

Toussaint left little to chance. His men were brave, had natural fighting ability, and knew the country. To these natural assets, he added discipline and drill. Marcus Rainsford, later a captain in the 3rd West India Regiment, witnessed a review of Toussaint's forces.

Two thousand officers were in the field, carrying arms, from the general to the ensign, yet with the utmost attention to rank...Each general officer had a demi-brigade, which went through the manual exercise with a degree of expertise seldom witnessed, and performed equally well several manoeuvres applicable to their method of fighting. At a whistle a whole brigade ran three or four hundred yards, then separating, threw themselves flat on the ground, changing to their backs or sides, keeping up a strong fire for the whole of the time, till they were recalled; they then formed again, in an instant, into their wonted regularity. This single manoeuvre was executed with such facility and precision, as totally to prevent cavalry from charging them in bushy and hilly countries. Such complete subordination, such promptitude and dexterity, prevailed the whole time, as would have astonished any European soldier who had the smallest idea of their previous situation.

Toussaint was adept at tactics, marshalling his troops in such a way as to negate the advantages of European regulars. He relied on the terrain, on weight of numbers and the element of surprise. This was guerrilla-like warfare designed to frustrate and confuse his opponents. His black soldiers often operated in small squads of 10 to 12 men which would converge on the enemy from different directions, perhaps emerging from the woods at dawn in an attack en masse, scattering if there was significant resistance, continuing to snipe from behind trees and undergrowth. Larger bands of mounted raiders, 60 to 70 horsemen, would suddenly appear to attack a convoy or plantation before slipping through the fingers of their weary pursuers. Toussaint never missed an opportunity to exaggerate the strength of his forces and he was skilful in selecting his own battlefield. Later in the wars, he became more proficient at defending his captured territories. That Toussaint and his army became capable of sophisticated movement in the field is apparent from his account of an encounter with Dessource's Volunteers in 1798.

The enemy had not taken the precaution to establish on the St Marc road reserve camps to protect his retreat. I used a trick to encourage him to pass by the highway; this is how. From the town of Verrettes he could see all my movements, so I made my army defile on the side of Mirebalais, where he could see it, so as to give him the idea that I was sending large reinforcements there: while a moment after I made it re-enter the town of Petit-Rivière behind a hill without his perceiving it. He fell right into the snare, seeming even to hasten his retreat. I then made a large body of cavalry cross the river, putting myself at the head of it in order to reach the enemy quickly and keep him busy, and in order to give time to my infantry which was coming up behind with a piece of cannon to join me. This manoeuvre succeeded marvellously.

Toussaint's army had already proved that it was capable in conventional warfare, successfully storming and capturing several forts.

British officers were at first dismissive of Toussaint's men. They complained that they 'fought like apes and were worse than Arabs'. The black troops were regarded as 'brigands', a derisory catch-all term used to describe all black and other disaffected elements who opposed the British. Toussaint was 'contemptible' and the guerrilla tactics he employed were considered to be underhand and cowardly. Any acknowledgement of the enemy's successes was grudging, generally attributed to perceived 'slavish' attributes such as cunning, toughness and an intimate knowledge of the ground. They thrived in the 'poisonous air' that the whites were unable to breathe. This perception changed with time, intelligent officers such as Thomas Phipps Howard still slow to praise but ultimately convinced of the daring, skill and military knowledge of the black and mulatto soldiers he faced. French officers were more forthcoming. Jean-Baptiste Lemonnier-Delafosse first encountered Toussaint's army in 1802.

> Fatal error! The French regarded these men as savages...Alas! Their perseverance in the struggle, their courageous resistance, destroying European science, proved the opposite to be true, and one could from that point predict the [French] failure which, later, would lead to the abandonment of the island.[4]

The British faced other redoubtable enemies in Saint Domingue. The mulatto leader, André Rigaud, was also a thorn in their side. Born in France, the son of a French lawyer and a mulatto woman, he was a natural convert to the Republican cause and his largely independent *Légion de Sud* operated against the British from the south of the colony. Rigaud had a reputation for cruelty, but he was also a talented and determined leader able to effectively manoeuvre his men. He was quoted as saying that the mulattoes' 'intuition' arose from the combination of black and white in their souls. They were well adapted to the warfare of the country, able to survive on a minimal diet, to operate barefoot, and skilled as horseman and sharpshooters. The *Légion de Sud* was a sizeable enemy force, perhaps numbering 5,000 infantry and 1,200 cavalry in 1796 and around 8,000 strong in 1798. British officers had respect for the mulatto army, General Simcoe comparing it favourably with the local militia. Another commander in the colony, Thomas Maitland, believed that Rigaud was a finer soldier than Toussaint and that the mulattoes were more dangerous than black troops.[5]

On St Vincent, British forces were resisted by the native Carib population, who favoured the French and who welcomed the Republican emissaries of Victor Hugues in 1795. It seems that that they were regarded by British troops as being good jungle fighters, but less reliable in the open. Private John Simpson found the Caribs to be an elusive foe. They were, he says, 'excellent climbers' who were capable of launching attacks from the densest forest. Whenever the British retreated, the Caribs followed them 'with as much rapidity as if they had sprung like monkeys from tree to tree'. We get a more rounded account of Carib fighters from French Republican Lieutenant of Artillery Alexandre Moreau de Jonnès, who was sent to St Vincent by Hugues to encourage action against the British.

> Already for a long time had the Caribs adopted the use of firearms, though from necessity and custom they continued to use bows, tomahawks, and a cutlass which they handled every cleverly. I had obtained from Guadeloupe powder, balls, and some muskets, and I extracted from the wrecked frigate ten times as much by means of the Carib swimmers. At the same time, my artillerymen became instructors, teaching the Caribs to handle their muskets and to manoeuvre like our light troops. Success was prompt and effective. These were no dull peasants, but active hunters, with a straight eye and sure foot, who had only to learn to work together.

Moreau de Jonnès says that the Caribs soon became expert shots. He thought them to be superior to the motley reinforcements sent to the colony by Hugues; 'They [the Caribs] were better disciplined than the soldiers, not so fierce as the negroes, and, besides, not so fond of drink as the sailors'.[6]

The Maroons of Jamaica were among the most daunting of Britain's adversaries. They were descended from slaves who had fled to the hills from their Spanish masters when Britain conquered the island in 1655. Under the terms of a treaty signed with the British in the early eighteenth century, the Maroons were granted an apparent degree of independence and limited land in return for their cooperation in suppressing the King's enemies and hunting down runaway slaves. It was a one-sided treaty, in the words of a modern historian the triumph 'of a literate, sophisticated, cynical society motivated by expediency and gain, over an illiterate, vigorous but simple community skilled only in warfare and physical survival'. The uneasy peace was finally broken in 1795. It is unclear how many Maroons there were at this time, possibly around 1,500. There were five Maroon towns including Trelawny Town in the parish of St James and Accompong Town in St Elizabeth.

Contemporary historians, including Robert Dallas who penned a famous history of the conflict on Jamaica published in 1803, were quick to denounce the Maroons, but they had to admit that they were formidable warriors. Dallas believed them to be superior to other races of African descent.

> ...erect and lofty...vigour appeared upon their muscles and their motions displayed agility. Their eyes were quick, wild and fiery... [and] they possessed most, if not all, of the senses in a superior degree.

West Indian planter Bryan Edwards, whose *History of the West Indies* appeared in 1806, broadly agreed with Dallas although he thought the Maroons' taste to be 'depraved' as they preferred rum to wine, a judgment he does not apply to British soldiers.

Allied to these physical attributes, the Maroons were willing to rally behind a good leader and were capable of, in Dallas's words, a 'regular and concerted system of warfare'. They used ammunition cautiously and fully exploited the Cockpits, narrow valleys enclosed by rocks and mountains which formed natural fortifications. Most of the island's paths led to a Cockpit entrance where the Maroons lay in wait.

At this mouth which looks like a great fissure made through the rock by some extraordinary convulsion of nature, from two hundred yards to half a mile in length, and through which men can only pass in single file, the Maroons, whenever they expected an attack, disposed of themselves on the ledges of the rocks on both sides. Sometimes they advanced a party beyond the entrance of the defile, frequently in a line on each side, if the ground would admit; and lay covered by the underwood, and behind rocks and the roots of trees, waiting in silent ambush for their pursuers, of whose approach they had always information from their out-scouts. These [British soldiers], after a long march, oppressed by fatigue and thirst, advance towards the mouth of the defile, through the track obscured by trees and underwood, in an approach of many windings, which are either occasioned by the irregularity of the ground, or designedly made for the purpose of exposing the assailants to the attacks of the different parties in ambush. A favourable opportunity is taken, when the enemy is within a few paces, to fire upon them from one side. If the party surprised return the fire on the spot where they see the smoke of the discharge, and prepare to rush on towards it, they receive a volley in another direction. Stopped by this, and undecided which party to pursue, they are staggered by the discharge of a third volley from the entrance of the defile. In the meantime the concealed Maroons, fresh, and thoroughly acquainted with their ground, vanish almost unseen before their enemies have reloaded. The [British] troops, after losing more men, are under the necessity of retreating; and return to their posts, frequently without shoes on their feet, lame, and for some time unfit for service.[7]

British soldiers faced similar challenges on Grenada and St Lucia. On the former island, the local revolutionary forces were led by the feared Julien Fédon. Again, officers were surprised by the obduracy of their mostly black adversaries, William Dyott admitting that Fédon's men were capable of stiff resistance. They were, he said, able to bear much suffering and were also extremely mobile; 'It is astonishing with what incredible alacrity the negroes got through the woods, and how nimbly they scrambled up and down the hills'. When Fédon's posts were captured, his notepaper, which was found to be headed '*Liberté, Égalité, La Loi*', left no doubt as to the insurrectionists' sympathies. British forces on St Lucia also endured prolonged periods of guerrilla-type warfare. When Thomas Henry Browne captured 500 prisoners he found, to his 'mortification', that there was not a single white soldier among them. John Moore confirms the commitment of the insurgents.

> Their attachment and fidelity to the cause is great; they go to death with indifference. One man the other day denied, and persevered in doing so, that he had ever been with them or knew anything of them. The instant before he was shot he called out 'Vive le république'.

Moore says that the insurgents carried out numerous atrocities, a fact he attributed to them being directed by 'vagabonds' from France.[8]

Finally, in this brief overview of Britain's enemies in the Caribbean, we should consider the troops of other European nations. The Dutch had significant interests in the region, including the colonies of Surinam and Demerara on the South American mainland. After the Treaty of Amiens in 1802, a number of light infantry (*Jager*) battalions and artillery detachments were sent to strengthen these garrisons. When the British captured Surinam in 1804 the prisoners were a mix of two *Jager* regiments (shown as chasseurs in the return) and Colonial White Chasseurs and Colonial Black Rangers in addition to engineers and artillery. Ralph Abercromby's assaults on Trinidad and Puerto Rico in 1797 brought his army into contact with Spanish forces. At Trinidad, the larger part of the garrison was actually made up of naval forces, but there was also a small army contingent consisting of the Trinidad Regiment and supporting artillery and engineers, in all about 600 troops. The raising of local militia and an uneasy combination of French Royalists and Republicans meant that it was a typically polyglot Caribbean force. On Puerto Rico, the Spanish garrison was both better motivated and stronger, including 1,200 regular soldiers. Denmark and Sweden both had minor possessions in the West Indies but they were only weakly garrisoned by their European troops who caused little trouble to the British.[9]

CAMPAIGNS

Chapter 3

The Crater of Vesuvius:
Saint Domingue 1793–1794

The hundreds of West Indian islands form an arc of 2,400 miles in the Caribbean Sea and can be most simply divided into two groups (see map 1). To the west are the Greater Antilles including Jamaica, Puerto Rico, the Dominican Republic and Haiti. The latter two countries together form the island of Hispaniola referred to as St Domingo in the late eighteenth century. The smaller group, the Lesser Antilles, form the Caribbean's eastern border and include the Leeward Islands (the Virgin Islands, Anguilla, St Martin, St Bartholomew, Saba, St Eustatius, St Kitts, Nevis, Barbudo, Antigua, Montserrat and Guadeloupe) and the Windward Islands to the south (Dominica, Martinique, St Lucia, Barbados, St Vincent, The Grenadines and Grenada). At the time of the French Revolutionary Wars, the division of Leeward and Windward was subject to variation. On the edge of the two Antilles groups of islands are the Bahamas in the north and Trinidad and Tobago off the Venezuelan coast.

For much of the eighteenth century this complicated geography was familiar to senior British politicians and military men. According to Bryan Edwards, 'Whenever the nations of Europe are engaged, from whatever cause, in war with each other, these unhappy countries are consistently made the theatre of its operations. Thither the combatants repair, as to the arena, to decide their differences'. In the 1750s, the French colonies of Martinique, Guadeloupe and Saint Domingue were both lucrative centres for the sugar trade and havens for French privateers preying on British and American shipping. William Pitt was prompted to launch an expedition to the region, culminating in the capture of Guadeloupe, a triumph attributed by Major General John Barrington to 'great perseverance' and achieved despite the troops succumbing to fever in alarming numbers. This early 'War for Empire' peaked in further Caribbean operations in 1762 and led to at least 41 British regular battalions being employed in the Americas. Even during subsequent periods of peace the number of redcoats in the region was maintained at significantly higher levels than in the earlier years of the century. Predictably, France also had designs on a wider role in the West Indian colonies; in the War of 1778–83 Britain was forced to relinquish Tobago and to grant her American colonies their independence.

In 1793, the West Indian islands were divided amongst the leading European powers. Britain maintained a hold on Jamaica, Bahama Island and the Bay of Honduras to leeward and, to windward, Barbados, Grenada, Antigua, St Vincent, Dominica, St Kitts, Nevis, Montserrat and the Virgin Islands. Her implacable enemy held sway in Martinique, Guadeloupe, the Saints, St Lucia, Tobago, Marie-Galante and in the western part of St Domingo (Saint Domingue). Spain retained the islands of Cuba, Trinidad, Puerto Rico and the eastern part of St Domingo (Santo Domingo), whilst the remaining islands were split amongst the lesser European players of Holland, Portugal, Denmark and Sweden.

On the eve of the French Revolution, Saint Domingue was one of the wealthiest colonies in the world and a colonial powder keg. The whites of the island, numbering only around 7% of the population, were, in the words of Mirabeau, 'Sleeping on the crater of Vesuvius'. The Revolution flowed like hot lava through the land we now call Haiti, tearing away the fabric of French colonial society. Wealthy white planters sought more autonomy from the mother country whilst the poorer whites, evoking *liberté* and *égalité*, claimed equal rights to their social superiors. Soon, the mulattoes were seeking equality with the whites and all groups were breaking free of traditional restraints imposed from France.

The unrest was not limited to a solitary island – a civil war was also erupting in Martinique – but it was in Saint Domingue that events took the most savage turn, with the increasingly anarchic behaviour of the white factions of *grand* and *petit blancs* and a suppressed mulatto uprising. This dissension in the upper echelons of colonial society led to unrest among black slaves, culminating in the 'Night of Fire' in August 1791 when 50,000 slaves revolted under the leadership of the priest Boukman and took brutal revenge for centuries of oppression, humiliation and torture. Now the white planters were dragged from their homes and gruesomely put to death. In a few days, 2,000 whites were massacred and almost 200 sugar plantations and 1,000 coffee plantations were destroyed. Historian David Geggus concludes that 'considering the reckless complaisance of most whites and the excessive suspicion of others, not to mention the provocation of troops arriving from France, perhaps the most surprising feature of the slave revolt is its slowness in coming'. The whites joined with the mulattoes and took predictable revenge, apparently bent on complete extermination of the blacks. Perhaps 10,000 slaves died in these reprisals.

A firm European response was needed, but France was unable to spare sufficient troops to either dominate the feckless whites or suppress the insurgents. In early 1792, the National Assembly in Paris granted equal rights to the mulattoes. Two new commissioners, Sonthonax and Polverel, were sent to the colony to root out racial discrimination and restore order. To implement the Jacobin revolution on Haiti, Sonthonax, the dominant commissioner, needed the mulattoes' cooperation and his activities alienated white opinion. His only allies at the end of the year were the increasingly confused mulattoes and a dwindling number of French troops. The slave armies, numbering around 30,000 men, continued to control large areas in the north. Such was the situation in February 1793 when the French Republic declared war on Britain.

In this apocalyptic scenario, Mirabeau's predicted volcanic eruption, it is unsurprising that some of Saint Domingue's white colonists sought help from Britain. Sixty planters arrived in London agreeing to transfer their allegiance to George III in return for British protection up to the time of a general peace. Royalist emissaries from Martinique and Guadeloupe, which had renounced the Paris revolution, were also in England. Ministers were initially wary of these approaches, but with the outbreak of war the case for an offensive strategy in the Caribbean was growing. Henry Dundas, surveying the globe for potential threats of conflict, concluded that the West Indies 'was the first point to make perfectly certain'.

British willingness to intervene in the region in the early 1790s was the result both of perceived opportunities and threats. The major gains of assimilating the islands were the exploitation of their undoubted wealth and the generation of naval power. The West Indies contributed substantially to British prosperity, being easily the country's largest overseas capital investment. In the British colonies there were almost 600,000 slaves and these islands exported products worth over seven million pounds. West Indian investments generated around 20% of all British trade. France's West Indian colonies were even more valuable and contributed close to half of all her foreign trade. For both countries the loss of annual income from the Caribbean would have inevitably led to a serious financial crisis. As the region was sparsely populated by European colonists, mostly concentrated on Jamaica and Barbados, this capital investment was unusually exposed both to foreign attack and to internal unrest.

The West Indian colonies also made significant contributions to Britain's and France's maritime power. In the late eighteenth century, trade with the Caribbean serviced over one-eighth of all British merchant tonnage and its trained seamen. This contribution to naval strength was in itself of such magnitude that abandonment of the islands was unthinkable. Furthermore, control of a number of strategic harbours, such as on St Lucia, potentially allowed control of the Atlantic and the extension of influence to South America. For France, the influence of the region on her naval power was arguably even more crucial; a quarter of her merchant tonnage and over a third of her seamen were reliant on her West Indian dominions. Loss of the islands would seriously undermine her pretensions to be a world maritime power.

There were more negative reasons for action. A passive non-interventional policy risked the spread of the chaos on the French islands to the British colonies. Disaffection was already growing among British colonists due to the home country's abolitionist tendencies. Although there had so far been no equivalent uprising on the British islands, mobilisation of the militia on Jamaica allaying initial alarms, there were potential trouble spots on Grenada, St Vincent and Dominica. Imitation of the Saint Domingue slave revolt was a real possibility.

In considering the factors – materialistic, maritime and defensive – which led to the Revolutionary and Napoleonic Wars in the West Indies, it is important not to view the region in isolation. Geggus points out that it is easy to over-rate the role of the islands in the Government's overall strategy.

> To depict [Prime Minister William] Pitt [the Younger] and Dundas as engaging in a headlong, purposeful pursuit of Caribbean spoils, and *la perle des Antilles* [Saint Domingue] in particular, is a little misleading. Although, within a deeply divided cabinet, proponents of an aggressive West Indian policy predominated, primacy was always accorded to the War in Europe.

Britain's first priority was to blunt the French threat to its interests in Belgium and Holland. Once war was inevitable, on the basis of European considerations, then the seizure of the French West Indies was a secondary but highly desirable objective, at once bolstering the empire and endangering French wealth and sea power. Thus it was, at the start of 1793, Dundas forbade the Governor of Jamaica to take any offensive action whilst peace endured, but added pointedly that in the likely event of war it was the Government's intention 'to extend the protection of His Majesty's Arms to the French West Indies, and secure to them the advantages of being subject to the Crown of Britain'.[1]

With war declared, the first British assault – the start of 22 years of intermittent fighting in the region extending beyond Waterloo – was against Tobago. Dundas believed that the island merited early attention as the overwhelmingly British white population had suffered loss of prestige and wealth after 20 years of French rule. One of the most prominent planters, Gilbert Petrie, had already been in contact with the Government. The French garrison, not reinforced since 1788, was, in the words of a French historian, '*très faible*'. Perhaps a further incentive for the capture of Tobago was that it was the only French colony from which the prevailing winds allowed any attack to be made on the key British possession of Barbados.

On 10 February 1793, Dundas sent a secret despatch to Major General Cornelius Cuyler at Barbados ordering him to attack Tobago as soon as he judged his force to be adequate. On 10 April, the naval squadron of Vice Admiral Sir John Laforey arrived and the expedition sailed three days later. Cuyler had not received reinforcements ordered in December and his small army was limited to a detachment of artillery, nine companies of the 9th Regiment and a small number of marines, in all about 470 men. On the 14th, the troops disembarked at Great Courland Bay on the north side of the island (see map 2). Petrie supplied the invaders from his estate but, contrary to expectations, most of the colonists kept their distance or even joined the Republican governor Monsieur Montel, lieutenant colonel of the 31st *ligne* (*Régiment d'Aunis*), who was occupying the French fort above Scarborough (Port Louis) on the other side of the colony. Cuyler's men marched across the island and summoned the fort two to three miles distant, but Montel refused to yield. It is likely that the small British expeditionary force was of the same size as the garrison, both numbering a few hundred. The British were regulars and, not having the means to undertake a siege, Cuyler decided to risk all on a night attack. This was despite the enemy's fortifications being much stronger than he had expected. The affair of the 14th was confused and disjointed, the best account being that of Cuyler who was himself wounded.

> The troops lay upon their Arms at the Place where we had halted until One o' Clock, at which Time we formed, and marched at Half-Past One, leaving the Artillery under the care of Lieutenant Hope and the Detachment. We had more than two miles to proceed. The men were positively forbidden to fire, but to trust entirely to the Bayonet; the Smallness of our Number not justifying a Diversion to favour the general Attack, which was determined to be on the North West Side where I had reason to believe that the Work was most imperfect.
>
> We reached the Town of Scarborough undiscovered, but here we were fired upon from a House by some of the French Inhabitants which gave the Garrison the Alarm; however no return of Fire or Delay was made.
>
> In consequence of a Negro, who served as a Guide to the Grenadiers, running away, a part of the Column separated in mounting the Hill; this occasioned a Delay and separation that could not be rectified during the Night, which was extremely dark. Separated however as they were, the Troops approached the Fort; the Light Infantry and a Part of the Grenadiers on the side where the fort was most defenceless, and where the whole were to have made their Effort.
>
> The other Part of the Troops having taken the Road which led directly to the Barrier, and the Enemy's Fire commencing on the Flank companies, the former advanced to attack the Barrier under a heavy Fire of Round and Grape Shot and Musketry, which drew the attack of the enemy to this Part of the Work; and the Flank companies at that moment pushing forward, very gallantly entered the work, upon which the enemy surrendered, and the Humanity of the British Troops accepted of them as Prisoners of War.

The night attack on Tobago, carried out by a small expeditionary force armed with the bayonet over unmapped treacherous terrain against a strongpoint held by an unpredictable and irregular enemy, was to foreshadow many of the British operations in the region during the remainder of the wars. Cuyler's force suffered three killed and 24 wounded. The French were reported to have 15 killed and wounded. When the fort was stormed, around a hundred armed inhabitants, including a number of mulattoes and blacks, fled the scene. Ninety-six French prisoners were taken, mostly men of the 31st *ligne*, and a hundred sailors were also captured. Cuyler immediately restored the British colonial constitution which the French had usurped in 1781.[2]

Attention now turned to Martinique in consequence of representations made by Royalists on the island to Major General Thomas Bruce that the arrival of even a small force, as few as 800 men, would induce the inhabitants to submit to British rule. News of the execution of Louis XVI and of the declaration of war between Britain and France had encouraged the Royalists to take up arms against the Republican governor, le Vicomte de Rochambeau. Bruce met the former Royalist governor of the island, the Comte de Behague, and decided to support the revolt. The general commanded a small army of around 1,100 troops consisting of the flank companies of the 9th Regiment, nine companies of the 4th Battalion of the 60th Regiment, some marines from the fleet, and the Black Carolina Corps. The men were embarked at Barbados on 10 June and sailed with Rear Admiral Sir Alan Gardner's squadron.

As the British plotted the capture of Martinique, events were conspiring against them. The Republicans were suddenly in the ascendency, Rochambeau capturing the main Royalist stronghold and all their artillery. Nevertheless, Bruce remained optimistic and he disembarked his men at Case de Navire between the 17th and 19th (see map 3). He believed that his force, now supported by around 800 Royalists, was 'perfectly adequate to the service proposed', the plan being to seize the commercial port of St Pierre where Rochambeau commanded a few hundred French troops. British progress was delayed by the need to bring up artillery, a number of 6-pounders, to their stations and also by a brief sally by the enemy. When the attack on the town was finally launched against the two defending batteries it was an ignominious failure, well described in Bruce's despatch to Dundas.

> We were to move forward in Two Columns, the one consisting of British Troops, the other of the Royalists; for this Purpose the Troops were put in motion before Day-break; but, unfortunately, some Alarm having taken place amongst the Royalists, they began, in a mistake, firing on one another; and their Commander [Gimat] being severely wounded on the Occasion, his troops were immensely disconcerted, would not submit to the Control of any of the other officers, and instantly retired to the post from which they had marched.

This conduct strongly proved that no Dependence could be placed upon them, and the attack against St Pierre must solely have been carried on by the British Troops, to which their Numbers were not equal; and, as they luckily were not yet engaged with the enemy they were ordered immediately to return to their former posts.

Senior British officers met the following day and decided that further operations were futile. All British accounts stress the incompetence of their Royalist allies as the reason for the failure of the expedition, but French opinions were predictably at odds with this view, The Royalist Behague thought the British troops precipitous retreat was due to tactical naivety, '...if they had the order to attack they did not do enough and if they didn't have such an order, they did too much'. Rochambeau was keen to take some credit from his enemy's debacle, attributing the route of the Royalists to an ambush made by three to four hundred of his men. Poyen believed the British withdrawal to be understandable, '...if one remembers that they had marched with the hope of the fort surrendering on their arrival and of taking possession of the island without spilling a drop of blood, and that they had much hesitated to undertake any military action, we should not be surprised to see them abandon their attempts after the first check'. Winter was now approaching and, on 22 June, the British fleet left for Barbados carrying the troops and 5-6,000 Royalist refugees escaping from Republican retribution.[3]

It was clear to Bruce and to ministers at home that a much larger effort would be needed to conquer the Windward Islands. This major expedition will be discussed in the next chapter, but we must first return to Saint Domingue to recount British fortunes on the colony which, as has been related, was in such a state of anarchy that sections of the population were seeking British help. It is important to note that Saint Domingue was that part of the island of St Domingo that belonged to the French. This made up little more than a third of the whole island, the western tract of land with two long peninsulas (see map 4). Within its 12,000 square miles, Saint Domingue had close to 200 towns; the largest were Cap Français and Port au Prince. Much of the wealth was in the hands of the white planters, although in the months prior to the British intervention the Republican Commissioners had transferred at least some of this white power to the mulattoes and the enormous potential strength of the blacks as successors to both was starting to be felt. Attitudes to the British were polarised; many of the planters favoured the 'English' or at least the French King, but the 'non-proprietors' often had Republican sympathies. Marcus Rainsford declared that the most intelligent of the planters favoured Britain, but he also thought that those planters who supported the French Commissioners mostly did so 'probably from principle'. Any conflict would have to be fought out in an environment alien to newly arrived Europeans. Although the terrain reminded visitors of Switzerland, the climate was hot, humid, damp and oppressive, encouraging a lifestyle, according to the French Governor, of 'laziness and debauchery'. Hector McLean, a British Inspector of Hospitals on the island, believed the colony to be remarkably unhealthy with 'fever in each treacherous breeze'.

It was into this 'hornets' nest' that Dundas plunged. He and General Sir Adam Williamson, Governor of Jamaica, had been encouraged by the Saint Domingue emissaries and particularly the planter Pierre François Venault de Charmilly. It is unclear whether Charmilly or his allies had the permission of the inhabitants to transfer their island from France to England, but the signature of the document effectively committed Britain to the protection of Saint Domingue. Fortescue describes this as a blunder, but modern historians have been more guarded as to the justification for British action. Geggus invokes the British desire to check the growing influence of the mulattoes and blacks – even at the 'eleventh hour' – but he also acknowledges that Pitt and Dundas's decision to intervene 'defies any simple explanation'. Chances of success on the island were not clear-cut. On the one hand, many of the whites had been aggrieved by the behaviour of France, at least some of the mulattoes were antagonised by the Commissaires' reliance on the blacks, and many of the blacks favoured their Royalist masters over the Republicans. Conversely, large areas of land had been desolated, the counter-revolutionary forces were not concentrated, and significant parts of the island were inhabited by alienated blacks and mulattoes with Republican sympathies. In the north, the black troops of Toussaint Louverture were becoming more organised.[4]

The first British landing on 20 September 1793 was at Jérémie on the southern peninsula. This was a propitious place to take the first step as the local white planters were under imminent threat from the mulatto leader André Rigaud's marauding army of slaves and mulattoes, and were desperate to treat on any terms. From his Jamaican garrison, Williamson raised a force of just under 700 men made up of the 13th Regiment, two flank companies of the 49th and a detachment of artillery. The men were boarded on the men-of-war of Commodore John Ford's squadron under the command of Lieutenant Colonel John Whitelocke of the 13th and were landed uneventfully at Jérémie where, according to Williamson, '...colours were hoisted at both forts with two salutes of Twenty-one guns and answered by the Commodore and his squadron. The troops were received with the loudest acclamation from all ranks'. Shouts of '*Vive les Anglais!*' resounded, a banquet was prepared and even a song composed to honour the invaders. The locals swore allegiance to the British King.

The capture of Jérémie gave control of the Grand Anse, a significant acquisition, and a greater prize immediately followed. Ford had been informed by a captured French officer that the inhabitants of Môle St Nicolas would also readily surrender to the British if they were promised support and protection. Accordingly, the commodore sailed across the Bight of Léogane and the Môle, one of the strongest naval bases in the New World, and its extensive dependencies, fell into British hands on the 22nd. Fifty marines took immediate command of the garrison and Williamson quickly sent to Jérémie for the grenadier company of the 19th and then further strengthened the garrison with five companies of the 49th from Jamaica. British gains included large quantities of stores and ordnance and the French Regiment of Dillon. This easy acquisition would not be so simple to retain; a recurrent theme of warfare in the Caribbean. The local population were not trustworthy and the local British commissioner thought a garrison of 500 men necessary. The people were anxious, he reported; 'it requires that no difficulties should appear among us'.

A small reverse at the beginning of October was a salutary reminder of the difficulties of cooperating with local factions. Tiburon, the neighbouring port to Jérémie, was important for the security of Grand Anse. It was decided that Whitelocke would attack from the sea whilst a sympathetic local planter, Morin Duval, leader of the colonial 'Army of the Grand Anse', would lead 500 men against the town from the landside. Whitelocke's troops were repelled from the beach by musket fire and, having initially underestimated the enemy's strength, were forced to retreat with the loss of around 20 men. The British, and later historians including Fortescue, were quick to blame Duval for the failure, but it seems that the two forces were poorly coordinated and ill-fated; Whitelocke had landed three miles distant from the planned point of disembarkation and, according to Rainsford, the wind intercepted Duval's signal and the local commander spent most of the day lost.[5]

Following the fall of the Môle, a number of other parishes clamoured for British protection. The reasons for this were probably the increasingly aggressive stance of the Spanish, whose plans to conquer the island were frustrated by lack of troops, the apparent support of Sonthonax for the blacks, and the news of the fall of the key naval base of Toulon. The commander of the Môle received submissions from St Marc and Gonaives in the Bight of Léogane, Verrettes and Petite Rivière to the east of St Marc, and Léogane and smaller towns in the south.

Reinforced only by a paltry 200 more troops from Jamaica, the British were reduced to sending small bodies of men, often measured in tens and twenties, to occupy these new possessions. At St Marc, Brevet Major Thomas Brisbane arrived with a force 50 strong to face down and force the surrender of a hundred or so French troops drawn up in the main square. The garrisons of the Môle and Jérémie were weakened to only a few hundred men and there were too few available for Brisbane to accept the surrender of Mirebalais. Overtures from Jacmel and other key towns in the south also had to be ignored. The capture of Léogane and its hinterland should have been a valuable asset, the sugar estates little affected by previous conflict, but the lack of British manpower allowed southern raiders to burn the land. Nevertheless, the gains were judged adequate for Ford to summon Sonthonax to yield up Port au Prince and Williamson was confident enough of the capital's eventual submission to send the 20th Regiment to Jérémie to be available to take possession.[6]

In reality, the British grip was weak. They had the support of a number of irregular corps of French colonists and of a body of ex-slaves led by the able Jean Kina. Britain and Spain co-existed on the left bank of the Artibonite, but it was unlikely that the Spanish could be persuaded to take offensive action. The mulattoes mostly remained suspicious, dissatisfied by British failure to grant them equal rights to the whites. Williamson and Ford had possession, if not control, of one-third of Saint Domingue. With only 800 soldiers in the colony, to press any advantage they needed either Republican defection or their own reinforcement. In the event, neither happened. Dundas had become distracted by events in Europe, notably in Flanders and at Toulon, and also by preparations for an expedition against the Windward Islands. In December, the minister announced the planned departure of two regiments from Ireland to Saint Domingue, but these were delayed for several months by the usual problems of sickness and poor weather. The only reinforcement actually received was of 400 men of the First Royals from Jamaica, a garrison that was now also dangerously weak.[7]

Lacking the resources to make a decisive military push, the British resorted to bluff; Ford twice appeared off Port au Prince in January and March threatening a bombardment and demanding the town's surrender, but he withdrew on each occasion without taking action. Bribes were offered to selected French generals. There was an unsavoury element to the British occupation described by Geggus as a mixture of 'cynicism, greed, impotence and empty threats'. However, where a military force could be deployed there was the potential for decisive action and even glory. Lieutenant Colonel John Whitelocke's capture of the strategically important stronghold of Tiburon on 2 and 3 February 1794 was, in Williamson's view, 'spirited and well done'. Commanding a small force of a few hundred men just arrived from Jamaica, Whitelocke planned to attack Tiburon from the beach. He instructed colonial auxiliaries camped at Irois to move to cut off the Republicans' retreat to the west. On the evening of the 2nd, a broadside from the three frigates appeared to clear the shoreline of enemy troops.

> Just before dark I [Whitelocke] ordered the Flank Companies to land and take possession of a house about 150 paces from the Beach, and well situated for Defence, and to protect landing of the whole. Major [Brent] Spencer commanded the Flank Companies and was not annoyed until the Moment the Boats grounded, when the Brigands appeared in

Line on the Beach, and fired on the troops, who, by the Major's Orders, were on Shore in an Instant, charged, and in a minute routed the Enemy and surrounded the Post.

Whitelocke landed at daylight with the 13th and 20th Regiments, the Marines, and British Legion. He estimated the enemy's strength to have been 650 blacks and 200 mulattoes and whites. Around 50 were killed and wounded, 150 surrendered and the remainder escaped, the colonists failing to cut off their retreat as planned. British losses were limited.

Perhaps believing that an offensive strategy was the best way of concealing his true weakness, Williamson decided to reduce enemy posts around Port au Prince to clear the ground for an attack on the capital. Two weeks after the capture of Tiburon, the same force attacked the Fort l'Acul. In another combined operation, the plan was for Whitelocke to march on the place from Léogane, around six miles to the east, whilst 200 colonial troops commanded by the Baron de Montalembert were to land and attack the fort from the sea at an appointed hour. Marching at four in the morning, Whitelocke led his small force of flank companies, the 13th Regiment, a detachment of Royal Artillery, around fifty colonial troops, two howitzers and two 4-pounders to within cannon shot of the fort, on the opposite flank of which the larger body of colonials were to commence their attack. Captain John Vincent was sent with the flank companies of the 49th and 120 colonial troops to support the latter. Unfortunately alcohol now played a vital role as one of the captains of the transports became intoxicated and Montalembert was unable to land. Ashore, the two opposing forces exchanged artillery fire. Realising that his colonial allies could do no more than serve as a diversion, holding the attention of the 200 blacks and mulattoes on the beach, Whitelocke decided to storm the fort.

About half past four, P. M., Major Spencer was ordered, with Two Flank Companies, to join Captain Vincent to advance and fire on the fort which he did according to a signal given, and Lieutenant-Colonel Whitelocke advanced in front under the Fire of Two Guns loaded with Grape, and a heavy Fire of Musketry. They ascended the Hill, which was rendered as difficult as possible by Trees placed in all Directions, gallantly pushed on with fixed bayonets, and drove the Enemy from their Works. Many of the enemy were killed; and had the Colonial corps been landed, not a man would have escaped.

The garrison was thought to have numbered around 600 men led by a Frenchman, De Lille, who, according to Williamson, was supposed to have murdered 300 of his fellow whites. The brigands fired the fort, accidentally setting light to an artillery wagon, which exploded causing a number of casualties including two British officers. Total British losses were five killed and 32 wounded.[8]

The British were apparently in the ascendency; the people of nearby Grand Goâve raised the Union Jack and took an oath of allegiance. There was, however, a growing realisation on the part of many of the inhabitants that Williamson's small army, never numbering more than 900 effective soldiers, was not sufficient to give them real protection. Promised reinforcements never appeared and distrust of the British grew. In Port au Prince, there was black insurrection; one of the French regular regiments was forced to seek British help at Léogane. Here and at l'Acul the garrisons were reduced to a skeleton by disease. The Republicans had lost ground but, encouraged by British inaction and the general unrest, they launched a major counter-attack. On 16 April, Rigaud threw 2,000 men, mostly insurrected blacks, against Tiburon. After the mulatto leader surrounded the fort at three in the morning, the defenders fought bravely for six hours, their task being made more desperate by the destruction of the powder magazine by a suicide agent. The Chevalier de Sevre, a local creole, made a sortie from the fort, ably supported by Jean Kina's black corps, and the enemy were eventually driven off. The intensity of the fighting was well demonstrated by the besieged force expending 40,000 rounds of ball cartridge. Of the 60 British troops of the 30th Foot in the garrison, 28 were killed. A similar number of colonial troops fell. The equally determined attackers left 170 men dead on the field. A frigate arrived the following day to provide naval protection whilst repairs to the fort were undertaken; a salutary reminder of the vital role of the navy in supporting isolated garrisons.[9]

The British were starting to suffer setbacks. In early April, mulattoes at Jean-Rabel, one of Whitelocke's outlying posts, rose up and surrendered to the Republicans. German settlers at Bombarde also rebelled and Whitelocke decided to take them by surprise. A force of 200 men composed mainly of marines performing garrison duty at the Môle were led by Major Brent Spencer. The British officer was accompanied by two Frenchmen, Monsieur Deneux, a major of artillery, and Lieutenant Colonel Charmilly, whose knowledge of the language was likely to be useful. Setting off at nine at night, the small force marched 15 miles through woods and mountains. When they arrived at Bombarde at three in the morning, they found it defended by 150 Germans armed with three pieces of cannon. Rainsford recounts the outcome.

Colonel Markham with half the detachment attacked the redoubt in the flank while the remainder approached the gate. The enemy suffered them to arrive within half-gun shot, when having three times called – 'Qui vive?' – Colonel Spencer answered 'England' and immediately the assailants received a fire perfectly well directed and kept up with so much order and briskness that the enterprise was obliged to be

immediately abandoned. Several of the officers advanced as far as the
ditch, supported by some grenadiers, but not being sufficiently
numerous, all retired in confusion.

Spencer lost 40 men killed, wounded or taken prisoner, a significant number in
view of the vulnerability of the Môle garrison. British weakness was becoming
increasingly clear to the Republicans and the semi-autonomous groups who
supported them. Two days later, around 1,500 blacks and mulattoes under the
command of the black leader Pompé attempted to storm Fort l'Acul. The
attackers showed the same valour as at Tiburon but were routed by the 400 men
of Montalembert's Légion and Léogane militia who made free use of the
bayonet.[10]

With the situation becoming critical, the arrival of the long-awaited
reinforcements at Môle St Nicolas, 1,500 men under Major General John
Whyte, boosted the British cause. In Rainsford's words, 'All spirits were now
resumed...' The troops were detached by General Charles Grey, whose major
operations to windward will shortly be described. The force now at Whyte's
disposal for offensive operations was made up of the 22nd, 23rd and 41st
Regiments in the transports (except for the flank companies which had been
left at Martinique) and a detachment from the flank companies of regiments
already in Saint Domingue. There were two obvious targets, the major
Republican strongholds of Port au Prince and Cap Français. The general
decided to assault the former, probably because it was more exposed, more
isolated by the British blockade, and because it contained the predominant part
of the Republican forces. The 45 merchant ships trapped in Port au Prince's
harbour were coveted by Commodore Ford, whose fleet sailed at midday on
30 May and anchored off the city. In addition to his regular contingent, Whyte
could also call upon the support of colonial troops around Arcahaye and
Léogane.

Ford's priority was to find a safe anchorage. It was this consideration that
made the assault on Fort Bizothon to the west of Port au Prince the first
objective. This fort, manned by a garrison of 500 men, both dominated the
coastline and controlled the main road from Léogane. As Whyte lacked a siege
train, the place was bombarded from the sea on 31 May by two line of battle
ships and a frigate. In the evening, after four hours' bombardment, Whyte
ordered 300 British and a number of colonial troops to be landed within a mile
of the fort. Under the command of Major Brent Spencer, this small body of men
advanced meeting little opposition. A violent thunderstorm now intervened and
'taking advantage of the lucky minute afforded to them by so favourable a
circumstance' the soldiers charged with the bayonet and carried the place.

The fall of Fort Bizothon effectively sealed the fate of Port au Prince. Whyte
describes subsequent events in his dispatch.

This great Point being carried, I repaired (with Lieutenant-Colonel Whitelocke, whom I ordered to take the Command of the Centre) to the opposite side of the Bay; and, having landed Major [Edward] Handfield with 200 British Troops to support the attack on the Port of Salines (the Frigate scouring the Beach and enfilading the Entrenchments) he attacked and carried the Post without loss and, continuing his March, the next Day he turned the Batteries which defended the Landings near to and on the Left of Port-au-Prince. The enemy being thus hemmed in on all sides, excepting in the Rear, and perceiving numbers moving out by a Road called the Charbonier, we determined on a general Assault, and the Fleet and Army advanced; when the enemy, perceiving our motions, struck their Flags and abandoned the place, having previously spiked their cannon on the Land Defences; and the Two Commissioners from France, Pulverele [Polveral] and Sonthonax with the Black General Monbrune (who was wounded with a Bayonet at Bizothon) escaped and I have not since been able to learn any certain Account of them...

The seizure of Port au Prince was a great British triumph and a bitter blow to the Republicans. Achieved with very few losses (13 killed and 19 wounded), enormous riches – 100 pieces of ordnance and 22 ships with cargos worth nearly half a million sterling – fell into the captors' hands. Whyte wrote to Dundas, 'the importance of this Conquest to Great Britain you, Sir, must know: There is more sugar now nearly ready to cut than in all Jamaica'. However, as inferred in the general's dispatch, the military objective had not been entirely achieved. The bulk of the Republican Army of the Western Province and its leaders had escaped towards Jacmel on the south coast.[11]

Saint Domingue remained a hotbed of racial friction and vested interest. It was not to be pacified by a single military operation. Following the capture of Port au Prince, the ubiquitous Charmilly, described by Fortescue as '...a rogue [but] assuredly no fool', had rushed to England with a letter of recommendation from Williamson. He petitioned Dundas and Pitt, apparently on behalf of the proprietors of the colony, for more British reinforcements, the strengthening of the black corps, and the raising of new colonial units. The latter included the Légion Britannique, which he would personally raise and which would require a substantial advance of funds. Ministers hesitated, but Charmilly eventually got permission to raise two corps, one of infantry and one of cavalry. Anglo-colonial relations remained cool. Whitelocke, mindful of the failings of colonial troops at Tiburon and Fort l'Acul, wrote to a fellow French officer, '*Je ne m'attends pas à aucun changement dans leur sentiments militaires*'. At the end of April, an uprising of black auxiliary troops against the Spanish garrison in Gonaives appeared a peripheral event, but it probably marked the first attachment of Toussaint Louverture to the Republican cause.[12]

Toussaint's volte face potentially brought an extra 4,000 black soldiers into the fight against them, but the British were nevertheless in a strong position in early June. The consensus among historians is that a vital initiative was now lost. According to Geggus:

> Recently reinforced, they had 3,500 armed men in Port au Prince, about 1,800, mostly mounted, in la Grand' Anse, garrisons at Saint Marc, Arcahaye, and the Môle, and a strong naval squadron. The psychological advantage was theirs. Port au Prince had fallen almost without a shot and amid mutual recriminations. The Republicans were in disarray and everywhere short of food and ammunition.

He argues that the British commanders squandered opportunities, failing to immediately attack Toussaint in the Artibonite, not attacking Jacmel in the south, and not pursuing Sonthonox's fleeing army through the mountains. The latter force was deeply divided, fighting breaking out between black and mulatto troops and dissension growing among the mulatto generals. Michael Duffy points out that the potential danger of Toussaint was not yet appreciated by many contemporaries. The failure of Rigaud's further attack on Tiburon in June emphasised both the constant enemy threat and the impotency of Republican forces at this time. Rigaud's men, weakened by famine, were massacred by the planter cavalry of the Grand Anse and the artillery of the fort and a navy frigate.

British ambitions were not helped by disagreement in their own camp. General Whyte, as senior military officer in Saint Domingue appointed by Grey, the Commander in Chief in the West Indies, expected to be in charge of affairs, but he discovered that he was to be held to account by Williamson at Jamaica. The two men had served together before and there may have been some antagonism between them. Whyte's strictly military authoritarian view of matters in the colony was at odds with Williamson's more conciliatory political approach and the Governor of Jamaica soon found fault with the general's 'inquisitorial' edicts. The British Government supported Williamson and the unsavoury episode was brought to an end when Whyte departed for England to be replaced by General Charles Horneck.

A more sinister force than internal discord was at work in the British army. It was to be a recurrent theme of the Caribbean campaigns that periods of military inactivity were marked by outbreaks of disease. Held in notoriously unhealthy Port au Prince at the start of the sickly season, Whyte's unseasoned men were horribly vulnerable to yellow fever. The flank companies of the 22nd, 23rd, and 41st – sent by Grey from windward in June to join their battalions – brought the disease with them. The death rate in some regiments soon exceeded 20% per month. Within two months, some 600 men were dead and by mid-November 1,000 British soldiers had been buried in the city. The navy was perhaps even more severely affected.[13]

With operations around Port au Prince brought to a halt by the ravages of disease, the military focus moved to St Marc where British hopes were invested in Captain Thomas Brisbane of the 49th Foot. This officer is eulogised by Fortescue.

> With no more than eighty British soldiers, a handful of French regulars, about three hundred reluctant Spaniards, the local militia, and a black legion of his own raising – in all about twelve hundred men – he was the terror alike of Republican troops and of negro brigands over an area of one thousand square miles. He brought the negro chief, Toussaint l'Ouverture, who was later to become the master of Haiti, to submission with surrender of the territory he had conquered...

In a more sober assessment of Brisbane's achievements, Geggus suggests that some of the concessions made to the British were a subterfuge on the part of Toussaint, who was preparing to strike at his 'duped and unsuspecting foe'. What is more certain is that when Brisbane left a small garrison of convalescents at St Marc whilst he attacked Gonaives, a mulatto rebellion broke out. Seduced by promises made by the French commissioners, the rebels massacred many of the inhabitants and burned much of the town. Rushing back, Brisbane fought off the repeated attacks of Toussaint's combined black and mulatto forces before the arrival of a frigate, a Spanish advance down the Artibonite, and reinforcements from Arcahaye allowed him to drive the enemy back across the Artibonite River. Whilst pursuing these operations, Brisbane was so weakened by fever as to be unable to write, instead having to dictate his military reports. Williamson commented, 'Too much cannot be said in his praise'.[14]

Brisbane's fortitude had preserved British possessions, but any alliance with the mulattoes in the area had been broken. Toussaint was able to consolidate a strong defensive position around Marchand. All towns without a British garrison or immediate naval protection were vulnerable to insurrection and attack. At Léogane, the mulattoes invited Rigaud into the town. There was little resistance, a number of blacks and whites fleeing to Port au Prince. Debilitated by disease, Horneck's small army was on the back foot. A return for October 1794 shows 1,862 British troops in Saint Domingue of whom 1,022 were sick or convalescent. Their colonial allies (640 men) were similarly afflicted. Williamson decried the political failure to declare equality between whites and mulattoes to please the latter; he was, he complained, beset by an increasing number of enemies. Rigaud's and Toussaint's forces, driven on by the promises of emancipation and now hopeful of repelling the European invader, fought with increasing confidence.[15]

The loss of Léogane rendered the western approaches to Port au Prince vulnerable and Rigaud was keen to exploit the opportunity. By the night of 5

December, the mulatto leader had secretly assembled 2,000 men under the works of Fort Bizothon, which was manned by 120 British soldiers of various flank companies and battalions. Supported by a cannonade from a brig offshore, the small garrison resisted heroically for about an hour against three enemy columns launched at two parts of the defences. All three officers in the place were wounded but, dressing their own injuries, they fought on and Rigaud was forced to retreat. British losses were 22 killed and wounded and the attackers left 250 men dead, a testament to the determined nature of the assault.[16]

Not deterred by this setback, Rigaud was resolved to make another attempt to take Tiburon. His intentions were known, but no ship could be spared to intercept his force, which sailed from Aux Cayes on 23 December; this was made up of a naval squadron of a brig of 16 guns and three schooners of 14 guns each and a military contingent of 3,000 men described by Rainsford as being of 'all colours and descriptions'. Arriving on Christmas Day, the mulatto general first sank a British schooner in the harbour before turning his attention to the fort. The Tiburon garrison was composed of 500 men, mostly blacks under the command of Jean Kina and also some British convalescents. Rigaud poured musketry and mortar shells into the place for four days until, on the 29th, a shell exploded in the ditch, leading to a panicky retreat by Kina's men who were close by. Led by Lieutenant John Bradford of the 23rd, the garrison's survivors fought their way through enemy ambuscades to Irois and finally to Jérémie. Around 300 of the defenders were killed, two-thirds of the original garrison. Little mercy was shown; many of the wounded were massacred. Lieutenant Baskerville was left behind and blew his brains out as Rigaud entered the fort.[17]

Baskerville's fate was in keeping with the depressing state of British interests in Saint Domingue at the end of 1794. New insurrections erupted at Jérémie and St Marc. Williamson understood that his army was as much threatened by the 'enemy within' as by any external foe. The hospitals were full and reinforcements a distant prospect. In the 15 months since the British landed on the colony they had received fewer than 900 men from England. The navy was also under strain, unable to either counter enemy expeditions or to rein in the privateers, or to stop Republican supplies of ammunition and stores. Fortescue places much of the blame on Henry Dundas, who made repeated plans for extra men but did not deliver. The War Minister gave contradictory orders with respect to West Indian reinforcements, but he was fighting a near impossible battle against adverse weather, sickness among the troops, and the demands of the campaigns in the Low Countries. A further reason for the failure of the promised regiments to reach Saint Domingue was the major expedition to windward, to which we will now turn.[18]

Chapter 4

With Spirit and Impetuosity: The Grey Jervis Expedition of 1793–1794

Dundas's implementation of Pitt's military policy was focussed on Martinique and Guadeloupe, islands in a less anarchic state than Saint Domingue and apparently ripe for capture and exploitation. As we have seen, Tobago had already been taken, but an attack on Martinique had been aborted. As early as May 1793, there was a plan for an expedition to be launched by September, timed to arrive in the West Indies at the end of the sickly season with six months of operations feasible. For his army and navy commanders, the Secretary of State appointed Lieutenant General Sir Charles Grey and Vice Admiral Sir John Jervis. Grey, 64 years old, was well qualified for the responsibility having seen much hard fighting in the Seven Years War in Germany, in several mid-eighteenth-century operations, and in the American War of Independence where he was a rare British officer to emerge with credit. His previous experience of both the Caribbean and of combined operations made him a propitious choice. Jervis, six years younger than Grey, was also an intelligent appointment as, although this was his first major independent command, he had knowledge of amphibious operations and had built a reputation as a good organiser. The two men were friends.

As for other foreign expeditions of the wars, the endeavour was subject to repeated false starts and changes in both the size of the available force and the stated objectives. Initially, there was a plan for the regiments already in the Caribbean to be brought up to a strength of over 6,000 men and to reinforce them with 1,800 troops from Gibraltar, 3,000 from Ireland, and over 5,000 from England; this would give Grey a total force of over 16,000 men to conquer Guadeloupe, Martinique and Saint Domingue. The delays now started. There were serious problems in obtaining sufficient ordnance – the communication between Dundas and the Master General of Ordnance, the Duke of Richmond, left much to be desired – and there were similar glitches in obtaining adequate engineers and medical cover. Bad news on the Continent, where the Duke of

York was retreating through the Low Countries, led to the diversion of manpower from the West Indies to Ostend. Grey was himself despatched to command these men in late October, although Dundas stressed to the general that this duty was temporary and was not to be interpreted as a change to the plan to send him to the West Indies.

By early November, Grey's Caribbean force was reduced to fewer than 11,000 men assembled from Spithead and Cork, with the tentative plan now to attack the French islands of Martinique, Guadeloupe and St Lucia. If he could spare sufficient forces, he might also attack Saint Domingue. In practice, the capture of all these islands appeared unrealistic. The reduction of Fort Bourbon on Martinique would probably be impossible due to a shortage of heavy artillery. Grey would have the final say when he arrived in the region.

In mid-November the general was back in London and expecting the imminent departure of his expedition. At this late hour, reinforcements were needed for the defence of the newly acquired British naval base at Toulon and the support of Royalist forces at St Malo on the western French coast. The only solution was to further dilute Grey's small army to just over 7,000 men drawn from Portsmouth and Cork. The expedition finally set sail from St Helen's Road on 26 November. It was roughly half the original planned strength and 18 weeks behind schedule. Dundas had supported it and was as eager to see it depart as its commanders, but the project had, in Duffy's words, 'stood at the mercy of every messenger who arrived from the Continent or the Caribbean'.[1]

No doubt relieved at escaping the uncertainties of the expedition's tortuous preparation, Grey and Jervis arrived at Carlisle Bay on Barbados on 6 January 1794. Here they were expecting to find the transports that had preceded them from Cork, but the bay was empty. This further anxiety was soon allayed by the arrival of the troops; by mid month all the hundred or so Portsmouth and Cork ships had arrived except three. Grey established his headquarters at Government House, a healthy situation about half a mile outside Bridgetown. General Bruce had returned home sick and the temporary command had been in the hands of Major General John Whyte. Grey found that the planned concentration of troops at Barbados had not happened. Lacking clear orders, his predecessors had only partly brought together the flank companies and had sent two regiments to St Vincent and Grenada. All necessary regiments to leeward would have to be retrieved against the trade winds. The manpower issues were worsened by outbreaks of disease, mainly scurvy and typhus, in the newly arrived men. There were soon 1,200 on the sick list, a situation exacerbated by the failure of medical supplies to reach the island.

It was typical of Grey that he used the enforced delay to his advantage. As the sickness levels gradually improved, the general made every effort to improve the morale and battle readiness of his soldiers. He ordered every officer of the light companies to attend a course of instruction given by Major General

Thomas Dundas in order to acquire 'the perfection of Light Infantry attained during the American war'. Training of the troops was undertaken between three o' clock in the morning and sunrise to protect them from the heat of the day. Jervis was equally busy. Cooper Willyams, chaplain on the *Boyne*, saw the sailors put through their paces, 'exercised and instructed in the use of small arms and pikes'.[2]

As these preparations gained momentum, Grey received an unwelcome letter from Dundas suggesting that Saint Domingue might be attacked first. British gains in the colony could be consolidated and all the West Indian targets could be achieved in a single campaign. Conscious of the immediate military imperatives and the realities of warfare in the region, Grey rejected the idea. Any change of plan would lead to even more delay; the campaigning season was already advanced and an all out assault on Saint Domingue would mean a thousand-mile voyage before having to return to Martinique against the trade winds. Any compromise, perhaps the sending of a detachment to Saint Domingue, would still undermine operations to windward. Grey was hopeful of great success in the Windward Islands. He had a high-quality force – the Cork troops were the elite of the Irish Army – and French émigrés' reports of enemy weakness led him to believe that even Fort Bourbon and Martinique could be taken. At least some of his officers shared their commander's optimism. Brevet Major Robert Irving of the 70th wrote home on the 11th, 'I suppose in less than three weeks we will attack Martinico...we expect it will be an easy conquest as there are few white troops and the slaves they have armed will not stand above one fire, much less allow the bayonet to come near them'.

Having identified Martinique as the first objective, Grey formulated his plan of attack. He had the rare advantage of good intelligence. Refugee French officers fleeing Martinique informed him that the defences of Fort Bourbon were weak, the island's governor, Rochambeau, was at odds with the mulattoes, and that the garrison and defences were of poor quality.

By the end of January, Grey had gathered in the troops from leeward and the British force had grown to just over 7,000 men with an escort of 19 ships of war. Mindful of the dispersed French defences, he decided on a strategy of multiple simultaneous attacks on the island. In his own words, the three separate landings would be, '...distant from each other, not only for the Purpose of dividing the Enemy's Force and Attention, but to alarm him in every quarter at the same Time...' The first of the three divisions of the force under Commodore Charles Thompson and General Thomas Dundas was to make for the Bay of Galion on the east coast of the colony (see map 3). Dundas was to capture the fortified refuge at Gros Morne in the centre of the island, thus threatening both St Pierre and Fort Royal from the rear. The second part of the force under Captain Josiah Rogers of the *HMS Quebec* and Colonel Sir Charles Gordon were to make for Case de Navire to the north-west of Fort Royal. This area was relatively well fortified with coastal batteries and defensive lines and the landing was intended to be a substantial diversion. The main landing, under the supervision of the two commanders, was to be at Sainte Luce in the south. Once ashore, part of this contingent, under the command of Major General Whyte, was to march along the coast to the west capturing the sea batteries while Grey was to move inland to join Dundas's force around Fort Royal Bay. British knowledge of the geography was good enough to allow detailed lines of march to be provided; these contained names of local guides and information pertaining to plantations and even individual houses. On 22 and 24 January, Grey issued general orders leaving his men in no doubt as to what he expected of them. The tone was optimistic. He praised their fighting qualities. If they were fighting the best troops in France, 'it would not be a contest of ten minutes', but their enemies on Martinique would be largely untrained. Rochambeau's defensive force was probably between 1,000 and 2,000 men, with only around 200 regular troops, 3–400 National Guards and 160 sailors, the remainder an indeterminate number of mulattoes and blacks. Most of the regular force was in Fort Royal. Jervis had so effectively cleared the surrounding seas of enemy ships that the British arrival caught the French by surprise.[3]

On the evening of 5 February, a small number of Grey's men landed at Pointe de Borgnesse and silenced the enemy batteries before re-embarking. The general was disinclined to land more men in the gloom and it was 3am on the following day before 2,700 troops of Robert Prescott's 3rd Brigade, the 3rd Battalion of Grenadiers and the 2nd and 3rd Battalions of Light Infantry started to go ashore at Trois Rivières to the west of Sainte Luce. The latter units were made up of the grenadier and light companies of the various line regiments. Within a few hours, the division was safely landed and Grey joined his men. He then immediately marched with one column along the difficult and mountainous road to Rivière Salée. The troops were under cover in the village by 7pm. The sufferings on this eight-mile march, one sergeant dying of heat exhaustion, were a brutal introduction to Caribbean warfare. In accordance with the plan, Whyte was detached westward with the 2nd Battalion of Light infantry to take the seaward batteries of Cape Solomon and Pointe Bourgos in the rear. The ultimate objective was to capture Pigeon Island, a heavily fortified enemy stronghold which was preventing the navy entering the harbour of Fort Royal Bay.

Rochambeau now made his first move, sending men from Fort Royal across the bay to the height of Morne Charlotte Pied to cut communications between Whyte and headquarters at Rivière Salée. Grey responded vigorously, ordering the 70th Regiment and two howitzers to dislodge them with a bayonet charge, a successful action which, according to the general's dispatch, was 'executed with great spirit'. By the next day, the 9th, Whyte had been reinforced by artillery, two companies of the 15th Regiment, and 200 seamen. Armed with pikes and pistols, the sailors made 'unequalled exertions' to bring up supplies through mountain and forest, thereby allowing Whyte to erect a battery on Morne Matharine only 400 yards to the south of Pigeon Island. The two 5½-inch howitzers opened up on the morning of the 11th, taking the island's defences in the rear and forcing the garrison to surrender after two hours' bombardment with the loss of 15 killed and 25 wounded out of 200 defenders. The capture of Pigeon Island opened Fort Royal Bay and allowed proper naval support for the land forces.[4]

Grey was now well established to the south of Fort Royal. To the north, Gordon had also made some progress. It has been noted that this force was landing on a more heavily guarded part of the island and Gordon's 1,654 officers and men suffered casualties from the beach batteries at Case de Navire before effecting a landing on the 8th at Case Pilote to the northwest. The coastal road to Fort Royal was strongly occupied by the enemy and the British force had to strike through the mountains in a turning movement. This was draining work for the troops but, by the 12th, the five enemy batteries between Case de Navire and Negro Point had been carried and the force was encamped within a league of Fort Royal. Contemporary and more recent opinions vary as to Gordon's efforts; Fortescue portrays his operation as being as triumphant as Grey's and indeed the army's commander was upbeat in his subsequent dispatch, applauding Gordon's 'complete success' and emphasising the gains. Not all Gordon's men were so impressed. Captain William Stewart comments that the force commander gave little instruction to his officers and that when the 12th company of Grenadiers were surprised by a night attack by a small party of the enemy, there was panic and confusion. Duffy describes Gordon's success as 'partial' and his occupation of the heights of St Catherine as a 'dead stop'.[5]

The third landing was made by Dundas at Galion Bay on the 5th. Here there was unequivocal success. A naval squadron silenced the shore batteries before Dundas landed his troops and moved on Trinité, which was defended by the mulatto commander General Bellegarde. After some skirmishing, Bellegarde set fire to the evacuated town, which was promptly occupied by British forces who managed to salvage much of the place. Poyen informs us that Bellegarde was later criticised by Rochambeau for retreating towards St Pierre rather than falling back on the strategically important fortified passes of the Gros Morne. Fully exploiting the enemy's error, Dundas reached this central position at midnight on the seventh. Leaving the 64th to hold Gros Morne and delayed only by heavy rain he then pushed forward again and seized the Heights of Bruneau, the site of an old fort six miles to the north-east of Fort Bourbon, at noon on the 9th. He was now within sight of the outposts of Fort Royal.

Three companies under Lieutenant Colonel Craddock took possession of Fort Matilde, a good landing place on the Cohé du Lamentin to the left of the force. On the 10th, Colonel Campbell was despatched with five companies of light infantry to seize Colon. Bellegarde's men made an attack on Matilde but they were repulsed by Craddock, the grenadiers of the 9th Regiment dispersing their opponents with a bayonet charge. Campbell was reinforced at Colon by Lieutenant Colonel Eyre Coote, and moved on to take possession of Lemaitre. Three enemy attacks during the night of the 11th were beaten off. The bulk of Dundas's men were dug in at Bruneau sheltering from persisting rain; on the 14th, they were joined by Grey's contingent moving up from Rivière Salée. A week into the operation, the junction of the two forces landed north and south of Fort Royal had been achieved.

Dundas now returned to Trinité with the 2nd Battalion of Grenadiers, the light companies of the 33rd and 40th and the 65th Regiment. This force was split into two. Under the command of Colonel Campbell, the two light companies and the 65th moved northwest with instruction to await the arrival of Dundas's men on a spur of mountain extending south-west from Mont Pelée. The latter force commenced their march on the evening of the 14th, first along the coast north of Trinité and then westwards to the pass of La Calebasse, 4,000 feet above sea level. These manoeuvres through the 'impenetrable' ravines, mountains and jungle of the interior of Martinique required considerable determination and some skill. When he reached La Calebasse, Dundas had travelled 20 miles through this terrain in just 12 hours. After a short respite, his exhausted men scaled the steep slopes and drove the enemy back before linking with Campbell's column (to the south near Montigné) which was also involved in heavy fighting with five or six hundred of the enemy. Dundas's intervention with his advance guard was vital, the French again repulsed. Campbell had been killed earlier in the day leading a bayonet charge at the head of the 40th light company. Fending off a final enemy counter attack, the British force took a well deserved rest on Morne Rouge.[6]

At daybreak on the 17th, two columns advanced towards St Pierre, the next objective. By the time Dundas reached the town, he found it already in the possession of Colonel Richard Symes, whose detachment of three light companies and the 58th Regiment had been disembarked to the north. A second force of five companies of the 1st Battalion of Grenadiers and five companies of the 2nd Battalion of Light Infantry under Colonel William Myers stood to the immediate south of the town. This wealthy commercial capital had been abandoned, those Republicans still willing to fight all retreating to Fort Royal. Willyams says that Symes's troops had occupied the place in good order. 'No man was suffered to quit his ranks, nor was the least injury done to any of the inhabitants, who, with the women and the children, sat at their doors and windows to see our army march in, the same as when troops pass through a town in England.'[7]

The fall of St Pierre meant that the only obstacles to Grey's mastery of Martinique were the defences of the town of Fort Royal, the fortifications of

Fort Bourbon and Fort Louis. Here, Rochambeau had concentrated his regular forces and was determined to resist for as long as possible. Time might prove to be the French commander's greatest asset; the sickly season was approaching, any delay frustrated Grey's ambitions with respect to the other islands, and there was still hope of reinforcement from France. Of the two forts, Bourbon was the more formidable, but it was dominated by the Heights of Sourier to the north. Grey concluded that he could not properly invest Bourbon without possession of this higher ground, which was occupied by Bellegarde with a considerable number of mulatto and black troops. The British commander planned his attack for one o'clock in the morning of 19 February but, as Grey himself describes, his adversary made an impulsive first move.

> At noon on the preceding day [18 February] a most fortunate Event anticipated my Wishes and his Ruin. Bellegarde, with part of his Troops, descending the Heights, attacked my Left, towards the Landing-Place, in a very daring and spirited Manner; to which Part Lieutenant-General Prescott led a Reinforcement, with great Judgement and in good Time, checking and charging the Enemy. Availing myself of this favourable moment, when Bellegarde's camp was weakened, I ordered from my Right, the 3rd Battalion of Grenadiers, commanded by Lieutenant-Colonel [Joseph] Buckeridge, and supported by the 1st and 2nd Battalions of Light Infantry, under Lieutenant-Colonels Coote and [Bryan] Blundell, who attacked his Camp upon the Left, in such a Superior Style of Spirit and Impetuosity, as to prove irresistible: and I got possession of it and his Cannon, with inconsiderable Loss; which might have proved very different if my Attack had not taken place until one o'clock the next morning...

The mulatto leader had played into Grey's capable hands. British losses were only 60 killed and wounded whilst Bellegarde had lost 200 of his men. The survivors of this rout fled to Fort Bourbon where Rochambeau, furious at Bellegarde's precipitate attack, refused them entry. Seven days later, Bellegarde and his 300 chasseurs surrendered. Poyen asserts that he was bribed by the payment of 200,000 *livres*, but it may be that he was more influenced by Rochambeau's antagonism. The captured general was sent to Boston.[8]

The cession of the Height of Sourier did not deter Rochambeau and he rejected Grey's offer of a negotiated surrender. The British made their siege preparations in unusually persistent and heavy rain which turned the ground into a quagmire. Progress was frustratingly slow but methodical, directed by the army's engineers and carried out by every available man. Entrenchment was made difficult by the rocky terrain and fascines were constructed to protect the batteries. The seamen moved guns and ammunition and dug roads. This brutal work was often interrupted by fire from the fort, the Republicans starting to find their range. Lieutenant George Colville helped to construct one of the batteries on Sourier and saw nine black labourers killed or wounded by a single cannon shot. Snipers were also a constant danger.

Despite the appalling weather and difficult ground, the batteries were ready. According to Grey, these were at a distance of four to five hundred yards from the fortress's walls. The effect of the subsequent bombardment of Fort Bourbon was witnessed by Cooper Willyams.

> At day-break on the 7th (the gun boats having as usual attacked Fort Louis in the night) mortars, howitzers, and great guns opened from five batteries at the same instant, keeping up an incessant fire on the fort and advanced redoubt all of that day and the night, from each of which it was returned with equal fury. All the following day the same spirited attack and defence was continued.

Other observers could see the houses in the fort collapsing as they were struck by shells 'which hit them in all possible directions'. The enemy made a sortie on the 9th on the side of Case de Navire but they were driven back by the 3rd Light Infantry and a company of seamen.

The defenders' problems are well documented in Rochambeau's journal. Fort Bourbon was not as strong as its reputation. Among its defects was a narrow front to the north towards Sourier, which meant that only a proportion of the 100 available guns could be turned against Grey's batteries. The French commander worked hard to overcome these physical flaws, but in the face of the powerful British attack and escalating losses – the first day's bombardment cost a twelfth of the garrison – he struggled to maintain his force's morale. On the 9th, Colville counted more than a hundred shots fired by the three 24-pounders. Three days later, Grey, conscious of the wider implications of a prolonged siege, again offered Rochambeau surrender terms. The Frenchman refused.

> 12 March – The general Grey and the vice-admiral Jervis have written to me, as well as to the local authorities and to the citizens of the town of the Republic to summon us to surrender the forts. They give four hours for a response...I replied that, resigned to the future, I will defend myself in a manner to deserve the estimation of the English generals and troops, and that we will restart hostilities when the parleying officer is returned.

At this time, a sixth of the garrison were affected by wounds and another sixth by dysentery.

The stubborn resistance of the depleted Republican garrison was starting to frustrate the besiegers. Grey was reluctant to storm Fort Bourbon along the ridge from Sourier, wary of the heavy casualties he was likely to suffer in first capturing the redoubt and then entering the fortress. The general and admiral instead decided to launch an attack against Forts Royal and Louis from the sea. The combined operation, planned for 20 March, would serve to isolate Fort Bourbon. This was to prove the breakthrough.

> Having concerted measures with the Admiral for a combined attack by the Naval and Land forces upon the Fort and Town of Fort Royal, and the Batteries of my Second Parallel being ready, those on Morne Tortenson and Carriere kept up an incessant fire upon Fort Royal, and all the other Batteries on Fort Bourbon, during the Day and Night of the 19th Instant, and on the Morning on the 20th following, till the Ships destined for this Service had taken their Stations. The Asia of 64 Guns, Captain Browne, and the Zebra Sloop of 16 Guns, Captain Faulkner, with Captain Rogers, and a body of Seamen in Flat Boats, the whole under Commodore Thompson, composed the Naval Force; and the Land Force consisted of the 1st Battalion of Grenadiers, under Lieutenant-Colonel Stewart; and the 3rd Light Infantry under Lieutenant-Colonel Close, from Prince Edward's camp at La Coste; with the 3rd Grenadiers, under Lieutenant-Colonel Buckeridge, and the 1st Light Infantry, under Lieutenant-Colonel Coote, from General Prescott's camp at Sourriere.

By this stage, the fire from the batteries in Fort Bourbon had much slackened. The intrepid Faulkner took his *Zebra* sloop directly against the high walls of Fort Royal under the enemy's guns. His sailors threw across bamboo scaling ladders from the rigging and stormed the place. They met little opposition and the bulk of the garrison fled up the hill to Fort Bourbon. At the same time, the land forces gained entrance to Fort Royal town and raised the Union Jack, changing its name to Fort Edward to honour the Duke of Kent, who had just joined the force.

Rochambeau's situation was now desperate. Following consultation with the local authorities and his troops, he decided to surrender. The French commander was covered in the blood of a wounded fellow officer, had few stores and little water, had lost half of his artillery, and was surrounded by demoralised men. Fortescue acknowledges that his defence of Fort Bourbon was 'gallant'. The British bombardment ceased after 2.30pm on the 20th and negotiations began. It was agreed that the garrison should march out with the full honours of war. Colville watched them from the side of the harbour road.

The Regiment of Turenne leading them, very weak in numbers but in general well looking men. The mulattos and blacks next followed in every respect a most despicable enemy, half naked and half starved. Between 6–700 souls marched out and a most pitiful appearance did they make.

Rochambeau was sent to America and his men were immediately embarked in transports to take them to France on condition that they should not serve again in the war.[9]

The siege of Fort Bourbon had delayed Grey for almost seven weeks but it was a valuable prize. Its occupation gave Britain a major strategic advantage in the West Indies. Deprived of this key naval base, the French would now be limited to small expeditions. Only by creating unrest and insurrection would the Republic be able to sustain the struggle. Grey had vowed to make every effort to preserve his troops and he had kept his word. The arduous operations leading to the capture of Martinique resulted in the loss of only around 300 killed and wounded. He did, however, have 500 men sick and a line infantry strength of less than 6,000. During the siege he had asked Dundas for reinforcement to continue the campaign, to capture and occupy as many French islands as possible before the start of the sickly season.[10]

The next target was the significantly smaller colony of St Lucia, thought to be defended by little more than a thousand men, a mixture of regulars, mulattoes and local whites. Grey was to repeat the strategy which had served him well on Martinique, landing his forces at several points on the island. Leaving a garrison at the new possession, his remaining force, 4,800 strong, departed Fort Royal on 30 March. It was composed as follows:

...the Brigade of Grenadiers, commanded by his Highness Prince Edward; the Brigade of Light Infantry, by Major-General Dundas; and the 6th, 9th and 43rd Regiments by Colonel Sir Charles Gordon, with Engineers, & c. under Colonel Durnford and a Detachment of the Royal Artillery with some Light Ordnance under Lieutenant-Colonel Patterson...

Reaching St Lucia on 1 April, troops were landed at Anse du Cap, Anse du Choc, Anse Latoc and at Marigot (see map 5). There was no resistance and, with Jervis's fleet safely anchored in Cul de Sac Bay, British forces were soon closing in on their ultimate goal, the fort of Morne Fortune, which dominated the port of Castries and which was under the command of General Ricard. This fortress was vulnerable with the works incomplete and a garrison of only a few hundred. Poyen describes the defenders as 'sick and deprived of everything'. Under the circumstances, Grey was confident enough to take the offensive immediately. On the evening of the 2nd, four companies of Coote's 1st Light Infantry Battalion surprised a redoubt and two batteries, bayoneting 32 men and spiking six cannon. According to Johnston Abercromby of the 3rd Battalion of Grenadiers this 'terrified' the defenders in the fort and the reverse was enough to induce Ricard to surrender under the same terms agreed at Martinique. The small garrison marched out on 4 April to be replaced by the 6th and 9th Regiments. Grey wrote to Dundas that the name of the fort had been changed to Charlotte and that the conquest of the island had been achieved without the loss of a man.[11]

After returning to Martinique, the British general turned his eyes towards Guadeloupe, made up of the islands of Basse Terre (often referred to as Guadeloupe) and Grande Terre (see map 6). These islands were separated by a narrow arm of the sea, called La Rivière Salée, which was navigable for vessels of 50 tons. Grande Terre is mainly low lying and Basse Terre more rugged and mountainous. Together, these islands were larger in both size and population than Martinique. Grey had just over 4,000 men at his disposal, whilst the number of Republican troops on the colony was uncertain. One estimate was that there were as many as 7–8,000 regulars in addition to sailors, mulatto and black contingents, but this is at odds with the local French commander General Collot's later assertion that, because of disease, he had only 120 regular soldiers to oppose the English invasion.

Grey and Jervis sent a squadron ahead to capture the small islands called the Saints; these could be used as a supply base and anchorage. The main force sailed on 8 April with the intent to seize Guadeloupe's main town, Point-à-Pitre, and the nearby fort of Fleur d'Épée on the south coast of Grande Terre. The fleet was dispersed by adverse winds and when the first ships arrived off Gozier to the east of Point-à-Pitre on 10 April other vessels, including many of the troop transports, were still two days away. It was an awkward situation which Grey tackled in typically aggressive style, choosing to put ashore a scratch force of two grenadier battalions, one company of the 43rd Regiment, fifty marines, and 400 seamen to defend the beaches until other troops arrived. The general was determined not to give his adversary time to reinforce potential landing sites. The disembarkation was assisted by the fire of the 32-gun frigate *Winchelsea*, which silenced the enemy's guns. The vessel's commander, Lord Garlies, was the only man wounded in the operation.[12]

By the following day, the 12th, the remaining transports had appeared, more troops were disembarked and Grey resolved to attack the Republican forces on Morne Mascotte and in Fort Fleur d'Épée. The latter was the most formidable of the enemy defences but it was controlled by Morne Mascotte, a hill only a musket shot to the rear of it. This fact determined Grey's plan of attack. A detachment under Prince Edward was to attack the Morne, a second under Thomas Dundas to assault Fleur d'Épée from the rear, and a third under Colonel

Symes to follow the road along the coast to cooperate with Dundas. Grey ordered his men 'not to fire but to execute every Thing with the Bayonet'. At five o'clock, a signal of the firing of a gun was given from Jervis's flagship, the *Boyne*, and the troops swarmed towards the fort. Willyams relates the dénouement.

> As they advanced to the first piquet the alarm was given; the outposts were driven in or put to death: and in an instant the sides of the hill on which the fort was situated were covered by our people, who scrambled up, under a most tremendous discharge of grape shot and musketry: some sailors jump into the embrasures, driving the enemy before: the soldiers, who had reached the gates, at length succeeded in forcing them open: the enemy still continuing to make a stout resistance were put to the sword in great numbers; at length, as many as could escape through the gates and embrasures, or by leaping over the walls, fled with the utmost precipitation towards the town of Point-à-Pitre.

Both sides suffered significant losses in this hard fought affair; the British 15 killed and 60 wounded (including 15 sailors) and the enemy 67 killed, 55 wounded and 110 taken prisoner. Of the prisoners, 78 were black, 18 mulatto, and 14 white, reflecting the mixed nature of the Republican force. The number of enemy captives casts doubt on Poyen's accusation that the victorious troops showed little mercy to the garrison.[13]

Grey now had effective control of Grande Terre. Leaving the 43rd Regiment to garrison Point-à-Pitre and Fort Prince Of Wales (the late Fort Fleur d'Épée) he embarked the 1st and 2nd Grenadiers and the 1st Light Infantry at twelve o'clock on the 14th and landed five hours later across the bay at Petit Bourg on Basse Terre. Here he was greeted with 'great demonstrations of joy' by local French planters. Grey now moved south along the coast road to Trois Rivières where he could see two enemy redoubts and the strong post of Palmiste near the town of Basseterre, where Collot and the bulk of his forces awaited the British attack. This was to be two-pronged as Dundas had sailed from Point-à-Pitre and landed with the 3rd Battalion of Grenadiers and the 2nd and 3rd Battalions of Light Infantry at Vieux Habitants and was approaching the town from the north. On the 21st, the two forces made their junction having turned the enemy out of the key defences of Palmiste and the Morne Houelle.

Collot's hold on Basseterre was weakened by insurrection. During the nights of the 17th and 18th, large parts of the town, including the hospital, were set alight. A council of war was assembled and it was concluded that the number of regular troops in the garrison was insufficient to defend the fort; at least 1,000 would be needed. Collot capitulated, surrendering Guadeloupe and all its dependencies including the islands of Marie Galante, Desiderata and the Saints.

The terms were the same as were agreed with Rochambeau at Martinique and Ricard at St Lucia. At 8 o'clock on the 22nd, the French garrison of 55 regulars of the Regiments of Guadeloupe and the 14th *ligne* and over 800 National Guards and others marched out of Basseterre's Fort Saint Charles (Matilda). Grey had lost only 11 men, killed, wounded or missing. The whole campaign was, in Fortescue's opinion, 'an extraordinary example of the power of a small and efficient army working in perfect harmony with a small and efficient squadron upon a fortified coast'.[14]

Grey wrote to Dundas of his latest triumph, emphasising the 'unanimity and extraordinary exertions of the Navy and Army' and listing the islands he had added to the British Empire. He was, however, running out of men. There was no question of a new offensive against Saint Domingue. Indeed, with a growing number of soldiers on the sick list, it was no easy task to defend his conquests. The general, no doubt believing his capture of the main military prize in the Caribbean, Martinique, to be a sufficient gain, was planning to return home in July. Modestly attributing his successes to 'good fortune', he informed Dundas that he was exhausted, '...my continuing here would reduce and weaken me to that degree that I am persuaded would prevent me being able to execute, to my own satisfaction, any service on which I might be employed in Autumn'. Grey's and Jervis's enjoyment of their West Indian triumphs – they were hailed as heroes at home where the canons in St James's Park and the Tower of London fired salutes – was to be compromised by accusations that they had illegally enriched themselves with prize money. Grey admitted that, as a military man, many administrative matters were beyond him. He was undoubtedly guilty of greed and nepotism.

In early May, battalion companies of the 22nd, 35th, and 41st Regiments from Ireland reached Grey at Martinique. He was warned by the British Consul that a French fleet was in Hampton Roads and that the Americans were threatening war; the 35th were retained but the remaining reinforcements were sent on to Jamaica with General Whyte and, as has been related, were subsequently employed in Saint Domingue. Grey now considered an expedition against the French colony of Cayenne, but this scheme was abandoned when it was learnt that there was a strong force on the island. The army's mounting number of sick remained a disincentive to active operations. Flank companies of the 22nd, 23rd, 35th and 41st were sent to rejoin their battalion companies in Saint Domingue.

At the end of the month, as the Government basked in the glory of Caribbean triumphs, peace seemed to have broken out in the region. However, the British hold on Guadeloupe and St Lucia was not as tight as it appeared. Only the larger towns and fortifications were secured; much of the interior of both islands was held only because of the goodwill of the colonists, which was being eroded by the perception that British commanders and soldiers were rapacious. French residents believed that they had 'changed one set of oppressors for another'. Grey thought that any French counter-attack could not begin before the autumn, the sickly season now starting, but he and Jervis were about to be unpleasantly surprised.

On 2 June 1794, nine French ships approached Point-à-Pitre. Aboard was a force of around 1,100 men comprised of a battalion of light infantry, a strong company of infantry of the line, and 150 canons arranged into two batteries. This expedition, which had departed from Rochefort 40 days earlier, was under the command of two civil commissioners, Pierre Chrétien and Victor Hugues. The approach of the force was noted by Lieutenant Colonel James Drummond, the commander of Grande Terre. This officer made hurried preparations but his regiment, the 43rd, was reduced to less than 200 men by sickness and the British response was also compromised by the death of the colony's governor, Major General Thomas Dundas, of yellow fever on the same day as the French arrival. Dundas's successor made belated efforts to help Drummond in Fort Fleur d'Épée but it was too late.

The Republicans came ashore near the village of Gozier on the 2nd and 3rd. Drummond had been reinforced by the merchants of Point-à-Pitre and French Royalists, bringing the strength of the garrison to around 300 men. A sortie by the Royalists on the 4th achieved little beyond disturbing the Republican pickets and they quickly retreated to the fort. At one o'clock on the morning of Friday the 6th, the Republicans attacked the fort with between 1,200 and 1,500 men. Drummond relates the outcome;

> ...the advanced Piquet came into the Fort and we then distinctly heard the Approach of the enemy along the road leading from the Village. We instantly commenced a Fire of Grape Shot from One Twenty-four-Pounder and Two Field-Pieces, which threw them into great Confusion and must have been attended with considerable Effect. The enemy halted for Two or Three Minutes, and then, at the Persuasion of their Officers, marched on to the Foot of the Hill, and began to Storm the Work. We kept up a very heavy Fire of Musketry for about Fifteen minutes; The Enemy were evidently repulsed, and I am persuaded that had the Royalists acted with Resolution at that moment, we might have maintained our Ground; but, on the firing ceasing, Numbers of them concluded the Place lost, and, abandoning their Posts, ran in Crowds towards the Gate. It was in vain for the Soldiers of the 43rd Regiment to Oppose their Progress; the Gates were laid open and nearly One Half of the whole Body deserted the Town. The Gates were again closed as soon as possible, and the small Body of the 43rd Regiment, which I had kept in Reserve, moved on to the Attack. They opposed the Entrance of the enemy for some Time, but one side of the Work having been abandoned,

and left entirely defenceless, we found ourselves nearly surrounded, and I then ordered the Soldiers I had with me to charge with their Bayonets, and retire a few Paces to a Spot where we might be better able to defend ourselves. Here we halted, and received a Volley of musketry from a Number of the enemy that had formed themselves in a Body in our Front. The Crowd of People that now came rushing from every Quarter toward the Gate rendered every effort by the Soldiers ineffectual: Overpowered as they were, they found themselves dispersed and obliged to retire.

Drummond now consulted with two or three of his fellow officers and, judging the fort untenable, he abandoned Fleur d'Épée, retiring to Fort Louis. Here he decided that prolonged resistance was futile and he embarked his remaining force and escaped across the bay to Basse Terre. When Lieutenant Colonel Blundell belatedly arrived with reinforcements on the 6th, the Republican flag was flying over the fort. Drummond was unsure of his number of killed and wounded, whilst Hugues estimated his losses as 90 men and believed his enemy to have suffered more than double this number of casualties. He had taken some French Royalist and British prisoners.[16]

In Duffy's words, the Caribbean war was suddenly 'more serious and deadly'. The Republican forces were struck by yellow fever, with the death of many senior civil and military officers. This meant that the command role devolved to the capable but merciless Hugues. In addition to strengthening his land defences, Hugues took radical steps to enlarge his army, summoning all Republicans and disseminating the contents of the decrees of the French Convention of 4 February 1794, legislation which emancipated the slaves. Now the blacks had equal rights to the whites and the Convention planned to rally the whole black population to their own cause, a threat not just to Guadeloupe, but also to other British islands.

Reports of the slaughter of the sick and wives of the 43rd Regiment at the hospital at Point-à-Pitre underlined the prevailing mood and the need for quick retaliation. Grey was determined to retake the initiative, writing to Sir Evan Nepean, Undersecretary for War, that he had no doubt of 'doing the business', even with his reduced forces, and that he believed it only a matter of 'being more alert and striking harder' than the enemy. He was prepared to resort to 'every means' to obtain his objective. The general and admiral boarded the *Boyne* and sailed for Guadeloupe, dropping anchor off Point-à-Pitre. British troops had been driven from Grande Terre to Basse Terre; the men were incensed at reports of Republican atrocities and were swearing revenge, emotions which their commander did not discourage. Jervis's fleet blockaded the French ships in Point-à-Pitre.

Whilst awaiting reinforcements from the other islands, Grey was given the opportunity to gain a morale-boosting victory. On the night of 13 June, the

French carelessly sent a modest detachment across the Salée to occupy Point St Jean, a headland on Basse Terre. They had been there only 48 hours when a British force, composed of the 39th Regiment and light infantry under the command of Colonel Francis Dundas, fell upon them with the bayonet killing 200 and causing others to flee into the waters of the harbour. The enemy's camp, colours, baggage and cannon were captured with only nine wounded and not a man killed. Grey praised his soldiers in General Orders promising that those who had particularly distinguished themselves would be commended to the King.[17]

By the morning of the 19th, sufficient reinforcements, including a number of flank companies, had arrived to allow the opening of operations against Hugues on Grande Terre. A landing was made 'without loss or opposition' on the beach of Anse Canot under the cover of two frigates. Once ashore, the grenadiers and light infantry moved on Gozier, which the enemy abandoned, burning some of the houses. Grey began to throw up batteries against Fleur d'Épée and there commenced several days desperate fighting around the fort. The British had 3–4,000 men and the Republicans perhaps around 3,000. Having seized St Ann's, seven miles to the east, Grey next ordered Lieutenant Colonel Gerrit Fisher to clear the road from Gozier to Fleur d'Épée, a task he performed with aplomb. This left the enemy still in possession of high and wooded country in front of Morne Mascotte and, on the 27th, they were forced back into Fleur d'Épée by grenadiers and light infantry under Brigadier General Richard Symes. Undeterred by this reverse, the enemy responded by 'arming Blacks, Mulattos, and Coloureds' and launching an attack against that part of the Morne held by Fisher and his men. Republican fire raked the top of the hill such that the grenadiers had to lay flat on their faces. When the enemy were within a few yards, the British sprang up and drove them back down the hill with the bayonet. Two days later, around a thousand mulatto and black troops, described by Grey as being clothed in the 'National Uniform' attacked the same post. On this occasion they had the support of round and grape-shot from the fort and a field piece on the right enfilading the grenadiers but the outcome was the same, the Republican assault repulsed with heavy losses by grenadiers and light infantry using their well-tested bayonets.

He had so far prevailed, but the incessant and intense fighting took its toll on Grey's men. In his later dispatch, the general explained his situation.

> The Rainy Season being already set in and this being the last month for acting before the Hurricane Season, at the same time that the Troops were exposed alternately to heavy Rains and a vertical sun, together with the circumstances of the great Slaughter recently suffered by the Enemy in the Two Attacks they made on Morne Mascot determined me to make an effort for finishing the Campaign at once...[18]

The British failure to capture Point-à-Pitre was one of the seminal events of the war. Grey entrusted the night attack of 1 July to Symes. The objective was the capture of Morne Gouvernement, the fortified post overlooking the town, or at least the destruction of the town's stores. Following Symes's anticipated success, Grey would storm Fleur d'Épée with the remainder of the army. Symes's force was made up of 800 men of the 1st Battalion of Grenadiers (under Lieutenant Colonel Fisher), the 1st and 2nd Light Infantry Battalions (under Lieutenant Colonel Gomm and Major Ross) and the 1st Battalion of Seamen (under Captain Robertson). There was a delay of two hours before the men moved off Morne Mascotte at 8pm. As later related by Symes, there were soon problems.

> The Troops marched with the utmost Silence through deep Ravines, in Hopes of reaching the Enemy undiscovered; but our Guides, whether from Ignorance, or the Darkness of the Night, led us in Front to those Posts of the Enemy which it had been proposed to pass by and which they assured us was practicable: To effect our Purpose by Surprise became therefore impossible.

Despite this setback, at 4 o'clock in the morning Major Ross and the 2nd Battalion of Light Infantry succeeded in driving in the enemy outposts and clearing the streets of the town with their bayonets, resisting heavy fire from Morne Gouvernement. The latter post had been reinforced and Symes judged that attacking it was now 'highly impossible'.

The general resolved to achieve his secondary objective of destroying the stores, but his men were under heavy fire both from the musketry of the defenders and the Republican ships in the harbour. He was taking heavy casualties and gradually losing control.

> ...by a Fatality as unforeseen as impossible to guard against we were prevented from completing what carried so fair an Appearance of Success. Our Troops, to whom you [Grey] have so strictly enjoined in Night Attacks never to fire, who have uniformly succeeded so often by a strict observance to that Rule, and who, till this Moment, had not in the Course of the Night fired a Shot, most unfortunately began to load and fire upon each other, nor could all the Efforts of the Officers put a stop to it.

The confusion was only increased by Symes himself suffering a severe wound to the right arm; he had not disclosed his orders to others. Sensing the opportunity, two senior French officers, Boudet and Pélardy, threw their men on Morne Gouvernement against the increasingly disorganised British force in the town. Captain of Grenadiers William Stewart saw his brother soldiers 'falling before our eyes under the swords and bayonets of a merciless enemy'. Ross and Fisher, fearing the complete destruction of their battalions, sounded the retreat and, with the gallant rear-guard action of the grenadiers and reinforcements furnished by Grey, were able to bring the remnants of the force back to Morne Mascotte.

The British losses are difficult to ascertain but they must have been great. An army casualty return for the period 10 June to 3 July shows 112 killed, 330 wounded and 56 missing; Fortescue estimates that more than 80% of these losses were sustained during the attack of 1 July. Other sources suggest over 500 soldiers and seamen lost including many of Grey's best officers. According to Poyen, '...two or three hundred French had put to flight two or three thousand English'. This is an exaggeration but the fighting spirit of the army was broken. Grey admitted as much, '...the troops had not the power in them; they were so completely worn down that they could not advance when ordered'. He did not blame them and he also stopped short of censuring Symes, who was to die from his wound. A year later, he confided to John Whyte that he believed that Symes had made a mistake in abandoning the high ground before charging into Point-à-Pitre. Officers on the scene thought Symes to be culpable. Bartholomew James accused him of not collecting his force properly before entering the town and of then 'harassing' his men. William Stewart agreed. The larger part of the force should have first stormed Morne Gouvernement to command the town and the failure to do this was in part due to the loss of guides, but also 'from the want of regular plan and exact arrangement which are so essentially necessary in all attacks and operations carried on by night'.

Whatever the cause of the debacle, the failure to storm Point-à-Pitre and thus capture the whole of Guadeloupe had profound implications for British strategy in the region. Without security to windward, always the strategic centre of the West Indies, it would be impossible to extend decisive operations to take and pacify Saint Domingue.[19]

It was obvious to Grey that he could not acquire Grande Terre immediately and he began to withdraw his forces to Basse Terre. Here he fortified a quadrilateral position around Berville on the isthmus west of the Rivière Salée. Breastworks were constructed with embrasures for field pieces and a strong abattis formed. On 8 July, Grey wrote to Dundas stating that he needed 1,200 to 2,000 troops simply to garrison the island already under his control and 6,000 men to retake Grande Terre. Leaving 48 companies, around 1,800 men (1st Battalion Grenadiers, 1st Battalion Light Infantry, 35th, 39th, 43rd, and 65th), at Berville camp under the command of Brigadier Colin Graham, Grey returned to Martinique on the 13th. Here he revised his estimate of required reinforcements to 10,800 and also exhorted Dundas to send out civilian governors to ease his administrative burden. The minister promised over 4,500 men to sail by late September and early November and inferred that Grey would be replaced and permitted to return to England on their arrival. Reinforcements were desperately needed: the sickly and ill-equipped British army believed that it had been forgotten by its political masters. By early September there were only 1,800 effectives with over a thousand men on the sick list. Berville camp, surrounded by unhealthy swamps, was a particular concern, 300 men dying in a few weeks in August, leaving only a similar number of men fit for duty. At the town of Basseterre, Governor Robert Prescott's force was also declining in an alarming fashion. Efforts to raise new soldiers on the islands were ultimately ineffectual. Unable to secure whites or mulattoes, Grey attempted to recruit black rangers but their number was limited to a few hundred. Grey's misery at the deaths of so many of his friends and troops was compounded when Dundas informed him that all his decisions relating to prize money were to be annulled. 'If this army be deprived of its prize money', the general replied, 'many of the officers must be ruined'.[20]

Anxieties regarding his reputation, or the wealth of his officers, were quickly overtaken by the deteriorating military situation in the conquered French islands. Grey's actions were limited to Jervis's naval blockade of Point-à-Pitre and a long-range bombardment from Berville camp. In contrast to the dramatic decline in British manpower, Hugues was able to augment his own sickly European forces with 2,000 black troops during August and early September and it was only a matter of time before he took the offensive against Basse Terre. A quick Republican attack was predicated by the need to preserve their own inactive forces from disease, the ongoing bombardment of Point-à-Pitre, and the fear of possible British reinforcements. On the night of 26 September, Jervis's blockading squadron drifted far enough to allow Hugues to bring his men ashore under the command of General Pélardy. The landings were at Lamentin and Goyave to the north and south of the British positions. The French plan was for a three-pronged assault on Berville, a third column attacking directly across the Rivière Salée via a pontoon bridge. Following his landing at Goyave, Pélardy quickly moved on Petit Bourg where the unfortunate James Drummond of the 43rd, commanding a small group of Royalists and hospital convalescents, was soon forced to surrender. Poyen tells us that the British lost 140 men and that a further 160 were taken prisoner whilst the French losses were only eight. The treatment of the prisoners is a matter of contention. Some witnesses, notably Cooper Willyams, insist that the sick not lucky enough to be evacuated by British ships were massacred. 'From the hospitals to the wharf was a continued scene of misery and horror, being strewed with the bodies of the sick, who were barbarously put to death as they were crawling to the shore...' At Lamentin, General Boudet advanced without meeting resistance to just north of the camp where he joined the central column under the command of Chef de Bataillon Bures, which had by now driven in the enemy outposts and crossed the Salée.[21]

The Republican plan had so far been well executed and Pélardy had seized extra cannon, munitions and supplies at Petit Bourg. Hugues ordered Boudet to attack Berville on the 29th with the two columns now under his united command. The Republicans had not properly reconnoitred the ground and they were beaten back from the redoubts with the loss of 400 killed or wounded. Boudet suffered a fractured shoulder. The small garrison, probably around 200 regulars and 300 Royalists, had fought for three hours with great resolve; Graham was severely wounded and his second-in-command killed. What happened next is uncertain. Poyen suggests that Graham was forced to surrender following a bombardment whilst Willyams claims that the Republicans made two more violent assaults on the 30th and on 4 October. What is certain is that, by the 6th, Graham's force of 125 men was in no fit state to make further resistance. His losses amounted to 27 killed and 56 wounded. The remaining men of the 39th, 43rd, and 65th Regiments and the flank companies from Ireland – 'fitter for hospital than to be under arms' – marched out of the camp to be made prisoners of war. Many of them subsequently perished in hulks in the harbour of Point-à-Pitre. Fortescue concludes that, '...the records of the British Army contain no greater example of heroism than this of the dying garrison of the Camp of Berville'. A few Royalists escaped but the unfortunates who fell into Republican hands were shot or guillotined.[22]

Hugues marshalled his 2,000 men along the coast to the town of Basseterre, burning and looting Royalist plantations. Grey's force was by now reduced to little over a thousand infantry fit for service and most of these troops were moved to Fort Matilda (known to the French as Saint Charles) at the southern end of Basseterre. Here, General Prescott was in a desperate state. To resist the impending Republican attack he had only around 500 men, mostly infantry but also a smaller number of marines, seamen, Royal Artillery and black corps. Offers of Royalist help were refused, either to protect them from brutal reprisals or because he believed them to be of little military value. The fortifications were in disrepair; a senior officer described the place as 'weak and irregular' and Prescott himself acknowledged that the works were even lacking lime to properly cement the walls.

The siege was to last for seven weeks. On the Republican side, Pélardy fell ill and was replaced by General Boudet, who vigorously opened the attack on the fort with two 18-pounders, two 24-pounders and a mortar. Local blacks helped to construct the wooden batteries. By early December, the attackers were running short of ammunition. Inside the fort, Bartholomew James bemoaned the mismatch of the two protagonists, '...where the loss of one man in the garrison was of more consequence to us than a hundred and fifty to the besiegers, whose force was not only excessively strong indeed, but which was increasing rapidly every hour; while sickness and havoc were every day reducing the few men that composed the garrison'. So desperate were the defenders, they were reduced to throwing glass into the ditches around the fort, '...well knowing they [the Republicans] did not abound in shoes and stockings'. On 9 December, Prescott believed himself to be under fire from 23 pieces of cannon and eight mortars. Making an inspection with his chief engineer, he concluded that the 'tottering' state of the defences enforced an immediate evacuation. All the guns at the Gallion Bastion were dismounted and the fortification a heap of ruins.

Prescott now skilfully embarked his garrison into the waiting ships of Rear Admiral Thompson. The operation was kept secret until the last possible moment and, by ten o'clock on the evening of the 10th, all the men were safely aboard without serious interruption by the enemy, who were apparently oblivious to Prescott's intentions. The general had preserved his garrison but Guadeloupe was lost. Poyen estimates the Republican losses in the siege to have been limited to 14 killed and a few wounded. Pélardy found the fort to be in ruins and the batteries almost all out of action. He well understood his adversary's decision to evacuate the place. Official returns show British losses during the siege as 16 killed and 82 wounded.[23]

Two weeks before the abandonment of Fort Matilda, Grey and Jervis, both weakened by illness and the demands of West Indian campaigning, had returned to England. The general was especially debilitated, complaining to Prescott of an attack of dysentery, '...if not quickly removed, I shall be laid completely fast'. Prescott was also ill. Despite the difficulties the military campaign had been, in large part, remarkably successful, a great example of excellent cooperation between the services. Even the feisty Prescott, who was not well disposed towards the navy, gave his thanks to Jervis for his support in first defending and then evacuating Fort Matilda. The ultimate failure of the expedition was due to lack of timely support from the British Government. Grey's growing disillusionment is obvious from his correspondence home; in a letter to a friend written as he waited for confirmation of the fall of Fort Matilda, he complains that the reverse of fortune was inevitable, '...should not the most ample reenforcements not arrive, not by piecemeal, the first falling victims to the Murderous Climate, before the second arrives, leaving us still in a weak state, our losses will not be confined to Guadeloupe'. The enemy, boosted by the support of emancipated slaves and by British weakness, would only grow in strength. To preserve the captured islands, Grey warned, '...a total new and powerful Establishment must come out, with a proper commander for I am so worn down as to be no longer fit to command'.

Of the officers who had accompanied Grey to Martinique, 27 were killed or died of their wounds and 170 fell victim to yellow fever or other tropical disease. The survivors were mostly invalids. As for the rank and file, it is difficult to be precise but at least 5,000, possibly as many as 7,000, of Grey's army were left in Caribbean graves. At Saint Domingue, of 4,000 troops who had landed there were only 1,800 alive at the end of the year. Many of the dead were raw recruits with little hope of survival, but the losses afflicted elite units including the flank companies of the Irish army. The navy suffered similarly. In the transport vessels, charged with the arduous task of landing troops, artillery and stores, more than a thousand crew had died of yellow fever. We cannot confidently state the total death toll but perhaps 12,000 British soldiers and sailors were lost in the West Indies in 1794.[24]

Chapter 5

The Flame of Rebellion:
The Uprisings of 1795

Fears that insurrection would break out in the British West Indian colonies proved to be well founded in 1795. The fundamental problem remained the lack of significant reinforcements to stabilise and defend the region. Extra troops promised since the autumn of 1794 failed to materialise. This was in part due to misfortune – regiments gathered at Portsmouth and Plymouth were forced back by bad weather and large numbers died of typhus on the crowded transports – but the nation's global objectives meant that resources were overstretched. Soldiers were also needed in Holland, India, Ceylon and the Cape of Good Hope. A few trickled through to the Caribbean; in December 1794, 1,780 officers and rank and file arrived at Martinique from Gibraltar.

Guadeloupe was lost, but Grey's conquests of Martinique and St Lucia remained under British control. The two islands absorbed around half the British forces in the region. It had been Grey's opinion, expressed in the summer of 1794, that the security of the Windward Islands demanded a garrison 11,000 strong. On Martinique, Grey's successor, Lieutenant General Sir John Vaughan, was less optimistic, asserting that the entire British army would not suffice to first capture and then defend all the islands. The realities of warfare in the region were more obvious to men on the scene and Vaughan urged Dundas to sanction the raising of black regiments. Williamson attempted a similar initiative in Saint Domingue, offering slaves freedom for long-term service. The army had so far relied heavily on the navy to protect vulnerable ports and forts but sailors were also dying of disease and the service was under strain.[1]

This increasing naval weakness was exposed in January 1795 when Hugues was able to penetrate the British blockade and reinforce his army on Guadeloupe. The Republican commander lost a transport carrying 550 men in a sharp action with British ships, but the remaining 1,500 troops were landed at Point-à-Pitre. Hugues was not much impressed by the help he had just received, complaining to the *Convention Nationale* that many of the weapons and ammunition were unusable and the soldiers mediocre. The 700 men of the Bataillon Antilles were a mixture of local whites and blacks who had previously been deported to France for political reasons. They were unlikely to stand up to the English. The poor quality of the new arrivals from Europe was less important than it might have been. Hugues was now bent on raising local manpower to usurp his enemy. He was quick to exploit his improved security on Guadeloupe to sow discontent and encourage insurrection on the neighbouring British islands. Republican delegations slipped out of Guadeloupe and made for St Lucia, Grenada and St Vincent.[2]

The first and most dramatic revolt was on Grenada. An English eyewitness on the island, Gordon Turnbull, was in no doubt as to who had incited the French colonists and slaves.

> We can more readily account for the defection of those of desperate fortunes, or of turbulent and malignant dispositions, differing only in colour from the *banditti* with whom they enlisted themselves, under the banner of rapine, treason and murder. Among these, there were several emissaries of the French Republic, who had, in the commotion of the troubles in the French Islands, emigrated from thence to Grenada, where, under the cloak of loyalty, and of suffering for its sake, they too easily found an asylum and were received with that generous compassion which is the particular characteristic of the British Nation.

These emissaries were eventually suspected of having ulterior motives, but they eluded capture.

> The general insurrection of the slaves which soon followed was undoubtedly the work of the same insidious instruments employed in spreading the flame of rebellion, disseminating discord, confusion and anarchy in the minds of all those who were susceptible of receiving the impression.

Many of the black inhabitants were French speaking and had easy connection with Republican sympathisers. On 2 March, the rebels seized the towns of Goyave and Grenville (see map 7). Many of the white inhabitants were massacred. The complacent governor, Ninian Home, was captured whilst traversing the island and held as a hostage by Julien Fédon, the mulatto who led the uprising. Fédon was quick to exploit his prize, issuing a grandiloquent proclamation, '...the tyrant Home, late governor of the island, Alexander Campbell [a local estate owner] and a great number of English having been made prisoner that their heads and the heads of all others shall answer for the conduct of those in authority'. The acting governor, Kenneth Mackenzie, was forced to concentrate his small force, probably some 500 regulars and militia, in and around St George's. According to Turnbull, the insurrection now became more widespread, thousands of blacks and French sympathisers rallying to Fédon's call.[3]

On St Lucia, there was similar unrest. The island was the most pro-revolutionary of the colonies and Hugues's demand that the inhabitants join the Republicans on pain of death was widely heeded. The British governor, Charles Gordon, was unpopular and the British commander, Brigadier General James Stewart, reported that the brigands were gaining ground. He held only the town of Castries and Morne Fortune (see map 5). This alarming news trickled through to Vaughan at Martinique. Unable to give simultaneous help to both islands, he decided that Grenada was the more urgent priority, actually removing 150 men from the St Lucia garrison and sending them to St George's under the command of Lieutenant Colonel Colin Lindsay of the 46th. Lindsay found that Mackenzie had already launched operations against Goyave but that little had been achieved. Reinforcements had arrived in the form of marines landed from three British men of war and also around 40 Spanish troops from the garrison of Trinidad. Lindsay reviewed the local militia, declaring that he was satisfied with their appearance. On 15 March at four o'clock in the morning, he marched off at the head of 400 regulars and militia to attack the rebels' camp at Belvidere close to Morne Felix. On the 17th, contact was made with about 150 enemy who were charged and chased into a wood. Lindsay's letter to Mackenzie, written the next day, gives no hint of impending tragedy.

> My Dear Sir
> I have great pleasure in testifying to you that nothing *could be better* than the behaviour of the militia in yesterday's affair which did not cost anything near the number of men we expected to lose. They showed the best countenance; and every soldier in our regular troops remarked that nothing could be better. Our whole loss is one Captain wounded, two rank and file killed, and sixteen wounded, chiefly of the ninth regiment who bore the brunt of the attack. We hope to be in their camp tomorrow.
> I remain, sir, your humble servant
> Colin Lindsay

Fédon's men lost about 20 killed and 40 wounded. Very heavy rain now rendered further forward movement impracticable and, in the early hours of the 22nd, Lindsay committed suicide. Whether this was because of the anxieties of command – he was frustrated both by the adverse weather and desertions from the militia – or illness is impossible to know. This popular and respected officer was replaced by Lieutenant Colonel John Bridges Schaw, but the opportunity had been lost. The Spanish troops were called back to Trinidad and Schaw judged that his remaining force was not sufficient for offensive operations. He withdrew to St George's and the island was effectively controlled by the enemy, now 5,000 strong. Mackenzie was forced to wait for reinforcements whilst British vessels attempted to stop Hugues landing arms and stores.[4]

Hugues's emissaries were also creating havoc on St Vincent. Here, both the French planters and the native Caribs had historical grievances against grasping British planters and they were ready converts to the Republican cause. French officer Moreau de Jonnès, sent to St Vincent by Hugues to stir insurrection, speaks of the Caribs' 'national hatred' for the English. The natives were no match for regulars in a pitched battle. When King Chateaugai threatened the capital Kingstown in March 1795, he was routed by a combined force of sailors and soldiers under the command of Captain Skinner of the *Zebra* and Captain Dugald Campbell of the 46th. The chief was killed and the Caribs suffered a hundred casualties. The Carib chief was not much helped by his allies. He had been supported by a battalion of infantry sent by Hugues but, according to Moreau de Jonnès, these men were a motley mixture of criminals from colonial depots, naval deserters, and runaway slaves. Vaughan, in a communication to Dundas, described the British losses as 'small'. Despite this success, and the antipathy of many of the island's blacks to the Caribs, Governor James Seton ceded most of the colony to the brigands. Denied the means to raise a black regiment, he kept his regulars, a handful of men from the 60th and 46th, and local militia of doubtful loyalty, in Fort Charlotte which guarded the entrance to Kingstown (see map 8).[5]

Dundas's promised reinforcements finally arrived at Barbados on 30 March but these were deficient in both quantity and quality. Instead of the anticipated 11 battalions there were only five, adding up to 2,700 men. Most of the troops were recent recruits, many of them little more than boys, equally unfit to bear arms or to survive the climate. Vaughan judged the 45th to be particularly weak, unsuited for service in any part of the world. He quickly decided to disperse the battalions around the various islands to try and check the insurrections. Thus, the 25th and 29th were sent to Grenada, the 34th and 61st to St Lucia, and the 41st to St Vincent. Including the units retained on Martinique, the total force in the Windward Islands in April was now 5,000 strong. The broad strategy was to occupy enough of the insurgent islands to starve the rebels of arms and stores from Guadeloupe. The weakened bands of brigands might then be driven inland, where a combination of British military strength and starvation would induce them to surrender.

Before describing the outcome of these operations it should be noted that, despite the chronic shortage of manpower in the region, Dundas had eyes on the Dutch colonies, proposing that a force of 600 men, the 3rd Battalion of the 60th, should be sent to Demerara 500 miles from Vaughan's base. There was no clear military objective; the minister was urged to take the colony by British merchants. Dundas did acknowledge to Vaughan that the security of the British islands must be prioritised and when the Dutch government refused to allow the 60th to land, the small detachment was sent on to Barbados. The outspoken Vaughan decried the Government's attachment to the opinions of 'self-interested merchants', criticised the poor quality of the new battalions, and warned that unless black regiments were raised the islands would soon be lost. 'The French blacks will invade us and gain ours by the promise of freedom'.[6]

The arrival of the additional two regiments on St Lucia allowed Brigadier General Stewart to take the offensive and attempt to recover lost ground. On 14 April, he landed at Vieuxfort on the southern extremity of the island (see map 5) with a force composed of a portion of the 9th, 61st and 68th Regiments, a company of the Black Carolina Corps, and one company of the new black corps of Malcolm's Rangers – in all, about 600 white and 400 black troops. After some skirmishing, Stewart entered the town on the 16th, the brigands abandoning a large amount of stores and ammunition. He now pushed on towards the enemy's strongest point at Soufrière on the west coast. Progress via the towns of Laborie and Choiseul was difficult, the marches severe and the four pieces of artillery having to be dragged over steep wooded terrain by soldiers and seamen. On the 20th, the flank companies of the 9th and Malcolm's Rangers fell into an ambush from which they gallantly extricated themselves at some cost to their assailants. Two days later, Stewart sighted the enemy's stronghold, well protected by the natural obstacles of mountain and swamp and also man-made breastworks and barriers.

The British commander, realising the strength of the centre of the enemy position, made turning manoeuvres to both right and left before cautiously sending a company of the 61st in advance of the guns on the road. This induced the enemy to open fire, which in turn led the rangers and other British soldiers to reply, thereby wasting much of their ammunition. The brigands now advanced along the road towards the British guns, showing great coolness and determination; only after suffering heavy casualties in two separate attacks were they repulsed by the light infantry of the 61st and 68th. Unfortunately these two companies made a precipitate pursuit of their foe and in turn suffered significant losses at the parapet of the defences. Vaughan later communicated that 'the contest continued warmly for seven hours and although the greatest exertions were made by the British they were finally compelled to retreat to Choiseul'. Stewart had little choice but to fall back, his ammunition spent and his men short of provisions and exhausted. Commissioner Goyrand, Hugues's man on the scene, declared that, 'The musketry of a handful of Republicans replied so well to the enemy artillery of two 6-pounders that the enemy general ordered the retreat as night approached...His losses are at least 600 men killed, wounded or made prisoner'. This was very likely exaggeration as the brigands made no serious effort to pursue the retreating force. British returns suggest losses of 30 killed, 150 wounded and five missing between 14 and 22 April. There was no denying that this was a serious British reverse, made more ominous by the unexpected obduracy and organisation of their adversaries. Not wishing to divide his main force, the chastened Stewart withdrew first to Vieuxfort where he placed a predominantly black garrison, some 200 strong; he then assembled the remainder of his troops around Morne Fortune in the north.[7]

The British foothold on St Lucia was tenuous. Stewart's force was demoralised and diminished by yellow fever whilst the enemy was strengthened by the receipt of artillery from Guadeloupe. In early June, Goyrand's men easily captured the post of Gros Islet and then, on the 9th, a key battery on Morne Fortune was seized. When, on the night of the 17th, the Vigie (a fortified peninsula to the north of Castries) also fell, it was clear to Stewart that he would have to evacuate the island. The peninsula was vital to maintain communications around the Carénage (the harbour of Castries). In the early hours of the 19th, the garrison of 1,200 was embarked onto HMS *Experience* and a transport at the mouth of the Carénage. The ships remained out of gunshot range and evacuated the fleeing army to Martinique. Goyrand was quick to draw parallels with the fate of Prescott at Basseterre, '...for the second time, in a short period, the English ships thus spared their generals the shame of a capitulation'. The flight was so hasty, the emissary noted, that the English had had to leave behind 60 sick and 36 women and children. Goyrand, who appears to have been more generous than Hugues, arranged for them to be returned the following day.[8]

The fall of one island encouraged Republican influence and insurgency on its neighbours. British operations on Grenada, where the force had also been strengthened from Barbados, recommenced at the start of April just before the events described on St Lucia. The new campaign opened inauspiciously. When Lieutenant Colonel Archibald Campbell of the 29th landed his own regiment and the 25th at Goyave he was called to interview by Mackenzie, who divided the force into three, the plan being to advance simultaneously from Goyave, St George's and Grenville against Fédon's stronghold on Mount St Catherine in the north (see map 7). Mackenzie was, as Fortescue pointedly reminds us, a 'civilian', and his methods were judged to be 'too Austrian'. Campbell was ordered to make a direct assault with 300 raw recruits and 150 seamen. This was against his better judgement as the enemy camp was atop a sheer mountain, very well fortified, and defended by several hundred rebels. He later wrote to Lord Cathcart, '...the service was in storming the stronghold of the insurgents, which ended in proving which must of been the opinion of every military person before it commenced, a matter without any probability of success'. The outcome is well described by eyewitness Gordon Turnbull.

Everything was now prepared for the assault which was made on the morning of the 8th [April]. Our troops were led on by Lieutenant Colonel [John] Hope; and, on their advancing, the enemy abandoned the lower post at Belvidere and retreated to the ridge of the mountain, on which they had two guns, but one much more advanced, that is to say, lower down on the ridge than the other. This was the first object to which the movements of a company of the 9th under Captain Stopford, on one side, and a part of the seamen led on by Captain Watkins, on the other side of the ridge, were pointed. The first was supported by Lieutenant-Colonel Hope with a party of the 29th and 58th, and the last, by a detachment of the 25th under Lieutenant Colonel Dickson. Both columns pressed forward with great ardour. Captain Stopford, notwithstanding the extreme difficulty of the ascent, had got within twenty yards of the gun, when he fell. Mr William Park [a civilian; editor of the Grenada Gazette], who had gallantly engaged in the enterprise as a volunteer, fell almost at the same instant. The troops now being exposed to a heavy and galling fire from the enemy, and finding it impossible to make their way through the fallen trees, were forced to retreat. On the other side, Captain Watkins, with Captain Blackett and thirty-five brave seamen had actually got within a few yards of the gun; but observing that Colonel Hope with his detachment was retreating, and the rest of the seamen not having come up, they were also under the necessity of retreating.

The withdrawal was well covered by a detachment of the 68th but three officers had perished and 80 rank and file were killed or wounded. Turnbull attributes the debacle to a combination of the wet ground littered with felled trees, the lack of adequate artillery support, the inexperience of the troops, and the failure to gain any element of surprise. Fédon massacred his prisoners including Governor Home and 50 British inhabitants captured early in the course of the attack. The rebel leader's army now increased by 10,000 men as the island's black population willingly joined the brigands.[9]

Hearing of the setback, Vaughan sent Lieutenant Colonel Oliver Nicolls to Grenada. His acting rank of Brigadier General left no doubt as to who was now in charge of the British military effort. Campbell voiced the general relief; 'Brigadier General Nicolls has lately rescued us from the command of a president of the Council who on the death of the military governor assumed the military command and issued orders for attack & c. with all the confidence of a veteran'. At first this change in command produced the desired effect. Nicolls discarded Mackenzie's strategy of dispersal and multiple attacks and instead concentrated his forces driving the enemy from Grenville and setting up strong posts in the town and also at Sauteurs and Goyave. He additionally raised five black corps each of 50 men. By the end of July, Nicolls had secured the principal harbours and the coast was under British control. There was hope that the rebels might be starved into submission and thus bring an end to what Campbell referred to as a 'blackguard war'. However, British resources were stretched and manpower dwindling by the day since the arrival of the sickly season; between the 7th and 23rd on the month, more than 250 men died of disease, reducing the army's effective strength to less than 900. The mortality among Campbell's men was so great that he feared that 'a few weeks will put a period to the existence of this deserted battalion'. The only reinforcement was a small detachment of the 68th from Martinique whilst the insurgents received more arms and provisions from Guadeloupe, thereby undoing much of Nicolls's laudable work.

The increasing British weakness culminated in a jolting reverse. On the night of 15 October, the rebels attacked an apparently strong British post on the heights above Goyave. This was manned by a captain, two subalterns, four sergeants, and 60 rank and file, and commanded the town and the harbour. The senior officer, Lieutenant Colonel Schaw of the 68th, later penned a detailed letter to Nicolls justifying his own part in the 'unfortunate business'. Schaw's account is confused but it seems that the piquet was surprised by an attack made on more than one front and, after initial losses, all attempts to recover the hill by the 68th were foiled by the enemy's superior numbers and their capture of a field piece from which they fired grapeshot. Schaw also invokes the steep and slippery state of the hill after incessant rain, but presumably this must have been equally the case for his audacious foe. The officer withdrew his men to St George's, 12 miles distant. About 40 sick from the 25th and 30 from the 68th were left at Goyave and fell into enemy hands. The return of the 68th also shows two sergeants and 34 rank and file missing following the action.[10]

Events far from the Caribbean now impacted on the struggle for Grenada. A French commissioner from Guadeloupe landed on the island. Extolling the more enlightened principles that had replaced the philosophy of terror in France, he demanded the arrest of Fédon for the atrocities committed by the rebels. From this time, the Republican war effort was to be humane and conducted with the primary aim of abolishing slavery. This change of direction, whilst commendable, increased British anxieties relating to the loyalty of the black populations on their colonies. As it was, Fédon escaped capture and remained at the head of an increasingly powerful rebel army, which continued to harass Nicolls's men. Even with reinforcement from Martinique, the British force at the end of 1795 amounted to less than 700 effectives. Republican reinforcements now had little problem landing on the island and, in late February 1796, two schooners of men arrived from Guadeloupe and invested Pilot Hill, the British post commanding Grenville Bay. The prompt evacuation of this strongpoint with the abandonment of five guns was attributed to a lack of water, but it was more likely caused by a shortage of defenders. In early 1796, British fortunes were at low ebb, Nicolls grimly hanging on to St George's and fearing his ejection from the colony.[11]

On St Vincent, there was intense fighting between April 1795 and January 1796. Vaughan informed Dundas of the uprising on the island: 'In St Vincent the Charibbs [Caribs], instigated by the French, and joined by most of the French inhabitants, sensed a favourable time, most treacherously, to attack the English inhabitants of that Colony. The arts of cruelty which they have committed upon defenceless men, women and children, are beyond description, and burning every plantation in their power'. At the beginning of April, Governor Seton was reinforced by the arrival of the seasoned 46th Regiment and the enemy were driven back allowing the British to establish posts outside Kingstown at Calliaqua, Chateau Belair and Sion Hill (see map 8). Hugues supplied the Caribs from Guadeloupe and Goyrand sent men and munitions from captured St Lucia. It was, in Poyen's words, a 'war of extermination', the Caribs massacring their prisoners and the British hanging captured Caribs, whom they regarded as rebellious subjects. Later in the month, Seton was able to eject the Caribs from their main camp, the attack carried out by a detachment of the 46th supported by black rangers and seamen. On 7 May, seven or eight hundred enemy appeared on the heights above Calliaqua and Seton anticipated an attack on Kingstown. Captain John Hall of the 46th commanded a party of a subaltern and 33 rank and file of the regiment, 40 militia, 40 of the corps of black rangers, five artillerymen and a 14-pound field piece, his mission to take possession of Dorsetshire Hill to the east of the town. At one o'clock in the morning, they were attacked by 300 French and Caribs and forced to retreat to Sion Hill. Realising his position to be untenable, Seton ordered a further attack at daybreak on the following day. A hundred men of the 46th and militia under the command of Lieutenant Colonel Christopher Seton of the rangers successfully stormed the hill through a hail of grapeshot. In the two attacks, the British lost 30 wounded and three killed whilst 23 French and 19 Caribs were found dead on the field.[12]

More reinforcements arrived at the beginning of June in the form of the 3rd Battalion of the 60th, the unit refused a landing at Demerara, and a detachment of Malcolm's Rangers. Governor Seton now sought to make gains on the eastern side of the colony. On the night of 11 June, a force under the command of Lieutenant Colonel Baldwin Leighton composed of detachments from the 46th and 60th Regiments, Malcolm's Rangers, Island Rangers, all the southern and windward militia, and the Royal Artillery, marched out of Kingstown and halted at a river about four miles from their destination, the Vigie. This was the principal position of the enemy, a heavily fortified post on a ridge (*vigie* is the French for 'look-out post') forming the south-west side of the valley of Marriqua (Mesopotamia), one of the most heavily vegetated parts of the island. The troops were divided into four columns and, by daybreak, the enemy were completely invested. The British first forced their way into two redoubts, the Carib defenders taking flight. French troops from Guadeloupe now took up the fight, sallying from their defensive positions before being forced back by British forces threatening their flank. Thomas Coke, an early West Indies historian, evocatively relates the denouement.

Never did troops display greater gallantry than did the British militia and rangers on this occasion. The whole seemed as if activated by one soul. Two six pounders from adjacent situations were directed against the batteries and works of the enemy, with unabating perseverance. Early in the attack a mortar was brought forward which scattered its destructive materials among them with considerable annoyance, while the smaller arms kept up an uninterrupted discharge. Thus was victory undecided for about the space of five hours, when the shot, necessary to support their great guns, became expended; and most of those who were acquainted with their management were killed or wounded. In consequence of this change of circumstances, their resistance gradually diminished; until at length, they felt it expedient to beat the *chamade*...

British killed and wounded were about 60 and the enemy probably no less than 250. Leighton sent out rangers to scour the surrounding area and destroy Carib huts. Leaving the 60th to garrison the Vigie, he marched up the east coast of the island with the remains of his force and reached Mount Young on the 16th. Here, he fortified his position and sent out parties to devastate the countryside, the objective being to starve the enemy and push them into the interior.[13]

The Caribs were a resourceful race and they effected a passage across the mountains, a considerable number of them appearing on a hill near the British post at Chateau Belair on the leeward coast. The new enemy position dominated the smaller British hill and before long they had unfurled the flag *de la liberté* and had opened fire with a small field piece imported from St Lucia. It was apparent that decisive action had to be taken and Seton reinforced the post with a detachment of the 3rd Battalion of the 60th Regiment and another from the northern corps of militia. In early July, he directed Lieutenant Colin Prevost to attack the enemy position with what proved to be an inadequate force of about a hundred local militia and British regulars. The commander of the storming party, Lieutenant Moore, was soon fatally wounded, the leaderless troops became disordered, and an ignominious retreat followed. Desperate for reinforcements from Martinique, Seton was instead forced to order Leighton to transfer part of his force across the island to retrieve the situation. After an exhausting eight-hour march, Leighton led 200 men of the 46th and 60th in a second attack against the French above Chateau Belair and, overcoming stubborn resistance, drove them into the woods, capturing two guns and ammunition. The 46th lost 14 killed and 30 wounded, the British casualties around 60 in total. Probably outnumbered by four to three, it was a significant triumph for Leighton's men, particular credit falling to the mauled 46th.[14]

British spirits were raised. Coke comments that the success '...compensated fully for recent disappointments and promised to greatly facilitate the annihilation of those who had wronged us'. This was overly optimistic and

Seton now overstretched his position, setting up multiple ill-supported posts in the windward part of the island. The main body of troops, perhaps 400 fit for duty, remained around Mount Young under Leighton's command. A further blunder was the failure to adequately defend Owia, a small town in the extreme north-east of the colony, which gave easy communication with French St Lucia. In early September, in the middle of the night during a thunderstorm, 600 enemy troops fell on the camp killing many of the black garrison and the commanding British officer. The survivors fled to Kingstown.[15]

Encouraged by this success, Hugues was hopeful of seizing St Vincent just as he had captured Guadeloupe and St Lucia. On the morning of 18 September, a French force of 800 men was landed from four vessels in Owia Bay. Hopelessly outnumbered, Leighton was ordered to abandon Mount Young and return to the vicinity of Kingstown. He slipped away leaving lights burning in the soldiers' huts to deceive the enemy. Vaughan now responded to the deteriorating situation by sending Colonel William Myers to take command on the island. The new commander could initially do little more than cede more ground, evacuating posts to leeward and windward and concentrating his increasingly demoralised men around Kingstown, the Vigie and Dorsetshire Hill. The small force on the Vigie, 100 British regulars and 100 black troops, was especially vulnerable, both short of provisions and dangerously isolated from Kingstown. Myers was determined to support the position and he ordered Lieutenant Colonel Ritchie of the 60th to escort a convoy of 200 of his regiment, 150 St Vincent Rangers and 80 mules carrying the necessary stores. This detachment proceeded from Sion Hill on the afternoon of the 24th, continued as far as Calliaqua, and then ascended towards the Vigie. The enemy were in wait and after a brief exchange of musketry they were forced to fall back. Captain William Cooper Foster of the 46th gave orders for an immediate charge to press home the advantage but he was ignored, the troops instead giving way and fleeing in all directions. Sixty men were killed and taken prisoner and the stores were lost. Ritchie was wounded as he made a fighting retreat with a small band of 20 men. According to Coke, the unexpected reverse caused 'consternation and dread' in British ranks. It was obvious that the Vigie would have to be abandoned. A large detachment of the 46th and Malcolm's Rangers was sent to Baker's estate within 15 minutes march of the enemy. This feint provided the necessary distraction and the Vigie garrison marched through the night to Calliaqua from where they were moved to Kingstown in boats.[16]

While every effort was being made to strengthen posts around the town, an unexpected reinforcement reached the island. This was composed of the 40th, 54th, and 59th Regiments and the 2nd West India Regiment; the St Vincent Rangers were now drafted into the latter unit. Major General Robert Irving was sent from Martinique to take command. These soldiers were not in ideal condition for campaigning in the Tropics, little trained and stressed by the voyage from home, but Irving judged the situation of Kingstown so precarious that an immediate attack on the Vigie was imperative. On 2 October, the troops set out divided into two columns of 750 and 900 men with, as Irving relates, the intent to make a two-pronged attack on the hill. As usual in the West Indies, the terrain and elements combined as a second enemy.

> I informed myself, from those best acquainted with the Country that a Height, called Fairbane's Hill, commanded the Vigie; upon this I formed my Plan of Attack. The Grenadiers and Light Infantry, with Four Companies of the 40th Regiment, were to gain the Hill on one Quarter, whilst the 59th Regiment, supported by Two Three Pounders, were to force it on another, the Whole Marched at Three o' Clock Yesterday Morning, so as to be at the Object by Day-break. The first Division gained the Heights early in the Morning, with considerable Loss, the 59th Regiment was early within fifty paces of the Enemy, and made several attempts to gain the Post, but the Natural Strength of the Ground, and the heavy Rain that unluckily fell at Day-break rendered the place inaccessible. The Troops having been exposed the Whole of the Day to great Fatigues, and the Weather being very unfavourable, from violent showers during the Day, and having no Possibility of providing the least shelter for them, I thought it most advisable to return to our former Quarters for the Night. Having sufficient Reason to suppose the Enemy had abandoned their Posts during the Night, I ordered out early this morning [3 October] a strong Detachment of the St Vincent's Rangers to take Possession of it; as I have the Satisfaction to inform your Excellency [Major General Charles Leigh] that the British Flag now displays itself there.

British losses were inevitably heavy; 46 killed and 107 wounded, the 59th suffering about half of these casualties. The enemy were presumably also badly enough mauled to induce them to abandon the Vigie, one estimate being that they lost 250 men.

Irving may have snatched victory from defeat but the mood remained gloomy. The commander cautiously moved north up the east coast, establishing posts near Mount William and Mount Young, but he was inhibited by a number of concerns. His adversary had been reinforced from St Lucia, his own reinforcements might have to be switched to Grenada, and morale was deteriorating. Myers wrote to General Grey in November that 'apathy and indifference' had affected both the troops and the colony's inhabitants. The latter were tired of the war and reluctant to give up their black workers to aid the British cause. The year ended with the British entrenched on Bellevue ridge (facing Mount William) hoping for the arrival of another 'great expedition', the subject of the next chapter.[17]

The initiative had been lost and at 3 o'clock on the morning of 8 January 1796 the enemy attacked a battery placed on a supposedly inaccessible tongue of land to the left of the Mount William camp. Despite taking the normal precautions of posting sentries and making patrols, Brigadier General Stewart, the officer in charge, was caught by surprise.

On the first Shot, I immediately ran out as fast as the Darkness would permit me and was met by Major [Henry] Harcourt, Field Officer of the Day. I found the Men all paraded and Brigadier General [William] Strutt who had just then received a Wound in his Face, exerting himself much with the 54th Regiment. I full proceeded to the Left, but, from the Darkness, could not distinguish the enemy from our own Soldiers...

Stewart did his best to marshal his men, but with many of his officers seriously wounded, all parts of the line eventually broke and he was forced to fall back south along the coast to Baiabu. Here he had no provisions and little ammunition and he necessarily continued his retreat to Kingstown 12 miles away. It was a shattering and costly defeat. From the five units engaged (the Royal Artillery, 40th, 54th, 59th, and the 2nd West India Regiment) there were 54 killed, 109 wounded and as many as 200 missing.[18]

A new officer, Major General Martin Hunter, was sent from Martinique to take command, but he could do little more than withdraw the remaining forces to the vicinity of Kingstown. On 19 January, he informed Major General Charles Leigh (the new commander-in-chief, see below) that he had concentrated around the posts of Dorsetshire Hill, Millar's Bridge, Sion Hill, Cane Garden, Keane's House, Fort Charlotte and Kingstown itself. The demoralisation of the army was highlighted on the 20th, when Lieutenant Colonel Prevost's attempt to attack an isolated enemy piquet was frustrated by the refusal of all but eight men to follow him. There was, however, enough resolve to repulse a French counter-attack. Hunter warned Leigh that unless he was reinforced he would soon have to withdraw into Fort Charlotte, the only post he was confident of holding against the enemy's full strength; '...the very hard Duty the Men and Officers are obliged to do cannot be supported for any Length of Time.' At the start of 1796, the British were, just as on Grenada, hemmed into a small corner of St Vincent waiting for help.[19]

On Dominica, the British garrison was weak and debilitated by disease. Hugues sent 470 men to the island in early June 1795 but the Republican attack was botched. General Pélardy informs us that the assault force remained in the boats for five days before disembarking, thus losing any chance of surprise. They were eventually landed at Pagoua Bay on the north-east of the colony and a small British force made up chiefly of parts of the sickly 15th and 21st Regiments and a handful of local militia was dispatched from Prince Rupert's

Bay to intercept them (see map 9). The French invaders were divided and the British, led by Captain John Bathe of the 15th, soon surrounded both encampments and forced them to surrender between the 17th and the 19th with the capture of around 350 prisoners. On 22 June, Lieutenant Colonel Edward Madden wrote to Vaughan describing the subsequent mopping up operation.

> There are a number of them [Republicans] in Two's and Three's in the Woods, that the English Negroes are in Pursuit of, and are hourly bringing some in – I am sending out small Parties of Militia (who have behaved uncommonly well) to the different Parishes in order to root them out entirely, and hope very soon to have to report to your Excellency that there is not a Brigand in the Island.

The efforts of the British regulars were also commendable, particularly when one considers that 40% of the rank and file were on the sick list and that the operation involved an exhausting march across the country. However, the key reason for the failure of the Republican attack was that the planter and black populations mostly remained loyal to the British. Hugues's strategy was almost wholly dependent on the locals; without their help, French forces acting in isolation could achieve little.[20]

The crushing of the French attempt on Dominica was a welcome fillip, but in the summer of 1795, in his headquarters on Martinique, Commander-in-Chief Vaughan was beset by problems. A lack of manpower remained the major concern. Reinforcements arriving in March and April increased Vaughan's total force in the region to 6,750 men. This was still well short of Dundas's objective of an army 10,000 strong and only approximately two-thirds of the available force was fit for duty. The new arrivals, as Vaughan was quick to point out to Dundas, were of poor quality and unlikely to survive the sickly season. 'It is only filling the hospitals and deceiving yourselves to send out raw or newly trained levies'. Unable to give any help to St Lucia, St Vincent and Grenada, the commander-in-chief was increasingly vulnerable on Martinique where his rapidly shrinking army was little deterrent against Hugues' inspired insurgencies. In June, Vaughan finally received permission to raise West India Regiments on the island but it was too late for him to act as he soon became one more victim of disease.

Vaughan's successor, Robert Irving, inherited a toxic command. The dramatic mortality continued and desperate appeals in early July to Major General Gordon Forbes to spare some of his 2,000 men bound for Saint Domingue fell on deaf ears. By 1 August, there were less than 3,000 fit soldiers in the Windward and Leeward garrisons. Just as Vaughan had done before him, Irving tried to impress the reality of the situation on ministers at home, informing Dundas that to retrieve St Vincent and Grenada and restore order to all the islands would require 20,000 men of whom only half would be likely to survive the campaign. With no hope of such reinforcement, Irving tried to mobilise the black regiments, but the planters were by now disillusioned with the British and little inclined to hand over their slaves. The arrival of the 40th, 59th, and 79th Regiments at the end of September was welcome but the new commander-in-chief, Major General Leigh, had no more answers than his predecessors. The constant threat was underlined by the landing of 60 Republicans at Vauclin on the south-east aspect of Martinique in early December. An initial sortie by a detachment of the 2nd Queens under the command of Major Lord Dalhousie was repulsed before a subsequent attack with the support of black rangers led to the capture of enemy forces and the hasty return of planned Republican reinforcements to St Lucia and Guadeloupe. Poyen attributes the French failure to the lack of local assistance.[21]

This completes the sorry account of events in the Windward Islands in 1795. Fortescue concludes that the campaign was, in its later stages, 'perhaps the most discreditable that is to be found in the records of the British Army'. He places the blame on the shoulders of the politicians whose aspirations for military control of the colonies were not backed up by the necessary battalions. We must now turn to leeward and the island of Jamaica and the colony of Saint Domingue. We have made little allusion to Jamaica. Here, white society had so far been spared the worst ravages of the French Revolution, but the colonial population was nervous, provoked by the abolitionist campaign in England. The island's Maroons, particularly the Trelawny Maroons in the north-east (see Chapter 2), were also agitated. Kept in check since a treaty of 1738, their control was now devolved to one man, Major John James, Superintendant General of the entire Maroon community. James was popular with the Maroons but he performed his duties in a desultory manner, apparently more interested in a property he owned 25 miles from Maroon Town (Trelawny Town). After a 57-year period during which the Maroons' freedom and independence had been gradually eroded, the summer of 1795 provided the catalysts for revolt. They had three main grievances; the Assembly's dismissal of the insubordinate James, the indignity suffered when two Maroon men were whipped for alleged hog stealing, and the desire for more land to support their growing numbers.

The colony was gripped by panic. It was feared that the Trelawny Maroons would be supported by other Maroon townships and the island's slaves. The magistrates in the parish of St James wrote to the British governor, Major General Lord Balcarres, on 18 July.

> We are sorry to find that a very serious disturbance is likely to break out immediately with the Maroons of Trelawny Town. They have obliged the [newly appointed] superintendant to quit the town. They have threatened the destruction of the two plantations nearest them. All the

people belonging to them have been called in; the women are sent into the woods; and, between this and Monday, they propose to kill their cattle and their children, who may be an encumbrance.

An imminent attack was anticipated. At first, the House of Assembly made placatory moves, distributing money to the Maroons and offering to discuss their complaints. This lull was short-lived. The constant dread of insurrection was fuelled by the rumour that French agents from Saint Domingue were supporting the Maroons. The colonists demanded strong action; on 4 August, Balcarres was given the powers of martial law.

Fortuitously, Balcarres's hand was strengthened by the arrival of reinforcements in mid-July. The governor had recalled the 83rd Regiment bound for Saint Domingue and a further detachment, originally heading for the same island, now landed and was detained on Jamaica. The total extra force, including the 83rd and 400 Light Dragoons, amounted to close to 1,500 men. To this could be added the depleted 60th and 62nd Regiments of the Line and the 20th Light Dragoons, all already on the island and together perhaps 500 strong.[22]

Balcarres's plan was to intimidate, outmanoeuvre and isolate his adversary. On 9 August, the governor sent an ultimatum to the Maroon leaders.

Every pass to your town has been occupied and guarded by the militia and regular forces. You are surrounded by thousands. Look at Montego Bay, and you will see the force brought against you. I have issued a proclamation ordering a reward for your heads.

Balcarres had underestimated the Maroons' determination. Although confronted by 2,000 regular troops supported by several thousand local militia, they resolved to fight and were encouraged by an early success. On 12 August, a small British force of dragoons and Trelawny militia under the command of Colonel Sansford attempted to surprise the Old Maroon town (see map 10). Falling into an ambush, the officer and around 40 men were killed. The disorganised remains of the party made their way back to Balcarres's Vaughansfield headquarters; some were so relieved to have escaped alive that they fired their guns into the air.

The Trelawny Maroons took refuge in the Cockpits, mountainous country ideal for defence and ambush and opportunistic raiding. It was desperately difficult terrain for the operations of European regular forces, particularly cavalry, and Balcarres responded by trying to surround the whole area including the Old and New Maroon Towns and the Cockpits around Petty River Bottom. Reinforcements of regulars and militia, the latter unreliable, were called up to destroy the provision grounds and the two towns. Balcarres believed that starvation was his best weapon. The governor's correspondence reveals increasing frustration as this strategy failed to produce the desired results. On 8 September, he writes to Major General Taylor, '...I am sorry I cannot close my letter as agreeably as I could wish. None of the Maroons have come in, and they seem determined to inveterate war.' Four days later, Colonel William Fitch, entrusted to carry out operations by Balcarres, walked into a Maroon ambush. Eight men, including Fitch, lost their lives. A month of warfare had cost the British more than 70 fatalities whereas, as the contemporary historian Robert Charles Dallas points out, not one Maroon was known to have been killed. The enemy had retired to their fortresses and the loss of the popular Fitch had 'cast a gloom over the whole island'. The regular troops were becoming exhausted and disillusioned. Captain Oldham of the 62nd had perished of nothing more than fatigue. Supplies were running out. The air of apprehension was not relieved by Balcarres's hopeful speech at the Assembly.[23]

The turning point was the appointment of Colonel George Walpole to the rank of Major General to succeed Fitch. In mid-September, Walpole left Accompong Town and rode hard through dangerous country to Fitch's old headquarters at Trelawny Town. Here, he found Fitch's men living in poor accommodation and disillusioned by the torrential rain and the apparent hopelessness of their task. Walpole quickly realised that their morale was such that any further defeat would be disastrous. He abandoned Balcarres's attempts at encirclement and instead pursued a determined strategy of land clearance and the building of outposts to guard nearby settlements. Whilst slave gangs chopped at the covering bush, Walpole trained his soldiers to emulate Maroon tactics, taking maximum advantage of available cover to fire and reload. Using howitzers to fire shells into the inaccessible ravines, he gradually dislodged the Maroons from their main stronghold into the more northerly mountains. As Maroon morale sagged, the spirits of the British troops began to recover.

By early October, Walpole was in the ascendancy; reinforced by detachments of troops under the command of Colonel Skinner, there were now thousands of well-armed and supplied regulars and militia at his disposal. In contrast, the Trelawny Maroon warriors numbered only around 250 men divided into two groups, one of them a raiding party under the command of a man called Johnson who imposed an iron discipline. It was probably Johnson's men who had ambushed Fitch and, despite their limited numbers, they remained a danger to unwary Europeans. Balcarres explained the threat to the Duke of Portland in a letter of 16 November.

As it is impossible to get up with these savages without first receiving the fire of their ambush, our loss in every affair is constantly from eight to twelve men killed and wounded; and as the ambuscade is generally formed within a few yards of the track the return of killed is often, unfortunately, greater than the wounded.

Walpole appears to have had a talent for jungle warfare and he methodically transformed the Cockpits from a Maroon refuge into a trap. He used local knowledge to cut off the Trelawnys from their meeting places. Maroon morale was further damaged by the arrival of dog handling chasseurs from Cuba. Balcarres had great expectations of the 'Spanish dogs' and he was not disappointed, exaggerated accounts of the size and ferocity of the animals soon reaching the enemy, who were left in no doubt that they would be employed if no peaceful settlement was reached.

Although no single great victory had been achieved, Walpole had succeeded in restricting Maroon movements and denying them food and water. Many were sick and they had become alienated from the local slaves, their normal suppliers. It was now only a matter of time. One group of Maroons surrendered to Walpole in December. They agreed to ask the King's pardon on their knees. Their lives would be spared and they would not be deported. Balcarres demanded a cessation of resistance by the remaining Maroons on 1 January 1796; at the end on the month, he wrote to Dundas.

> Three weeks having elapsed without any apparent Intent on the Part of the Maroons to fulfil the Treaty, I ordered the Honourable Major General Walpole to move forward, on the 14th instant, with a strong Column of Regular Troops. He had only advanced some Yards when a Message was delivered from the Maroon Chief [Johnson] begging that no further hostile step should be taken. As we had experienced Duplicity and Evasion, it was judged expedient to move slowly on, and the line of March was so arranged as to give the Maroons an Opportunity of coming in with safety. This had the desired effect. The Maroon Rebellion I think is drawing to a close.

The governor estimated that 500 Maroons had surrendered with only a handful of warriors still at large. They would capitulate within weeks. More than 20 actions had been fought to crush 'a most daring, unprovoked, and ungrateful Rebellion'.

There remained the question of the fate of the defeated Maroons. Against Walpole's wishes – he had originally agreed in his December treaty that they would not be deported – the island's Assembly voted for their removal from the colony. The majority had surrendered after 1 January and were not covered by the treaty and even those who were chose to accompany their comrades. They were transported to Nova Scotia in June 1796 where, unsurprisingly, they failed to adapt to the working conditions and climate. The British Government finally relented to their demands and, in 1800, they were moved on to the colony of ex-slaves formed at Sierra Leone. The Jamaican colonists had been placated. The number of Maroons remaining on the island was small and, daunted by the fate of the Trelawny Maroons, those to windward took an oath of allegiance to the King.[24]

We must now return to Saint Domingue where, at the end of 1794, Tiburon had disastrously fallen to Rigaud and the country was wracked by internal strife (see Chapter 3). The number of fit British troops on 1 January 1795 was less than 1,100 and their hold on parts of the colony – Môle St Nicolas, Jérémie, Irois, Léogane, Fort Bizothon, Port au Prince and an area to the north of the capital around the Bight of Léogane – was at best precarious. The loss of Saltrou in the south to insurgents was not in itself of great strategic significance but an ominous sign of British vulnerability.

Brisbane continued his heroic operations against Toussaint in the Artibonite acting in concert with forces from Arcahaye and Mirebalais. The region was crippled by the combination of continuous warfare and drought and, by February, there was famine. Many locals fled to the Republican zone. Toussaint was hampered by lack of ammunition and the Anglo-Royalist forces' stubbornly maintained posts on the left bank of the Artibonite. The death of Brisbane on 4 February, shot in the head during a reconnaissance on the river, was a blow to British hopes; this officer was hugely admired and was seen as crucial to the defence of the area around St Marc. A second highly respected British soldier was killed the following month at Fort Bizothon. Lieutenant Colonel Markham fell making a sortie against Rigaud's besieging army. Montalembert's cavalry caused numerous casualties in Rigaud's ranks but the siege continued. Naval attempts to make a diversion at Léogane came to nothing and St Marc remained under attack by Toussaint. There was serious consideration of pulling all British forces back to the Môle.

A number of factors prevented the evolution of this perilous situation into catastrophe. Firstly, some reinforcements arrived from England; around 1,700 troops on 17 April. This relieved some of the immediate pressure and, most notably, Rigaud abandoned the siege of Fort Bizothon. Williamson left Jamaica at the end of the month to take personal command, reaching the Môle on 12 May. The second factor working in Williamson's favour was his successful raising of colonial corps with the cooperation of Royalist planters. It was Dessources's 200 chasseurs who repulsed Toussaint's attack on St Marc in April, routing the rebel forces who were forced to evacuate the Artibonite. A further pro-British factor was the Spanish presence on the east side of the island (Santo Domingo). Although the two countries collaborated only loosely, Spanish attacks in early 1795 distracted the Republicans. Finally, the discord which had compromised British operations in Saint Domingue equally affected their adversaries. There was friction between mulattoes and blacks and the loyalty of apparently pro-Republican factions could not be assumed. Their leaders were often unwilling allies; Rigaud was able to work with Toussaint but failed to gain help from Dieudonné and Pompé.

These mitigating elements gave the British some respite. The most likely short-term outcome was a period of stalemate. Williamson could not have been cheered by his first inspection of his small army. Predictably, many were sick and even those on the fit list were exhausted by endless duty, sleep deprivation and the climate. At St Marc, almost every soldier in five British companies was hospitalised. On 1 June, of the 3,000 soldiers on the colony, only 1,300 were registered fit for duty. Williamson could derive some encouragement from reports of further reinforcements from home and the increasing number of black troops in British service. The arrival of Major General Forbes with a detachment from Jamaica might have brought relief, but the erosive effect of disease, mostly yellow fever, was relentless and, at the end of June, the number of fit men had actually fallen to around a thousand, approximately half of the force.[25]

A month later, the Spanish were expelled by a local uprising in the area around Mirebalais and the nearby mountains of Grand Bois and Trou d'Eau. This remained a fertile region containing over 400 plantations worked by local blacks. The other inhabitants were largely mulattoes, but there were also around 500 whites who had emigrated from the north. Toussaint nominally controlled this territory but it is probable that only a minority of the locals actually supported the Republican cause. When Williamson received more reinforcements – the 82nd Regiment on 9 August – he was confident enough to sanction the easterly advance of his colonial forces. On 15 August, the whites under the leadership of the Creole Lavergne capitulated without resistance. Toussaint immediately responded by sending his colonial ally Christophe Mornet to 'exterminate' the Royalists, but the colonial troops, led by Montalembert and Lapointe, pressed on through the mountains in pouring rain gaining local support. The campaign was not entirely successful – Mornet escaped with his plunder and Dessources's column was largely destroyed by Toussaint's counter-attack at Verrettes – but Mirebalais was captured. This had immediate implications. A productive region was secured, Toussaint had suffered a setback, and the communication between enemy forces in the north and south was broken. Montalembert was given the local rank of brigadier general in acknowledgement of his achievement.[26]

The raw recruits of August had little formal training and even less immunity to the prevailing diseases. A fresh epidemic during September and October sent another thousand men to their graves. Potential reinforcements from Jamaica, where Balcarres was fighting the Maroon War, failed to materialise. News that Spain had surrendered Santo Domingo to France was alarming, although it was possible that the Spanish planters would side with the British. On a more positive note, Dundas announced that the futile trickle of reinforcements would stop and that a substantial army was about to be sent to launch an offensive in both the Windward and Leeward Islands. This was the long-awaited expedition of Sir Ralph Abercromby, the subject of the next chapter. Sixteen thousand troops were promised for Saint Domingue, to arrive before the end of the year; these were to be commanded by General Forbes, Williamson being allowed to return home although he did not depart until the following March.[27]

Encouraged by the prospect of significant help, Forbes made plans for the conquest of Cap Français, Port de Paix and the Northern Province. There was growing appreciation that military aggression might not be enough to pacify Saint Domingue and Dundas granted Forbes £15,000 to win over the black and mulatto leaders. This financial incentive was joined to legislation favouring the mulattoes and the promise of eventual emancipation for black soldiers fighting as British corps. The latter initiative was vital to recruit black troops and was taken locally by Forbes against Dundas's orders. There was already dissension in the Republican factions. Reports of the imminent arrival of a large British expedition in the region exaggerated pre-existing splits and there was extensive fighting between mulattoes and blacks in the north and south of the colony. In the south, black bands led by Pompé and Pierre Dieudonné defected from the Republican cause. Forbes won over black auxiliaries formerly attached to Spain; two of their leaders, Titus and Gagnettes, committed the support of their 5–6,000 followers. The combined effect of skilful British negotiations and Republican disorder was such that, in February 1796, Williamson declared himself more secure than ever at Port au Prince, despite having only 200 men fit for duty. Forbes, who had sailed from the Môle with the hope of meeting the expected convoy from Cork and leading an attack against Cap Français, was less optimistic. As was so often the case, the actual reinforcement fell well short of ministers' promises. In early January 1796, the 66th and 69th Regiments, under General Henry Bowyer, landed at the Môle and, by 15 February, the 1,600 men transferred to Port au Prince were ready for action. A week later came the news that the larger force of 16,500 men had been detained by storms and that, in reality, there would be no more than 4,500 extra troops, largely foreign and with an uncertain arrival date.

This was bitterly disappointing for the British commanders. Williamson's assessment of their security suddenly appeared complacent. The spreading news that a large British force was not about to appear only served to spur on the enemy; Rigaud remained active, negotiations with Dieudonné broke down, leaving some of his men to throw in their lot with Toussaint, and a number of lesser chiefs attached themselves to the Republican flag. Neither side had a clear advantage; in early March Toussaint complained that he was cornered by his enemies on land and sea. In this maelstrom of shifting loyalties, it was crucial to grasp the initiative. Following the failure of the talks with Dieudonné, Williamson used the extra troops at Port au Prince to attack positions held by black troops overlooking the capital. On 28 February, Dessources's 500 chasseurs clambered up the mountain and cleared the enemy, destroying 2,000 huts. Camp Turgeau was captured and a strongpoint established to guard the town.[28]

With Williamson's final departure on 14 March, Forbes was left in sole command. Williamson had achieved as much as could be expected and his successor, commander by default in the absence of a more able candidate, struggled to maintain his position. He decided to attack Léogane. Geggus argues that this was a mistake and that Gonaives, Toussaint's link to the outside world, was a better target. To be fair to Forbes, a number of others including Williamson, Montalembert, and the commander of the squadron, Admiral Hyde Parker, all strongly supported the operation. In the event it was a debacle. Parker related the outcome to Evan Nepean.

On the 21st [March 1796], the Army was landed, in Two Divisions, to the Eastward and Westward of the Fort and Town, covered to the Westward by the Ceres and Lark, and to the Eastward by the Iphigenia, and Cormorant and Serin Sloops, with the Africa and Leviathan placed against the Fort, and the Swiftsure to cannonade the Town. The Fire of the latter [ship] was interrupted in the Course of Half an hour from the situation of the Army on shore, but the Two former kept up an unremitting Cannonade for nearly Four Hours, against the Fort until Dark, and the Land Wind coming Fresh, the Ships were moved off to a proper Anchorage. The Day following, the Army were chiefly employed reconnoitring, and the next Day, from what they had observed and the Intelligence gained, the Enemy were found so exceedingly numerous that it was resolved best for His Majesty's Service to re-embark the Army, &c and postpone the Operations for the present.

The admiral understates the ignominy of the retreat and the friction between the services. Commodore John Duckworth, his second in command, described the expedition as 'blundering and undigested'. Léogane was much stronger than had been anticipated, surrounded by a palisaded ditch. Forbes had insufficient artillery for a siege and his suggestion that his 750 troops be supported by 4,000 seamen and heavy guns brought ashore received short shrift from Parker, who had already had two ships disabled by enemy artillery. The force returned to Port au Prince to be eaten away by inactivity and yellow fever.

Forbes's next reinforcement, reaching the Môle on 1 May, was the remnants of the Cork expedition. This was the largest single body of men ever to reach Saint Domingue and it raised the total British force to 7,500. The new additions were in poor shape, effectively the men Abercromby did not need to windward. Many of the 1,800 troops were had been sick on the voyage and were destined to die within a few months. More soldiers arrived in June under the command of General Whyte; these included a regiment of British Light Dragoons, some Dutch artillery, Hompesch's Hussars and Montalembert's Legion. The foreign cavalry had no horses and were unprepared to fight on foot. Despite this influx, the toll of yellow fever was such that, by 1 July, the number of men fit for duty had actually fallen to less than 6,000 with 2,500 reported sick. Two tropical months had claimed 1,300 British lives. One consequence of the mismanaged attack on Léogane was that the damage to the *Leviathan* and *Africa* meant that the navy were unable to maintain sufficient strength off Cap Français to prevent the French landing their own reinforcements. On 11 May, a squadron of 10 Republican warships brought nearly 3,000 troops and National Guards in addition to ample supplies of arms and powder. Toussaint Louverture was able to bolster his army to 10,000 infantry and two cavalry regiments, whilst Rigaud now commanded over 5,000 infantry and 1,200 cavalry. More French reinforcements, perhaps as many as 10,000, were expected.[29]

Forbes's situation had deteriorated but he still hoped for help from Abercromby. Forced on the defensive for most of May and June, he decided to make a second foray targeting the town and fort at Bombarde on the road to the Môle. This settlement was important both for the security of the Môle and for food supplies. The march on Bombarde highlighted Forbes's unsuitability for command. Three thousand men were readied on the evening of 7 June but, for reasons that are unclear, their departure was delayed until the next day which was exceptionally hot. Harry Ross-Lewin was a major in the 32nd Regiment.

> The troops were disembarked with the least possible delay. Brigadier-General Forbes, with part of the 13th Light Dragoons, and the 32nd, 56th, 67th and 81st Regiments of the line proceeded to take the fort of Bombarde, distant sixteen miles. We had the option of approaching this point by either of two roads; the one was crossed by streams in two or three places, while along the other there was no water, and the latter unfortunately was chosen. The General's reason for preferring it I have never heard: all I can say is, that the consequences were very disastrous. The troops only moved off at 9 A.M. and before that the greater number of the men had emptied their canteens; for a considerable distance, we had to pass through a deep and close ravine, and were half suffocated by clouds of red dust; we had not advance above two miles when the sergeant-major and thirteen privates of the 67th expired...

Ross-Lewin notes that the general was 'fortunately well supplied' with drinks. The force reached Bombarde in a desperate state but the garrison, only 350 strong, was intimidated by the British arrival and they surrendered on the condition that they be allowed to escape to Republican territory. It was to be a hollow victory, Bombarde actually absorbing resources from the Môle. Whyte, commander of the Môle since June, struggled to maintain communications by land, due to ambushes, or sea, due to swarms of French privateers, and the isolated settlement won with so much suffering was evacuated after a few weeks.[30]

Despite poor military leadership, the situation in Saint Domingue in the late summer and early autumn of 1796 was quite positive for the British. Forbes had almost 7,000 British and European and 10,000 colonial troops at his disposal. His adversaries had a significantly larger force, perhaps 25–30,000 men, but they were mostly untrained and racked by internal divisions. The arrival of white troops from France fanned these flames; André Rigaud now despised the French more than the British. Indeed, the Republicans found themselves under attack from all parties – the British, blacks, mulattoes and Spaniards. There was fighting between mulattoes and blacks and the two Republican commissioners, Rochambeau and Sonthonax, quarrelled, the former leaving the colony. Pitted against such fractured opposition, the British had some notable successes. During August, Rigaud's attacks on Irois and other posts were driven off by General Bowyer. Although October brought heavy rain and this, combined with sickness, halted operations, Forbes was optimistic, writing to Dundas on the 9th:

> I am happy to have the power of assuring you that our situation in St. Domingo [Saint Domingue] is by far more favourable at this Time than since His Majesty has been in Possession of any Part of It.

At the end of the month, the general claimed that with 8–10,000 troops he might gain complete control. 'Now would be the time to strike a blow'. This chance, if it existed, was soon lost. Between the summer of 1796 and February 1797, the British and allied foreign forces dwindled to around 1,500 men, mostly unfit for active duty. When Spain declared war in October a number of regiments had been removed to other islands. The Government, and public opinion, had tired of the constant drain of lives and money demanded by the occupation of Saint Domingue. It was obvious at the outset of 1797 that more progress would entail prohibitive cost. Geggus well describes the dilemma.

> The irony therefore, was double. The British Government gave up hope of the reconquest of Saint Domingue just when the military situation was at its most favourable and the occupied zone was showing signs of prosperity. Now that success seemed within Britain's grasp, however, it was increasingly certain that the colony would prove a profitless, if not untenable, conquest.

Saint Domingue was neglected, in large part, because there were no available troops. Britain was on a path of economy which would eventually lead to withdrawal. Manpower was now required elsewhere, not least to supply the great expedition to the Windward and Leeward Islands.[31]

Chapter 6

Winds of Change:
The Abercromby Expeditions, the
Loss of Saint Domingue and the
Peace of Amiens, 1795–1802

In the summer months of 1795 a new great expedition was planned. Under the command of Sir Ralph Abercromby, it was to consist of an army of 30,000 men – the largest military force ever to sail from Great Britain – to be carried to their destination in 100,000 tons of shipping, more than 200 vessels. As the redcoats gathered on the south coast of England and at Cork, instructions were sent ahead to the West Indies for the raising of extra black corps and the construction of hospitals.

Abercromby was a sensible choice to lead the second great push in the Caribbean. The 62-year-old general had fought with distinction in the Netherlands in 1793. He was to build a reputation for utter integrity, intelligence and humanity. He demanded high levels of discipline and training, writing to Dundas in 1794, 'If we are to have another campaign, order, discipline and confidence must be restored to this army'. His faults, such as his poor eyesight and a tendency to command too close to the front, were only likely to endear him to his officers. Sir Henry Bunbury remembered him as 'a noble chieftain: mild in manner, resolute in mind, frank, unassuming, just, inflexible in what he deemed to be right, valiant as the Cid, liberal and loyal as the proudest of Black Edward's knights'. John Moore, one of his ablest lieutenants, was close to Abercromby in the coming West Indian campaign.

> Sir Ralph is very short-sighted. Without a glass, he sees nothing, but with it he observes ground quickly and well. He has the zeal and eagerness of youth, and for his age has much activity of mind and body.

Henry Clinton agreed that their leader 'bore fatigue better than younger men'.

This respected army commander was to have Hugh Cloberry Christian as his naval colleague in the combined operation. Christian had only been promoted to rear-admiral in June but, crucially, he had both experience of the Transport Board and the West Indies. Like Abercromby, he was popular. Mariner William Richardson describes him as 'good, brave, and persevering'. However, his appointment to naval command of the expedition was complicated by issues of seniority; Christian was inferior in rank to the ageing Sir John Laforey who would have nominal command in the wider Caribbean. Following army complaints at this confusing arrangement, practical considerations trumped naval etiquette and Laforey was recalled.

Abercromby received his initial instructions on 9 October. These ran to several pages, with a number of contingencies, but his first objectives were to be the capture of Guadeloupe and St Lucia. To achieve this, he was to remove as many troops from the garrisons of the Windward and Leeward Islands as he judged necessary and feasible. His secondary objectives were to quell the lingering unrest on Grenada and St Vincent (see Chapter 5) and to acquire the Dutch settlements of Surinam, Berbice and Demerara. Once all these opportunities had been seized, he might then dispatch forces to leeward to intervene in Saint Domingue. Abercromby reported to Dundas on the 27th.

> I have now had an Opportunity of considering the Instructions you sent me, and of Comparing the Means given me, with the Ends proposed. The Number of Troops required for the Windward and Leeward Island Service, has been furnished; in general, they are well equipped, and are healthy. The Transports on which the Troops are embarked are, in general, unexceptionable. The Hospital Staff is nearly complete. Regulations for the Care of Men on Ship Board, and on their arrival in the West Indies, have been framed by Military and Medical Men of Judgement and Experience, and no pains or Experience have been spared to furnish the Troops with every Article for their Accommodation and Comfort, in Health and in Sickness. The Artillery and Military Stores now embarked will prove Sufficient for the Service. I have the fullest Confidence in the Temper and Professional Abilities of the Naval commander with whom I am to act.
>
> With all these Prospects and Advantages, it would be too presumptuous to count on the Certainty of Success, some of those Accidents and Disasters that have befallen other conjunct Expeditions may attend us.

The general was doing everything in his power, but his final words proved to be prescient. The launch of a large combined expedition was a daunting task and some delays borne out of the interactions of the numerous civil, army and navy departments were almost inevitable; on this occasion, the Ordnance Department attracted the most criticism. The damage caused by human frailty was soon to be dwarfed by elemental forces. On 16 November, the transports set out from Portsmouth under the protection of Christian's squadron, but on the evening of the following day a violent storm struck the fleet. It continued through the night with hurricane-like fury and, by the following afternoon, many of the ships were aground or driven back to seek refuge. Several were lost; on one Dorset beach the bodies of 250 soldiers were washed up on the pebbles. This was catastrophic enough, but when the rapidly repaired fleet attempted a second voyage on 3 December, it was again afflicted by a gale and widely dispersed. By the end of the year, a hundred transports were still unaccounted for; how many were sunk was impossible to know. The admiral had been three weeks at sea but was only three days from the British coast and still failing to make much progress against the relentless storms. The seasick troops were in a miserable state and even seasoned sailors were prey to the doubters. William Richardson was one.

> Varying were the reports in England about our second time being driven back: some said it was a judgement from God, for sending so many men to the West Indies to die; others said it was a judgement against the nation for going to war with France, which we had no right to do...

Midshipman William Dillon complained that when he was forced to return to shore he heard 'nothing but sad tales of woe and distress'. This pessimism was fuelled by the news that the convoy from Cork taking troops to Saint Domingue had also been scattered by bad weather.

The steadfast admiral, now regarded by many superstitious sailors to be unlucky, finally got the main part of the expeditionary force away at the end of February 1796. By this time, Abercromby had departed for Barbados in the frigate *Arethusa* and, in his absence, there was a lack of proper organisation. Brigadier General John Moore found Southampton to be in a state of confusion; '...everything is in disorder and the expedition will sail in as bad a state as ever an expedition did sail from this country'. The extensive damage sustained in the storms and the attendant delays meant that both the scale of the expedition and its objectives had to be repeatedly reassessed. Despite taking the best troops from units destined for the Mediterranean and India, Dundas struggled to raise the planned force of 30,000 men. The first sailing in November had carried nearly 19,000 troops and the second in December a few hundred more soldiers. After the second storm, about 12,000 troops were forced back to Portsmouth and, at the start of February, it could only be hoped that many of the 7,500 missing had gone on to the West Indies. Individual regiments were broken up with significant numbers stranded in England whilst their compatriots had sailed for the Caribbean.

A new plan was needed. Dundas agreed with Abercromby that a concentration of available manpower would be made at Barbados prior to a campaign targeting the Windward Islands. The priorities were now judged to be St Lucia, St Vincent, Grenada and Demerara. It was expected that at least 5,000 troops would have reached Barbados. To these, Dundas undertook to add the remnants of the six regiments of whom the majority of men were presumed already in the Caribbean, the Cork force of 7,300 men, and 6,000 foreign troops. Abercromby would have to decide how many men to spare, predominantly cavalry and foreign infantry, to pursue British aims in Saint Domingue. When the general arrived in Carlisle Bay, Barbados on 17 March, he found that a third of the 6,000 troops who had preceded him had been sent on to the beleaguered colonies of St Vincent and Grenada. This meant that he had a paltry 3,700 British regulars at his disposal. The number and nature of the local forces was also a disappointment. Attempts to raise West India Regiments had failed and there were only around a thousand under-trained temporary black corps (including Malcolm's and Druault's Rangers) and a few thousand pioneers (largely unwanted slaves) brought together with great difficulty by Quartermaster General John Knox. The arrival of the first transports of the Cork contingent coincided with that of Abercromby, but these filled the hospitals more quickly than the ranks. The general would have to wait for the promised convoys from Portsmouth to launch his major offensive.[1]

The help sent to Grenada included a first reinforcement of approximately 600 men of the 10th, 25th, 29th and 88th Regiments, followed by detachments of the 3rd, 8th and 63rd. Their arrival allowed Nicolls to retake the offensive and he attacked fortified enemy posts south of Port Royal (St Andrew's Bay) on 25 March. After initial failure, the 88th and a black corps (Loyal Black Rangers and Captain Brander's Company) being forced to retreat, the attack culminated with Brigadier General Campbell leading the 3rd, the 8th, 63rd and 29th Regiments against enemy positions.

> They soon gained the top of the ridge, the enemy then ran towards their redoubt, and were followed by our people, who scrambled in at the embrasures, Captain [Joseph] Clary of the 29th being the first that entered. The enemy then fled in the utmost terror in all directions some throwing themselves down precipices, whilst others tried to escape down the hill through brush and other wood; but there was so heavy a fire kept upon them by our people that they endeavoured to escape along a bottom, where the detachment of the [17th] Light Dragoons under Captain [John] Black and the St George's troop of Light Cavalry under M. Burney (that had previously been formed under the hill to profit of any occasion that offered) seeing the enemy fleeing rushed on them...

According to Nicolls, few of the enemy in Port Royal, mostly '*Sans Culottes* companies' from Guadeloupe, escaped. British losses were 20 regulars killed and 95 wounded and eight killed and 32 wounded among the colonial troops. The enemy, who had suffered losses five or six times as great, promptly evacuated Pilot Hill and Nicolls now occupied the ports, thus blocking Republican help from Guadeloupe. The insurrection was effectively crushed and further active operations could wait until later in the year.[2]

With Grenada at least temporarily secured, Abercromby soon achieved another secondary objective. The Dutch possessions of Demerara and Curaçao had offered to surrender in return for British protection. The British commander was still awaiting the arrival of his main force and he took the pragmatic decision to use the available Cork troops to intervene on Demerera. The force – 1,200 men of the 39th, 93rd and 99th Regiments under General Whyte – left Barbados and reached the South American coast on 20 April. As related by Army Physician George Pinckard, the landing at the mouth of the Demerera River was not straightforward.

> At length the little fleet of sloops, schooners and other small vessels, calculated, as it was believed, for the shallow sea they had to pass, got under weigh, and stood direct for the shore. The larger ships were unable to approach near enough to give any protection to the landing. The small light vessels into which the troops and stores were removed were some of them brought with us from Barbados for the purpose – and some taken after our arrival on the coast; but, unfortunately, it proved that even these, light as they were, drew too much water for this muddy shore; for, about five o'clock, we had the mortification to learn that our little fleet was fast aground deep fixed in mud. Finding the small vessels in this dilemma, our ship, together with the others which had sailed through a very confused channel towards the fort [William Frederick] came to anchor near the entrance of the Demerera river, having the fort, also a Dutch frigate, and a number of shipping in full view before them. This was a more unhappy accident than the breaking loose of the boats with artillery stores, and might have proved of serious consequence as the troops were compelled to remain until the next flood of tide, being equally unable to reach the shore or return.

It was a relief when the fort's Dutch governor promptly surrendered, allowing Whyte to gloss over the difficulties in his report to Abercromby, '...the Unanimity with which the Service was carried on between the Fleet and Army was pleasing to all concerned...' The Dutch frigate and a cutter were added to the fleet and Whyte's men marched on the capital Stabroek. Here, the capitulations of Demerera and the colony of Essequibo were negotiated. The neighbouring colony of Berbice soon followed suit and the Dutch garrison of all these acquisitions entered the British army.[3]

The arrival of Cornwallis's convoy in mid-April meant that Abercromby had an available force of between seven and eight thousand men and enough shipping to deploy them. He was ready to attempt the first major objective of the expedition, the capture of St Lucia. Once this island was acquired, he could turn to St Vincent and also complete the subjugation of Grenada. As so often in the region, this sequence was determined more by the prevailing winds than by purely military considerations. The fleet sailed from Carlisle Bay on 21 April and anchored on the 23rd in Marin Bay on the southern part of Martinique. This stopover had been planned by Laforey and was resented by the army's officers, who believed that all the necessary preparations could have been completed on Barbados. Moore notes in his lucid and detailed journal that both Abercromby and Christian, who had just arrived from England, disapproved of the delay. The latter's assumption of the naval command was welcomed by both soldiers and sailors. On the evening of the 25th, the expedition sailed on for St Lucia.

Abercromby's plan of attack was to make multiple landings on the north west of the island around Castries. This was very similar to Grey's strategy two years earlier. Three attacks were to be launched under cover of divisions of the fleet. The first and most northerly was to be at the Bay of Anse du Cap (between the Pointe du Cap and Pigeon Island); the second at Anse du Choc, a few miles to the south; and the third at Anse la Raye, five miles to the south of Castries (see map 5).

The strength of the enemy was a matter of conjecture. Lieutenant Colonel Henry Clinton wrote home to his brother that it was thought that they were 4,000 strong and occupying the posts of Morne Fortune, Soufrière and Vieuxfort. Abercromby was later to estimate the Republican garrison on Morne Fortune to contain 'about 2,000 well disciplined Black Troops, some Hundred Whites and a number of Black People who have taken refuge...' This was, he admitted, only the best information to hand. French sources are not explicit, but Poyen tells us that the British attack was expected by the French Commissioner.

At St Lucia, Goyrand, who had knowledge of these [British] preparations and who realised that he would be the first to be attacked, had prepared his defence with great energy; he had built new batteries, organised two companies of cannoniers, pallisaded the forts, and requested from his comrades at Guadeloupe that which he lacked, especially flour and ammunition. He made careful observations and watched ceaselessly himself 'with his telescope' all the coasts of the island, to prevent any surprise...

Goyrand called on all men fit to bear arms to join him to support the cause of *'liberté'*.

The first ships were off Anse du Choc on the morning of the 26th but the remainder of the fleet was strung out all the way back to Marin Bay. The plan was for 1,900 troops under the command of Major General Alexander Campbell to land at Anse du Cap and the 14th Foot and the 42nd Highlanders were soon ashore with no enemy in sight. By the time Campbell joined them he had received a letter from Abercromby requesting him to delay the landing. This was a difficult instruction to comply with, as John Moore explains; 'It was already part executed; to re-embark was impossible; to put off the march to Trouillac [on the Heights of Anse du Choc] till next morning, dangerous. The enemy was already apprised of our descent; they might therefore assemble, attack and tease us upon our march, perhaps completely impede it'. Moore was assertive and Campbell ill and the more junior officer's opinion prevailed. A message was sent to Abercromby who sanctioned a night move to the south. By now, other units had landed and the march began at three o'clock in the morning. Moore's aggressiveness paid off as Goyrand pulled his men back to Morne Fortune and the British arrived on the Heights of Anse du Choc to discover two abandoned enemy batteries. The admiral and general made the second landing at Anse du Choc on the morning of the 27th.[4]

With the two northern landings expedited, Abercromby now had to clear the way for an attack on the fortress of Morne Fortune. The capture of Morne Chabot, an eminence to the east of Castries and Morne Fortune, was a vital first step. This was achieved, but it was a close run affair, the attack being poorly conducted and the troops showing their inexperience. Two detachments under the command of Moore and Brigadier General John Hope were ordered to assail the Morne Chabot from two different sides. Moore set out at midnight on the 27th by the more circuitous route with seven companies of the 53rd, 200 men of Malcolm's Rangers and 50 of Lowenstein's Chasseurs. Hope took the more direct road with 350 men of the 57th, 150 of Malcolm's and 50 of Lowenstein's. The total British force amounted to around 1,100 and Goyrand's Republican defenders near to 750. The objective was to make a simultaneous attack at dawn but, despite the difficult ascent, Moore's column made contact with an enemy piquet one and a half hours before the appointed time and he had little option but to push on and attack alone. The terrain was difficult and the troops hesitant and Moore drove them forward, leading by example. The outcome was in the balance when the men at the front, who were reluctant to charge with the bayonet, received friendly fire from those behind them but some forward momentum was maintained and the enemy was finally forced off the summit, a number bayoneted and a handful taken prisoner.

We will return to Moore's account in Chapter 10 but here it is sufficient to say that the officer admitted that he had never 'made greater efforts or ever run more personal danger'. The soldiers had shown willing, but they were not the disciplined, battle-hardened warriors of Grey's campaigns. British losses were 60 to 70 killed and wounded; Abercromby estimated that 50 of the enemy were dead. Moore informed Hope that he was in possession of Morne Chabot. The second column had only reached the bottom of the hill at the time of the attack by the first. The two commanders agreed to leave the 53rd and some riflemen on Morne Chabot and to consolidate their position by also occupying Morne Duchazeau three miles to the south. This post was thought to be of 'infinite importance' as it was adjacent to and higher than the enemy stronghold of Morne Fortune and ensured communication between the troops already ashore and landing to the north of Castries and those of the third division which was to land at Anse la Raye to the south. Moore set up camp on the peak and ridge of Duchazeau and threw up advanced posts within 1,200 yards of Morne Fortune. These were only six to seven yards from the enemy's forward positions.[5]

On 28 April, Major General William Morshead disembarked his 1,900 men at Anse la Raye. The coming ashore was uneventful but there was sharp skirmishing with Republican outposts before Morshead's force was able to take up its assigned position on the Cul de Sac River to the south of Morne Fortune. Abercromby was under no illusion that the capture of the Morne would be straightforward. On 2 May, he confided to Dundas that he was daunted by what he saw; '...the difficulty in reducing this island will be greater than I apprehended, not from any increased number of blacks in arms but totally from the natural strength of the country'. The Morne was more of a hill than a mountain, standing at 700 feet, but it was well fortified with various works and artillery and held by Goyrand's determined 2,000 strong garrison. A summons for its surrender on the 28th had been summarily rejected.

The first step to reduce the Morne was to clear enemy batteries from the lower slopes on the side of the Cul de Sac. This task was entrusted to Morshead and 'to render the Success more Sure', he was given the support of Hope's detachment from Morne Chabot made up of 350 men of the 42nd, the light company of the 57th and 200 of Malcolm's Rangers. The plan was for Hope to attack the Seche battery and spike the guns whilst Morshead's two columns, 1,200 strong, were to attack the Ciceron battery; the whole were to then join up and take up a position between the Morne Fortune and the sea. John Moore was an anxious spectator of the operation on 3 May.

> At daylight, I saw our troops retreating through the valley of the Cul de Sac attacked on all sides. Our people seemed, however, to move with great regularity, though the country was woody and exposed them to be much harassed. General Hope reached his point before daylight, and sent Colonel Malcolm to attack the battery. He was killed, poor fellow,

before he reached it. The men, however, got in, and even turned the guns against the enemy, but they had no spikes, and were driven from it with loss by the guns from the Fortuné. Colonel Riffel [Riddle], who commanded one of General Morshead's columns, gained one of the batteries he was ordered to attack [the Chapuis] but, daylight coming on, he, being unsupported by the other column which had never crossed the river, was attacked and obliged to retire with loss. General Morshead had the gout and had entrusted his column, which was to have supported the other two, to Brigadier-General [James] Perryn. The latter, I understand, found his men fatigued with their march to the river which runs through the Valley de Cul de Sac, had not crossed it, and left Colonel Riffel and General Hope in the lurch. The whole retired to General Morshead's camp with the loss of about 100 officers and men killed and wounded. The Commander-in-Chief is, I understand, infinitely displeased.

Moore understood correctly. Morshead was immediately replaced by Major General Charles Graham. Perryn, described by Abercromby as a 'madman', was ordered to escort the foreign cavalry to Saint Domingue.[6]

This abject failure made it obvious that Abercromby would have to undertake a proper siege of Morne Fortune. He could not rely on help from the local population, who had mostly fled the area, or Republican weakness. He lacked Grey's elite troops but did, however, have a substantial force. The arrival of three new regiments (the 27th, 31st, and 57th), originally intended to form a reserve force at Barbados, increased the besieging army to 12–13,000 troops. This allowed the divisions of Moore and Graham to be connected and strengthened the investment of the Morne. There was optimism that French resistance would be quickly overcome. Henry Clinton wrote home that, 'as the enemy have neither casements nor embrasures', he expected that the Morne would be captured within a few days. Inside the fortifications, the obdurate Goyrand already had to ration his resources, '...I decided to prolong my defence as long as possible and to manage the powder even more. One can't imagine the quantity that is consumed during a siege'. He established a workshop to make cartridges. The French commissioner estimated the enemy to be 17,000 strong, not allowing for seamen and black troops. He sent out letters in English in an attempt to incite disaffection and desertion among the attackers.

Goyrand admits that his propaganda had little effect, but Abercromby had his own problems and British progress was frustratingly slow. The construction of roads in the rugged terrain was punishing work, horses were scarce, and it was difficult to get supplies to a line of investment 10 miles long and interrupted by the Morne. The men disliked the siege work and became dispirited. Foreign cavalry refused to serve as infantry and had to be re-embarked. Abercromby was distant from the front line at headquarters at Anse du Choc and his energy was badly missed. His most senior officers – men such as Moore, Hope and Knox – were worked into the ground. On 16 May, eight pieces of ordnance opened fire but with little immediate effect. More parallels were under construction and the commander hoped that he might be in possession of the Morne in 10 to 12 days. He admitted to Dundas that the enemy's defences were 'in a high degree difficult to be subdued'[7]

Despite British efforts to isolate Goyrand, a French convoy had entered the Carénage bringing vital provisions to the besieged men. Abercromby decided to tighten the screw by taking the Vigie peninsula to the north of the harbour; this would also shorten his line of attack and silence the Vigie's batteries which were a danger to the fleet. The attack followed a land and sea bombardment.

...on the night of the 17th, the 31st Regiment, happening to be the Regiment nearest at Hand, was ordered to march immediately after it was dark to take Possession of the Vigie, where the Enemy had not apparently more than from One Hundred and Fifty to Two Hundred Men. The first Part of the Attack succeeded to our Wish, A Battery of Three Eighteen Pounders, which was feebly defended, was seized, the Guns spiked and thrown over the Precipice. There remained on the Summit of the Hill One large Gun and Field Piece, which the Regiment was ordered to take Possession of: unfortunately the Guide was wounded and the Troops became uncertain of the right Approach to the Hill: While in this Situation the Enemy's Grape Shot took Effect to such a Degree, as induced Lieutenant-Colonel Hay to order the Regiment to retreat, which it did with considerable loss.

Poyen gives the more heroic French version of events, '...the brave Vacherat, Lieutenant of the Bataillon des Antilles, seeing them [the 31st]; he cried with all his strength, *'Camarades de la Vigie, l'ennemi s'avance; faites feu!'*". Vacherat's fellow officer, Lemaître, held his fire until the last possible moment; two further attacks were repulsed and British casualties were estimated at 800. The British return suggests less catastrophic losses, around 200 killed and wounded. Captain Lasalle de Louisenthal of Lowenstein's Chasseurs asserts that the confusion was such that many were victims of friendly fire. Sailors watched the disaster from their ships and drew their own conclusions. William Richardson was reluctant to blame the troops, '...someone unknown ordered the retreat to be beat...but the villain could not be found out'. William Dillon saw the 'splendid effects' of British musketry in the dark but was left lamenting the loss of life. On the following day, he watched enemy troops strip the dead of their clothes.

The second failed attack in quick succession led to soul-searching in the army. John Moore was unforgiving. 'The attack was planned in a hurry and executed without spirit or judgement. The regiments are in general extremely bad; it is hard to say whether the officers or men are worse.' He notes that even the successful attack on Morne Chabot nearly met the same fate and implies that Abercromby had been complacent. His chief was 'hurt and surprised' and certainly the commander felt the need to issue general orders in which he gave encouragement to his men but also stressed the importance of pushing on with the bayonet until they had achieved their objective, '...he trusts that in future he will never be disappointed'. His officers were more explicitly rebuked, being publicly reminded of the need to display zeal, industry and courage.[8]

Morne Fortune was not to be saved by British ineptitude. The bombardment was starting to drain the morale of the defenders; perhaps as many as 1,700 shells were falling on the fortress each day. Goyrand was plunged into despair by his inability to find bread for the women and children – 'useless mouths' – or medicines or linen for his wounded. The two main water cisterns were empty. On the 24th, the British made what was to be the decisive move, the capture of an enemy post near a flèche which formed the easterly outcrop of Morne Fortune. The energetic Moore was in the thick of the action.

> About six o'clock a few of the guns were turned upon the enemy's advanced post, and particularly upon a flèche to the right of it. When these had fired a sufficient time to dislodge whatever troops were supposed to be in and about it, the Light Infantry and Grenadiers of the 27th Regiment under Lieutenant-Colonel Drummond advanced. I placed myself between the two companies when we reached the top. We were fired upon by thirty or forty men from the flèche. No resistance had been expected. The General's orders were not to advance to the flèche, as the road to it was exposed to grape-shot from the fort, but to lodge ourselves on the reverse of the height we had gained till such time as a covered road could be made to the flèche. I immediately perceived that without the flèche and the ridge on which it stood, the possession of the first height would be of no use and that the fort would not dare fire upon us for fear of hurting their own men. I therefore ordered the two columns to attack it. They advanced briskly and the enemy abandoned it; we lost two men. The flèche stood upon a narrow ridge which ran to within 500 yards of the fort.

Goyrand launched two sorties to regain the flèche but both were beaten back by the outnumbered British grenadiers and light infantry. Moore had been critical of the soldiers, but these were among the best troops in Abercromby's army and the Republicans were no match for them in hand to hand combat. The desperate nature of the action is clear from the casualty figures; the valiant 27th lost 120 killed and wounded and the French close to 200 men. The flèche was secured and two 6-pounders placed in it. When another party of men emerged from the fort they were carrying biers for the dead and wounded; it was obvious that no more counter-attacks were to be made.

Further resistance was likely to be futile. The Morne owed its strength to its inaccessibility, not its fortifications, and the besiegers were now dug in close to the walls. Goyrand had lost 1,400 men in the siege and the commander accepted that there was now an overwhelming case for surrender.

> The bombardment continued; it was very destructive. Pressed by wise representations based on the exhaustion of the powder, the cisterns, the poor quality of the stagnant water which it was necessary to desalinate, on the cries of women and children demanding bread, on the protection of republicans who had survived this memorable siege, I hesitated no longer to listen to the voices of suffering humanity.

A flag of truce was sent out on the 25th and the capitulation signed the next day. Moore watched proceedings, '...we formed a lane from the gate and the garrison to the amount of 2,000 marched out, laid down their arms and were conveyed to the Vigie and from thence on board transports. The garrison consisted chiefly of blacks and men of colour'.

When the British flag was raised above Morne Fortune there was cheering on the ships of the fleet. Midshipman Dillon says that all was 'joy and cheerfulness' but the success had been expensive in lives, money and time. British casualties were significant; 566 officers and men killed, wounded or missing between the assault on Morne Chabot on 28 April and the final action on Morne Fortune on 24 May. The financial bill was perhaps £500,000 and the operation had cost Abercromby a full month, time he could ill afford as the rainy season was approaching. The victory was not complete. Many Republican sympathisers had fled into the wooded interior and remained a threat. Abercromby admitted that he had made a 'barren conquest'. The general wrote to Dundas that the island could be considered no more than a 'military post' and that the black population remained 'complete masters' of the place. He was forced to leave his best officer, John Moore, in charge of 4,000 men to undertake the unenviable task of suppressing the insurgents and maintaining some form of peace in the colony.[9]

The disillusioned Moore believed that Abercromby should have stayed longer on St Lucia to consolidate its capture using the whole army; 'The General and Admiral think they have cleared themselves from all trouble by running away from it'. This was a harsh and self-interested judgement. Abercromby had wider objectives and was running out of time. The weeks spent at St Lucia effectively precluded an attack on Guadeloupe; but he was determined to recover St Vincent and Grenada. He sailed first to Cariacou Bay with the Grenada division and then on to St Vincent where he arrived on 7 June. Here, the situation had stagnated with the British garrison in Kingstown dominated by French Republicans and native Caribs on the fortified heights of the Vigie a few miles to the east (see map 8). Troops were disembarked on the 8th with the intention of launching a decisive attack on the Vigie the following day. Abercromby's plan was for a frontal assault by three columns under Fuller, Morshead and Hunter, whilst two columns under Dickens and Knox worked their way around the enemy's rear. The attacking units totalled 2,800 and the encircling force 1,250 men. The commander was no doubt mindful of the debacle on the St Lucia Vigie and, at 7 o'clock of the morning of the 9th, he opened an artillery bombardment to soften up the defenders. This had some effect, a significant number of Caribs fleeing before their escape route was closed, but the white contingent and the troops imported from Guadeloupe and St Lucia bravely held their positions. By early afternoon, it was judged 'absolutely necessary' to storm the heights as daylight would soon be lost. Abercromby describes the successful outcome to Dundas.

> From Major-General Hunter's Divisions on the Right a Part of Lowenstein's Corps, and Two Companies of the 42nd Regiment, with some Island Rangers, availed themselves of the Profile of the Hill, and Lodged themselves within a very short distance of the Fort. At Two o' clock the Two remaining companies of the 42nd Regiment, from Major-General Hunter's Column, and the Buffs [3rd Regiment], supported by the York Rangers from Major-General Morshead's, were ordered to advance to the attack. The enemy, unable to withstand their Ardour, retired from the first, second and third Redoubts but rallied round the New Vigie, their principal post. They were now fully in our power...

Knox and Dickens had closed the trap and at 5pm the French commander, Marinier, surrendered. British losses amounted to 38 killed and 141 wounded. Abercromby estimated the number of prisoners as around 700 with perhaps 200 of the insurgents escaping into the jungle with the Caribs. Private John Simpson of the 42nd witnessed the capitulation; '...the next morning [10th] the French marched out with Drums beating and Colours flying and passed the English Army who stood with presented Arms. They consisted chiefly of Negroes and the nake[de]st set of ratches [wretches] ever was seen...'

Moreau de Jonnès believed Abercromby's surrender terms to be 'honourable but very hard'. The Vigie garrison was treated as prisoners of war except for the wounded who were to be returned immediately to France. The fate of the native Caribs on the island is a more tragic story. They were widely dispersed and the British set about systematically destroying their infrastructure. Private Simpson relates that the Caribs were in large numbers in the woods but difficult to catch; in one typical encounter, seven of his comrades were killed and eight wounded by an invisible enemy hiding in the trees and the undergrowth. This led, he explains, to more radical measures; '...by sending parties as far in to the woods as they [the British] could and destroyed all the fruits and roots they could come at, every day for a considerable time till we at last got them reduced to a state of starvation'. The black rangers were vital in this jungle war. A contemporary English historian admitted that, 'on negroes depend the preservation of the colony of St Vincent being separated from Great Britain'.

By the end of October, more than 5,000 black Caribs were captured and it was decided that they should be deported. British correspondence suggests no more sinister intent, Dundas twice emphasising to Abercromby that the captives should be managed with humanity. In the event, affairs were clumsily handled, the Caribs being first evacuated to the tiny island of Balliceaux in the Grenadines where they were devastated by disease and then to the underdeveloped island of Roatan in the Bay of Honduras. By 1802, the survivors had begun to colonise the Central American coast. The attitude of British historians to the episode has evolved. Fortescue, writing in 1915, is dismissive; 'with this incident the Black Caribs vanish from history, none too soon for the peace of St Vincent'. Modern authors have understandably taken a dimmer view, Duffy referring to Balliceaux as a 'concentration camp' and, in considering previous deportations of entire communities, he describes the Caribs' treatment as that which 'came closest to genocide'.[10]

The British were also taking control on Grenada. The reinforcement of 3,000 men from St Lucia had landed at Palmiste on the west coast (see map 7) on 10 June to join the 2,000 men already on the colony. The plan was for the new force under the command of Nicolls to attack the enemy at Goyave whilst the garrison force, under the leadership of Brigadier General Campbell, would advance from the windward side of the island to attack the enemy's rear. Nicolls quickly overpowered token French resistance at Goyave on the 11th but the Campbell column was still only half way across the colony and Fédon was able to escape with 1,000 insurgents to his camp at Belvidere on Mount Quoca (Mount St Catherine, 2,500 feet). Abercromby made it explicit to Nicolls that only Fédon's unconditional surrender was acceptable; 'The Atrocity of his Character and the Cruelties of which he has been guilty, render it impossible to treat with him upon any other Terms'.

Having completed his conquest of St Vincent, Abercromby joined Nicolls on 16 June to find the enemy invested. Nicolls was keeping a respectful distance and all operations had been slowed by the heavy rain. The stronghold was formidable and is well described by William Dyott.

Mount Quoca is the highest mountain in the island of Grenada, extremely strong by nature, as it is a ridge, one end of which is almost perpendicular. The enemy had added greatly to its natural strength, having by dint of negro labour got some heavy cannon to the top. The place from the beginning of the resurrection had been their grand camp and principal place of assembly, and it is a most remarkable situation. It consists of three heights, one rising above another, on each of which they had cannon.

The rebels had named the three heights the *Camp de Liberté*, the *Camp L'Egalité* and, the highest, the *Camp La Mort*. The latter had been used for massacring their prisoners. There was a second enemy camp called 'Asche's' four miles to the north east of St George's.

Abercromby grasped the nettle on the night of 11 June, ordering Count Heillemer of Lowenstein's Chasseurs to storm Mount Quoca whilst other units were deployed to block the insurgents' escape and to take Asche's camp. The choice of the foreign corps to make the main assault was propitious. Dyott saw the light infantry 'scrabbling through the woods, getting behind trees and taking a shot when they could get an opportunity'. Captain Lasalle de Louisenthal of the Chasseurs describes them using their swords as scaling ladders to climb the sheer incline and take the enemy in the rear. It was an audacious and overwhelming attack, Heillemer killing more than a hundred of the enemy for the loss of only seven men. Louisenthal saluted the achievement of his unit, *'Au début, personne ne voulut croire à ce success extraordinairement rapide. Personne ne pouvait le comprendre!'*. Fédon fled after slaughtering 40 white prisoners. Total British losses between 9 and 19 June were nine killed and 60 wounded.

The back of Fédon's forces had been broken. Asche's camp fell to another determined assault by Lowenstein's Chasseurs and light infantry. According to Dyott, the foreign troops had to be pressed on by British regulars; '...they would have played the very game the brigands were practising and have bush fought them all along the ridge'. It only remained to take retribution. Nicolls informed Abercromby that 'we were divided in search of the Monsters in every direction...' By October, Major General Charles Graham was able to report that the island was tranquil. There were still a few insurgents in the woods but they were causing little trouble, '...they rather deserve our Contempt than merit our Resentment.' Fédon had not been captured but was rumoured to have drowned from a canoe while attempting escape.[11]

The subjugation of Grenada completed Abercromby's campaign in the Windward Islands. This can be judged to have been a qualified success. The gains had restored the situation to that at the end of 1794 with the addition of the Dutch colonies. On the other hand, St Lucia remained vulnerable to

French intervention, Guadeloupe had not been attacked, and the whole project had drained vital resources from Saint Domingue. Exhausted by his exertions, Abercromby returned home in August 1796 leaving General Graham in command. As was the norm in the West Indies, the subsequent period of relative inactivity was marked by a virulent outbreak of yellow fever. In the Windwards and Leewards, around 2,500 British soldiers perished from disease between April and October. John Moore's retaining force on St Lucia was similarly afflicted, being reduced from 4,000 strong to 1,000 men fit for duty between June and November. There were 5,000 sick on Dominica alone.

The decimation of their West Indian forces – we will return to the precise losses in Chapter 11 – might have deterred ministers from taking more initiatives in the region. There was a growing realisation in London that the available forces were inadequate to obtain full control of Saint Domingue or to launch a fresh assault on Guadeloupe. Abercromby had thought it necessary to have an army in excess of 12,000 men to recapture the latter and Forbes wanted at least 8,000 fresh men to gain ground on the former. However, the changing political and military situation dragged Dundas's attention inexorably back to the Caribbean. The declaration of war by Spain in early October raised the prospect of an attack on the vulnerable Spanish colonies of Trinidad and Puerto Rico. Abercromby was instructed to return to the region to undertake the new conquests. He was faced with a daunting task. The garrison to windward was perhaps 3,000 men short of the 12,000 thought necessary to ensure security and he could expect few reinforcements, in all likelihood mostly German mercenaries of dubious motivation and quality. There were some compensating factors. He was at least absolved of any responsibility for Saint Domingue; the final operations here were left to General John Graves Simcoe. Also, the threat from Hugues was subsiding. The Republican leader was involved in infighting, had a shrinking army at his disposal, and was more interested in self-aggrandisement than insurrection.[12]

Abercromby arrived at Martinique on 17 November. He was resolved to make Trinidad his first objective. The necessary reinforcements, around 2,000 men including the 2nd Regiment of the Irish Brigade and Hompesch's Light Infantry, arrived at the end of January 1797. With troops collected from Barbados, Tobago and St Vincent this brought Abercromby's total force to close to 3,750, comprised of approximately 2,500 British regulars (2nd Queens, 14th, 53rd, 3rd flank companies, detachments of the 38th and 60th Regiments) and 1,000 men of the two foreign corps, Hompesch's and Lowenstein's Chasseurs. This small army was to rendezvous at Cariacou Bay in the Grenadines before being transported to its final destination, Port of Spain, on the 13-ship squadron of the Martinique station naval commander, Rear Admiral Henry Harvey. It

Recruiting to the Army. The West Indies was an unpopular destination and recruits were often reluctant and of poor quality.

The capture of Tobago, 1793.

Lieutenant General Sir
Charles Grey.

Vice Admiral Sir
John Jervis.

A View of Fort Louis, Martinique.

The storming of Fort Louis in February 1794. Captain Faulkner leads his men across the beach.

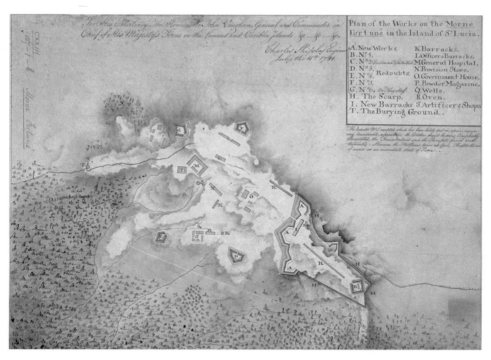

Plan of the military fortifications on Morne Fortune, St Lucia, 1781. Made for Commander-in-Chief Sir John Vaughan with a list of repairs appended.

Batteries at the entrance of the Carnage, St Lucia. View from the La Toc battery.

View of the bridge over the River Gallion from Fort Matilda, Guadeloupe, 1794.

Victor Hugues recaptures Guadeloupe from the British in June 1794.

A Maroon
captain.

A Maroon ambush on Jamaica, 1795.

Lieutenant Colonel William Fitch who was killed in a Maroon ambush in 1795. The posthumous portrait shows Fitch with his sisters.

Sir Ralph Abercromby.

Rear Admiral Christian's fleet battling the storms of late 1795.

TOUSSAINT LOUVERTURE,

Toussaint
Louverture.

No 1

It appears to be our whole intention to wait the cork
Hesto decide on any thing the critical situation
of grenada and St Vincents make reinforcements
necessary if Suger can remain after this I think
St Lucia will be the next Object there are 8500
other here eleven hundred Blacks well drilled
and 2000 pioneers &c 25 march vir Sts
to goes to ut Domingo in July.

No 2

3500 men.
Remainder of Portsmouth armament   4500
Sea nigro Battn   1000
Seamen and marines

   3600
   4500
   1000
   ——
  10,000

St Lucia is the first Object, the enemy supposed
to be about 6000 strong, occupy the ports of morne
fortune la vuifiere and vieure fort, there are to
be attacked, at the same time for which your men
and from hence at var est and make 3 landing
in the course of the next day once maker of
that grenada and st vincents are not yet

No 3

```
41 74 42 4  7 651 3 50 45 41 50 64 46 40 51 49 15 64 41 34
46 6 67 10 64 60 25 45 64 46 47  642 574 242 616 49 42 40
51 49 62  72 58 45 50 6 51 56 5784 41 15 26 65 49 64 59 47
16 25 41 51 46  51 49 66 44 65 6 44 47 9 49 42 56 50 42 20 76
51 64 6 42 11 56 51 64 44 17 63 64 6 11 63 50 259 46 61 37
50 41 6 49 42 47 70 30 52 38 60 57 3 46 40 36 41 82 55 32 62
32 93 55 40 308 22 116 63 20 69 25 70 69 61 34 10 64 64 745
17 0 36 70 26 69 37 2 36 25 70 64 70 69 8 11 18 11 53 69 40 25
70 11 67 36 49 56 20 37 66 636 2 61 11 865 70 67 2 43 1019
36 70 64 67 20 69 56 64 37 64 69 9 67 2 0 11 15 20 59 67 20 6
45 62 116 9 6 65 25 207 017 420 60 34 16 56 627 70 66 690
22 6 216 687 06 40 627 75 36 70 66 643 670 157 67 15 24
70 69 18 27 70 367 0 40 70 60 70 657 0 15 69 51 28 67 670 28
66 508 08 019 16 6 64 45 119 470 6 47 28 36 20 60 2847 6
69 28 47 55 57 67 62 6 20 69 70 36 116 26 58 1016 432
74 4 64 47 27 36 41 60 32 47 63 59 41 18 20 57 49 656
32 57 34 1 13 67 40 34 2013 34 63 20 34 39 13 27 59
55 1 57 40 69 55 40 54 26 49 46 75
```

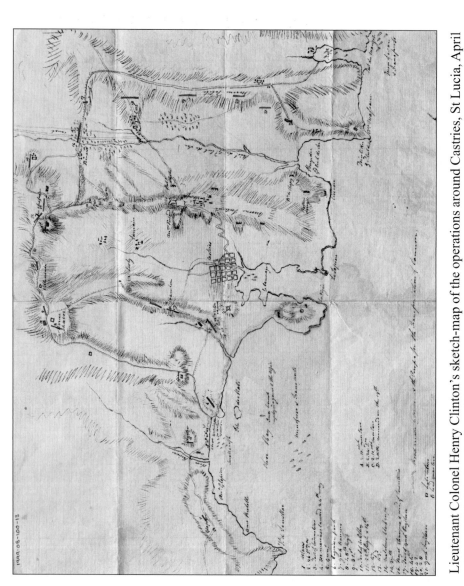

Lieutenant Colonel Henry Clinton's sketch-map of the operations around Castries, St Lucia, April – May 1796. (National Army Museum)

Polish troops in French service fighting black troops in Saint Domingue, 1802.

Lieutenant General Sir George Beckwith.

The British capture Martinique in 1809. A crude contemporary woodcut.

A French view of the British attack on Martinique, 1809.

A Private of the 5th West India Regiment.

The 3rd West India Regiment in action against French troops on the Saints, 1809.

Idealised view of Beckwith's capture of Guadeloupe, 1810. Compare with Beckwith's formal portrait, Illustration 20.

Lieutenant Colonel Henry Clinton's sketch-map of his voyage to the West Indies. He departed Portsmouth on 20 February 1796 and arrived at Barbados on 20 March. (National Army Museum)

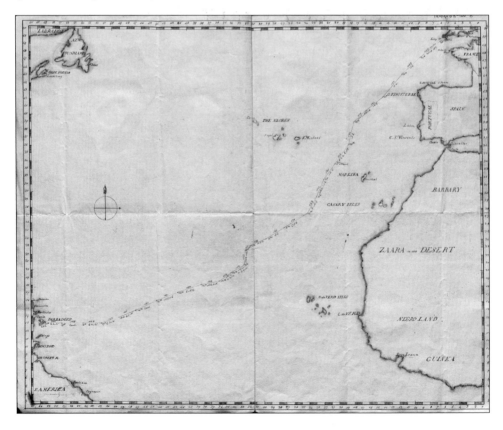

A street scene in St Pierre, Martinique, 1794.

A typical market of the West Indies.

The Torrid Zone or Blessings of Jamaica.

French graveyard near Castries, St Lucia.

seems that general and admiral had struck up a good relationship, a vital ingredient for a successful combined operation.

Port of Spain was Trinidad's main town and was protected by three forts. The Spanish garrison was 600 strong and there were also 1,600 marines and seamen aboard five Spanish ships anchored a few miles along the coast. This may have added up to a formidable obstacle; but the land defences were weak, the ships were seriously undermanned and the Spanish governor, Don José Chacon, had no stomach for a fight. In fairness to the governor, his garrison was a toxic mixture of French Republicans, French Royalists and Spanish; many of the second and third factions were antagonistic to the first and saw potential gain in British intervention.

It transpired that the most spectacular event of the attack on Trinidad was the self-immolation of the Spanish fleet on the night of 16 February. Thomas Brisbane witnessed the destruction.

> When we came off Port d'Espagne we found the enemy's fleet...As the sun was setting it was too late to attack them that night but it was resolved to do so at daylight the following morning. About ten o'clock that night we discerned a fire among the enemy's ships which presented a most awful appearance. As the fire extended to the guns they went off in succession, and on the flames reaching the magazines they exploded with a tremendous crash, while the burning fragments and sparks were seen for a considerable period high in the air.

Spanish Rear Admiral Don Sebastien Ruiz de Apodaca had taken the drastic step to deny the British the use of his ships. Abercromby landed a few hundred men about four miles to the west of the town on the 17th. Brisbane says that Port of Spain was occupied 'after a very trifling resistance' and Ensign David Wainwright confirms that he and his comrades met little opposition. Abercromby later communicated to Dundas that the town and its environs, with the exception of the two smaller forts, were quickly under his control. Chacon was weighed down by the defeatism of his small garrison and the lack of provisions and ammunition. He gratefully complied with Abercromby's polite summons to surrender, '...I see with sorrow his [Chacon's] troops are without hope of being able to carry out his wishes'. It was fortunate that the enemy was feeble as the landing, not for the first time in the campaigns, was unduly prolonged and there were well documented instances of drunkenness and plundering committed by the invaders. Captain Lasalle de Louisenthal claims that the 3rd Regiment were the main miscreants. 'If Don Chacon and Admiral Apodaca had attacked and if they had come out of the fort with only a hundred men, they would have been able to annihilate almost the entire army...happily this thought did not enter their heads'.

The single fatality of the attack on Trinidad, Lieutenant Villeneuve of the 8th Regiment of Foot, Brigade Major to Hompesch, was very likely a victim of friendly fire. Only a handful of men were wounded. In contrast, the spoils were great. More than 2,000 Spanish soldiers and sailors were made prisoner, and about a hundred guns and a surviving ship of the line captured. The colony was, in the words of one officer, a 'valuable acquisition'; all the troops would later receive significant prize money.[13]

Abercromby left a 1,000-strong Trinidad garrison under the command of Lieutenant Colonel Thomas Picton and turned his attention to Puerto Rico. He approached this venture with an optimism based more on perceived Spanish weakness that the strength or quality of his own forces. The new batch of reinforcements, 1,600 men of the 87th and a detachment of Lowenstein's Chasseurs, was of poor calibre and a total force of just over 4,000 men was not obviously adequate to overcome real resistance. On 17 April, Harvey's fleet of some sixty ships anchored off the north-east coast of Puerto Rico near San Juan which was the capital, a major port and, more significantly, a substantial fortress.

At dawn on the following day, troops were put ashore in landing craft, Abercromby accompanying them in a dangerously advanced position. The Spanish Governor, General Don Ramon de Castro, sent out a small detachment of perhaps a hundred men and a few guns. Private Simpson says that the enemy initially subjected them to heavy musketry fire from a wood and that field guns and ammunition were brought ashore, '...after which we moved forward keeping a good distance between each file, on purpose to make the enemy think that we had a great force on this advance; we was very much fatigued with the great heat'. Brisbane agrees that there was 'considerable resistance' before the Spaniards were driven back to the walls of San Juan.

Abercromby could now see for himself the strength of the fortress. This was on a narrow island on the northern side of San Juan Bay (see map 11). The combination of man-made and natural defences was such that the British commander decided that there was only one possible direction of attack, from the eastern side across the San Antonio Bridge. Even this approach was well defended by entrenchments and ordnance and Abercromby reluctantly concluded that his only hope was to first sap Spanish morale. 'The only Thing left was to endeavour to bombard the Town from a Point to the southward of it, near to a large Magazine abandoned by the Enemy'. This was not Trinidad. Not only were the fortifications much stronger, but the Spanish commander, Castro, was also a veteran with military experience against the English and his garrison of perhaps 4,000 men – mostly Spanish regulars and militia with some French and local black troops – was at least equal in numbers to the besieging force and determined and resourceful. Castro declined Abercromby's invitation to surrender.

The artillery exchange proved to be one-sided. British guns caused some damage to Spanish defences, but the counter-fire from the fortress was more destructive, silencing a number of British pieces and damaging magazines. The defenders appeared on the ramparts shouting insults and throwing stones. For the attackers it was brutal and unrewarding work. Brisbane later recalled that 'we had the severest duty I ever experienced, as, independently of living on salt provisions we had no other covering but our cloaks and the sand of the sea-beach for our couch'. Enemy militia had made an appearance in the British rear and were harassing outlying entrenchments and foraging parties.

Abercromby was frustrated at the lack of progress and the failings of his troops. Desertions were increasing, mainly from the German regiments. He decided to abandon the attack, fearing that a change in the weather might leave his small army marooned and at the mercy of the Spaniards. Disembarkation was no simple undertaking but the army was spirited away, marched to the beach during the night of 30 April and loaded on to the transports the next day. Tents were left in place to confuse the enemy who kept up a constant fire on the camp for several hours after the sudden departure.

British losses were 31 killed, 70 wounded and 124 missing. Abercromby's gamble had failed and the assault on Puerto Rico marked the end of the last major West Indian offensive of the Revolutionary Wars. Manpower was not sufficient for further attacks and even if more acquisitions were made it was unclear what would be accomplished. John Moore was pessimistic; 'It is to be regretted that we ever made the attempt [on Puerto Rico], but I doubt if not getting possession of that island is a misfortune...such numerous and extended possessions must ever be in danger'. The Government had reached the same conclusion. Abercromby was replaced by Major General Cornelius Cuyler who was instructed to desist from any aggressive operations and to consolidate the hold on existing British colonies at the least possible expense.[14]

We have seen that the over-worked Abercromby was at least spared the responsibility for Saint Domingue where General Simcoe took command in February 1797. His instructions were vague, reflecting the lack of British certainty regarding the current state and future of the colony. He was to reduce expenditure to £25,000 per month – no small challenge as £700,000 was spent in January – and permitted to pull back troops to the Môle if judged necessary. This place was to be held at all costs as a potential bargaining tool and because it bolstered the defence of Jamaica. He was promised some recruits, supplies and the services of Lieutenant Colonel Thomas Maitland. Both Simcoe and Maitland agreed on the importance of Saint Domingue but the latter officer took a more conservative view of the military options. Certainly, offensive operations would have to acknowledge the low morale of the colonists; corruption, infighting and desertion were everywhere. Simcoe's heterogeneous army, alluded to in the first chapter, was made up of 5,000 European troops of whom around 40% were non-British, in addition to 5,800 black chasseurs and three to four thousand local militia. This is a paper return and sickness and desertion significantly reduced the force available for immediate action. He was opposed by Toussaint with an army of approximately 20,000 men and Rigaud with around 12,000. Only at sea could the British boast superiority and Léogane and Gonaives were blockaded to stem the flow of Republican supplies.[15]

Simcoe had hoped to form a strike force of picked troops which could be launched from the sea against selected coastal targets. This opportunity never arose and he instead had to focus on defending occupied territory. In late February and March, Toussaint's forces overran the outposts around Mirebalais. A relief force under Montalembert was ambushed with heavy casualties. By the beginning of April, the enemy was approaching Port au Prince from Léogane; there was fear that Toussaint and Rigaud might join forces in the Plain of Cul de Sac and make a concerted attack on the capital. The determination of émigré officers, men such as Montalembert and Viscomte de Bruges, was questionable. On 11 April, Maitland arrived at Port au Prince with 600 troops of the 40th Regiment of the Irish Brigade and other small detachments. Simcoe used the extra men to force Toussaint back from the town and sought to follow up this success by pushing on towards Verrettes with the ultimate objective of capturing Mirebalais. The attack had to be abandoned at Arcahaye when news was received that Rigaud was besieging Irois in the south.[16]

Simcoe responded to the new threat by immediately despatching a relief operation towards Jérémie under the command of Maitland. Irois's tiny garrison was composed of 50 men of the 17th Foot and colonial artillery. On 20 April, Rigaud's army of 1,200 men made a vigorous attack against which the intrepid group of defenders resisted long enough to allow 350 of Prince Edward's Black Chasseurs to reach the place and drive the attackers back. Rigaud had started a regular siege when, by pure good fortune, two British frigates arrived to sink the enemy flotilla and completely defeat Rigaud's land forces. Brigadier General George Churchill, reporting to Simcoe, estimated the Republican losses as at least 800; around Irois there were 250 bodies, mostly mulattoes and whites. By the time that Maitland appeared, the crisis had passed. That officer was, however, unimpressed, commenting that British survival was now a matter of rushing troops around the colony.[17]

Leaving Maitland at Jérémie, Simcoe was resolved to retake Mirebalais. Toussaint was taken by surprise and the place was captured cheaply at the end of May, the Republicans escaping across the flooded Artibonite. There was more anxiety at St Marc where the British garrison came under attack from a substantial Toussaint army approaching from Gonaives, perhaps as many as 14,000 men. Ground was ceded and the besieged force retired to Fort Churchill, where a bombardment was followed by a violent attack by 1,500 of Toussaint's best fighters. The fort and town were saved by the timely arrival of Dessources in the harbour. Lieutenant Thomas Phipps Howard of the York Hussars describes the reaction.

> ...to the inexpressible satisfaction of the Garrison, the vessels were found to be Colonel Dessources's Sloop with Transports having on Board a reinforcement of 500 men ...Colonel Dessources was received in the Town as a Saviour.

It was one more example of a British West Indian garrison being rescued from the sea.

As Rigaud and Laplume were preoccupied fighting each other, Simcoe sensed an opportunity to strike a decisive blow against Toussaint's retreating army. He hoped that the combination of troops under Churchill, Dessources and Julien Depestre would trap his foe on the left bank of the Artibonite. Churchill's dispatch describing this operation is strangely triumphant, but Simcoe's assessment, communicated to Dundas, is more realistic.

> The Brigadier General's [Churchill's] Letter will inform you of the Success of the Expedition but I have to regret that from some Delay of the Columns they did not move with the Exactitude and Concert I had hoped, by which Circumstance a considerable Object of the Expedition failed of success...

Churchill was not of the same calibre as Maitland and he had not displayed the necessary energy. To be fair, he was not helped by the torrential rain and the disillusionment of Dessources and Depestre. Simcoe still had some hope of seizing Verrettes but, by late June, the British army was bogged down in the fields around Arcahaye, more likely to perish of disease than in decisive action.[18]

Simcoe was frustrated. He was disgruntled by the perceived poor performance of his troops and an increasingly strained relationship with the navy. The situation was not entirely unfavourable for the British. The Spanish and the black population in the north were potential allies, Rigaud was at odds with the black leaders and Toussaint's power had been blunted. However, the exploitation of these positives required more manpower and more money, both commodities the commander was denied by the over-riding demand for austerity. Simcoe bemoaned the missed opportunity, claiming that with just a few extra thousand men he would have 'finished the business'. Having written a report to Dundas in June, making clear his view that it was impossible to protect Saint Domingue with the available resources, he left the colony in the company of Maitland in July, passing the command to Major General Whyte. Following the return of the two officers to London, the Government issued notice that a proposal had been made that the islands of St Domingo and Jamaica should remain neutral and that British troops in Saint Domingue would be withdrawn to the Môle and Jérémie. The citizens of Port au Prince would be offered support for either self-defence or escape. It appears that Maitland's views had prevailed. He was more tuned in to the Government's political and financial mood that the belligerent Simcoe.[19]

The man entrusted to impose this new policy on Saint Domingue at the start of 1798 was Major General Colebrooke Nesbitt. Maitland was also to sail from England as his chief of staff. Nesbitt fell seriously ill at Madeira and it was Maitland, only a lieutenant colonel in rank, who would effectively act as commander-in-chief; he arrived on the colony on 12 March. The early months of 1798 had seen General Whyte forced to cede ground to his enemies. Both Toussaint and Rigaud launched major attacks against the occupied zone in late January. Toussaint advanced from the Artibonite, forcing the abandonment of Grand Bois and the withdrawal of British troops in the Cul de Sac back to Croix des Bouquets. Mirebalais was surrounded and soon capitulated. In the south, Rigaud was besieging Irois and Laplume had captured the mountain stronghold of Lacoupe. Whyte remained passive; nearly all the combatants in these actions were black troops in uniform.[20]

Maitland was faced with a rapidly deteriorating situation. He was unable to work with Whyte, who returned to the Môle in a huff, handing all responsibility to his opinionated colleague. In mid-March, the cordon of the plain of Arcahaye, a series of forts, was abandoned by its commander, an officer of the Irish Brigade. Fortescue describes this action as 'treacherous', but the forts had a total garrison of 300 and were faced by 4,000 soldiers of Toussaint and Christophe. The colonial cavalry of Lapointe and Depestre could only slow the Republican advance and Port au Prince was now threatened. Maitland decided to follow through on his original plan to sacrifice the capital. On 23 April, he approached Toussaint offering to surrender Western Province in return for a five-week cessation of hostilities to allow the unhindered evacuation of British forces from St Marc, Arcahaye, and Port au Prince. His opponent quickly agreed, the negotiation tacitly acknowledging his precedence among the black and mulatto leaders. Maitland imposed martial law and embarked his troops and all locals who wished to go; by 18 May, the British had left Port au Prince.[21]

The British commander had not discounted the possibility of a final offensive. Part of the evacuated force was sent to the Môle and then moved to Jérémie where Maitland joined them. He still had approximately 2,000 British regulars and 7,000 colonial troops fit for duty and he was resolved to strike a blow against Rigaud by capturing Tiburon. Maitland blamed the officer in command in the Grand Anse, Brigadier General Brent Spencer, for allowing Rigaud's army of 4–7,000 men to dominate him; 'Spencer's failure', he opined, was due to 'the received and practised mode of carrying on the war in this island – that of stuffing all his men into posts without leaving any moving force, so that when one of his posts was attacked, he could not hope to relieve it'. Operations were delayed by torrential rain until mid-June when Maitland left Jérémie with 800 British and 2,300 colonial troops, At first, things went to plan, the naval squadron bombarding the fort of Les Anglais whilst 1,700 of Dessources's Volunteers moved through the mountains to cut Tiburon off from the north. The defenders were surprised but the weather and sea conditions, adverse winds and a heavy surf, prevented the landing of more men from the ships and, after three days, Maitland gave up.[22]

Negotiations with the enemy were opened to allow discussion of the final withdrawal of the British from Saint Domingue. This required some fortitude on Maitland's part as there were many parties who were against the decision. Apart from a number of ministers at home, Balcarres on Jamaica and Admiral Hyde were strongly opposed. At the end of July, Maitland received both the necessary approval from Dundas and a conciliatory approach from Toussaint. His subsequent arrangements with the black leader showed perspicacity. Although the British evacuation could not be viewed as anything other than a defeat, Maitland contrived to leave the colony in as non-threatening a state as possible. The agreements with Toussaint ensured that his interests substantially coincided with those of the British and that he would pose no danger to Jamaica. Indeed, within a short period he was the dominant force, had turned against Rigaud and the Directory, and had become an open enemy of France. The last British troops sailed from the Môle in October. Saint Domingue remained a trap for unwary Europeans, but it was now baited for the French.[23]

In the years immediately following the departure from Saint Domingue, there was limited British offensive action in the Caribbean. The emphasis was now on defence and economy; in the nine months leading up to March 1800, only one complete regiment and two half-strength units were sent to the West Indies. The lack of a major French counter-offensive did, however, give a breathing space for some opportunistic conquests. In August 1799, a British expeditionary force just over a thousand strong, under the command of Lieutenant General Thomas Trigge, sailed from Martinique to capture the Dutch colony of Surinam on the South American coast. The local governor had previously been softened with inducements, which was just as well as the operation was badly mishandled. The divided landing force was greatly outnumbered by Dutch and Spanish regulars, but the governor duly capitulated, allowing Trigge's men to first march into New Amsterdam and then to occupy the capital, Paramaribo.

In September 1800, Dutch Curaçao and its dependancy Aruba were seized in another bloodless coup. More easy catches followed in the spring of the following year. In March, the small island of St Batholomew, close to Guadeloupe and Sweden's only West Indian possession, was surrendered without a fight. The island of St Martin, part Dutch and part French, put up some resistance but soon followed suit. The Danish islands of St Thomas and St John and the Dutch islands of St Eustatius and Saba were all part of the British Empire by the end of April.[24]

This rapid-fire acquisition of small dependencies proved to be the last action of the war against Revolutionary France in the Caribbean. In the summer of 1801, Dundas's expansionist West Indian policy was unpopular in war weary Britain and the new Prime Minister, Henry Addington, was keen to sue for peace with France. The subsequent negotiations, at Amiens, were conducted by Lord Cornwallis and the final treaty was signed on 25 March, 1802. The terms were widely criticised in Britain, regarded as a diplomatic triumph for her enemy. French dominion in Europe and British superiority in India and on the high seas confirmed the status quo. The West Indian colonies were pawns in this game of aggrandisement. All Britain's hard-won conquests were returned to France and Holland, and only Trinidad, taken from Spain, was retained.[25]

Chapter 7

An English Lake:
The Short Peace and the
Napoleonic Wars 1802–1815

The resumption of hostilities in 1803 marked a change from the ideological warfare of the 1790s to a more traditional conflict between Britain and France. The Duke of York's reforms had created a better trained, more professional army now much more comparable to the navy. This was reflected by the very rapid remobilisation of both army and navy after the short uneasy peace. By the end of 1804, the two services totalled 600,000 men; between 11 and 14% of the adult male population had been raised, three times the ratio achieved in France. During the Napoleonic era, the Caribbean theatre was increasingly overshadowed by the herculean struggle in Europe, notably the Iberian Peninsula where Wellington and his Spanish and Portuguese allies waged war against the French between 1808 and 1814. However, as previously discussed (see Chapter 1), there was still a significant commitment of manpower to the region, the Government striving to consolidate financial and maritime ascendancy over France. The availability of these forces, and their relatively good quality, allowed the British to make a number of re-conquests, the last of these actually taking place after the Battle of Waterloo. These Napoleonic actions are broadly divisible into three periods: the years 1803–1805, then 1807–1810, and, finally, 1815.[1]

We must first briefly review two French initiatives which were both launched by Bonaparte in 1802. In April, General Antoine Richepanse, a veteran of the Revolutionary Wars, commanded an expeditionary force of 3,800 men against mulatto-led insurgents on Guadeloupe. The threat of the return of slavery only served to exacerbate the insurrection, but the French forces prevailed, crushing the rebellion with great brutality and deporting 3,000 alleged black insurgents from the colony. Richepanse and many of his poorly supplied army were to die of yellow fever, but the Guadeloupe episode was to be overshadowed by the attempt to wrest power from Toussaint Louverture in Saint Domingue. The expeditionary corps, under the command of General Victor

Emmanuel Leclerc, Bonaparte's brother-in-law, arrived in February 1802. It was allowed free passage by the British who were cautious of growing French influence but not averse to the end of black autonomy in the colony. Leclerc's sizeable army, around 35,000 men, achieved initial military success, soon forcing Toussaint's submission, but the French were ultimately to lose a savage war against the overwhelming resistance of the black population and tropical disease. By October, a desperate Leclerc was writing to Bonaparte, 'Since I arrived here I have seen only the spectre of burnings, insurrection, assassinations, of dead and of the dying...I struggle here against the blacks, against the whites, against the misery and the shortage of money, against my army which is demoralised'. The general soon succumbed to yellow fever and there was little left of the French force by the end of 1803. Rochambeau took command of the remnants and after a prolonged campaign of terror and sporadic fighting against the Spanish (by this time allied with Britain) around the town of Santo Domingo during 1808, the last survivors of Leclerc's original corps surrendered to the British general Hugh Carmichael in 1809. This was to be the end of all fighting to leeward. As many as 40,000 French lives had been sacrificed to Napoleon's colonial ambitions.[2]

Another event in 1802 caused great alarm in the British West Indian islands. On 9 April, troops of the elite flank companies of the 8th West India Regiment mutinied at Prince Rupert's Bluff on Dominica. Three British officers and all the white non-commissioned officers were murdered by the mutineers, a mixture of African-born soldiers and French-speaking Creoles. It appears that they had rebelled because of a rumour that they were to be reduced and sold as slaves. The West India Regiment had been already used to remove brushwood and drain swamps near to the fortifications and they believed that this work – probably ordered to stem the prevailing sickness – was a ploy to assess their suitability for cutting cane. A resident, who has left the best account of the affair, describes the local reaction, '...so strong was the apprehension that these proceedings were a first step towards a general insurrection among the slaves, that the white inhabitants only whispered their terrors to each other, afraid to declare, in the hearing of the black population, *all* that had taken place at Prince Rupert's'.

The island's governor, Cochrane Johnston, invoked martial law and a force of 1,800 men made up of the 68th Regiment, a detachment of the Royals, marines, and the St George's Militia was quickly raised to tackle the rebels, estimated as 450 strong. The two parties confronted each other on the 12th.

> The Royals, 68th Regiment, and marines having taken up their ground in front of them [the mutineers], Governor Johnston rode up to address them. Scarcely, however, had he addressed his regret and sorrow, that the corps of which he was the colonel and which had distinguished itself at the capture of the Danish settlements [St Martin, 1801] should so have

acted, when the angry feelings betrayed by the mutineers led him to wheel a little round; and, again fronting them, he, without losing further time, gave the word for them to order, and ground their arms. A few only obeyed this order; and one of their ringleaders, stepping out, called to them 'not to lay down their arms, as Governor Johnston would cheat them'.

At this point, the Royals fired a volley and the 68th and the marines advanced with the bayonet. After returning a few shots, the mutineers fled down a steep precipice. Over a hundred were killed in the action and several prisoners who were subsequently court-martialled and found guilty of mutiny were executed. Those British officers who had been held captive by the miscreants escaped unhurt. Following this episode, the governor resolved not to discharge black soldiers back to their local community during the peace but to keep these men, such as those from the disbanded 8th West India Regiment, in British pay.[3]

The Peace of Amiens was always likely to be short-lived. Both Britain and France treated it as no more than a short interlude in their titanic struggle. Ministers were distrustful of Bonaparte and the regular army, 132,000 strong, remained more than twice the size it had been at the end of the previous war in 1783. The navy, with 32 ships of the line and more than 50,000 seamen and marines in service, was also well prepared for the renewal of fighting. Britain's sudden declaration of war in May 1803 caught Bonaparte off guard, with half his warships committed to the Saint Domingue expedition. In the wider West Indies, neither the British fleet nor the army had been placed on a peace footing and, in early 1803, there were close to 10,000 men – a mixture of white regulars, West India Regiments and other troops – in the Windward and Leeward Islands. In the twelve years of impending Caribbean warfare, Britain's enemies at various periods were to be the French but also the Spanish, the Dutch and the Danes.[4]

The news of Britain's declaration of war in the West Indies formally arrived in the region in mid-June 1803, but army and navy commanders on the scene had been given early warning of the inevitable end of peace. Lieutenant General William Grinfield, the commander-in-chief in the Windward and Leewards, had toured the islands 'for the purpose of awaking the drowsy soldiers'. Now, he took aboard supplies for 4,000 men who were themselves prepared to embark at 24 hours' notice on Commodore Samuel Hood's fleet. Grinfield was given orders to attack one or more of Martinique, St Lucia and Tobago; he judged the first place to be too strong but he believed capture of the latter two islands to be feasible with his 3,000 strong force (2/1st, 64th, 68th, 3rd West India Regiment, Royal Artillery, Royal Military Artificers, black pioneers).

St Lucia was the first objective and the bulk of the force was disembarked in Anse du Choc, the bay to the north of the town of Castries, on 21 June (see map 5). Enemy outposts were driven in and Castries taken. The French commander, General Jean-François-Xavier Nogues, a veteran of Marengo, was holed up on the Morne Fortune with only a handful of troops. Poyen criticises the French strategy of dividing their forces *'en petits paquets'* among the islands. Nogues's desperate efforts to organise the defence of the Morne were witnessed by Lasalle de Louisenthal, formerly of Lowenstein's Hussars, who had joined his family on the colony.

> Diseases had decimated the French. General Nogues had scarcely 160 men of which 50 had been detached to Gros Islet. They called up the militia but very few were mustered. Most hid themselves away. For others the journey was too long. The general placed his men in front of the breach [on the Morne], placed six cannons in the front and awaited his enemy. Summoned by the English to surrender, he replied *'L'Empereur a donné ordre de ne pas rendre une fortresse avant qu'elle n'ait été attaquée, je m'ens tiens à cet ordre'.*

Nogues bravery was laudable but his paltry forces were no match for the British troops who attacked the Morne on the 22nd led by George Prevost and Robert Brereton. Grinfield, in his peremptory dispatch, describes the assault commencing at 4 o'clock and lasting for half an hour. Most of the fighting was borne by the Royal Scots and the 64th. A number of senior officers on both sides were wounded; the brother of General Nogues suffered a severe wound to the thigh and was only saved from the wrath of the rank and file by Brereton who took him in his arms. Louisenthal expresses his surprise that the overweight British general (*'son extraordinaire embonpoint'*) had reached the top of the Morne. The British total losses were 20 killed, 120 wounded and eight missing, reflecting the stiff French resistance. Despite the intensity of the fighting there was a good relationship between the adversaries, Grinfield commenting that, '...no sooner were the Works carried by Assault and the Opposition no longer existed, that every Idea of Animosity appeared to cease and not a French soldier was either killed or wounded'. Six hundred and forty French prisoners were sent back to France and Nogues and several of his officers were permitted to return to Martinique. The victorious Grinfield garrisoned the new acquisition with the 68th Regiment and three companies of black troops under Brereton's command.[5]

The next target was Tobago. Most of the island's inhabitants were British and the chief town and fort of Scarborough (see map 2) was defended by a French garrison of little more than 200 soldiers and sailors under the command of General César Berthier. Hood and Grinfield sailed from St Lucia and reached Tobago on 25 June, the greater part of the troops being landed by the late afternoon. It was, as Grinfield related in his dispatch, a bloodless coup.

...the two leading columns [the most advanced column of two companies
of the 64th and five companies of the 3rd West India Regiment under
the command of Brigadier General Thomas Picton] marched forward
towards Scarborough and meeting with no Opposition in the Defiles of
St Mary's, advanced to Mount Grace, from which place I sent a
Summons to the Commandant-General Berthier, who returned an answer
by proposing Terms of Capitulation...

These were quickly agreed, the French garrison marching out and laying down
their arms with the full honours of war. Grinfield praised Hood for his
exemplary naval cooperation and the commodore, in his own dispatch, noted
the general's 'superior energy'. French plans to make Tobago a naval depot had
been frustrated and the colony was garrisoned by eight companies of Royal
Scots and a detachment of black troops. Grinfield now returned to Barbados.[6]

It was often easier to conquer Caribbean islands than to safeguard them.
The commanders in the West Indies had a firmer grasp of this reality than
ministers in London. Any new acquisition of a 'valuable' sugar island sucked
in resources to ensure its adequate supply and protection from French reprisals.
Much of the power remained in civil hands and military considerations were
often subjugated to local needs. Governors remained reluctant to call out their
militia. Grinfield had little control of local shipping and Commodore Hood's
fleet was not strong enough to frustrate all enemy movements. When Henry
Addington's ministry ordered the assimilation of the Dutch colonies of
Demerara, Berbice and Surinam, Grinfield pointed out that his expeditionary
force would soon be nothing more than several weak garrisons. St Lucia and
Tobago required 2,000 men and the former Dutch possessions would consume
most of the rest. Promised reinforcements, a battalion from Gibraltar, did not
arrive. Grinfield's objections were not due to any ulterior reluctance to undertake
military operations; his case for conserving the status quo was pragmatic.

The general's reservations were ignored. Dutch colonists on the South
American mainland had been unnerved by a visit by Hugues and had appealed
to Britain for help. The temptation of another easy conquest was too great to
resist for the army's political masters. By August 1803, Grinfield had
intelligence that Demerara would indeed make little resistance and on 18
September his force of 1,300 men was anchored off the main settlement of
Georgetown. A flag of truce was immediately sent to the Governor of Demerara
and Essequibo with a summons and orders to wait only one hour.

The Commander in Chief of the Land and Sea Forces of His Britannic
Majesty being fully assured of their decided Superiority to the Forces
of the Batavian Republic [the successor of the Republic of the United
Netherlands, extant 1795–1806], in these Colonies, and certain of being

able to prevent Succours being thrown in...with the View therefore to prevent unnecessary Effusion of Blood, or the Mischief which must ensue to the Colonies, should the Troops be under the necessity of making good the Landing, and the Ships to enforce a Passage, the Commander in Chief thought it right to trouble your Excellency with this summons...

The Governor complied with the demand for immediate surrender of the two colonies under his jurisdiction. Berbice capitulated five days later to a detachment under the command of Lieutenant Colonel Nicholson of the Royals. Again there was no fighting. The Dutch garrisons, around 1,500 men, entered British service as the York Light Infantry Volunteers.[7]

Grinfield and many of his men died of yellow fever, but this did nothing to stem the political momentum for acquisition. In March 1804, the new commander-in-chief, Sir Charles Green, was instructed to combine with Hood to attack Dutch Surinam (now the South American Republic of Suriname). The planters were thought to be friendly, but this was not likely to be a repeat of the meek submission of the other Dutch colonies. More resistance was expected and the attack would be complicated by the labyrinthine local geography and significant Dutch fortifications. In his later explicit dispatch, Green explained that the coastline '...is of very difficult Approach, shallow, and full of Banks; that a Landing is only to be attempted at the top of the Tide, and at particular Points; the Coast is uncleared, and from Wood, and the marshy Nature of the soil, it is impossible to penetrate into the Interior except by the Rivers and the Creeks'.

The major river, the Surinam, was the key to the capture of the capital Paramaribo, ten miles upstream, and the subjugation of the colony (see map 12). Accordingly, the Dutch engineers had constructed a series of powerful fortifications, also well described by Green. At the mouth of the river was the battery of Bram's Point with seven 18-pounders; then there was Fort Amsterdam at the confluence of the Surinam and Commewyne (Commewijne) with 80 pieces of ordnance; 2,000 yards away on the right bank of the Surinam where it met the Commewyne was Fort Leyden with 12 heavy guns; Fort Frederick with 20 heavy guns was 1,200 yards lower down; Fort Purmurent with 10 guns stood nearly opposite to Fort Amsterdam on the river's left bank; finally, Fort Zeelandia, a battery of 10 guns, defended Paramaribo. The fire of all these works and batteries was intended to prevent ships going up the river.

It was obvious that a substantial effort was required and that effective army and navy cooperation was paramount. On 25 May, Green and Hood, both aboard the *Centaur*, anchored about 10 miles off the mouth of the Surinam; most of the remainder of the fleet had joined them by the following day. There was an available force of 2,150 men divided into an advanced corps, the 1st and 2nd

Brigades, and Royal Artillery ordnance. Green describes the opening of the campaign.

On the 26th, a Corps [the advanced corps], consisting of the Flank Companies of the 16th and 64th Regiments, the Rifle company of the 2nd Battalion 60th Regiment, made up by Detachments from the Battalion Companies of the 16th, 64th, and 6th West India Regiments, to about Six Hundred Men, and the 1st Brigade [Battery] of Royal Artillery, besides Armed Seamen, was detached in different Vessels under Convoy of His Majesty's Ship Hippomenes, Captain Shipley. This Corps was commanded by Brigadier-General [Frederick] Maitland, who was directed to effect a Landing at the Warappa Creek, about Ten Leagues [thirty miles] to the Eastward of the Surinam River, where the Enemy occupied a Post. The Object of the Operation was to obtain a Water Communication with the Commewyne River, to procure Plantation Boats in sufficient Number to transport the Troops down that river towards its Junction with the Surinam, and thereby facilitate our Approach to take a Position in the Rear of Fort New Amsterdam; and also with a view to cut off a considerable Detachment of the enemy stationed at Fort Brandwacht [a lesser fortification close by], on the Mud Creek. On the same Day, Preparations were made for landing a Body of Troops to take Possession of Bram's Point...A Detachment of Troops under Brigadier General [William Carlyon] Hughes immediately landed and took Possession of Bram's Point, making Prisoners a Captain and Forty-four men. The Entrance being thus secured, the Commodore made Signal for the Ships to go into the River as soon as possible; in the Course of that and the following Day, the most considerable Part of the Fleet anchored in the River.

Green sent a flag of truce up the river to the Dutch Governor whose refusal to yield was received on the 28th. The British General resolved to lose no time in driving in the enemy posts but an attempt on Fort Purmurent by a detachment of the 64th and some seamen was frustrated by the state of the tide.

The winning of Surinam was as much about overcoming jungle, swamp and water as defeating the human enemy. On the 29th, intelligence was gained that there was a way through the woods by which the troops might be brought up to the rear of Forts Leyden and Frederick. On the same night, Hughes took command of a party of a detachment of the 64th supported by a lesser number of the 6th West India Regiment, some seamen and soldiers from the Artificers Corps, in all about 180 men. They were led along the path by local guides.

A great Quantity of Rain having recently fallen, it was found that the Path, at all Times difficult, had become almost impassable, but no

Obstacle could damp the enterprising Spirit of our Seamen and Soldiers, who, with persevering Courage, after a laborious March of five Hours arrived near the Rear of Frederici Battery [Fort Frederick]. The Alarm having been given, a considerable Fire of Grapeshot was made upon the Troops, before they quitted the wood, while forming for the Attack, and of musketry as they approached the Battery. The Assault of our intrepid Seamen and Troops with fixed Bayonets was so animated and rigorous as to prevent any further Resistance. The enemy fled to Fort Leyden, having set Fire to the Powder Magazine by the Explosion of which a few British Officers and Men were severely wounded.

Hughes now moved against Leyden with similar results, his force again making an impetuous attack in the face of grapeshot and musketry. The fort quickly surrendered. Most of the 150 strong garrison were captured but some escaped across the Commewyne to Fort Amsterdam.

This action, described by Green as a 'brilliant affair', meant that a position was secured whereby a bombardment could be made against Fort Amsterdam. A communication with Maitland's detachment had been opened and the country now controlled 'abounded with resources of all kinds'. On the 30th, the army and navy commanders went ashore to inspect the shelters designed to give the newly captured works and occupying troops some protection from the intermittent fire of the fort. Two British mortars threw some shells in return and the Dutch fire was soon silenced. Green had by this time received a report of Maitland's successful landing at the Warappa Creek. The commander sought to combine his forces, the plan being for the bulk of his troops, still on the ships, to disembark at Fort Leyden and march up the north bank of the Commewyne to eventually link with Maitland on the opposite side of the river. All stores, supplies and artillery were conveyed along the river in naval vessels.

On 3 May, Maitland appeared on the Commewyne, his corps carried in plantation boats, and landed at a plantation on the south side of the river. He was soon joined by the 16th Regiment and, on the following day, he moved through the woods to within a mile of Fort Amsterdam. A few shots were fired by enemy patrols which then promptly retired. Green and Hood, at headquarters on the Commewyne, now received a flag of truce from the Dutch commander, Lieutenant Colonel Balenburg. Terms were quickly agreed and Surinam was a British colony. Two thousand prisoners were taken; these were mostly Dutch white troops (the 5th and 8th *Jagers*, Colonial White Chasseurs and artillery) but there were also 400 men of the Colonial Black Rangers. The strength of this force, and of the fortifications, suggest that an even stiffer resistance might have been made. British combined army and navy losses were surprisingly light, only seven men killed and 21 wounded. This implies that the fire from Forts Frederick and Leyden was not as murderous as described in Green's dispatch.

The locals had given little help to the British, only coming around when the outcome was certain. Victor Hugues' proximity on Cayenne meant that a garrison of 1,500 men, in part composed of Dutch soldiers, was judged necessary.[8]

British success was not universal. Rear Admiral John Thomas Duckworth's attempt to capture Curaçao in early 1804 came to nought. Overstretching his authority, resources and ability, he had sailed from Jamaica and landed 800 troops. Lacking any artillery support, he was impotent in the face of a Dutch garrison of 600 men placed behind fortifications and he had little alternative but to make a hasty retreat. His quest for prize money may explain his willingness to play the soldier as well as sailor. This failure was probably fortuitous; Surinam was arguably a conquest too far. Each new British dependency was a potential liability. A return of the spring of 1804 shows the number of British forces in the Caribbean to be 11,000 but scattered over 13 different islands and settlements with an average sick list of 2,000. William Myers, the commander-in-chief of the Windward and Leeward Islands, pleaded for reinforcements but, by the autumn, ministers were too preoccupied with the threat of a French invasion of England to send more men to the West Indies.[9]

Under the circumstances, it is unsurprising that the only significant British action in the region in 1805 was defensive in nature. Napoleon's expansionist policy included the launch of two fleets under Admirals Pierre-Charles Villeneuve and Edouard Thomas Burgues de Missiessy. The Emperor expected great things of his sailors, but the master commander on land had little understanding of the realities of the war at sea. The former fleet was forced back to Toulon by adverse weather, but Missiessy arrived at Martinique on 20 February. After consultations with General Joseph Lagrange and Admiral Louis-Thomas Villaret it was decided that British-held Dominica, vital for communication between Martinique and Guadeloupe, should be the first target. By midnight on the following day the force, possibly 4,000 strong, was moored off the Dominican town of Roseau on the south-west coast of the island. The French had hoped to take the British by surprise and, as related by a British resident, they were ready to employ subterfuge.

> Returning to Fort Young, I found the ships fully in view, and really within gunshot. There were five sail of the line, six heavy frigates, and several brigs and schooners. The fort hoisted the British colours and the enemy's ships immediately *did the same*. The Governor, at that moment, received dispatches from Barbados, by a schooner, which had arrived during the night. This, however, mentioned nothing of either a British or French force having been seen. Though the ships displayed English colours our naval men were not to be deceived...

General George Prevost, the British commander on the colony, ordered a shot to be fired across the fleet; the British Ensign was promptly lowered and the Tricolour raised.

The French plan of attack was for three landings on the island's west coast. General Lagrange was to disembark south of Roseau with 900 men; a second column under Adjutant-Commander Barbot was to land north of the town, and a third column of 900 men under General Claparède was to target Prince Rupert's Bay (see map 9). To defend Dominica, Prevost had only 300 soldiers of the 46th Regiment, 400 of the 1st West India Regiment, a few Royal Artillerymen, and some companies of local militia. This modest force was necessarily divided between Prince Rupert's Bay and Roseau.

The first French wave came ashore south of Roseau, Prevost's left flank, and was opposed by detachments of the 46th and the 1st West India Regiment and militia. Moreau de Jonnès, aboard the invading fleet, could see 'strings of men in red coming down the hills and winding down the sides of the streams on the way to dispute our landing'. Prevost had given orders that 'not an inch of ground' was to be yielded and the French advance was vigorously resisted with the support of two field pieces manned by gunners and sailors. The troops were heroically led by their officers. Major Abraham Augustus Nunn of the 1st West India Regiment was mortally wounded and his place taken by Captain Maurice Charles O'Connell of the same unit. Despite also being wounded, O'Connell fought on, in Prevost's words, '...[the wound] could not induce him to give up the Honour of the First, and he continued in the Field animating his men, and resisting the repeated charges of the Enemy until about One o'clock, when he obliged the French to retire from their advanced position with great Slaughter'.

Frustrated to the south of Roseau, the invaders landed a column a mile and a half to the north of the town near Morne Daniel. Prevost had few resources to resist this second attack, only a hundred or so militia who were shaken by fire from French frigates close in to the shore. They soon had to fall back and Barbot's men pushed on to take a redoubt on Morne Daniel, the 1st West India Regiment and militia defenders overwhelmed by the number of their adversaries. The column originally destined for Prince Rupert's Bay had been becalmed and these men were now landed to join the second column with the intent of cutting off Prevost's retreat. Roseau was in flames having received a heavy bombardment from the French fleet. The dry roofs of the houses were highly inflammable. The town was protected only by a howitzer, a 6-pounder, and a part of a light company of militia. Prevost realised that the situation was desperate with his right flank conceded and a real danger of the British force being encircled and trapped. He decided to surrender Roseau and to leave the negotiations to the local governor. The general then made an audacious escape with the remainder of his force to Prince Rupert's.

...I crossed the Island, and, in Twenty Four Hours with the Aid of the Inhabitants, and the Exertion of the Caribs, got to the Garrison [Prince Rupert's] on the 23rd – After Four Days' continued March through the most difficult country, I might almost say existing.

Roseau and its local militia had been sacrificed but Dominica saved. The French had no appetite for a regular siege of Fort Cabrits at Prince Rupert's Bay and when Lagrange's summons for surrender was refused they decided to evacuate. Lagrange had fallen out with Missiessy and was deaf to the pleas of General Jean Augustin Ernouf, who offered extra troops to capture the island. After destroying the remaining defences at Roseau and disarming the militia, the French fleet sailed from Dominica on the 28th, first to Guadeloupe and then to the smaller islands of St Kitts, Nevis and Montserrat where contributions were levied. British losses in this brave defensive campaign were 21 killed, 21 wounded and eight men, all of the Royal Artillery, captured by the enemy. Prevost estimated French losses at about 300. Poyen's figures are, as always, significantly different, British casualties being given as close to 200 and the French as little more than half of this. Moreau de Jonnès comments that there were '300 or 400 wounded' aboard his ship and that they were taken to the hospital at Martinique.[10]

A period of British and French naval manoeuvring now followed. We will only briefly review these events as their greater significance lay beyond the West Indies. Missiessy returned to Rochefort having stopped at the port of Santo Domingo to land reinforcements and supplies. Napoleon was still determined that his navy would influence affairs and, on 14 May, Villeneuve finally arrived with part of his fleet at Martinique. The Emperor's intentions were unclear – was the foray to the Caribbean a feint? – but the British Government was concerned enough to plan to send more troops to the region under the command of Sir Eyre Coote. Myers at Barbados was acutely anxious, fretting that the strength of the enemy was such that none of the islands were safe. Villeneuve was, however, receiving conflicting signals from Paris. He was awaiting reinforcements, but meanwhile was given free rein to attack St Lucia, Dominica and other islands so long as he was able to return to Boulogne at short notice. In the event, the only offensive action was the capture of Diamond Rock, a tiny British-held dominion off Martinique. The Emperor's eyes were by now focussed more on the grey waters of the Channel than the blue expanses of the Caribbean. The British navy had not been idle and, in early June, Nelson brought his fleet into Carlisle Bay; although inferior to the French armament, the British admiral embarked a force of 2,000 troops and moved to protect Trinidad, passing Tobago and Grenada. Myers and the troops were disembarked at Antigua and the fleet turned north following the elusive Villeneuve. The French had stopped operations and had flown the West Indies. Nelson sent ahead warning of Villeneuve's return to Europe and himself returned to Gibraltar. Napoleon's directive to Villeneuve to make him 'master of the Channel for the space of three days' was never fulfilled and his plan to invade England was abandoned by August. The naval duel was to culminate in Nelson's crushing victory at Trafalgar in October 1805.[11]

The following year saw little military activity in the West Indies but ministers, despite the persisting high mortality among the troops garrisoning the islands, remained determined to diminish French power in the area. There was still a will to control the Caribbean. Napoleon's invasion of Spain in 1808 was to influence policy both to leeward and windward as the Spanish were now allies and their colonies, such as Cuba, had to be protected from the French. We must remember that Britain's enemies included Holland and, from 1807, Denmark, and it was against the Danish islands of St Thomas, St John and St Croix that the next decisive action was taken. General Henry Bowyer assembled a force of 2,500 men from Barbados and other British islands and, sailing with Rear Admiral Cochrane's fleet, arrived at St Thomas on 21 December 1807. The Danish commander-in-chief, Casimir Wilhelm Von Scholten, was summoned to surrender the island and, after establishing that he was faced by overwhelming force, he duly complied. Bowyer left a garrison of 300 men of the 70th Regiment and moved on to St John and St Croix, which both succumbed without resistance within a few days. The benign nature of the coup was reflected in Bowyer's platitudinous dispatch to the Secretary of State for War, Castlereagh; 'I am convinced that had it been necessary to have called for the Exertions of the Sea and Land Forces employed upon the Expedition, that they would have added another Laurel to the many already acquired by British Valour and Discipline'. The troops and sailors had readied themselves for a landing and were left deflated by the prompt capitulation of the Danes. Midshipman John Luard was 'disgusted' at the lack of action, 'It was not for this that I joined the navy'.[12]

Troops were hastily collected to reinforce the naval occupation of Marie Galante off Guadeloupe, a cause of some ill-feeling as the islet was a rich source of naval officers' prize money. The navy was also struggling to effectively blockade Guadeloupe and Martinique. The latter appeared close to starvation in early 1808 but, during the summer, French corvettes slipped through Cochrane's cordon to bring in more men, stores and provisions. Guadeloupe was also supplied by the end of the year. Frustrated by his inability to either starve the enemy on land or to defeat him at sea, Cochrane urged General George Beckwith to attack Martinique. The successful assault on the island in 1809 and the subsequent capture of Guadeloupe in 1810 were the major West Indian actions of the Napoleonic period.

Beckwith had a substantial force at his disposal for the conquest of Martinique. His army of 10,000 men was organised into two divisions. The

First, under the command of General George Prevost, totalled 7,071 troops and was divide into a 1st Brigade (the 7th Regiment, 23rd, detachment 1st West India Regiment, Royal Artillery), a 2nd Brigade (the 8th, 13th, detachment 1st West India Regiment, Royal Artillery), and a Reserve (flank companies 25th, 3 and 4/60th, 4th West India Regiment, Light Infantry Battalion, Royal Artillery). The Second Division under the command of General Frederick Maitland totalled 3,710 men and was divided into a 3rd Brigade (63rd, Royal York Rangers), a 4th Brigade (flank companies of the 15th and 46th, battalion companies of 15th, York Light Infantry Volunteers, detachment 8th West India Regiment) and a 5th Brigade (the 90th, 3rd West India Regiment and Royal Artillery). The French defending force, under the command of the governor, Admiral Louis Thomas Villaret, was 3,500 strong, made up of 2,400 infantry, 300 sailors, and six battalions of National Guard. There was artillery support with 280 to 290 pieces of ordnance. The quality of the French troops was variable; in the 26th *ligne* there were veterans of Egypt and Italy, whereas the 82nd was weaker with more foreign elements (see Chapter 2). Their senior officers were mostly of low calibre, some of them aged and lacking the confidence of their men. Villaret was an experienced seaman but had done little fighting on land.

The British strategy was very similar to that of Grey 15 years earlier, the plan being to force the entrance to Fort Royal Bay and to seize the dominant position of Morne Bruneau to the north of Fort Royal (see map 3). The French strategy, determined by the insufficiency of the garrison, was to concentrate forces in the immediate vicinity of Fort Desaix (formerly Fort Bourbon but renamed by Napoleon). On 31 January, Maitland disembarked the bulk of the Second Division at Sainte Luce in the south of the island, detaching the York Rangers to land further to the west at Anse d'Arlet, where they quickly took the batteries at Cape Solomon gaining a safe anchorage for the fleet. Pigeon Island soon surrendered to a bombardment. Maitland himself pushed on to Lamentin, meeting no resistance and accepting the submission of a number of local militia. By the 3rd, he was entrenched within gunshot of Fort Desaix covering the potential landing place of the Cohé du Lamentin.

Prevost's First Division also landed on the 31st at Malgré Tout on the Bay Robert to the south of the Bay of Galion on the east coast. Again this was unopposed. After waiting four hours for the disembarkation of the artillery horses, the troops set out on the night march south through difficult country towards the River Lézarde. The horses had still not come up and the light artillery pieces had to be dragged by men on their hands and knees. Five miles was achieved with great difficulty. The enemy at first fell back but then made a stand in a strong position on a hill adjacent to Morne Bruneau. Prevost was still without his artillery, but he nevertheless ordered a general assault by the 1st Brigade and the Light Infantry Battalion of the Reserve. There was to be a frontal attack by the 7th and the 1st West India Regiment and turning movements to the French right and left by the remaining troops. The outcome is best related by Captain Thomas Henry Browne of the 23rd.

> The action began about nine o'clock in the morning [1 February], the Fusiliers leading, supported by the Light Companies which had been formed in to a Brigade. Two companies only of the 23rd were at first engaged, but the opposition of the French was so serious, that the remainder of the Regiment moved up and commencing a steady and brisk fire they began to give way. Our men cheered loudly and chased them with the Bayonet. We pursued [the French] to a second hill called Mont Sourrirè [the Heights of Sourier] where they rallied and received great reinforcements. We attacked again – they made a vigorous stand for several hours, and we were engaged within half musket shot. This sort of work would not do as we were expending ammunition and not gaining ground. We were ordered again to the charge and they gave way.

Lieutenant John Harrison of the same regiment confirms the obstinate resistance, '...the French repeatedly returning to the attack with drums beating'. It was by now becoming dark and Prevost controlled the heights, the enemy taking refuge under the guns of their redoubts. The British troops made fires and slept among the sugar canes protected by strong piquets thrown out to their front.

On the next day (2 February), Beckwith ordered the Light Battalion and the 7th Regiment to take the troublesome redoubt. The attempt was repulsed with the loss of 200 men, but during the night the redoubt was abandoned and occupied by the British. The defenders had retired into the fort, spiking their guns. On the 5th, Maitland led his men around the north of Fort Royal to Negro Point, effectively completing the investment of Fort Desaix. The capture of this fort was now the final objective, its fall ensuring the mastery of Martinique. Work began on the construction of gun and mortar batteries whilst more cannon, mortars and howitzers with their ammunition and stores were landed and dragged to the points designated by the engineers. There was incessant rain. Browne describes the siege work as 'exceedingly tedious'. Morale, however, remained good. Inside the fort, Villaret watched his foe at work and prepared for the siege; he refused to read a letter sent by Beckwith. 'We were occupied day and night with the defensive works'. In his journal, he notes that he went into the town to visit the 700 sick and wounded. His own house and some magazines had been pillaged and he ordered veterans to take up arms to 'control the blacks'. French batteries fired at intervals, but both Villaret and Beckwith agree that they had little effect against the besiegers.

The grip was tightened on 9 February when St Pierre in the north capitulated to a detachment of the 63rd Regiment under the command of Lieutenant Colonel

Barnes. The troops had been carried up the coast in a small naval convoy and marched into the town unopposed, accepting the surrender of the French National Guard commander. The bombardment of Fort Desaix commenced at 3pm on Sunday, 19 February; 14 pieces of heavy cannon and 28 mortars and howitzers opened fire. Sailors helped to construct and man the British batteries, among them James Scott.

> The embrasures were unmasked, and at the prescribed moment bang went one of the twenty-four pounders, and the swallow-tailed flag proudly fluttered over our heads. The next shot was the signal to commence, and in one instant the din and roar of shot and shell from all quarters was stunning. The besieged appeared determined to keep pace with us; their fire was well kept up, and the accuracy with which they dropped their shells into our battery obliged us now and then to discontinue the fire of some of our pieces to repair our embrasures and parapets. For four hours the discharge was uninterrupted, when the guns became so heated that we were forced to slacken our fire.

Thomas Browne believed that 500 shells and large quantities of roundshot were fired into the fort in the course of the day.

Behind the walls, Villaret was undaunted, 'We have replied [to British fire] with a vivacity and a precision which has astonished the English...' Over the next days the British bombardment continued relentlessly, Villaret estimating on the 21st that he had received more than 2,500 roundshot and shells in the previous 24 hours. The French commander ordered a sortie against British forward positions, but this achieved little and when one of his powder magazines blew up the situation was deteriorating rapidly. By the 23rd, Villaret was forced to admit that the enemy fire was 'more lively than ever' whilst his own had been almost extinguished by the loss of cannons and the poor state of the batteries. At daybreak on the 24th, three white flags appeared on the ramparts and the French flag was hauled down. Villaret had accepted the inevitable and was ready to talk. His initial demands were rejected, but the articles of capitulation – that the garrison should march out with the honours of war and the commander and his aides-de-camp be allowed to return to France – were soon agreed.

Total British casualties for the Martinique campaign amounted to around 550 of all ranks killed, wounded and missing. The heaviest losses were suffered by the 7th, the 23rd, and the Light Infantry Battalion, the latter unit made up mostly of black troops. A hospital return for the month of February shows 380 admissions for gunshot wounds and a slightly larger number of disease cases, mainly 'fevers' and 'fluxes'. There remained the fate of the 2,500 French prisoners. They were marched down to the transports on the 25th, their behaviour catching the attention of Drummer Richard Bentinck, '...though having so shortly before parted with their Eagles [four regimental eagles were captured by the British], [they] were seen laughing and singing and dancing on the decks, just as they would have done in any little cabaret near Paris...'

Their optimism was misplaced. It had originally been agreed that they would be sent to Quiberon Bay and exchanged, but Napoleon's refusal to release British captives scuppered the arrangement and all those who were fit enough to make the voyage, over 2,000 men, were dispatched to England. On his return to France, Villaret was tried and stripped of his rank. Beckwith and Cochrane basked in the glow of a well-managed and triumphant campaign. The general declared that his 27-day command at Martinique would be a source of pride for the remainder of his life and he thanked the navy for their 'indefatigable exertions'. The admiral reciprocated, stressing the amicable collaboration between the services, '...British troops led on by such officers as we have had the Happiness of serving with in the Reduction of this Island, are invincible...'[13]

The smell of success rarely lingered long in the spice-scented air of the Caribbean and Beckwith was soon grappling with the usual manpower issues. He requested a 3,000 strong garrison for Martinique but Prevost's division was sent back to Nova Scotia and he was under pressure to provide soldiers to help man the fleet. In early April, a French squadron of three sail of the line and two frigates from L'Orient took shelter in the Saints, islands to the south of Guadeloupe (see map 6). Here they were blockaded by Cochrane. Beckwith immediately sent a corps of 2,800 men under the command of Maitland to cooperate with the navy in the reduction of the islands and capture of the French shipping. Maitland sailed from Fort Royal Bay on 12 April and landed two days later on Terre en Haut (Terre-de-Haut), the most easterly of the small island chain. The French garrison on the Saints was surprisingly strong, but it did include a significant number of raw conscripts destined for the 66th *ligne*. These forces were usually distributed between the several French forts on Terre en Haut and the neighbouring smaller island of Cabrit.

Once ashore, Maitland found that the enemy were established in force on Mount Russell, at 800 feet the most elevated point on Terre en Haut. This was a daunting natural obstacle, the slope at an angle of 50 degrees and covered with bush and prickly pear. The invaders were distracted by a cannonade from Cabrit. Maitland ordered the rifle companies of the 3rd Regiment and of the 4th Battalion 60th Regiment to dislodge the enemy, a task they performed with élan, inflicting heavy losses. The British general now had the high ground, able to survey the French forts of Napoleon and Morelle on the northern aspect of Terre en Haut and the troublesome works on Cabrit. Batteries were constructed and a fire opened on the French squadron which soon fled, chased by Cochrane.

It was difficult to make progress along the west side of the island and Maitland therefore re-embarked the bulk of his troops and landed close to Fort

Napoleon. A detachment left ashore was ordered to descend from Mount Russell
to dislodge the enemy and protect the landing site. Mortar batteries pounded
the enemy forces. On the night of the 15th, French piquets were driven from a
ridge between the forts of Napoleon and Morelle and the short campaign was
in its final phase. The denouement is described by Maitland.

> ...about eight next morning [17 April] the enemy advanced from Forts
> Napoleon and Morelle to recover this Ground. A Sharp Action took
> place, the whole of the York Rangers and the Rifle Companies of the
> 60th supporting our Black Troops. The Ground lay open in great Part to
> the Grape Shot from Forts Napoleon and Morelle and to Round Shot
> from Islet de Cabrit, but all our Troops were undaunted; none were more
> brave or active than the Flank companies of the 3rd West India
> Regiment, and a Flank company of the 8th West India under Major
> Allen. The enemy was driven back with loss and our Possession of the
> Ground completely secured.

By noon the French had surrendered and by late afternoon the forts were flying
British flags. Maitland's slick occupation of the Saints had cost only six men
killed and 68 wounded. Poyen gives French losses as six killed, two wounded
and eight sick, but this is very likely a gross underestimate.[14]

Beckwith had the small prize and now he wanted Guadeloupe. He was given
lukewarm approval for the new campaign in September, ministers specifying
that it must be 'easy of accomplishment'. His soldiers were sickly but he could
still bring together just over 7,000 men, the small army divided into two
divisions and a reserve. The First Division, under the command of Major
General Thomas Hislop, was made up of a 3rd Brigade (2nd Light Infantry
Battalion, 90th, 8th West India Regiment) and a 4th Brigade (detachments of
13th and 63rd, York Light Infantry Volunteers, 4th West India Regiment): the
Second Division, under Major General George Harcourt, of a 1st Brigade (1st
Light Infantry Battalion, 15th, battalion companies 3rd West India Regiment)
and a 2nd Brigade (Grenadiers Battalion, 25th, 6th West India Regiment): and
the Reserve, under Brigadier General Charles Wale, of the 5th Brigade
(Grenadiers Battalion, Royal York Rangers, Royal Artillery). We have less detail
of French forces on Guadeloupe. General Ernouf probably had 8–9,000 men
for the defence of the whole colony. They were mostly stationed near to the
critical stronghold of the town of Basseterre. Beckwith later estimated that he
was opposed by 3,000 troops in this area.

Cochrane and Beckwith sailed from Martinique on 22 January 1810. After
a 48-hour delay at Prince Rupert's, Dominica, due to some transports having
fallen to leeward, Guadeloupe was reached on the 27th. The First Division and
Reserve anchored near the islet of Gozier and came ashore near Capesterre (see

map 6) meeting no opposition. Hislop's force then marched south and reached Trois Rivières; the French briefly threatened to defend some fortified positions but they abandoned these posts 'with precipitation' leaving the ordnance behind. Remaining at Trois Rivières until 2 February to allow the landing of provisions from the fleet, the corps then marched in two columns to take the heights of Palmiste a few miles to the east of Basseterre. On the following day, Beckwith crossed the River Gallion and posted his men on the roads leading northward from the town.

The Second Division under Harcourt had made a feint against Trois Rivières before heading north and landing at Vieux Habitants on 30 January. Harcourt's corps moved inland threatening the rear of Ernouf's right flank and forcing the enemy back over the Bridge of Noziere on the River Noire. By 3 February, Ernouf was hemmed in. Basseterre and its fort (the Fort Matilda of 1796) was the key to the colony and the French general had concentrated his troops, mostly militia and new recruits, in the mountains to the north-east. This position allowed him to threaten the British flanks and force his enemy to tackle him before approaching the town. He was now faced by the British First Division on a ridge to the south and the Second Division a little further to the west on the ridge of Beaupaire. A French sortie was beaten back with some ease, but Beckwith hesitated to make a direct assault. Ernouf had intelligently selected and fortified his position, his left apparently covered by the mountains and a river in his front. Beckwith was faced with a difficult decision.

> The Enemy being now compressed within narrow Limits, the Difficulty, (and that a considerable one), was the passage of the River Noire, to the Defence of which he had paid the utmost Attention; it appeared to me to be necessary to turn his Left by the Mountains not withstanding all the Obstructions of Nature and of Art which opposed this decision.

The onerous task was given to General Wale and the Reserve, who immediately benefitted from some luck. Wales's dispatch reveals that he met an 'intelligent Guide who promised at the Forfeiture of his own Life to lead my Brigade across the River [Noire] at less than Half the Distance of the originally intended Route...' The guide's only condition was that the march should be made in the day as the road was difficult. At 4 o'clock on the 3rd, Wale set off with the Royal York Rangers, the Grenadier Battalion ordered to make a diversion to the left.

> We proceeded to the Banks of the River without meeting any Resistance from the enemy but a few random shot and shell. The Pass of the River de la Pere [actually the River Noire, a branch of the des Pères] was by Nature most difficult, and was made still more so by Abbatis lined by

Troops and every possible Obstruction thrown in our Way. Here it was the Enemy opened their Fire of Musketry; but our brave Troops, superior to all Difficulties, soon forced this Passage. Having passed the River, we continued our March for about 100 Yards through rugged Rocks and Bushes, when the front Companies branched off into three Columns rapidly ascending the Heights, the three leading Companies reserving their Fire till they gained the same, the Remainder firing to their Flanks on the Enemy, but still following the Van; as we approached the Summit of the Height, the Ascent became more difficult, and about 500 of the enemy's best Troops poured down upon us a most destructive Fire.

Major Henderson, with the Three Companies who first ascended the Heights, found the Enemy posted behind Abbatis and Stockaded Redoubts. This intrepid Officer did not return the Fire of the enemy till within about Twenty-Five Yards Distance, and immediately closed with them, followed by the rest of the Regiment, and in a few minutes completely routed them; it was about One Hour and a Half from our being first engaged with the enemy.

It was 90 minutes that settled the fate of Guadeloupe. Beckwith's bold strategy and the bravery of the Reserve had left Ernouf with little choice but to surrender which he promptly did, the capitulation being signed on 6 February. The garrison, by now much reduced in size, was accorded the honours of war. Ernouf was sent to England before being exchanged and returned to France to face the inevitable inquest into the loss of another French Caribbean possession. British losses were 52 killed, 250 wounded and seven missing. The gallant Royal York Rangers suffered almost half of these casualties. Enemy losses were estimated at around 600 sick and wounded and a 'considerable number' killed and missing. It was a second notable triumph for Beckwith which, as he pointed out in his dispatch, had been achieved in eight days against a strong enemy position in difficult country with little artillery support. The British commander quickly followed up the subjugation of Guadeloupe by seizing the much smaller islands of St Martin and St Eustatius in mid-February. The two minimal garrisons, a mixture of French and Dutch troops, surrendered without resistance.[15]

In early 1810, Fortescue's vision of the Caribbean as an 'English lake' was close to fruition. Beckwith was left to oversee several years of relative inactivity in the region. The threat from France was almost non-existent but West Indian waters remainder troubled. There were 17 separate British garrisons on the islands and there remained the potential for a repeat of the insurrections of 1795; in 1811, an uprising on Martinique was quickly suppressed. Beckwith's calls for high-quality reinforcements – two good British battalions – fell on deaf ears, the Secretary of State for War, Lord Liverpool, informing him that there would be no additions to the 10,000 troops in the Leeward and Windward Islands. Men were urgently needed for the Peninsula and to replace those lost from 'Walcheren fever'. In vain did Beckwith retort that the West Indies was 'a perpetual Walcheren'. The Government trusted that British naval superiority was a sufficient deterrent to French attack. In truth, the West Indies had been relegated to the second division of military policy, overtaken by the wars in Europe and insecurities at home. In late 1813, Castlereagh confided to Lord Cathcart that, 'Antwerp and Flushing out of the hands of France are worth twenty Martiniques in our own hands'.

The hostilities in Europe culminated in the defeat of Napoleon in 1814 and the negotiation of the Treaty of Paris in May of the same year. Louis XVIII was restored to the throne of France and the former Emperor forced to accept the victors' demands, his abdication being followed by incarceration on Elba. The terms of the treaty were surprisingly generous to France, the allies being willing to agree a moderate peace to conciliate the vanquished and to allow the establishment of secure government. This philosophy was reflected in the arrangements for the West Indies where all the captured French colonies were returned except St Lucia and Tobago. Dutch colonies were also handed back. British ministers were not entirely convinced by this magnanimity, but they were talked round by Castlereagh, even allowing the payment of a million pounds to Sweden to give up a claim on Guadeloupe so that this island could also be unequivocally French.

In the event, the allies achieved little by such moderation. Factions in France remained loyal to Napoleon and British celebrations at the demise of her nemesis were cut short by his escape from Elba and landing in southern France in March 1815. The subsequent Hundred Days campaign and Napoleon's final defeat are ground well trodden by historians, but it is less well known that there was also fighting in the West Indies, the last action in the third British invasion of Guadeloupe taking place 53 days after the Battle of Waterloo.[16]

Military intervention was catalysed by the presence of significant numbers of Napoleonic sympathisers on the islands of Martinique and Guadeloupe. When the news of Napoleon's escape filtered through to the Caribbean, Britain had to act to ensure the French colonies' continued allegiance to Louis XVIII. Sir James Leith, the commander in the Leeward Islands, was making a tour of the area in a frigate when he received intelligence of the extraordinary events in France. He quickly returned to Barbados to prepare the army for any necessary action. On reaching Martinique in late May 1815 he found the situation on the island to be critical.

> ...for the troops of the line, consisting of thirteen hundred men, who possessed the forts, showed too much of the same disposition which had manifested itself in France. The majority of the officers were decidedly

for Bonaparte, some putting up the tri-coloured cockade, and others, with similar sentiments, less avowed, pretending that they only wished to return to France.

Fortunately, the island's French governor, the Comte de Vaugiraud was a staunch royalist and had already taken steps to defuse the situation, threatening that any disobedience would be punished as an act of mutiny against Louis XVIII. Leith quickly reached a cordial agreement with Vaugiraud such that 2,000 British troops were landed on the colony to occupy Fort Royal, Fort Bourbon and other key posts. This was an auxiliary force, the island remaining under the sovereignty of the French King and Vaugiraud in charge of its government. The local militia, 6,000 strong, and the British officers adopted the *cocarde blanche* in a demonstration of their allegiance. On 10 June, Leith wrote to the Secretary of State, Earl Bathurst, reassuring him that the island was pacified.[17]

Vaugiraud urged Admiral Comte de Linois, the governor of Guadeloupe, to follow his example. At first, Linois also professed fidelity to his sovereign but he fell under the influence of his second-in-command, the Bonapartist Colonel Boyer-Peyreleau. On 18 June 1815, the day of Waterloo, the tricolour was raised and Guadeloupe declared for the Emperor. Receiving news of the coup, Leith immediately collected as many troops as he could find to suppress it. The general, a Peninsular veteran, had to be obdurate as his naval colleague, Rear Admiral Sir Charles Durham was dubious of attempting a landing at that time of year, July through to September being the hurricane months. The British expeditionary force was assembled on the Saints. It was divided into three brigades, commanded by Major Generals Sir Charles Shipley, Edward Stehelin, and Robert Douglas and made up of the following units; 1/15th, 1/25th, 1/63rd, The Royal West India Rangers, The York Chasseurs, Royal York Rangers and detachments of the 1st West India Regiment.

The French were estimated to be 6,000 strong, a mixture of regulars and militia spread between Basse Terre (Guadeloupe) and Grande Terre. Leith's plan was to land three columns at separate points on Basse Terre and to prevent the enemy concentrating their forces. Accordingly, the first landing was made on 8 August at Anse Saint Sauveur to the south of Capesterre (see map 6). Here, 850 Royal York Rangers under Lieutenant Colonel Stark threatened the enemy's rear. Later the same day, the 1st and 2nd Brigades were landed at Grande Anse on the southern tip of the island. This was facilitated by a preliminary bombardment from the sea, a gunboat being lost in the tremendous surf. French forces fell back inland to Dole, their morale undermined by rumours of Napoleon's defeat at Waterloo and the ineptitude of their commander Colonel Boyer-Peyreleau. On the morning of the 9th, British troops moved in two columns on Dole and Palmiste, turning the enemy flanks and forcing them back to their main position at Morne Houel where they had eight guns.

Whilst the 1st and 2nd Brigades made progress to the south, Douglas landed the 3rd Brigade at Baillif to the north of Basseterre with instructions to seize the latter town and threaten the enemy's rear. The light company of the 63rd pushed forward valiantly on to the heights, repulsing the attack of 300 of the enemy. Intelligence was now received that French troops on Grande Terre were endeavouring to reinforce their beleaguered comrades on Morne Houel. This also raised the possibility of the combined French forces falling back on the strong point of Fort Matilda and Leith promptly responded by sending a detachment of the 1st West India Regiment to line the banks of the River Gallion and block the French advance. Night fell, the men of both armies saturated by the torrential rain. After what Leith described as 'these laborious movements', the columns were readied for the attack on the formidable position of Morne Houel at daybreak. The French defenders were heavily outnumbered, less than 500 men of the 62nd Ligne remaining. At 11pm, Linois attempted to surrender but Leith refused. On the morning of the 10th, as the troops started to move off, a white flag was seen on Morne Houel. Leith's demand that this should be replaced by the Union flag was met and the last fight against Napoleon's soldiers was over.

As the ex-Emperor sailed for St Helena on the *Northumberland*, the articles for the capitulation of Guadeloupe were agreed. The terms were harsh, the French having to give up all their eagles, flags, magazines, arms and 'treasures'. Colonel Boyer-Peyreleau was discovered hiding in a wine cellar and, according to Captain John Anderson of the York Chasseurs, was treated with kindness. This was generous as the Bonapartists had planned to mark Napoleon's 46th birthday, 15 August, by executing their Royalist prisoners. Leith gradually restored order, reporting to Bathurst that the 'sanguinary phrenzy' of the slaves incited by the French had dissipated. The third conquest of Guadeloupe had cost 16 men killed and 40 wounded.[18]

Martinique and Guadeloupe were both restored to France in the second Treaty of Paris, signed on 20 November 1815. France was handled more severely after Waterloo than in the first treaty signed six months earlier, but the final distribution of the West Indian colonies was unchanged. Britain returned all its conquests except for Tobago, St Lucia, Trinidad and the former Dutch colonies of Berbice, Demerara and Essequibo. The restoration of Martinique and Guadeloupe helped to give the new Bourbon regimen some credibility and the retention of the St Lucia naval base enabled French colonies to be closely observed. These arrangements also acknowledged wider European sensibilities. The settlement proved to be successful; after a generation of almost constant war, Europeans now enjoyed a generation of near-continuous peace.[19]

SOLDIERS

Chapter 8

A Sense of Terror:
Voyage and Arrival

Most soldiers set out on their West Indian adventure with a heavy heart. The anxiety induced by the mere mention of the region was such that, on occasion, whole regiments took action to try and stay at home. In the mid-1790s units recruited in Essex and Newcastle refused to sign the muster book, the men of the 8th Regiment reported ill en masse, and rioting troops in Cork brought the city to a standstill, protesting that their conditions of service had been broken. When there was a delay before departure some chose to desert or disable themselves with self-inflicted wounds. Recruits from the militia were eventually promised that they would not have to serve outside Europe.

This negativity is well reflected in the some of the diaries and journals written by soldiers destined for the Caribbean. John Moore acknowledged that the West Indies was 'not popular', but he was determined to 'make no difficulties and not to give a handle to any people whatever to accuse me of backwardness'. Moore's fortitude was shared by another officer who returned to Jamaica in 1807 after 33 years of active service. 'I am a soldier and it shall never be said that John Irving sold out, because ordered to a climate where I have suffered so much, and which may be fatal to me'. Soldiers who were punished with West Indian service such as Andrew Bryson, convicted for treason after the 1798 Irish Rebellion, predictably took an even dimmer view of their fate; '...had it been left to myself I would have soon as been hanged as consented to have worn a Red Coat'. Sailors were no more optimistic. 'We are bound for Grave's End' was a popular joke among tars leaving the London docks for the Caribbean. William Dillon admits that his fellow midshipmen were alarmed. Dillon's colleagues were 'talking of nothing else but the yellow fever'. 'Death stares them in the face', he tells us. There is no doubt that it was the profound fear of a lingering demise from disease that gave West Indian service its particular odium. George Pinckard, an army physician who served in the region, describes the opinions prevalent in 1795:

> A degree of horror seems to have overspread the nation from the late destructive effects of the yellow-fever, or, what the multitude

denominates the West India plague; insomuch that a sense of terror attaches to the very name of the West Indies – many, even, considering it synonymous with the grave; and, perhaps, it were not too much to say, that all, who have friends in the expedition, apprehend more from disease than the sword.

Such discouraging sentiments I am sorry to find have not been concealed from the troops. The fearful farewell of desponding friends is every day, and hour, either heedlessly, or artfully sounded in their ears. People walking about the camp, attending at a review, or a parade, or merely upon seeing parties of soldiers in the streets are heard to exclaim, – 'Ah, poor fellows! You are going to your last home! What a pity such brave men should go to that West India grave! – To that hateful climate to be killed by the plague! Poor fellows, good bye, farewell! We shall never see you back again!

Assistant Inspector of Hospitals Hector McLean agreed that soldiers bound for the region were terrified by accounts of the infectious nature of yellow fever and that many thought themselves doomed.

Well-connected officers might be protected from service in the Tropics. John Gaspard le Marchant was provisionally posted to the West Indies in 1797 with the 29th Light Dragoons, but he was instead appointed Lieutenant Colonel in the 7th Dragoons. 'I would not have you go to a bad climate', the King informed him, 'and am glad of the opportunity of removing you'. Others escaped by serendipity. Arthur Wellesley, the future Duke of Wellington, was only spared a period in the Caribbean in 1796 by a sudden change in military planning which diverted his regiment, the 33rd Foot, to India.

For some, the rousing prospect of adventure in a distant land outstripped all other considerations. Jonathan Leach remembers that the news of his regiment's posting to the West Indies 'caused some long faces among a few of our old hands who had previously served in that part of the world; but the greatest part of us being young and thoughtless, the order for moving, being a novelty, was received with pleasure rather than dislike'. For more thoughtful and ambitious men there was at least the hope of prize money and rapid advancement. Lieutenant Henry Sherwood of the 53rd was bent on gaining promotion, as he notes in his diary for 12 March 1798.

Colonel Thornton was very kind and recommended my exerting myself to purchase a Lieutenancy which might be effected in a Regiment in the West Indies as the yellow fever was raging there and some difficulty found in filling up commissions in that country. He knew my determination was to run all risks in the way of my profession and so I ought to get on as fast as possible.

These sentiments were shared by other European soldiers. Officier de Santé André Nicolas-Joseph Guilmot went to Saint Domingue to 'make his fortune', hoping that in such a remote place he might jump several grades in the medical hierarchy.

Many had more basic aspirations, trying to convince themselves and those close to them that they were going to survive their exposure to the West Indies. George Pinckard, very well aware of the dangers, insisted that 'not withstanding all the depressing rumours of the moment, and the trembling alarm of friends and relatives, I do not feel the slightest personal apprehension...I shall embark with confident assurance of returning to my friends and to old England'. Lieutenant Thomas St Clair, bound for Demerara, faced his foreign service with a 'joyous heart', undaunted by a lecture from his mother regarding the perils of the climate. In trying to reassure another anxious parent, Lieutenant Colonel Edward Pakenham resorted to quoting the literature of the enemy, '...I confess myself a disciple of the wise doctor Pangloss, viz "Every things for the best". In 1806, Lieutenant Edward Teasdale of the 54th wrote from Colchester barracks to his mother that he 'didn't mind much' about going to the West Indies, '...if I should never come back I leave it with you to dispose of what property I have left'.[8]

The voyage to the Caribbean most often departed from the large naval stations of the south of England, the cities of Portsmouth, Southampton and Plymouth. Lieutenant Thomas Phipps Howard of the York Hussars found the Portsmouth of 1795 to be 'one of the finest and most commodious' ports in the country. The fortifications were extensive and formidable. The shops were well stocked and there were several good inns and a playhouse. He notes that the 'principle commodity' of the place was women, '...of which there is no want & constant market'. George Pinckard agreed that many of the local populace eked out an existence by fleecing the endless stream of hapless soldiers and sailors. The city, he says, verified its reputation for 'unpleasantness and vulgar immorality'. During times of peace, grass grew in the streets but when a fleet arrived or departed it was suddenly busy with the emergence of 'a class of low and abandoned beings, who seem to have declared war against every habit of common decency and decorum'. The doctor preferred Southampton and Quartermaster William Surtees of the Rifles describes the Plymouth of 1814 in surprisingly complimentary terms – '...we met with every kindness from the inhabitants in general who are upon the whole, I think, an excellent and a moral people' – but it seems most likely that all the major ports were dens of iniquity.

Embarkation was rarely straightforward. A naval captain, writing from Portsmouth in 1794, complains that the army's officers were unable to embark their men in an organised manner. Too much was left to chance and even senior soldiers were ignorant of what a ship was capable of carrying. It had, he lamented, been so in all the wars he had participated in. Certainly, the eyewitness accounts of officers' departures to the West Indies are often testaments to poor planning. The proficient John Moore became embroiled in the mess, as is revealed by his Plymouth journal entry for 4 March 1796; 'The fleet was to sail the next morning; I had nothing prepared, and did not even know in what ship I could get a passage'. He obtained a berth on a transport only by gaining the help of a commissioner of the Transport Board; 'It was not pleasant when I was going upon the King's service to be obliged thus to solicit a passage...' Pinckard had a ship but could not find it, spending a frustrating day with a medical colleague rowing across the fleet at Portsmouth. He eventually learnt from the Transport Office that it had sailed for Cork and he had to seek an alternative, ultimately embarking on the *Ulysses* at Spithead. He well relates the mounting anticipation and near chaos as the fleet prepared to depart.

> ...multitudes pressing into, and overflowing the shops – people running against, or tumbling over each other upon the streets – loud disputes and quarrelling – the sadness of parting – greetings of friends, unexpectedly met, and as suddenly about to separate – sailors quitting their trulls [prostitutes] – drunkards reeling – boatmen wrangling – boats overloaded and upset – the tide beating in heavy sprays upon the shore – persons running and hurrying in every direction, for something new, or something forgot – some cursing the boatmen for not pushing off with more speed and others beseeching and imploring them to stop a minute longer.

The sailing of the fleet was signalled by the firing of guns, but this system was prone to error. Surgeon James McGrigor describes the scene in Portsmouth in 1795 where 200 sail destined for the Mediterranean were mixed with Admiral Christian's fleet bound for the Caribbean. 'The signals now made were for the former; but this not being generally understood, much confusion ensued; so that a great many of the transports for the West Indies got under way, in the belief also, that the signal was for us'. McGrigor hired a sloop and, unable to find his own ship, the *Jamaica*, he opportunistically boarded the *Betsey* off the Isle of Wight and proceeded to Barbados. As this ship had also inadvertently left officers behind he was well lodged and the men of the 48th Regiment provided him with shirts and stockings and other necessities left ashore. In a similar vein, William Surtees and his comrades lost all their carefully acquired provisions when the ship they had joined sailed so precipitately that the vital supplies were thrown about the deck and destroyed. The soldiers received little sympathy from the ship's crew and Surtees was left to rue that such things were commonplace in a soldier's life. 'It was therefore vain to fret'.

No doubt there must have been significant numbers of officers and men who set sail for the Caribbean uneventfully. It is the nature of eyewitness records that they emphasise the unfortunate or extraordinary. However, it does seem that uncertainty persisted once the troops were aboard, not least regarding their destination. Surtees, actually on a voyage to Barbados, believed that he was probably headed for America but no one could be sure, '...the nature of the service being kept a profound secret, we scarcely knew what articles of equipment to prepare'. Lieutenant Colonel Archibald Campbell of the 29th, awaiting his departure from Plymouth in 1795, bemoaned the fact that despite being embarked for a week he had no idea why. That it was a West Indian expedition did not become clear until the transports were off Cape Finisterre. Private John Simpson of the Black Watch watched the men of his regiment 'breaking open their instructions' in the Channel to discover that they were going to Barbados. When the York Hussars embarked at Portsmouth in 1795 they were pleased that they were bound for the English capital. On the third day afloat, staff officers read the orders that they were to proceed immediately to Saint Domingue. Norbert Landsheit admits that he and his German countrymen had not the least idea where this was; '...the colonel, who followed the cortege, explained that it was a place where gold and silver abounded; and that the King of England sent us to that favoured spot, in order that we might return, each man with a fortune'. Misinformation took various forms, perhaps the most extreme being the case of the 87th Regiment which, in 1797, was told that it was going to the Cape of Good Hope rather than its true destination of the Caribbean in order to ensure a more orderly and complete embarkation.[2]

The Transport Board was responsible for providing troopships for the West Indies passage, although the control of transports was contested by the army and navy throughout the wars. Some navy ships were adapted for the carriage of soldiers, but most of the vessels used in the Caribbean expeditions were privately owned merchant ships. The British merchant fleet was substantial, over 14,500 registered ships in 1793, but only a small proportion of these vessels were both suitable for military use and available to the Board at any given time. For Abercromby's first expedition, the Board resorted to hiring ships from Germany and from the East India convoys. The relentless demand for transports – over 135,000 soldiers were carried overseas during the French Revolutionary Wars – meant that they were worked very hard. Their quality was variable. At best, they were specialist vessels, ideal for a voyage to the Tropics. John Moore assured his mother in 1796 that he had secured an excellent ship at Portsmouth, '...a West Indian trader, coppered'. George Pinckard was equally fortunate to make his voyage on the *Lord Sheffield*.

> ...a very fine West India ship...she is conveniently fitted out for passengers, and is, expressly, calculated for the West Indies, having awnings, scuttles, port-holes and all the necessary accommodations for the climate.

At the other extreme, troopships were unfit for purpose and even unseaworthy. Pinckard had earlier boarded the transport *Bridgewater* for a planned transfer from Portsmouth to Cork. He was lucky that there was a quick change of plan as he judged the vessel to be ancient and potentially unsafe. The *Admiral de Vries*, a captured 68-gun third-rate man of war on which Andrew Bryson sailed from Ireland to Barbados in 1799 was no better.

> The vessel had been very leaky all the Passage insomuch that the Pumps had to be kept Going 14 out of the 24 hours. This afternoon, however, we had been pumping as hard as possible with all the 4 Pumps and Could not Get her dry. At 12 o' clock at night Purss & I had to take the works for 4 hours & after working as hard as we could with 32 men for an hour, we could not find that the Water seemed to Get any lower...

Only when all the rank and file were called on to man the pumps was the four feet of water removed. Bryson says that the army officers remained oblivious of the problem, '...but on taking up their heavy Baggage it was all Rather!!!!!!' With so many ships in similar condition, soldiers were forced to be pragmatic. When Norbert Landsheit and his comrades of the York Hussars returned from Saint Domingue they were dismayed to discover the wretched condition of their transport. 'Our scruples were finally overcome by the assurance that other vessels were just as miserably provided...'[3]

Many of the soldiers' complaints relate to overcrowding. This was despite regulations in place from the 1790s specifying the number of men to be embarked dependent on the size and destination of the vessel. More transports were required for the West Indies than for a Continental expedition as extra space was allocated for voyages over longer distances and to warmer climes. Thus, soldiers bound for the Caribbean were allowed two tons per man compared with one to one and a half tons for local and European destinations. Officers were variably allotted the tonnage of two to four privates. This all meant that a regiment of 700 men required 1,400 tons of shipping. Since most merchant ships used as transports were between 150 and 300 tons, on average six troopships would be needed.

Once on board, the troops were accommodated in hammocks or in berths or a combination of the two. The former were more comfortable and healthier but they consumed more space; a ship capable of carrying 300 men in hammocks might carry 500 in berths. Often, for instance in Abercromby's expeditions, hammocks were recommended but subsequently rejected by the Transport Board as being impracticable and uneconomical. Such compromises are reflected in the eyewitness accounts of living conditions on the troopships. At worst, there were hardly any preparations for the boarding troops. George Pinckard was shocked to find that HMS *Ulysses*, a converted 44-gun frigate, had no particular arrangements for their accommodation. 'Not a cot was flung; nor any sleeping places allotted'. He eventually found a bed and endured a difficult introduction to his new life at sea.

> Our first night has been restless and disturbed – the unpleasant heaving of the ship – the creaking of bulk-heads, and other noises – the uneasy motion of the cot, and a whole host of annoyances, prevented me from sleeping. At each movement of the ship, or the cot, my feet were stuck against the bulk-head at the bottom of the ward-room; or I was bumped upon the huge cannon standing under me; or had Cleghorn's feet roughly presented to my head.

William Surtees, departing Portsmouth for the West Indies almost 20 years later in 1814, was also aboard a crudely converted man of war. Twenty-four officers were forced to share one cabin. He complains that 'all the discipline and strictures' of the ship made the men's situation even more intolerable; 'In fact, we wished our fortune had placed us upon a transport...'

Once the West Indies was reached there were still the frequent shorter voyages between the islands and conditions were often no better than on the original passage out. James McGrigor, transferring from Barbados to Grenada in 1795, found the man of war to be 'choke-full'. 'We were sadly crowded; there was not room for all of us to lie down at one time, at night, to sleep; every floor and deck of the ship being crowded'. McGrigor's medical colleague, Physician Pinckard, suffered similar indignities between Barbados and Saint Domingue. The ship, a West Indian trader, was a good one, but she was soon packed with more than 300 troops, many of them drunk. The decks were so full that it was difficult to move about. 'Negroes, sailors, soldiers, and officers all mingled together, in one hurried and anxious mass...' On the upper deck, soldiers were forced to lie down with no covering using their arms or knapsacks as pillows with less than a foot between them. In such conditions, it is unsurprising that vermin thrived. Norbert Landsheit's ship returning from the Caribbean was infested with 'swarms of rats, musketos, cockroaches and other reptiles'. The battle against the rats was a constant one; seasoned sailor William Richardson remembers that they took possession of his ship, HMS *Tromp*, at Martinique, 'by their fighting and their noise night and day'. Eventually, a rat-catcher was employed. We have no record of the number of rats on voyages to the West Indies but Thomas Swaine, a naval rat-catcher operating in the 1780s, documented the killing of 2,475 animals in the hull of the 90-gun ship *Duke* and 1,015 on the flagship *Prince of Wales*.[4]

For many soldiers the greatest misery of the voyage to the Caribbean was seasickness. Army Physician Benjamin Moseley, who served in the West Indies, notes that the affliction often only lasted for the first day or two but that it was 'extremely harassing' and that some unfortunates were attacked for longer periods and only relieved by the end of the voyage. Moseley himself was so severely affected that on his arrival at Jamaica he could hardly walk. He tells us that a common remedy among sailors was a draught of seawater. Thomas St Clair, making for Demerara, experienced the 'horrors' of the disorder. When the sea became rougher, his fellow passengers came down to their small and filthy cabins appearing 'as pale as ashes'. The reluctant soldier, Andrew Bryson, attended a company roll call soon after the departure from Ireland where three out of every four men were vomiting 'till their hearts were like to come up'. Some sufferers had to have their hammocks cut down to force them up on to the deck. Although affected himself, he could not help laughing at the appearance of his comrades drawn up in ranks.[5]

As the sight of home was lost and the ships made for the Bay of Biscay (see illustration 26 for a typical route to the West Indies), a daily routine was established by the military officers. The primary objectives were to promote order and to preserve health. The troops were divided into three watches so as to keep one-third upon deck at one time. This was intended to reduce the overcrowding below. From 8 to 10 in the morning, the men were brought up on deck for bathing and to allow the berths and surrounding areas to be cleaned. Toileting included washing of hands and face, the hair combed and tied and clothes to be brushed and shoes cleaned. Inspection by the officers was followed by a 10am parade. Activities during the remainder of the day were more variable and might include washing and drying of clothes and cleaning and oiling of arms and accoutrements. Soldiers were back on deck at half past six for parade, during which the floors between decks were swept. In general, the men occupied the decks less when it was raining. Saturday evening was reserved for entertainment, often dancing for the officers whilst the rank and file made their own amusement below deck. On Sunday morning, there was a religious service.

This routine was underpinned by formal guidelines, for instance, the *Regulations for the better preservation of the Heath of Troops at Sea and on Service in hot climates* produced by military and medical officers consulted at the behest of Sir Ralph Abercromby in September 1795 and used during his first major expedition to the West Indies. Further suggestions included the whitewashing of decks and the transfer of sick men from transports to hospital ships accompanying the fleet. We will return to the wider measures used to prevent disease on sea and land in more detail in a later chapter.

Most private soldiers apparently complied with the stringencies of the regulations but there were subversive elements. Bryson and his fellows usurped the system designed to allow only two companies to be on deck at a given time by painting an extra number on the reverse of their caps. Most officers strove to impose the rules and to protect their own and their men's wellbeing. Captain Thomas Powell of the 14th Regiment, on a voyage to Barbados in February

1796, was proud of the low mortality among his charges compared with another vessel attended by his ship's surgeon.

> On the [other] transport there was 73 sick and they had thrown 12 overboard out of 170 which was the number at first embarked. We had in the Frances and Harriet, exact the same number, 170, we did not lose a man, nor had we a single sick man in the ship, when they came on board, which astonished them a little.

Powell describes the rigorous interpretation of the regulations including the regular fumigations with a mixture of gunpowder, vinegar and tar. William Dyott was convinced of the merits of a salt water bath, managing to give himself 'a most complete lavage, in which I stood great need, as the dirt (I may say filth) accumulates most wonderfully on board ships...' More significantly, he had tubs prepared and fixed on the forecastle in order that his men could also wash themselves. This, he explained, was both to preserve their health and give them relief from the heat.

The victualling of the fleet was also described in contemporary regulations. Troops were normally supplied with food and drink at two-thirds of a sailor's whole allowance; thus six soldiers were victualled the same as for four seamen. Women and children received lesser allowances. This meant that the provisions given in one week to six soldiers on board a transport bound for the Caribbean would be 28 pounds of bread, 28 half pints of spirits, 12 pounds of pork, 8 pints of pease, 16 ounces of butter and 32 ounces of cheese. In reality, there were often deficiencies in both amount and quality. Lieutenant Thomas Phipps Howard describes the regret of all aboard his Barbados bound ship when the last potato was consumed; 'A vegetable being some kind of relieve [relief] when nothing but Salt Provisions were issued out'. Harry Ross-Lewin says that his shipboard rations were of the worst description, the cheese being riddled with 'long red worms'. The round of boiled beef was too large for the cupboard and was instead hung up in a cabin, its perpetual movement only serving to exacerbate the men's nausea. When the officers complained to the ship's captain they were informed that the food was 'good enough for soldiers'. The salted diet was poor in vitamin C; William Dyott was lucky enough to be able to bring aboard his own cask of vegetables – carrots and turnips – and also a hamper of apples. Ordinary soldiers could not afford such luxuries and the impact of scurvy will be discussed later. Good drinking water was also at a premium, George Pinckard being forced to consume 'putrid and offensive' water on the HMS *Ulysses*. He found this to be a particular misfortune as he was averse to wine and beer. Most had no such reservations regarding alcohol. Powell says that his men had half their rum mixed with water and half not and that they drank porter with their biscuit.[6]

The maintenance of a good relationship between soldiers and sailors was a priority for both military and naval officers. This was a controversial subject in the 1790s. Regulations stipulated that soldiers and army officers on board transports were not subject to naval discipline and it appeared in the regulations of 1795 that this also applied to warships. Senior naval figures, notably Lord Spencer, First Lord of the Admiralty, argued that troops aboard warships should be answerable to naval law to ensure the efficient working of the vessel and to emphasise the primary position of the ship's commander. It seems that the disagreement was partly defused at the time of the Abercromby Christian expedition when the awkward regulations were ignored and discretion left to army and navy officers. Pinckard, always observant, comments that the sailors were liable to mock the soldiers, especially those who were seasick, 'Steward! Why don't you give the gentleman a piece of fat pork to settle his stomach'.[7]

Both soldiers and sailors were understandably preoccupied with the weather. The passage could be remarkably uneventful. Lieutenant Henry Clinton wrote to his brother from Barbados in 1796 that he had just experienced 'the finest voyage ever made' with moderate weather and a smooth sea, '...a glass of water placed upon the capstan would have run hardly any risk of being spilled'. James Aytoun, a rare voice from the ranks, had an idyllic passage out on a transport. 'I believe there is no voyage in the world equal to that to the West Indies. The weather was fine, the wind always blowing to the point where we were bound for'.

Of course, few were this fortunate and there are many graphic accounts of storms at sea. Unusually severe gales lashed Western Europe in 1794–96 and Thomas Phipps Howard's journal entry for Wednesday 9 March 1796 is typical of many accounts.

> Much wind with Rain. The Sea agitated in a most frightful Manner. The Vessel rocked so much that every wave broke directly over, so that no fire could be lighted; & the Soldiers in the Hold were almost drowned inspight [sic] of every thing I could invent to keep the Water from them. At Daybreak the Sea washed away one of the forward Necessaries while an Hussar was sitting on it; & what was almost next a Miracle, the next wave washed the Man on the Deck again. In the Even: the Wind abated.

The Reverend Cooper Willyams, sailing with the Grey Jervis expedition of 1793, describes similar events at the height of a storm. Soldiers and sailors were thrown about the deck and the sides of the vessel appeared to twist and bend as it rolled through the swell. The heavy guns hung out on one side and pressed against the other. It was, he admitted, 'a scene of surprise and alarm to the inexperienced voyager'. Lightning could inflict extensive damage. Thomas Henry Browne, making his passage in late 1808, relates a direct strike against the top of a mast, possibly attracted by an iron cap. One man was killed on the spot and a dozen soldiers, including Browne himself, were knocked over. The mizzen-mast was split from top to bottom. After the Union Jack was raised as a sign of distress, carpenters and a surgeon came aboard from another frigate in the convoy. Browne says that the effect of the 'flash' was such that he had impaired vision and hearing and a shrivelled left arm. 'One of the men who had been struck, lost his senses, and was I believe, subsequently discharged from the Regiment as an idiot'.[8]

Whereas death or insanity caused by lightning must be regarded as unlucky, there was a real risk of perishing from shipwreck and sinking. When the ships were crowded the casualties from these accidents often exceeded those from sea battles. In the course of the Abercromby expedition hundreds of troops were drowned in the Channel and the Bay of Biscay. We have, of course, only the tales of the survivors. Major Thomas Brisbane of the 53rd took control when his vessel ran aground in November 1795:

> Our ship, the William and Mary, a Newcastle collier, commanded by Captain Gordon, separated from the fleet; and after our vessel had sailed alone for some weeks, the master came to my cabin one morning at four o'clock, and awoke me, to say that they had made the land; but he was afraid it was the main continent. I immediately got upon deck, and found the ship among the breakers; and the captain upon seeing the danger said, 'Lord, have mercy on us, for we are all gone!' I said that is all very well, but let us do everything we can to save the ship. He ordered the helm to be put hard down; but so completely were the seamen paralysed by their awful situation, that none of them would touch a rope. With the assistance of the officers, I, with my own hands, eased off the main boom to allow the ship to pay off, and the sails to draw upon the other tack. Most providentially the wind came from the coast and filled the sails, and though we were from four till ten in this critical juncture, yet we found ourselves at length off the bank.

Brisbane was determined to shorten the odds of his future safety at sea and he later bought books on navigation and nautical instruments. Captain Thomas Powell was shipwrecked a month later, the vessel lying on its side for three minutes. He says that everyone expected to perish. 'All the sailors were praying and most of the soldiers. In fact no one had any idea but that of going to the bottom that night...'

Medico James McGrigor was a victim of poor navigation on two occasions, first shipwrecked in the Grenadines and later having a narrow escape on his return voyage home. During the latter passage on a transport, many of the sailors, including the original captain and mate, died of yellow fever and the command of the ship was devolved to a drunkard. Eventually, seven army officers took over and Captain Vandeleur, an ex-midshipman, was made responsible for navigation. He got them safely home, but only after entering the River Mersey believing it to be the Downs.

There were other perils short of wrecking. Fire was a constant hazard. Andrew Bryson describes a conflagration just before his ship's arrival at Barbados. He claims that the army officers 'were all Gathered about Doing no Good' and that it was left to the rank and file and the sailors to prevent the flames spreading from the galley to the rigging. The threat of disease must have been constantly in men's minds. Thomas Phipps Howard describes the working of air pumps between decks to allow the hussars to 'Sleep Healthy'. There were also external dangers, any ships isolated from the main convoy a potential target for foreign privateers. Pinckard relates that, 'When any strange vessel appeared in sight, it, commonly, caused some apprehension, from our being alone and badly armed...' All these factors made many of the doctor's fellows anxious passengers; he contrasts the sailor blithely performing his routine tasks with the soldier who was 'restless and inpatient – listening in terror to the wind – and shrinking in agitation at every sound'. Each moment brought new alarms and 'a thousand questions dictated by a thousand fears'.[9]

Pinckard may have exaggerated the soldiers' trepidation. As the convoys ploughed across the Atlantic towards the Tropics, at least some were relaxed enough to enjoy the change in climate and the novel sights and traditions of the ocean. William Surtees's vessel fell in with the trade winds after passing close to Tenerife and the other Canary Islands, '...our voyage now became delightful, for a gentle and refreshing, but constant and steady breeze carried us on at the rate of about five or six knots an hour...' Contemporary journals document sightings of turtles, porpoises, dolphins and sharks. Normal holidays and anniversaries were observed – Colour Sergeant William Nichol ate his Christmas dinner just before arrival in the West Indies in 1808 – but one event takes precedence in all accounts. The 'crossing the line' ceremony was most commonly performed at the Tropic of Cancer and was particularly designed to initiate sailors who had not crossed before. William Dyott gives us a flavour of proceedings:

> One of the sailors is made to personate Neptune, who is supposed to rise from the sea, accompanied by his wife, Amphitrite. They are clad in a most ridiculous manner, in order to represent the high and mighty god and goddess of the ocean. These deities have two attendants, one of which is supposed to be a very humble inhabitant of the deep, on earth yclept [called] a barber. Mister Neptune greets you with a welcome to the tropic and an offer of a *bottle of milk* and a newspaper that he is supposed to have got a few days before from ashore, adding he shall order a prosperous gale to carry you to your intended port.

After this benign opening, the unfortunate sailors were subjected to various indignities including imbibing seawater, ducking in a tub of water and crude shaving. In general, the ceremony was conducted in good humour. Soldiers and sailors used telescopes to view the activities on the other vessels.

The redcoats were mostly spared. When Thomas Henry Browne was paraded before the gods of the sea, he had the good sense to part with a dollar. 'The messengers were then about to be dispatched for some of the Soldiers, but as we did not wish them to pass thro' this filthy ordeal, we interfered and expressed our hopes that His Majesty would consider tribute money as the purchase of their freedom of the Seas as well as our own.' The ceremony could get out of hand and be mischievously used to exact retribution against an unpopular individual. Such a case occurred on Andrew Bryson's ship where a targeted army officer was unable to escape by hiding or paying the usual bribe.

> He then offered him [Neptune] a Crown: No. Then half a Guinea: No. Then a whole one: No. 'You have detained me from Dinner this half Hour & you Shall pay for it with a Vengeance. Officers, & you Barber, do y[ou]r duty.' Notwithstanding all his out-cries and Strength, they tied up his eyes & placed him on the bason. One of the men poured a little water down his cheek, on which he Gave a Shout & the Barber Crammed his brush full into his mouth & rammed it half down his throat.[10]

With fine weather and favourable trade winds the voyage to the West Indies could be made in as little as 30 days, but 40 to 50 days was more typical. Pinckard notes that the 'sad uncertainties' of the passage were well illustrated by the simultaneous arrival in Carlisle Bay of a transport of the Cork division and a merchantman of his own division, despite them departing a month apart in 1796. For many the voyage had become boring. William Dyott complained that nothing could be more unpleasant than being cooped up in a transport 'with eight or ten men you never saw till the day you got on board.' The time, he says, had become dull and tedious. The first sighting of the West Indies was therefore often a moment of relief and even joy. Pinckard is again our most descriptive witness, recounting the excited shouts of 'Land! Land!' when the boatswain spotted the higher points of Barbados, thereby winning the customary prize of a bottle of rum or brandy.

> It required the eye of a sailor to distinguish the all-delighting terra firma, amidst the clouds: the passengers looked, and looked in vain! A nearer approach of yet some leagues was necessary to render it visible to the eye of a landsman.

The relief of finally seeing the destination was proportional to the length of the voyage. John Skinner, lieutenant colonel of the 16th Regiment, had spent nearly 17 weeks at sea. 'Our men were almost wild with joy at landing...'[11]

In their journals, diaries, memoirs and letters home, the new arrivals strain to give their European brethren some conception of the remarkable appearance of the West Indies. For soldiers and sailors what had emerged from the horizon was a beautiful and strange world, both intoxicating and threatening. Most were awed by the spectacular scenery that met them as they first approached the shore and then landed. There is much repetition in these accounts, but we will select a few representative excerpts. Thomas Phipps Howard's journal entry for Tuesday 19 April 1796:

> The Morn: cloudy. The [Jolly] Boat went onshore early. At 12 oClock the Signal was made to weigh [anchor] & at about ½ after 12 got under Way for the Island of St Domingo [Saint Domingue]. The Boat returned just as the anchor was tripped. The Servant not returned therefore conclude he is run-away. Nothing can equal the beauty of the Sight that presented itself to us at 5 in the Even: A fleet of about 170 sail, crossing each other in all directions. The beautiful Island of Barbadoes on our Right; the mountains to their very tops thick-set with Villages, Plantations etc. etc. In short, I never saw so grand & − at the same time − pleasing Sight before.

Cooper Willyams was greatly impressed by the splendour of Fort Royal Bay, the white stone of Fort Bourbon with its tricolour making a stark contrast against the verdure of the surrounding mountains. Andrew Bryson was also moved by the vistas of Martinique:

> The Beauty of the Prospect as we passed from Fort Royal to St. Pierre far exceeded anything I had either Seen or had any Idea of. In every little Val[ley], of which there are a prodigious number, there was a plantation [at] the bottom of the Vale planted with plantation trees, the leaves of which were 6 feet long & 2 broad and on each side of the Banks the Negro huts [were] arranged in straight lines...In all there places, Tho' Nature had laid the Foundation, yet art had almost outstripped her in the Superstructure which, could it but be Viewed with-out reference to the Back Ground, it would indeed defy the Pencil of .... to do Justice to it.

The novel and, at times, surreal nature of this new environment led some to depict their surroundings in near-poetical terms. Thomas St Clair, landing on the coast of South America, was astonished by the 'tints of the foliage' of the forest trees, lit by the 'clear ethereal sky'. A Scottish soldier was delighted by the 'bright serene atmosphere' of Barbados, a place which was, in the words of William Dyott, 'picturesque almost to a degree of enchantment, and really makes you fancy it a fairy island'. John Moore was not inclined to hyperbole but he records in his journal that St Lucia was beautiful with all in great abundance; 'The situation of my post is very romantic...' The army's and navy's doctors should have been aware of the more sinister aspect of the islands, but naval surgeon John Augustus Waller was as seduced as others by his first view; 'The next morning, at day-light, displayed one of the most enchanting prospects my eyes ever beheld. It is at this hour that the West India islands appear in all their glory, and resemble a paradise'.[12]

Once ashore, the first challenge for all European troops was the alien climate. The most obvious change was the intense heat. Europe being a little cooler than it is today, the contrast may have been even greater in the Revolutionary and Napoleonic eras. There are plenty of anecdotal accounts of the effects of the sun, but we obtain hard facts from medical men who exhaustively documented the climate in attempting to explain the prevailing diseases. Colin Chisholm, inspector general of the ordnance medical department in the West Indies, collected data on Grenada in 1793. Using his mercury thermometer he determined that the summer temperature in the shade had usually reached 80° Farenheit by 10 o'clock in the morning, only lower than this if there was rain or wind. Taking his instrument into direct sunlight at noon he obtained a temperature reading of 120° and even as high as 130° in an enclosed yard.

Thomas Phipps Howard felt this midday sun in Saint Domingue in August 1796, comparing it to a furnace; 'The heat we experienced cannot be expressed by Words: broiling on a gridiron must be fools play to it'. In Port au Prince, soldiers fainted in the heat. Chisholm tells us that the temperature at night on Grenada fell to around 75°, which was some relief, although men still struggled to sleep. Lieutenant Henry Sherwood of the 53rd, on St Vincent in November 1798, wrote home that he got little rest at night, 'When this letter reaches you, I daresay you will be warming yourselves by a good fire in a close pent up room whilst, if I am alive, I shall be in a room with all my windows open and shall be unable to bear my coat'.

The only sure way to escape the heat was to move to the higher ground of the interior. William Dyott noted the marked contrast when campaigning on Grenada. Posted in the mountains in the north of the island, the nights were now chilly. 'We made large fires and rolled our blankets close round us, our lodging not much calculated to keep out either wet or cold.' Half of each day was spent in the clouds. The rainy season in the West Indies varies between the islands but generally runs from May to December. The rains often come suddenly and fall in torrents. The negative impact of heavy rain on the army's fighting capacity has been alluded to in the campaign chapters.

The winds, when moderate, were pleasant and mostly regarded as healthy. As was the case for the temperature, the breezes were believed to impact on the common tropical diseases and army doctors were quick to analyse their significance. In describing the winds of Guadeloupe, Inspector of Hospitals William Fergusson is careful to distinguish the sea breeze from the 'night land-wind from the mountains'. Extreme weather conditions were not unusual and there are several accounts of the destructive effects of the hurricanes which blighted the region between July and October. The raging winds can exceed 140 miles per hour and can destroy a city or an island's whole economy within hours. Mariner William Richardson was shipwrecked by a hurricane which struck Bermuda in 1798, the ship left lying on her side and the masts and sails blown away. 'It is almost incredible that the wind should have such power but it is actually true'. Thomas Phipps Howard experienced several violent storms in Saint Domingue, the rain falling as if a river was descending from the clouds, the trees cracking in the wind, the thunder echoing off the mountains and the lightning so bright that after every flash his men were forced to stop for half a minute to recover their sight.

The exotic flora and fauna of the islands were a source of fascination for the more curious British soldiers. Howard regarded Saint Domingue as a fine field for a botanist and he methodically lists many of the varieties in his journal, admitting that there were 'ten thousand' species with which he was unfamiliar. On his first journey on Martinique, Andrew Bryson saw 'Oranges, Limes, Saursap, Guave, Sugar Apple, Mungos, Mammy Apples, Alligator Pears, Cocoa nuts & Cabbage Trees'. Those soldiers arriving in the winter were astounded to see the brilliant greens of the landscape. Jonathan Leach, who reached the islands at Christmas, struggled to reconcile what he witnessed, '...above all the total absence of snow, frost, and the dark and lowering clouds emblematic of that season in Europe'. The exotic views were matched by the smell, Thomas Henry Browne immediately noticing that there was 'a sort of perfume in the air'. Many others appreciated the distinct odour of the spices, the sugar plantations and the myriad scented flowers.

Less savoury were the swarms of insects which were almost constant companions to the troops. Pinckard makes numerous allusions to them, commenting that the heat would have been supportable 'were it not for the addition and greater torment of musquitos, ants, centipedes, jack-spaniards [large wasps] and the multitudes of other insects biting, buzzing about our ears, crawling upon everything we touch and filling the whole atmosphere around us'. As we shall see, doctors did not understand the sinister role of mosquitoes and other insects in spreading deadly tropical diseases. Benjamin Moseley instead elaborated on the dangers of the various species of snakes before, in more optimistic vein, pointing out that the West Indies lacked many of the 'greater evils' of South America such as tigers, lions, bears and wolves.

Another natural phenomenon added to the other-worldly ambience of the islands. Physician Chisholm witnessed five earthquakes in his five years on Grenada. The worst of these lasted for two minutes, accompanied by a 'hollow rumbling noise'. Howard also relates his experience of more than one episode and says that it was widely known that Port au Prince had been almost totally destroyed less than 50 years earlier with the loss of 2,000 people. Most of the tremors were minor with minimal damage and the soldiers were reassured by the phlegmatic locals who would often hardly interrupt their work, pausing briefly to seek God's protection. When an earthquake shook Martinique in 1809, Browne noted that the inhabitants crossed themselves and uttered Ave Marias for a minute or so before they dispersed and moved on 'laughing to their several occupations'.[13]

With such a complex mix of sensations and emotions, it is difficult to generalise regarding the dominant feelings of British officers and rank and file encountering the West Indies for the first time. We must presume that these were almost as varied as the islands themselves. There was the simple relief at a safe arrival; George Pinckard, not prone to understatement, expressed his joy at reaching Barbados, 'How delightful an element – how cheering – is the solid earth!' This optimism was shared by Captain Joseph Anderson who disembarked on the colony almost 20 years later. His first impressions led him to hope for a 'continued happy residence' in the place. The garrison was apparently healthy, but he was soon disillusioned by the onset of yellow fever. Most soldiers were more jaundiced in their initial assessment; Jonathan Leach admitted that the Caribbean islands were 'interesting to the Johnny Newcomes' but he says this novelty soon wore off and that, barring the spectacular scenery, nothing much excited him. It is perhaps inevitable that those whose recruitment involved coercion were the most crushed by their posting. Andrew Bryson consoled himself that 'there was little probability of my living So long'.

The Irish recruit's attitude to the black West Indian population was typical of the xenophobia displayed by British soldiers in their accounts of the wars. His depression was deepened by the prospect of living close to the local inhabitants; his heart 'sickened at the very idea' and his blood was 'chilled' by the mere sighting of a row of 'negro huts'. Thomas St Clair and his comrades viewed the 'native negros' of Demerara with horror and disgust, 'so powerfully do our European ideas of decency affect the imagination'. Quartermaster Surtees shared this low opinion, whilst blaming the dissolute European colonists for many of the perceived depravities of the black population.

Here [Barbados, 1814] (I think I shall not far err if I say) you behold man in his lowest state: the savages of the woods are, in my opinion, much higher in the scale of being than those whom our cursed cupidity has introduced to all our vices, without one alleviating virtue to counterbalance the evil. But how could the poor African learn anything that is good from those who do not practice good themselves.

The new arrivals were targeted by the locals who, in Browne's opinion, looked 'as disgusting as possible'. He believed that he was entering 'the squalid darkness of the negro' and he accuses the local traders of cheating the troops 'by every means in their power'. The black women who the ungrateful Browne met in the market at Bridgetown gave him advice which was very likely well intended, 'Ah Massa Johny Newcome go back to Shippy, too hot for him here, kill him'.[14]

Soldiers' broad descriptions of the black population rarely extend beyond these myopic sketches, but there was one element of black existence which attracted more attention and even attempts at analysis. Many officers described the infrastructure of slavery – particularly the slave ships and the sales – and expressed their opinions, a complex mixture of distaste and justification. The eyewitness accounts are often contradictory, perhaps reflecting the reality that the lot of slaves was not entirely consistent. Several soldiers visited slave ships. Surprisingly, William Dyott thought the Liverpool vessel he inspected at Carlisle Bay in 1796 to be clean and well kept. 'The females were all in the after part of the ship and the males forward. They all appeared very happy...' George Pinckard was equally approving of an American slaver, making comments very similar to Dyott regarding the 'cheerfulness and contentment' of the captives. 'I am most happy to conclude my report of this visit by informing you that we discovered no marks of those horrors and cruelties said to be practised on board the ships occupied in this sad trade of human flesh'. He saw no restraining chains and believed the slaves' comfort and health to be have been fully addressed.

Conversely, Harry Ross-Lewin was shocked by the sight of a slave vessel which came close to his own ship near Puerto Rico. The occupants had only enough room to stand and were all naked. The two ships were at times so close 'that we could fling to the poor wretches on board a quantity of biscuit for which they scrambled with great avidity'. Thomas St Clair was also horror-struck by the American slaver he saw at Berbice. 'The whole party of blacks were such a set of scarcely animated automata, such a resurrection of skin and bone, as forcibly to remind me of the last trumpet, they all looked like corpses just arisen from the grave.'

The slave sales ashore also attracted much comment. Dyott may have approved of the slave ship, but he was taken aback to later see the human cargo 'sold just as a flock are sold in a fair in England'. St Clair made a similar comparison, watching the white planters examining their captives just as dealers in the horse fairs of home. The able-bodied men sold for £100–150 and boys from £40–50. He appears uneasy at the 'traffic in human flesh', but one of his fellow officers actually purchased two boys of 11 or 12 years of age. Pinckard attended a sale where the slaves were sold naked in a large barn-like building. He admits that he was curious to witness the event but he obtained from it only 'painful gratification'. It was something he would never forget. At the sale attended by vicar Cooper Willyams, 149 slaves had died on the passage. The survivors accompanied their new owners to the plantations where they were clothed, provided with some simple tools, and attached to an older slave.

There are eyewitness accounts of slaves receiving both sympathetic and cruel treatment. Pinckard describes both extremes on the South American mainland. Female slaves were whipped mercilessly and, in one particularly gruesome episode, a male slave was tied face down to the ground and brutally flogged. It was unclear whether he had deserved any punishment, but a European woman, probably the wife of a plantation owner, asked the army doctor if he wanted to watch, '...as if it was a pleasant sight for strangers, or something that might divert us'. On a later occasion, he came across a plantation owner whose kindness to his charges was so well known that when there was a threat of French attack the local slaves offered to risk their lives to protect him and his home. Others confirm that although the practice of slavery was universally abhorrent, the experience of the individuals held in bondage was inconsistent. James Aytoun believed that many slave owners were wrongly accused of cruelty, indeed he tells us that they had little incentive to behave in such a way; 'If you look at a set of black slaves, they appear contented and healthy'. This was not an opinion consistent with Ross-Lewin's graphic account of a French slave owner in Saint Domingue punishing a slave boy by burning and laceration with hot irons. The child cried for three days and died on the fourth.

Such dramatically differing experiences fuelled a range of attitudes to slavery. Many soldiers were themselves inconsistent. When he is theorising on the subject, St Clair condones it; '...it will appear that the injustice of the slave-trade exists more in name than in reality; that in fact when Europeans take inhabitants of Africa from their native soil, they do not add to the number of slaves already in the world, but merely transplant them from a land of ignorance and superstition to one of civilisation and improvement'. However, shortly after witnessing a slave ship and a subsequent sale, he felt 'all the disgust and horror of slavery'.

Officers made justificatory judgements of slavery based on a comparison of the lives of slaves and the oppressed impoverished peasantry of Britain. This is the commonest theme relating to the slave trade in contemporary military accounts. Jonathan Leach was a supporter of gradual abolition but he viewed the hardships of slavery with ambivalence.

> ...an unfortunate negro, writhing under the lash of the merciless slave-driver, for laying aside his spade for a few minutes in the heat of the

tropical sun, or for some offence equally trivial, is infinitely better off, decidedly more happy, and in a more enviable situation, than the labouring peasant in the mother country. Facts are stubborn things...

Almost identical views are expressed by Thomas St Clair, George Pinckard, Cooper Willyams, William Dyott and Marcus Rainsford. St Clair also compares the lot of the West Indian slaves with the peasants he later saw toiling in the Iberian Peninsula and Aytoun even draws a comparison with the army's rank and file; 'The negros have a great deal more liberty than soldiers'.

Although frequently obscured by an archaic terminology which is an anathema to modern readers, some soldiers and officers did have more than a one-dimensional view of the slaves. Aytoun informs us that many of his comrades thought them to be ignorant. He disagreed; 'They may be so in respect of religion but they are shrewd and acute and are capable of conducting themselves as well if not better than a great many of the white slaves in the British Isles'. John Moore was a free-thinker on military and social matters. In his St Lucia journal, he notes that he did not discriminate on the basis of skin colour or political persuasion. 'All men were entitled to justice, and they should meet with it from me without distinction or partiality, whether white or black, republican or royalist.' He admits that these sentiments were not universally popular.[15]

Chapter 9

Nancy Clarke and Susy Austin: Life in the Garrison

The anonymous author of *Sketches and Recollections of the West Indies* has left a brief description of a typical day in the Tropics for the resident European planters and officials.

> The hour of rising in the West Indies is generally five. When the glorious luminary of day ushers in the morn, a gun is fired from the respective forts and garrisons; and this is the general signal for starting. In warm climates, if the cool of the morning is lost in bed, the time for exercise is gone. The custom, therefore, is for those who have horses, to mount them as soon as dressed and to ride several miles before the breakfast hour, which is from seven to eight. Breakfast despatched, business commences. At two P.M. the shops, stores, and offices are shut; and it is then customary for the inhabitants to seek repose, stretched on their beds or couches, in their *robes de chambre*, until it is time to dress for dinner, which is served at four or later. This important meal seldom occupies more than an hour, except when parties are assembled to be convivial. The business over, the day ceases entirely at six, except on packet-days when the night, as well as day, is often devoted to letter-writing, accounts, & c. After five, the ladies and gentlemen enjoy their ride, or walk in the cool of the evening until sunset...

Only a very small fraction of soldiers' time in the colonies was spent on active campaign. The daily routine of the British garrisons scattered through the West Indian islands was, as for the locals, shaped by the unforgiving climate. Soldiers were woken in the dark and the first parade of the day commenced before sunrise. After an hour or two of drilling, as the first rays of the burning sun filtered through the damp air, bugle calls and drum beats signalled the first meal of the day, morning mess. Following this the men were confined to barracks, hidden from the direct glare of the sun but oppressed by the heat. The midday hours were only interrupted by the main feed of the day, the dinner meal at half past noon. Back in their barracks by two o'clock, the next bugle call announced evening parade at 5pm; there was more drilling, kits were inspected and any general orders read out. At sundown, the soldiers were again in their barracks, the officers having returned to their more salubrious quarters. Last call was at 10.30pm and an eerie silence marked the end of another day. This routine was often inexorable although there might be some variation in the duties of the rank and file. James Aytoun notes that the standing orders in Dominica were for three field days a week and six drill days. In reality, the field days were limited by the unpredictable rainstorms. Officers were also forced into an unfamiliar routine, albeit less rigid than that of the men and more akin to the European locals. William Dyott, on Grenada in 1796, rose half an hour before sunrise and rode on the beach until 7am before breakfasting. He sat in his tent until one and then rode to headquarters where he dined at three. In the evening he took another ride.[1]

The most vital, and most demanding, parts of the soldier's day were the morning and evening drills. At the end of the eighteenth century, he was expected to be proficient in the five fundamental skills; the manual exercise, the platoon exercise, the evolutions, the firings, and the manoeuvres. These terms are partly self-explanatory. Essentially, he had to be able to perform basic tasks such as loading his musket and using the bayonet, and also to be able to move and fire in concert with his comrades. This could only be achieved by robotic repetition, as was experienced by James Aytoun on Dominica.

> ...the adjutant commanded and at those times the manual exercise and platoon firings were all done by only one word of command and one motion followed another with such rapidity that the fogleman [in front of the soldiers as an example or model] who stood with his back to us, frequently had three or four motions to do after the regiment was done. On the day I have hinted at, the regiment was repeatedly in the middle or some part of the [drill] manual and the stop was ordered when the adjutant observed any of the men make a wrong motion or miss one which, among three or four hundred men, was almost unavoidable. I have been in the ranks on such occasions and have begun the manual and platoon exercises twenty times and the man who was so unlucky as to cause the exercise to be stopped was sure to receive a severe beating.[2]

The drill was crucial for the movement of bodies of troops in battle but it was also designed to create an atmosphere of unquestioning obedience. A regimen of harsh discipline was maintained throughout the West Indian garrisons and there is little doubt that it was necessary. Historian Roger Buckley has made a detailed study of the makeup and criminality of the British troops in the region and he reaches some interesting conclusions. For instance, the proportion of prisoners in the army in the Windward and Leeward Islands between 1799 and

1802 was approximately 20%. Secondly, there was always relatively more criminal activity in the West Indian garrison than elsewhere. If we take 1804 as an example, only 6% of the army's strength was in the Caribbean, but an astonishing 48% of all courts-martial were held in the region.

Breaches of discipline can be broadly divided into a systemic disorder, perhaps affecting a particular regiment or company, and individual misdemeanours. Senior officers strained to prevent both via proclamations in the general orders; Grey at Martinique in 1794 threatened the immediate execution of any soldier guilty of looting. More widespread infractions often reflected poor leadership. Lady Maria Nugent, wife of the governor of Jamaica, George Nugent, complains that the 4th Battalion of the 60th Regiment, stationed on the colony in 1805, were guilty of 'continual broils, insubordination, and constant cabals...' The commanding officer had little respect, being determined to return home '...leaving the horrible climate'. John Moore and William Dyott make allusions to more general breakdowns in discipline. Levels of misbehaviour were often greater during periods of epidemic disease when men perhaps felt that they had little to lose. All European armies in the region were afflicted. Antoine Métral describes the chaos in Saint Domingue where many French soldiers perished from yellow fever. '*Lorsque la contagion fut dans toute sa force, le débordement des folles passions humaines vint se mêler à ce torrent destructeur.*'

Individual misdemeanours varied from the trivial to the horrific. At the lower end of the spectrum, at least from a modern perspective, were looting and pillaging. Grey's directive is, however, a reminder that this was not tolerated in a British army on campaign. Cooper Willyams confirms that the general followed through on his threat; William Milton of the 10th Light Dragoons and Samuel Rice of a colonial corps were found guilty of looting a house in Salée on Martinique and were both hanged in front of the whole army. General Thomas Dundas also hanged two soldiers, a drummer and private of the 58th Regiment, for robbing a shop.

Grey's general orders issued on Guadeloupe in June 1794 warned soldiers and sailors not to straggle from their camps. Rolls were to be called every two hours and any man absent was to be punished 'in the most severe manner'. Miscreants might be vulnerable to enemy posts and also might be tempted to desert, a crime which greatly exercised the authorities. Buckley is again the best secondary source, showing that levels of desertion were particularly high during periods of military inactivity, presumably motivated by hardships and the boredom of army life in the Tropics. In 1803, desertion accounted for more than 90% of all serious crime in the West India garrison and in several other years during the Revolutionary and Napoleonic period it was the cause of more than half of the courts-martial. Prisoner soldiers such as Andrew Bryson were bent on desertion from the moment of their arrival in the Caribbean. Bryson's journal is dominated by allusions to escape; when admitted to hospital with fever his main regret was that he would now be less likely to 'get off' the island. Foreign mercenaries in British service were notorious for their propensity to desert. When Thomas Picton was made governor of Trinidad in 1796, he offered a reward for any German deserter either apprehended or killed. Fourteen of the worst offenders were court-martialled and executed. Few eyewitness accounts of the West Indian campaigns make reference to violations against the local population. Lasalle de Louisenthall's accusation of attempted rape made against soldiers of the 3rd Regiment on Trinidad is unusual.

We can glean more detail of the routine workings of army law from Charles James's voluminous work, *A Collection of the Charges, Opinions, and Sentences of General Courts Martial*, published in 1820. This contains records of a number of West Indian trials and gives a very useful insight into procedure and subsequent sentencing. Unsurprisingly, alcohol was at the root of a significant number of cases of insubordination. Ensign John Carnody of the 1st Battalion 63rd Regiment was found to be guilty of 'infamous and scandalous conduct', disobeying his orders '...and continuing to parade the streets of Fort Royal in a state of intoxication'. Other officers are guilty of financial misappropriations and 'ungentlemanly conduct'. Two lieutenants are charged in Jamaica in 1813 for throwing bricks and stones at a fellow officer's quarters. These disagreements could lead to duels. Thomas Phipps Howard relates a duel between two officers of his regiment shortly after their arrival in Saint Domingue. The reason was 'trifling' but it culminated in one of the adversaries being shot in the chest. The ball was extracted and, despite losing a large quantity of blood, he made a full recovery in six weeks. Thomas St Clair notes that there was a bad atmosphere in the regimental officers' mess in Demerara. One dispute had already led to a fatal duel and St Clair resolved to keep his head down.

The mutiny of the 8th West India Regiment on Dominica in 1802 has been described. There was no instance of mutiny in home-based British troops in the West Indian campaigns, but this was a constant anxiety with respect to the less reliable parts of the colonial corps in British service. At Saint Domingue in July 1798, Colonel William Stewart relates a mutiny breaking out in the Chasseurs de George and Malabre's following a series of petty disputes. Two chasseurs were shot and one received 500 lashes, the punishment inflicted in front of the hundred men of a garrison picket.

Flogging was the mainstay of corporal punishment for the erring rank and file. Buckley has analysed West Indian courts-martial records and he shows unequivocally that the brutality of this punishment was even greater in the region than in other theatres. Between 1800 and 1807, the average sentence exceeded 1,000 lashes; on occasion, sentences of 2,000 lashes were issued to unfortunates found to be guilty of crimes such as disobedience or desertion. Women were not spared; those found plundering received the same retribution as the men. James Aytoun makes several allusions to the tyrannical military regimen on Dominica. Soldiers were ruthlessly flogged for minor misdemeanours. A good man dropping off to sleep in the middle of the day was likely to be sent to the guard house and prosecuted for being drunk. It was not unusual for 13 men to be punished in a single morning. Once the sentence had been carried out the victims received rudimentary medical care from their comrades; every day a man was sent into the country to gather plantain leaves to soothe the lacerated backs.

Soldiers were appalled by their first view of flogging. Andrew Bryson soon understood that no infractions would be tolerated on Martinique.

> The next morning there was to be 4 men punished & I was called on, along with the rest, to See it. The punished [were] in the inside of the room to prevent the Negroes from seeing them. When they began they placed us So near the Triangles [the wooden structures to which the victims were tied] that [with] every lash they Gave, as soon as the skin was cut, the blood flew in my face. Shocked with this, & overcome with the fatigue of Standing So long, I fainted before they had half Done. The Capt. followed me down stairs & ordered me a Glass of Wine and as Soon as I was recovered, 'You See', Said he, 'what the effects of Misconduct in the Army [are] and as the punishment of another has affected you So much, you had need to take care lest you Subject yourself to Suffer.

Hanging was the most common method of execution. Again, this was often performed publicly to act as a deterrent. Grey's hanging of looters on Martinique clearly made the desired impression as it is referred to in a number of memoirs. Cooper Willyams expresses his surprise that two soldiers robbed the locals on the first day of campaigning despite the clarity of the warning in general orders. Executions were sometimes clumsily performed; William Richardson witnessed a mishandled hanging from a yardarm where the unfortunate survived long enough to reach up and grab the noose, effectively ending his own life. Execution by firing squad is less often mentioned, Stewart's account of the fate of the mutineers in Saint Domingue being one example. A few luckier individuals were pardoned, thereby avoiding the full force of military justice. Willyams recounts a case on Martinique where a soldier escaped a delayed sentence of 800 lashes as Grey, although approving the severity of the punishment, believed that the man's already prolonged imprisonment was enough. The commander hoped that the display of lenity would render the offender 'a good and faithful British soldier to his King and country'.[3]

Deficiencies in pay were a cause of disaffection among soldiers and sailors. The West Indies were expensive; the cost of just feeding a soldier was more than twice his daily allowance before deductions were made to cover costs such as clothing and hospitalisation. There is no shortage of grumbles about money from all ranks. Lieutenant Henry Sherwood ran short on St Vincent in 1799 although this seems to have been in part his own fault, '...I was put to great expense more indeed than was necessary for from my openness of character I advanced small sums to the officers and was not repaid'. His monies at home were invested and not easily available and he relied on his aunt to settle a bill of £100, a debt which he says had made him ill. Another profligate officer, Edward Pakenham, admitted to his mother from Barbados in 1802 that he had 'drawn most most devilishly', spending £500 in a year. 'I have thought it Right to take advantage of your goodness.'

The rank and file had no such recourse. James Aytoun recollects that his pay was normally six months in arrears. It was uncommon for a man who died in Dominica to be out of debt to the pay sergeant. When significant arrears did arrive, there was a temptation to part company with the windfall immediately. On St Vincent in 1796, the men pocketed the balance of 18 months' pay, John Simpson enthusing that as it was the first settlement they had received since arriving on the colony '...we got 3 days to spend our money'.[4]

A number of adaptations were made to the British infantryman's clothes and kit to meet the demands of a tropical climate. This is reflected in the army's regulations, the following taken from the report of the board appointed by Abercromby to make recommendations for the preservation of the health of his men in the West Indies in 1795.[4]

> The Board highly approves of the Troops being provided with Two Flannel Waistcoats, One Pair of Flannel Drawers for Night Duty, Two Pair of Worsted Socks each man, also a Flannel Cap or Welch Wig, and Two Pairs loose Trousers, made of Cotton Cloth, or Russian Duck. Half Gaiters of Cloth have been found useful as a Defence against Insects. The Hats should be White, they should be round, to shade the face from the Sun, and high in the Crown, to defend the Head from the Heat. Top Coats should be Short Skirted, and made sufficiently large to admit of buttoning across the Body. Each Regiment should be amply supplied with Watch Coats. The Stocks should be made of Black Cloth, in Preference to Leather, as better adapted to a warm Climate. The Knapsacks should be made of painted Canvas.

Frederick Maitland, the deputy adjutant general, trumpeted the use of flannel clothing, claiming that that it allowed the wearer to better tolerate the temperature extremes of day and night. He did admit that it was 'very dangerous' to put on wet flannel and that if worn for too long it was prone to 'putrescence'. Others were not convinced. Physician Hector McLean believed flannel to contribute little to the health of men in the Tropics, '...the soldier feels encumbered, hot and uneasy in his exertions'. Black Watch veteran David Stewart was unimpressed by the radical alterations to the Highlanders' uniform in 1795, the plaid, kilt and bonnet replaced by the regulation Russian duck pantaloons and round hat. The trousers and hat absorbed rainwater to the extent that the troops had 'a very unseemly and unmilitary appearance'. The felt hats hung down like the ears of a bloodhound. Some directives were subsequently reversed, for instance the white shakos, prone to mildew, were replaced by the standard black shako in 1813.

The dress initiatives fell down both because of inadequate supplies and because they did not go far enough. As early as Grey's first expedition, senior officers were forced to plead for flannel shirts for the men. It was commonplace throughout the West Indian campaigns for troops to fight without proper shoes. The shortages were, of course, not limited to the Caribbean, but the harmful climate and noisome insects meant that the deficiencies were especially damaging.

Despite the well-meaning concessions most soldiers reached the West Indies fitted out in heavy, tight-fitting uniforms and burdened with a great weight of kit. The steady trickle of recommended adaptations to the European pattern uniform still left redcoats burning up in the tropical sun. Aytoun set out from Edinburgh on his West Indian adventure loaded down with 'six shirts, three pairs stockings, two pairs of shoes, two pairs of gaiters, two pairs of breeches, an extra waistcoat, red jacket and a compleat regimental suit, besides arms, accoutrements, and ammunition'. The troops landing on Martinique in 1809 were equipped for 'light marching', but still carried a coat, shoes, other spare clothes, a canteen, a haversack, 60 rounds of ammunition in their pouches and 20 in their pocket. Officers were expected to wear long-tailed coats and bicorns when on duty – George Pinckard describes himself clad in scarlet and gold, '... a very lobster' – but throughout the period they had their own unofficial order of dress in the Caribbean with round hats, short-tailed jackets with white linen pantaloons, and boots or half-boots. There were also some adaptations to cavalry uniforms with the variable issue of lightweight coats, tin helmets and pantaloons.[5]

The importance of the early morning and midday meals in the routine of the garrison has been alluded to. A typical daily ration for a British Napoleonic soldier was 1½ pounds of bread, 1 pound of beef or ½ pound of pork, ¼ pint of pease, 1 ounce of butter or cheese and 1 ounce of rice. The food was routinely consumed in 'messes', several soldiers pooling their rations and eating together. There is a common notion that the soldiers' fare was dull, endless salted beef, but this was not the case in the West Indies where the diet was easily supplemented by abundant local produce. An excerpt from the section devoted to diet in the official recommendations for Abercromby's first expedition gives a flavour of this.

> The Board considers the Regulation of Diet in the West Indies as an Object of the first Importance – The Men should be divided into Messes, and should have Two regular Meals a Day; for Breakfast, Coffee or Cocoa, with Sugar; for Dinner Salt Provisions, with Yams, and the Vegetables of the Country and seasoned with the Spices of the country – Fresh Provisions should be served to the Troops as often as is practicable...

The lacing of the food with local ingredients was not only good for nutrition, but also provided novelty and helped relieve boredom. Many soldiers have left accounts of exotic Caribbean foods. James Aytoun, perhaps our best witness of the mundane life of the garrison, tells us that the men sold their standard rations – butter, rice, pease, beef and pork – to buy green plantains, roast coffee and treacle. Soup was thickened with Callaloo leaves and spiced with Cayenne pepper. Surprisingly, the seafood was mostly overlooked. The men were, Aytoun says, 'fed like fighting cocks' and the only thing in short supply was firewood. The quality of the basic rations was variable. In Demerara, the beef was sourced locally and, according to St Clair, it was often so poor that soldiers refused to eat it.

Officers were allowed even more freedom in their diet, either messing with their comrades in camp or in their own accommodation or eating outside the garrison. Vegetables and fruit were easily available but fresh meat not always so. In Demerara, Pinckard complained that he had to eat salted meat, a routine broken only by the rare procurement of a Muscovy duck, chicken or suckling pig. He admitted to having developed a 'Creole appetite', feasting on yams and plantains. The local potatoes were disappointing, a consignment from home being treated as a great delicacy. Other English articles might arrive every several months in merchant ships to be sold at exorbitant prices. Pinckard's enrolment into the regimental mess meant that he at least did not have to seek his own provisions. Dinners outside the garrison were unpredictable. When William Dyott visited General Leigh at his home on Barbados the repast was '...quite West Indian, consisting principally of poultry'. There was, he says, 'one joint of mutton, which some people said was as good as they ever ate. I pitied their taste'.

The diet of officers and men in the West Indies varied depending on the availability of supplies from home and the state of the local markets. However, the shortages were relative and genuine hunger was rare in the British garrison. Despite the difficulties of provisioning a theatre thousands of miles distant, the army's administrators did fill the mouths of their soldiers. Henry Sherwood on St Vincent in 1799 describes his men cooking rats, but this was probably because they preferred them to the meat rations rather than because they were actually starving. Sherwood was tempted but admitted that he could not 'muster the resolution'. In contrast to the British experience, the French suffered from severe hunger in Saint Domingue. In 1802, Sergeant Major Philippe Beaudoin complains of being without bread for three weeks and of being forced to subsist on root vegetables. Later, the troops were reduced to eating rotten biscuit and any animal they could kill including dogs, cats, rats and mice.

All European soldiers in the region needed a constant supply of clean drinking water. Barrack accommodation had its own water cisterns, usually with a curved roof and a square hole through which buckets of water were drawn. Rainwater was collected from the roof or specially constructed catchments and then filtered to remove mud and other debris. The remains of these systems can be still seen at Shirley Heights in Antigua and at the Brimstone Hill Fortress on St Kitts. Despite such initiatives the end of the rainy season could quickly lead to shortages. Jonathan Leach points out that there was not a single spring of fresh water on Antigua and that the troops and inhabitants were entirely dependent on rainfall and the filling of the cisterns. From January to June 1804, there was a drought and the men were placed on a small allowance of water. This would have been even more problematic if sloops had not been constantly employed bringing barrels of fresh water from neighbouring Montserrat. Leach concedes that his regimental comrades were 'by no means addicted to the use of water as a beverage' but they still suffered from its scarcity. There are other examples of water rationing; on Guadeloupe in the summer of 1794 the men were short of all supplies and limited to two quarts of water per day.

The most acute water deprivation and instances of severe thirst occurred on active campaigning. This happened throughout the wars. The men besieging Fort Bourbon in 1794 risked enemy shells and their officers' wrath to slake their thirst in a rivulet. The troops landed on Puerto Rico were equally afflicted. In Saint Domingue, many of the natural sources of water were tainted. Phipps Howard refers to *Les Sources Puante*, a well-known series of springs between Arcahaye and Port au Prince. The water was tinged with green and emitted the worst smell he had ever experienced. Harry Ross-Lewin witnessed men sucking sweat from their jackets and drinking their urine. Cavalryman Norbert Landsheit also campaigned in the colony.

> There was no water to be had along the road, and the little which the men had brought in their canteens was all exhausted. Numbers had, therefore, become so faint, that they could scarcely sit on their horses and some had even fallen to the ground. In particular, I recollect seeing a poor fellow stretched by the wayside, whom an officer saved from death, by pouring the last drop out of the canteen which he himself carried, into the sufferer's mouth; – and before two hours were passed, I saw the same officer perish for the lack of that which he had generously given away.

Such a valuable commodity could be used as a weapon. At the siege of Fort Matilda in 1794, the British water cisterns were stagnant, the French having cut the aqueduct supplying them. Prescott was forced to send men to collect water from the nearby River Gallion. These twice-daily armed parties were covered by the firing of grapeshot from the fort.

Leach's assertion that he and his comrades were not overly partial to water reflects the reality that alcohol was regarded by the army and navy as an essential thirst-quenching drink. Normal army rations contained an allowance of alcohol and in the West Indies this was a quarter of a pint of rum. Regulations from 1795 stipulate that this was to be at least a year old – to avoid the harmful effects of 'new rum' – and diluted with three parts water. During periods of excessive fatigue men might receive extra alcohol, preferably porter but more rum if only this was available. That rum was regarded as a prerequisite for the normal functioning of the army is underlined by William Dyott's shocked response to the lack of rum for his men fighting on Grenada; 'A soldier never murmurs at the shortage of provisions but if his grog is stopped he is completely defeated'. The local grog shops allowed the troops to further indulge themselves; the below description is from Antigua but other islands had similar institutions.

> ...where to the heterogeneous mass of eatables, crockery and tinware, is added the more exciting articles of brandy, rum, gin, porter and wine; and where of an evening amid fumes of every description (from Yanky cheese to Virginia tobacco) and dim smoky oil lamps, parties of soldiers, sailors and unfortunate females – ay, and men of better rank in life who ought to blush to be found in such places – love to congregate and barter health and money for dirty goblets of fiery liquids.

There was a wide choice of alcoholic drinks. In Barbados, Pinckard found the favourite tipples to be Madeira and claret wines, punch, sangaree (a tumbler of Madeira, sugar and nutmeg diluted with a wineglass of water), porter and cider. The combination of easily available alcohol and a life of alternating boredom and extreme danger led to much drunkenness. Excessive consumption was encouraged by the prevailing opinion that alcohol gave some protection against deadly tropical disease. Dr Theodore Gordon, deputy inspector of hospitals in the Windward and Leeward Islands, saw drink being downed by the troops with 'a degree of desperation that is scarcely creditable'. Gordon's medical colleague, William Fergusson, witnessed the same behaviour in Saint Domingue.

> ... I have seen the troops then in such a state that no parades could be formed for days together, and it was matter of difficulty to procure men in fit condition to take the ordinary guards. This occurred regularly once

a month and a vigilant enemy might then have easily surprised our strongest garrisons.

Fergusson says that the officers generally shunned the local rum, but there is no evidence that they deprived themselves. On the voyage out, Thomas Phipps Howard and a fellow officer had 360 bottles of port as their 'sea stock', enough, he thought, to last them to Barbados. Dr Hector McLean was an advocate of cautious alcohol consumption, limiting himself to draughts of sangaree and Madeira during the day and a bottle of claret after dinner. We will return to alcohol to discuss its insidious effects on the health of the West Indian garrison in a later chapter.[6]

Barrack accommodation for the men varied widely in its siting, size and construction. Most typical were functional brick and stone buildings such as still exist at Shirley Heights and at the Brimstone Hill Fortress. At the latter, there was accommodation for 800 men, although it seems to have been rarely fully occupied in the Revolutionary and Napoleonic periods. The barracks on Richmond Hill in Grenada, about two miles above St George's, could accommodate 600–800 troops and the three barracks at Barbados, described by Phipps Howard, were each capable of taking 1,000 men. There was little useful building material on Barbados and the barracks were constructed with wood brought from England. Some accommodation was deliberately built at altitude, up to 2,000 feet, the so called 'hill' or 'health stations'. These were most common in Jamaica. Other barracks exploited local buildings; the 99th Regiment in Dominica was housed in a spacious cotton works.

Whatever the precise nature of the barracks, they were tightly controlled. General regulations demanded that the accommodation should be 'roomy' and that men should ideally be housed in the upper quarters, sleeping in hammocks or cot frames with legs. A series of articles relating to the barracks in Jamaica in 1801 give an insight into barrack life. Some of the lengthier entries have been paraphrased.

> Article 1: The Island Barrack Master is to immediately appoint Barrack Masters to act at the different Island Barracks.
> 2: Every Barrack Master shall attend the arrival of such regiment or detachment as should be ordered to quarter in the barrack under his care: and having with the commanding officer viewed the conditions of the said barrack, and every room and part thereof, and the furniture and utensils, shall deliver the same, with an inventory under his hand stating the particular condition thereof.
> 3: No regiment should be given excessive rooms/furniture/utensils.
> 4: Each Barrack Master should make frequent inspections.
> 5: The use of every room to be indicated on the door.

6/7: Barrack Master to provide detailed returns for the Barrack Master General when a regiment arrives or leaves and routinely every three months.

8: Barrack Master to keep barracks clean and free from insects.

9: Barrack Master not to be absent from barracks without permission.

10: Barrack Master must be accountable to the commanding officer of the troops in barracks.

11/12: re: Management of wood supplies.

13: re: Regulations to promote discipline in barracks.

14: Officer of the day to inspect the messes (messing of the soldiers is of the utmost importance) to ensure the food is wholesome and sufficient and to check the rooms are clean and beds made up. No man to be permitted in the day time to lie on the bed. No things to be permitted that may tend to prevent that cleanliness which is necessary for the health of the troops (e.g. entrance of tradesmen).

15: If a regiment leaves a barracks dirty the commanding officer of the newly arriving regiment is to report the fact to the commander in chief.

The regulations imply a degree of order that was not always achieved in practice. Barrack accommodation was sometimes deficient in quantity and quality. On Jamaica in 1798, Balcarres complained that the entire windward part of the island lacked a barracks or any other soldiers' accommodation except for 170 men. Balcarres's replacement, George Nugent, inherited the problem. The temporary barracks at Up Park near Kingston had poor buildings and an inadequate water supply. More isolated postings were even more likely to lack proper accommodation. A detachment of the 7th West India Regiment stationed on Trinidad in 1804 had no access to barracks and the men were housed in shoddy cane huts.

The situation on Trinidad had not improved four years later, despite promised new accommodation. It appears that the construction of necessary barracks was often delayed by administrative and financial constraints. When troops arrived at the Môle in 1796, they were held on the transports because the new barracks were not finished. George Nugent laboured to solve the problems on Jamaica despite the sanctioning of a plan to build a permanent barracks for 1,000 men on high ground in the interior of the island.

The Embarrassments which a military man labours under upon this Establishment are very great as he cannot under the present System, direct the driving of a Nail, without the consent of the Board of Works, let the Exigency of the Service be ever so great.

The expenditure of the barrack department in Jamaica between 1796 and 1802 was almost £70,000.

There was a contemporary view, particularly among the army's doctors, that most of the barracks in the Caribbean were overcrowded. William Fergusson says that he had never seen a barracks where the men would not have been better moved to separate houses or even hovels. Hammocks were favoured as they allowed men to be crammed together, each soldier allowed only 22 to 23 inches. Many of the barrack buildings were in poor repair. At Brimstone Hill, there were problems with drainage and ventilation and at Up Park on Jamaica the floors were damp. Some institutions, for instance the St John's barracks on Antigua, were known to be 'sickly'. We have few accounts from the ranks of the details of barrack life in the West Indies. Men were probably pleased to be under cover and protected from the elements. Private John Simpson thought the barracks on St Vincent to be comfortable despite the men having no beds or bedding except their camp blankets.[7]

When not in barracks, soldiers slept in the open or in tents or huts. On campaign, it was not always possible to carry tents and troops bivouacked in the open air. In good weather this was tolerable, but men suffered during the frequent tropical storms. Thomas St Clair describes a typical downpour.

> ... [the rain] penetrates at once cloak, and coat, and all, to the very skin, nay more, through the skin itself, chilled to the marrow of one's bones. The bivouac instantly becomes a scene of desolation and dismal solitude. Jokes, laughter, and fires at once extinguished, the dripping crowd sought shelter where they could...

Thomas Browne endured this misery on Martinique in 1809, the troops wet through but at least able to start fires and cook their food. Many officers, Phipps Howard among them, believed that bivouacs were harmful.

> Baggage is so very difficult, if not impossible, as to totally hinder the carrying of Tents...The Men are obliged to sleep in the open fields, exposed to the heavy showers known by the Name of the West India Rains, not to be conceived in Europe; and the Damps arising after them, & exhalations of which, nothing can be more prejudicial to health.

Regulations dictated the optimal placement of tents. It was suggested that hammocks be installed in the round version and that a trench should be dug to aid drainage. John Moore tacitly approves their use on St Lucia, citing the protection given against sun and rain. However, soldiers did not necessarily appreciate the cover, William Dyott claiming that, 'To experience misery in extreme is to live in a tent in the West Indies'. His own tent was infested by insects and mice and was as wet and muddy as the surrounding ploughed field.

He believed them to be 'of very little service'. Several eyewitnesses testify that they were easily blown away in storms. Physician Fergusson also weighs in against tents which, he says, caused the soldiers to lie on cold ground in a confined space. They were 'hot beds for the generation of dysentery'.

Huts were an alternative form of temporary accommodation and they were sometimes constructed with care and ingenuity. Lieutenant Henry Sherwood was proud of the efforts of his regiment on St Vincent in 1799:

> We built our huts in the following form. Six uprights with forked heads about six feet from the ground. The piles across lying on the forks. The rafters from the pole to a ridge pole. Then tying split bamboo or rather canes like laths we take the feathery top of the cane and, breaking it through the lath, leave the leafy part hanging outwards and tuck the stalk under the second lath within, tying a second lath on the outside which holds it all firm. Thus is built an excellent hut for less than six pounds having two rooms.

This was a serious undertaking. Sherwood's own 'house' was thatched by a 27-man working party. Dyott notes that huts were widely used on Grenada, housing the 25th Regiment, and David Stewart confirms that soldiers on St Lucia also erected them as the only option to provide shelter. Huts were not well suited for the climate and had their own set of problems. Surgeon James McGrigor was cooped up with five other officers in a small 'bombproof' on Richmond Hill on Grenada. It was intolerably hot and he soon developed dysentery.

On active campaign, officers often had to rough it like their men. Many spent uncomfortable nights in soaking clothes. At other times, they benefitted from better barrack facilities or admission to an inn or a billet in a local planter's house. The officers' quarters blockhouse at Shirley Heights was constructed towards the end of the eighteenth century and is the largest remaining building on site. The cool front colonnade provided a pleasant informal meeting place whilst the interior was divided into a number of comfortable rooms, some of the original plaster still surviving. To the immediate rear of the quarters are a kitchen, servants' house and stables. At Brimstone Hill, there were separate barrack buildings for the infantry, artillery, engineer and medical officers. Again the quarters were imposing and fronted by colonnades.

Local taverns and inns were popular among the officers who put up in them. They were usually named after the owner and the most famous of all was Nancy Clarke's, commonly referred to as Nancy's, in Bridgetown. This was such a successful institution that the proprietress died a wealthy woman. Thomas St Clair, coming ashore in the town, heard the local blacks singing a ditty referring to the two most patronised inns of the time.

If you go to Nancy Clarke,
She will take you in the dark;
When she get you in the dark,
She will give you aquafortis.
If you go to Susy Austin,
She will take you in the parlour;
When she take you in the parlour,
She will give you wine and water.

The allusion in the first verse was to an incident in which Nancy Clarke allegedly threw aquafortis (nitric acid) into the face of a young woman in a fit of jealousy. The standard of accommodation was not, according to George Pinckard, 'precisely what a Bond Street lounger would expect in St James's Street', but it was comfortable enough.

Houses could be commandeered as temporary barracks; Pinckard and his medical colleagues in Demerara were accommodated on a cotton plantation. The rooms were commodious and the house conveniently close to the hospital. Alternatively, individuals or smaller groups of officers might be billeted with local families. Often they were well received, Norbert Landsheit being very pleased to find himself in the home of a fellow German in Port au Prince. He refused his countryman's offer to marry one of his daughters, admitting that it was tempting but that he did not dare to desert. Conversely, some billeting of officers was resented by the local population. The Privy Council in Saint Domingue repeatedly complained that army officers were allowed to lodge in the best houses in Port au Prince, leaving the local administration to pay the rent. This was one small example of the corruption endemic in the British military occupation of the colony.[8]

Women were an integral part of the British army presence in the West Indies. A return of November 1795 reveals that 808 women accompanied Abercromby's expedition, a ratio of roughly one woman for every 20 men. In the garrison of the Windward and Leeward Islands nine years later, there were 758 women, a rather higher proportion of the 12,500 strong force. Regulations from 1800 stipulated that soldiers' wives could follow the army in the proportion of six to 100 men; in the 1790s it was probably left to the discretion of senior officers. There are only fleeting references to the lives of these women in memoirs of the wars, this information supplemented by sparse instructions in the army's regulations and general orders. The adjutant general on Martinique in 1794 directs that the barracks 'ought not be crowded with women'.

Officers' wives had a relatively privileged existence, but they still needed stoicism to flourish in the climate and the atmosphere of doom induced by the prevailing diseases. Lady Maria Nugent's diary entries give an insight into the routine life of a senior officer's family in Jamaica.

October 15, 1801 – Very unwell; and I mean, as symptoms arise of any illness, always to mention it; because, if I should die in this country, it will be a satisfaction to those who are interested about me, to know the rise and progress of my illness, & c.

October 5, 1803 – Hear that poor Captain [John] Murray has the fever. Of late I have omitted to mention illness, for it only makes one melancholy and miserable; but there are, in fact, only three subjects of conversation here, – debt, disease and death. It is, indeed, truly shocking.

January 17, 1804 – Doctor McNeil came early to tell us that General C. [Hugh Carmichael] was in great distress, and very ill, too, himself. His nephew, Mr Cowen, died in the night, of convulsions, after the fever had left him, and he was supposed likely to recover. These awful circumstances, do indeed affect the spirits, but we must try not to think of them.

The lot of the wives of the rank and file was immensely worse. It appears that they were only grudgingly tolerated by the army's senior administrators as they were suspected of spreading venereal disease, plundering supplies and dealing in rum. They were mostly accommodated in the ordinary barracks, only a hanging cloth between them and the other soldiers for privacy. At Brimstone Hill, there was a small amount of married accommodation in the 1790s but this was in the form of decayed and condemned huts. In such extreme circumstances, it is understandable that at least some of these women and their spouses had flexible loyalties. Aytoun refers to this.

I know a man whose name was Daws, whose wife had been anything but a vestal. He sold her to the ninth of a man, whose name was Robert Lee, for fourteen dollars and a pair of silver buckles. I knew two women who changed from their husbands just as a servant would leave one family and go to another but they certainly mended their conditions by getting better men who kept them comfortable during life.

Undoubtedly some women made vital contributions to the garrison and there are instances of them playing an active part in combat. Lieutenant Colonel Stewart of the 42nd recalls the wife of a soldier of the regiment joining the assault on the Vigie Ridge on St Vincent in June 1796. Her husband was behind the lines looking after the knapsacks.

When the enemy had been beaten from the third redoubt, I was standing giving some directions to the men and preparing to push on to the fourth and last redoubt, when I found myself tapped on the shoulder and I saw my Amazonian friend standing with her clothes tucked up to her knees;

and seizing my hand, 'Well done, my Highland lads!', she exclaimed. 'See how the brigands scamper like so many deer! Come', added she, 'let us drive them from yonder hill.' On enquiry, I found that she had been in the hottest fire cheering and animating the men, and when the action was over she was as active as any of the surgeons in assisting the wounded.

There were children in the garrison; the previously quoted return from 1804 shows that there were just over 500 in the Windward and Leeward Islands. They are mentioned in contemporary accounts even less than their mothers, but their presence is confirmed by the toys found among the artefacts of old West Indian military camps. Infant mortality was high. A tombstone at Brimstone Hill is dedicated to Elizabeth, wife of Sergeant William White, who died in 1810 and shared her grave with four of her children. Other records document births on the islands. Ensign David Wainright and his wife Elizabeth had 13 children of whom the first two, a boy and a girl, were born on Martinique in 1795 and 1796.

Officers and men had different sorts of relationships with the local women. A number of memoirists testify to the general lack of morals. Thomas Phipps Howard claimed that, '...there is no Country in the World where the Inducement to dissipation & Libertinism are greater than is to be met with in the West Indies – & that in every point of View. In the first place Morality is scarcely known'. He blamed the heat for the inflammation of passions, '...a Man inclined to Libertinism finds here perhaps the largest field in the World to gratify himself in'. George Pinckard agreed, noting that it was commonplace for his South American hosts to offer him female company. There were essentially two forms of common prostitution in the region. The most numerous were the licensed prostitutes, slave women who had the approval of the army to serve the garrison's soldiers. Unlicensed or civilian prostitutes operated in the brothels of the hotels of the larger towns.

The relationships formed between officers and local women were potentially more complex. Here we are referring to 'mistresses' or 'concubines'. These liaisons may have arisen from mutual attraction; British soldiers often found the Creole women to be irresistible and they in turn were not inured to the glamour of a scarlet uniform. Money might be involved but this was not viewed as a form of common prostitution. Aytoun refers to a 'mulatto woman's daughter' in Demerara. 'Her father had been white. She was not a common prostitute but hired herself to officers etc. by the week or month...' That this arrangement was not always of an entirely monetary nature is suggested by the reaction of a drummer whom she refused to marry. He tried to hang himself and was only saved by a comrade who cut the cord. Thomas St Clair tells us that it was usual for Europeans arriving in the Caribbean to take a mistress and that the usual price was £100 to £150. They performed 'all the duties' of a wife. Two of his fellow officers kept two such girls in their barracks; '...one in Demerara, Lieutenant Myers, had a beautiful young mulatto and Lieutenant Clark in Berbice, had with him a handsome black woman'. St Clair says that he disapproved of these relationships but he had to acknowledge that the women formed a strong and sincere attraction to their new partners. As will be discussed in a later chapter, soldiers often benefitted from the excellent nursing care provided by these women.

Mistresses of senior officers could, on occasion, exert significant influence. When Thomas Picton was governor of Trinidad, it was alleged that his mulatto mistress had the fuel contract for the garrison and the means of retribution against local inhabitants who offended her. Another possible liaison was that between British soldiers and sailors and European women resident in the colonies. William Dillon came across a Dutch family at Curaçao in 1801; 'There were 6 or 8 very handsome girls, of splendid fortune for that place, with good landed estates who wished to unite themselves with the English officers. But, strange to say, none of them received an offer.' One naval colleague did marry a European woman but she had very little property. 'Sailors', Dillon concluded, 'do not manage well in these matters'.[9]

Most officers and men on service in the Caribbean had only time to kill. Cavalryman Norbert Landsheit remained for some months in the vicinity of St Marc in Saint Domingue in 1794.

> ...I could not avoid remarking to them with whom I associated, that if this were indeed war, we had no cause to wish, at any moment, for the return of peace... as to military operations there were none; our most perilous duties never going beyond a patrol, or at the most, an escort of stores to headquarters.

The centrality of the garrison regimen has been described. Ordinary soldiers were given routine housekeeping tasks to punctuate the hours of inactivity. Andrew Bryson recalls a dozen men of his company being picked out to wash their dirty clothes in the river. They were embarrassed to find themselves in the company of black women and quickly moved on to a more solitary spot. The officer class could take on servants to spare them such indignities, the regulations of 1795 making this explicit.

> It is not permitted in the West Indies that an Officer should be allowed to keep a white soldier as a servant. As an Equivalent to the Officer for this necessary Restriction, they will be allowed a just sum to have Blacks or Mulattoes, which will be paid at stated Periods by the Commissary General.

A field officer was permitted three black servants, a captain two, and a subaltern only one.

Officers thus had plenty of leisure time to divert themselves with various entertainments. Dancing was popular, especially in more developed areas. A ball at Jérémie in Saint Domingue was a major event bringing in 200 people from the surrounding countryside. Thomas Henry Browne makes reference to dances held at Susy Austin's hotel-tavern. Where there was a continuous British presence, such as on Jamaica, more sophisticated balls could be expected. Maria Nugent describes an elaborate affair arranged in Spanish Town.

> Dress soon after 7, and at 8 all the company were assembled – General
> N. [Governor George Nugent] and I then went down to the Great Hall,
> at the door of which all the staff were paraded, and we marched up to
> the sophas, at the upper end, to the tune of 'God Save the King'.

The formal introductions preceded the commencement of dancing. After a midnight supper, Maria admits that she 'forgot all dignity' and joined in a Scottish reel.

During daylight hours, officers frequently took the opportunity to explore. George Pinckard fills a considerable portion of his three volumes of recollections with accounts of perambulations around Barbados and the South American mainland. This activity ranged from a local hike – he and a medical colleague walked for several hours around Bridgetown in the early morning – to more ambitious 'Marooning excursions', which involved longer trips on horseback accompanied by slave guides and ample provisions. These journeys, he informs us, were pursued 'in the Marooning spirit of making a home wherever we might require it, or wherever we might find it, availing ourselves of whatever dwelling might present itself in our path'. Intrepid explorers, the Reverend Cooper Willyams among them, often received lavish hospitality from the plantation owners.

Participating in or watching various sports were other common pastimes. Hunting was limited by the lack of hounds and foxes, but shooting was very popular. Phipps Howard describes a shooting party near St Marc in 1796 where he and his fellow sportsmen, a small group of senior officers, 'amused ourselves for an hour or two, & shot a Number of Birds of the Snipe Species which are very abundant in this island...' The tropical wildlife was fair game, George Pinckard returning from a day spent shooting and fishing 'having shot two pelicans and a number of other birds'. As proof of their exploits, some officers got their kills stuffed and sent home.

Horse racing had been introduced to the islands, Jonathan Leach describing a circular course near St John's on Antigua. Physical pursuits included running races and swimming, but not all the participants took into account the vagaries of the climate and natural history. Maria Nugent dismissed the competitors in a race as 'silly boys of the 85th, who will, no doubt, suffer severely for their folly'. They were unlikely to be as unfortunate as one of Pinckard's hospital assistants, who went for a swim and was carried off by an alligator.

Officers' reading material included letters, journals and newspapers sent from Britain, all voraciously consumed to dull the homesickness felt by many. News of battles in Europe arrived with the papers carried by vessels arriving at the islands. Bookshops were rare in the West Indies, Edward Pakenham commenting that 'it might be strongly recommended to all Johny Newcombes to this country, to bring out a less stock of Quack medicine and a few more Books'. Works eagerly perused included Edward's *West Indies*, a comprehensive history of the region in three volumes.

Fortescue bemoans the lack of memoirs from the West Indies in the Revolutionary and Napoleonic periods and there are certainly far fewer existing eyewitness accounts than from the Peninsula or the Waterloo campaign. However, as the bibliography of primary sources in this work proves, there are more than might be thought, particularly if the researcher is prepared to delve into the archives. Men did survive the dreaded West Indies and write their memoirs and, even among those who perished, letters and journals have survived. Most were not attempting to immortalise their story but were content to maintain a tenuous link with loved ones and friends at home. Lieutenant Edward Teasdale of the 54th, one more victim of yellow fever, had earlier corresponded with his mother in 1807, promising to write to her from Kingston.

> ...there is no reason why you should not, in the meanwhile, write to me for you may depend upon it, I shall get it safe in Jamaica. And when you write, have the goodness to tell me a little more of the family – my poor cousins may be dead for all I know.

We have less of a written record from the ranks where most were illiterate. Johnston Abercromby, on Guadeloupe in 1794, apologises to his wife for his 'imperfect account' of the campaign 'as I have not time to think of any more at present'. He was, he tells her, determined to keep a journal. The joy of his correspondence is palpable.

> I cannot express the gratitude I owe to my god that after all the dangers and fatigues I have gone through I am well and able to write once more to my All on Earth.[10]

Chapter 10

Muzzle to Muzzle:
In Action

The central events of the West Indian campaigns have been related. In this chapter we will consider particular aspects of the fighting and also more fully address the human element of the conflict. It is not easy, or perhaps advisable, to glibly define the nature of a war stretching over 22 years and fought in a region as diverse and fragmented as the Caribbean. However, the limiting factors and vital stages of a 'typical' West Indian campaign can be tentatively described.

Most expeditions commenced with what the military commanders judged to be an inadequate force. This, as we have seen, was the inevitable consequence of political inconsistency and the demand for manpower elsewhere, especially in Europe. Both the timing and direction of campaigning was influenced by the weather. Fighting was best limited to the healthier winter months and the prevailing trade winds meant that this proceeded from east to west (windward to leeward), hence the strategic importance of the Windward Islands. The normal strategy for an assault on an island was to make multiple simultaneous landings, the amphibious operations requiring sophisticated cooperation between army and navy. Once ashore, there was usually a march to be made, sometimes over a significant distance. Any enemy outposts would have to be driven in prior to the storming of the enemy's main stronghold atop a dominant hill. A more substantial fortress might lead to a formal siege. Impenetrable mountains and jungle and the weakening effects of disease often proved greater obstacles than manmade defences. After the targeted strong-point was captured, the campaign had perhaps only just started, there remaining the difficult business of subjugating the rest of the island and its insurrectionary elements.

Officers were keen to stress to ministers and others at home that this was a type of warfare entirely different to that of the European theatre. Abercromby informed a colleague that it was 'most uninteresting' before elaborating.

> ...you see perhaps one or two days in the Campaign the Troops you command; the moment you begin to act you are obliged to parcel out your little army in small detachments, and the instant the Service is over they go on shipboard to return to their respective garrisons. The real

service of a campaign here might be comprised in the operation of a fortnight in Europe.

Formal operations all too often evolved into agonising struggles where, in the words of an eighteenth-century colonial governor, the main challenge was not to beat the enemy but to see him. In Saint Domingue, Thomas Phipps Howard complained that he faced adversaries who were unacquainted with any 'regular System of Tactics'; it was a 'war of Ambuscades'. This protracted guerrilla war was both hard and bewildering for officers and men trained in the manoeuvres of the European battlefield. On St Lucia, John Moore admitted that he had endured more fatigue in five weeks than most officers would suffer in five campaigns. The wearisome nature of West Indian warfare for the rank and file is best encapsulated in a letter written by Private Johnston Abercromby to his wife from Guadeloupe in 1794.

> Marched 7 miles up hill and lay in a field all night. The 19th we marched up another hill which was five miles high, the like of which I never beheld for we was forced to climb up by bushes and in danger of falling every minute and still raining, as soon as we gained the hill each man got an extraordinary share of grog and then stormed a small battery of 5 guns, the French all running away on seeing us coming. The 20th marched up another hill...[1]

The ordinary soldier could be forgiven for not distinguishing one hill from another. Senior commanders had varying levels of intelligence of the islands they were attacking. In 1794, Grey had copious information on the defences of Martinique thanks to contacts with émigré Frenchmen on Barbados. He knew which potential landing beaches were defended and those that were vulnerable. In stark contrast, Ralph Abercromby had to rely on snippets of information from local smugglers to plan his assault on Puerto Rico three years later. Deserters were another possible source of intelligence and there were undoubtedly spy networks in place for much of the period. British agents operated in the shadows of Saint Domingue, making contacts with sympathetic elements. Republicans were equally active in espionage, Victor Hugues making reference to a spy in his service who received 1,320 *livres* per month for information relating to British operations. Lieutenant Henry Clinton felt the need to write his letters to his brother in England in 1796 in code (see illustration 16).

Moving around the islands' interiors and maintaining good communications were constant challenges. Accurate maps were in short supply. In July 1795, Balcarres was forced to write to Sir Adam Williamson asking for a large map of Jamaica, '...if you can lay your hands on it, I need not say how very useful it may eventually be to us'. Under the circumstances, there was much reliance on local guides. Transmitting information over any significant distance was also difficult. John Moore vents his frustration against the postal arrangements on and around St Lucia. 'The vessel I had dispatched with my letter to Sir Ralph returned without finding him. This perplexed me much.' Later, the senior commander's reply failed to reach Moore. Dispatches sent home via the Post Office packets risked capture by enemy privateers. Signal stations were an alternative technology in place on some of the islands. Their primary role was to give early warning of infringements by the enemy and they variously used coloured flags, semaphore and alarm guns.[2]

Disembarking troops onto the beaches of an enemy-held island was commonly the first decisive step in an offensive campaign. We have the directives of the general orders to elucidate what was expected. Beckwith's instructions for the landing on Martinique in 1809 are typical.

> Upon a signal being made for the troops to land, the men will get into the boats as expeditiously as possible, but without disorder. They are to sit down in the boats, and in rowing on shore perfect silence is to be preserved. The Troops are not to load, until they are formed on the beach, nor are Bayonets to be fixed till that time, unless the landing be disputed. The formation to be effected as soon as possible. The men will fall in, in line opposite to where they disembark. They are to land in the lightest marching order...

The flat boats would have been assembled at a pre-determined place and the soldiers entering them carried a few days' provisions and other necessities such as blankets, camp kettles, water kegs, canteens and hatchets.

Most landings were not contested and this was just as well as it was difficult to coordinate the fleet carrying the troops and, as a result, they too often came ashore in a piecemeal or haphazard fashion. Examples include the landings on Guadeloupe in 1794, Demerara in 1796 and Trinidad in 1797. As these expeditions were under the military command of men such as Grey and Abercromby and experienced naval officers, we may assume that the difficulties were considerable. Maitland's account of the landing on the Saints underlines the challenges posed by the weather, tides and topography.

> The disembarkation was fixed to be at six o'clock in the morning of the 14th [April 1809], but a bad night separated our ships. By ten they were collected. Soon after the Acasta led in, through a very narrow channel, which was buoyed on either side; the Gloire, Narcissus, and Circe followed, the Intrepid about an hour after, but the Dolphin not until next day. His Majesty's Ships anchored opposite to the little bay Bois Joly. The landing was meant to have been at the next to the eastward, called

Ance Vanovre. As much time, it was then seen would be lost by persevering to go to Ance Vanovre, because the boats would have had a long row against wind and current, we landed at Ance Bois Joly, a secure landing, though a stony beach, protected by the fire of the frigates.

The first men ashore, often light infantry, were normally instructed to occupy any local strong-points, high ground or houses, thereby covering the landing of the remainder of the force.[3]

The next stage in the archetypal island campaign was a march. In Europe, 15 miles was judged a good daily distance in action. During the Peninsular War, troops often set out an hour or two before daylight and halted for 20 minutes every three or four miles. These efforts were liable to be wearisome and destructive in any part of the world, but there is no doubt that punishing marches through almost impenetrable terrain and in stifling heat were a particular feature of the West Indian campaigns. Examples include Dundas's 20-mile transit to La Calebasse on Martinique in 1794, Leighton's move to Mount Young on St Vincent in 1795, Maitland's march across the mountains in Saint Domingue in 1795 and Hughes's foray through the Surinam jungle in 1804. These marches brought significant strategic gains, the enemy surprised and the campaign potentially shortened. There was, however, a cost. It was estimated that three-quarters of European soldiers arriving in the region would succumb under such duress.

When men had to traverse jungle paths they were given cutlasses to hack their way through. Marching on roads was easier, but they were often of execrable quality. Major General Hugh Carmichael reported that there were only two practicable roads for the army on Guadeloupe, the 'Grand Road' leading along the coast and a difficult track over the heights of Cap Terre. Other islands and colonies were no better served. In Saint Domingue, the tracks through dense forest were virtually impassable, cut by streams flowing from the mountains, overgrown and blocked by fallen trees. According to Aytoun, the roads of Dominica were suitable only for pedestrians as they were intersected by 'bridges' made of single tree trunks laid across deep valleys. John Moore, bogged down in a struggle to exert control on St Lucia, complained that a march of three miles took as many hours He employed workmen to clear the roads. Difficult terrain and crude roads required compromises. General orders issued in January 1809 for the Martinique campaign specified that, due to the narrowness of the roads, the troops were to form two deep and march in files. Captain William Stewart confirms that the island's immense woods necessitated 'Indian-file marching for miles together'. In wet conditions soldiers commonly sank to their knees in thick mud and lost their shoes.

The tropical heat was the greatest enemy of the marching soldier. Thomas Phipps Howard saw men and animals toil and die in Saint Domingue.

Owing to the Troops leaving the Mole at such an ill-judged hour they suffered terribly by their March; the Sun being so extremely hot & not a drop of Water to be met with on the Road. None but those who have been obliged to March in this Country can have an idea of the Extremities to which the Army was reduced. So great was it that before they halted, which was about 3 o Clock in the Afternoon, no less than between 50 & 60 men had absolutely perished with thirst & were lying dead along the Road. The Horses employed in dragging the Artillery & Commissaries stores, not having been properly broke to the Service, & the Roads being so extremely bad, the greatest part was obliged to be left behind which greatly added to the Distress of the Troops.

Night marches were an obvious expedient, but these had their own problems. William Dyott declared that he was against this strategy, having endured a night march on Grenada where, even though there was a tolerably good road, it took nearly 10 hours to journey eight miles with considerable confusion. In Saint Domingue, a regiment of hussars which chose to travel mainly at night took 77 hours to cover the 60 miles between St Marc and Port au Prince.[4]

The first contact with the enemy might be a clash of patrols or a confrontation with advanced posts. The army's commanders stressed the need for vigilance, general orders issued in 1794 from Barbados reminding officers that the safety of the army relied on the alertness of outposts; 'It is the greatest disgrace that can possibly befall an officer; and so much so in the General's opinion, that any officer or non-commissioned officer who shall suffer himself to be surprised, must not expect to be forgiven'. Grey later returned to the subject, exhorting advanced parties to remain alert and 'in case of an insult, to meet it coolly, not risking themselves in darting forward...' Abercromby used similar language in 1796, informing his men that it was 'not wise to despise their enemy' and that they must guard against complacency whilst on outpost duty.

Patrolling and reconnoitring duties were generally undertaken by light cavalry units. Howard describes such actions in Saint Domingue, on one occasion making an eight-hour round trip to within a quarter of a mile of an enemy camp and later leading 40 cavalrymen in an information-gathering mission on the banks of the Artibonite. The greater mobility of cavalry was well suited to these tasks but its offensive role in the West Indian campaigns was limited to occasional shock tactics against demoralised or distracted opponents. Howard describes an attack on pillaging brigands.

...the Cavalrie, having bridled took a short turn round the back of the Camp while the Brigands were employed in tearing-up the Tents [and] fell upon them Sword in Hand before they had time to stand to their Arms. Instantly the deroute became general...

One hundred and eighty enemy were killed. In a later incident near St Marc, the brigands, terrified by the sudden appearance of the hussars, were 'cut down like so many sheep'. This potential shock role of the cavalry arm was appreciated by Balcarres who requested two regiments of light dragoons to be sent to Jamaica to 'awe the Maroons and the Negroes'.

Howard admits that his unit was sometimes returned to headquarters as the terrain was unsuitable for its deployment. Most of the islands were unfavourable for the use of cavalry regiments and many contemporary observers talk down their usefulness. Major General Gordon Forbes, writing to Dundas from Saint Domingue in 1796, declared a newly arrived cavalry contingent to be 'absolutely ineffective' for any offensive operations. Colonel Charles Chalmers agreed; the plains of the colony were 'exceeded at least twenty to one by mountains which seem almost inaccessible to cavalry'. David Stewart of the Black Watch believed the same to be true on Guadeloupe, St Lucia, St Vincent and Grenada. The terrain of all these islands was more rugged than his native Highlands and the cavalry regiments were 'totally useless', their horses dying in such numbers that they struggled to even carry dispatches.[5]

The infantry were the warriors of the Caribbean campaigns. Some aspects of their organisation have already been addressed in the introductory and campaign chapters, but here we will consider in a little more detail the tactics on the ground, including the use of light infantry and the human experience of fighting in the West Indies. Organisation and tactics varied during the years of conflict, but we can make some generalisations. Larger forces, designed to capture a major island such as Martinique or Guadeloupe, were normally organised into divisions, brigades and regiments. Thomas Beckwith's army for the attack on Martinique in 1809 was broadly divided into two divisions, each of which was subdivided into three brigades or two brigades and a reserve. The brigades were each composed of three or four regiments, although at least one of these might be reduced, perhaps made up of only four or five companies or only the flank companies. Two divisions of approximately 5,000 men, making up a total strike force of 10,000 operatives, was not unusual. Field artillery (discussed below) would be attached to the division independent of the brigades. Foreign regiments and black native troops might be outside the brigades and be returned as separate contingents. Similar organisational units were used by Grey and Abercromby.

Grey's tactics for his West Indian campaigns of the 1790s were drawn from his earlier experience in North America in the 1770s. His reliance on the bayonet had earned him the soubriquet of 'no flint Grey'. In 1777, Grey's troops were praised for their steadiness in charging without firing a single shot. The general's orders for the assault on Martinique in 1794 do not suggest any great evolution in his thoughts. His men were instructed that they were to march in two files to adapt to the narrow roads and that, when they attacked the enemy, judged to be weak and demoralised, they were to employ the bayonet to force them into precipitate flight. This was especially the case for night assaults, as they could then manoeuvre without revealing their position or strength and the risk of casualties or disorder caused by friendly fire was nullified. He also emphasised the importance of surprise; a classic Grey attack would be made with the bayonet in the night against a stuporose enemy. Abercromby, whose troops were in general much rawer than Grey's, appears to have followed suit, directing his charges at St Lucia in 1796 to preserve their fire and to be ready to follow through an attack with the bayonet until their foe retired.

The exact formation adopted depended much on local geography. For the assault against Morne Chabot on St Lucia, well related by John Moore, the troops were divided into two columns with the light companies and grenadiers at the head. That any formal arrangement was subjugated to the vagaries of the local ground is confirmed by Moore's comment that his column was soon marching in single file. Only when the path opened out close to the enemy were six or eight of the grenadiers able to form up.

Questions arise as to what extent 'light infantry' were used in the West Indian campaigns and whether colonial warfare was an essential catalyst for the growth of this arm in the British service, the feared Light Division playing a central role in the Peninsular War. The Black Rangers and West Indian Regiments have been discussed in the first chapter; these were de facto 'light infantrymen' despite never being formally designated as such. They were 'special battalions designed for a particular type of irregular warfare'. It is difficult to make such a generalisation with regard to the indigenous British regiments. Some sources suggest that Grey, influenced by his American experience, schooled some of his troops in light infantry procedures following their arrival in Barbados in 1794 (as described in Chapter 4). He was, apparently, straining to recreate the 'perfection of light infantry that was attained during the American War'. He made organisational change, joining his grenadier and light companies together to form new battalions.

Grey was not alone in trying to impose the views of the 'American school' on his West Indian army. Abercromby and Simcoe both stressed the importance of light infantry work. Beckwith created rifle companies on Martinique and Guadeloupe. More junior officers – Walpole on Jamaica, Moore on St Lucia – came to regard light infantry tactics as central to achieving their objectives against an irregular enemy secreted in the mountains and forests. It is no coincidence that men who subsequently played a prominent role in the training of Britain's light infantry, officers such as Moore and Coote Manningham, served extensively in the Caribbean.[6]

West Indian islands were won a few feet at a time in hand-to-hand fighting. Perhaps the apotheosis of this close-quarter warfare was on Jamaica where Walpole trained his men to share the carrying of their weapons to allow them to clamber across the rocky slopes of the Cockpits. There are, however, many other examples. In Saint Domingue, Phipps Howard relates many skirmishes with the brigands in the woods. On one occasion, in July 1796, a clash involved a small advanced detachment and an indeterminate number of the enemy. After exchanging musketry for two hours, the British are forced to fall back; 'The Brigands seeing them retreating in rather a disorderly manner followed them with a ferocity scarcely to be conceived & absolutely pushed several with their Bayonets down the Mountain...'. The men were only saved by the intervention of artillery.

The best eyewitness accounts of active operations in the West Indies during the Revolutionary era are penned by John Moore. His words bring us as close as possible to the realities of the fighting. In his diary entry for 25 May, 1796 we find a prolonged description of the desperate defence of a post on Morne Fortune, the following being a short excerpt.

After a short time the enemy ceased to molest us, and I went back to make my report to the General [Abercromby] and to hurry on the working parties. I found him in one of the batteries. Whilst I was speaking to him we observed a body of [enemy] men marching out of the fort [Charlotte] and advancing towards the post I had just taken. Orders were immediately sent to the most commanding batteries to fire upon them. I ran to the post, which was attacked almost immediately. The ground and some houses in our front favoured the enemy's approach. I sent a detachment to reinforce a party I had posted on the left flank, but they were never able to form so as to occupy the ground I directed. The fire from the enemy was brisk and well-directed. They had the means of covering themselves, and they were clever in availing themselves of it; our men were falling fast. I ordered the Grenadiers and Light Infantry to advance and charge them. Colonel Drummond headed them, cut down an officer with his sword, drove them with the bayonet, and followed them some way; they suffered on their return from grape-shot. Drummond had scarcely returned when the enemy were reinforced and returned a second time. I ordered another company to advance and line a hedge to my left. This order was, however, only very imperfectly carried out. The fire from the hedge would have swept a valley, or rather a dip, by which the enemy could advance under cover within twenty yards of me. The second attack was more spirited than the first. The enemy took advantage of the hedge not being properly lined, and advanced close to us with great boldness. The front I could present was small. Many officers and men had already been knocked down; more were falling every moment. The regiment [27th] showed great spirit but the enemy's force was superior to ours. The ground was so confined that the whole of our men could not be brought into action or to support each other, and if the men continued to fall so fast, it was to be dreaded they might give way.

Moore was eventually able to bring up another two fresh companies to save the vital post.

The later campaigns were characterised by many small scale clashes of arms. Companies of men fought at close quarters in confined spaces. On Martinique in 1809, Drummer William Bentinck relates an action on the Heights of Sourier. The numbers involved were not insignificant but this was still an intimate form of war, dictated as much by the terrain as by early nineteenth-century tactics.

> The red blazes from their muskets played as unflinchingly and so nearly as to dazzle the eyes of the British, who as before had to fire at random into the dense jungle in which the foe was posted on every bund. A general charge with the bayonet effected some clearance, but at a great sacrifice, as our men had as much as they could do to force a way through the cane-break and many were actually put to the bayonet as they were fast entangled in the immense briars and creepers. The combat was muzzle to muzzle.

Bentinck's company lost 35 men and officers from a strength of 100. Fighting could be on the smallest scale. Thomas Brisbane calmly recalls an episode on St Vincent in 1796 where he ended up on the floor grappling with the Carib chieftain Taquin.

> As I was unarmed, I seized hold of his knife, which he made an attempt to grasp, and told him that if he did not remain quiet I would instantly despatch him; as he was still determined to escape, I was obliged to carry my threat into execution.

An assault uphill against an enemy stronghold was one of the commonest scenarios, repeated many times through the campaigns. Moore's tactical approach to the storming of Morne Chabot has been discussed in Chapter 6. The culmination of the night attack is worth relating. Again, Moore's words give a rare insight into the haphazard nature of such operations and the crucial importance of good leadership.

> I was at a loss to know the ground I was going to attack. The guide was brought up and pointed it out. The ground was tolerably smooth in my front, and sloped gently to my left; close to my right was a thick hedge: I feared it might be lined with infantry. Exhorting the grenadiers not to

fire but to use the bayonet, I ordered them to advance again. We followed the direction of the hedge for a couple of hundred yards. A wood then appeared in my front, a fence in the hedge to the right. The guide said that beyond the fence was the road. I directed the men to pull it down but it was too strong. I then ordered them to leap over it, and upon their hesitating showed them the example by getting over myself. They immediately followed and formed. The enemy were at this time drawn up crowning the hill. They fired upon us with great effect, and, notwithstanding every effort, I could not prevent our men from firing or induce them to advance with the bayonet. They received repeated discharges within twenty or thirty yards. Those in our rear began also to fire, so that no situation could be more distressing. The two companies were much broken. The obscurity of the night and perhaps the fears of the enemy prevented them from seeing our real situation. Our men were always rather gaining ground, though not in the order nor with the rapidity necessary. I was hoarse and exhausted with calling to them.[7]

The fog of war was as thick in the jungles and mountains of the Caribbean as on the battlefields of Europe. Moore's energy prevailed, his men 'putting to the bayonet' some prisoners who had not had time to flee from the summit of the Morne. We have seen Grey's predilection for the bayonet and Moore makes many allusions to the weapon, at one point noting that the French 'who were superior to us in firing, could not stand the bayonet'. The utility of the bayonet in the wider Napoleonic conflict has been the subject of great debate, some historians quoting the apparent rarity of bayonet wounds and claiming that the 15-inch piece of steel was virtually useless. In the Peninsular War, a hand-to-hand fight with the 'white weapon' was a rarity, one of the very few instances occurring at the combat of Roncesvalles in 1813.

How then do we explain the ubiquity of the bayonet, the repeated emphasis on its employment in the general orders and eyewitness accounts of the West Indian Campaigns of the Revolutionary and Napoleonic Wars? It appears that there were several reasons for the preference for the weapon. The bayonet had been used extensively in the American War and officers such as Grey were, to a degree, just carrying on the same. It was especially effective in mass attacks on an irregular or ill-trained enemy and had particular utility at night, as Abercromby explains in general orders in 1794.

The soldiers will bear in mind the use of the bayonet, which in possession of, they can have no excuse for retreating for want of ammunition, the bayonet being the best and most effective weapon in the hands of a gallant British soldier; in which mode of attack (the General assures them) no troops on earth are equal to them. In case of

night attack, ammunition and firing are totally out of the question, and
the bayonet is ever to be preferred and made use of.

The general further explains that men attacking with the bayonet do not reveal
their numbers or situation by their fire. Beckwith's general orders in 1809 also
advocate the bayonet for night assaults.

We have no accurate data for the types of wounds inflicted on Britain's
enemies in the West Indian campaigns but even if, as in other theatres, there
were few bayonet wounds, this would not necessarily undermine the case for
the weapon being widely used and effective. Abercromby's assertion that the
threat of the weapon induced the *'precipitate* flight' of the enemy is revealing.
The bayonet charge was, in Rory Muir's words, 'a test of will and resolution:
whose nerve would break first'. Most often, certainly in the West Indies, the
examination favoured the British infantryman, the regular soldier and the
aggressor.

After the initial exchange of arms and perhaps the fall of a key stronghold,
the campaign often developed into a struggle marked by ambush and
insurgency. Prolonged periods of attritional warfare occurred throughout the
period and this was very much the nature of the fighting in the 1795 uprisings.
On Grenada, British officers had difficulty coming to terms with a near
invisible foe. Lieutenant Colonel Archibald Campbell writes to Lord Cathcart
in April 1795:

> We seem entirely left to poke out our own way in the dark wilds, and
> fastnesses, not yet having found a guide who knows a yard beyond the
> beaten tracks, which are here improperly called roads, neither can you
> get for love or money a person who will venture a hundred yards to gain
> intelligence, consequently we either fall into ambuscade, or are led to
> error through false information.

The enemy might be 'Banditti', but these constant ambushes caused a
demoralising number of casualties. William Dyott expresses similar sentiments
a year later:

> Our march for the last three miles was literally up and down precipices,
> half-way up the leg in clay, and through a wood where I believe no
> human foot had ever before stepped... they [the enemy] annoyed us all
> the evening with their bush fighting from the woods...

In Saint Domingue, Harry Ross-Lewin acknowledged the celerity of the
Republican forces, particularly the native troops. 'In a war against a savage
enemy, there is nothing to be so much feared as surprise'. He and his comrades

were harassed by repeated calls to arms during the night. On Dominica, soldiers of the 9th West India Regiment fell into a forest ambush laid by rebels; pits had been dug containing sharp stakes and disguised with foliage. On Jamaica, Balcarres also fought a jungle war. A secret pre-printed letter issued to officers in December 1799 directs them to enter the 'negro homes belonging to the planters' to seize all arms and round up all persons 'of every description' who had no clear role on the estate. They were to be confined until further notice.[8]

As inferred by the title of this book, the British soldier sent to the West Indies was more likely to die of disease than win a commendation or a medal. Nevertheless, there were notable examples of heroism, both by individuals and whole forces. Fortescue, whose magisterial and traditional work on the British army is vulnerable to criticism by modern academics, must take belated credit for almost single-handedly keeping alive the memory of some of these actions. Examples include Graham's last-ditch defence of the Camp of Berville in 1794, the brave attack of the 46th at Chateau Belair on St Vincent in 1796, the defence of Morne Daniel on Dominica by the same regiment in 1805, and the valour of the 3rd and 8th West India Regiments on the Saints in 1809. Senior officers frequently led by example. In April 1794, Abercromby personally led the attack on Puerto Rico. According to Charles Stewart of the 53rd, '...he was the first who touched the shore, drew his little hanger [short sword], cheered and run in to a thicket like a Yager...'George Prevost's leadership of his grenadiers at the assault on Fort Desaix on Martinique in 1809 was approvingly noted by his French opponents.[9]

We have discussed the role of infantry and cavalry, but have so far made only secondary references to the employment of artillery. The herculean efforts made to ship significant amounts of ordnance to the West Indies suggest that senior army officers believed that cannon, howitzers and mortars were vital in the conquest and defence of the islands. In practice, the role of the Royal Artillery was limited by the difficult terrain, the lack of horses and the variable quality and supply of guns and ammunition. Pieces of ordnance, especially the lighter guns, were theoretically manoeuvrable by men and horses, but keeping them up with the action was a constant problem. On Martinique in 1809, artillery officer James St Clair, the brother of Thomas, describes his men approaching the front around the Heights of Sourier:

> Then indeed came the tug of war: up hill and down hill, through mud and through water did my poor fellows haul the weighty pieces of artillery after them; and, oft-times, these poor eager soldiers, anxious for a share in the fight, pulled on all-fours for hours under a burning sun, only to encounter disappointment; for no sooner was one height gained than another presented itself...

On Grenada in April 1795, Governor Mackenzie was frustrated by the lack of basic artillery supplies. 'I am at a loss how to issue orders respecting ammunition for the artillery. Lately, their quantity, bulk and weight were matters of inconvenience; and now there is not enough'. Balcarres complained to Dundas that the whole of his field artillery on Jamaica was useless, '...the carriages are rotten, and have been filled up from time to time with putty, merely to deceive the eye.'

Accepting these caveats, there is evidence in the eyewitness record that the Royal Artillery played a significant supporting role in both general operations and sieges. The lighter pieces of ordnance might be employed to defend troops forced back by the enemy or, more commonly, to 'soften up' enemy positions prior to their storming. Republican and insurgent forces had their own artillery and duels sometimes developed. Thomas Phipps Howard makes several mentions of artillery skirmishes in Saint Domingue, on one occasion 12 and 18-pounders from Fort Brisbane seeing off a brigand assault on a British detachment. Moore stresses the importance of artillery in gaining higher ground on St Lucia, several batteries, including mortars, playing on enemy positions around Morne Fortune. As is clear from his diary entries in May 1796, the British artillery fire was neither unopposed nor entirely effective.

> 17th: The batteries opened yesterday morning at eight o'clock. At first the enemy seemed much alarmed. They soon recovered and commenced a fire from three mortars and seven guns. Our batteries are distant, our fire ill-directed; it has had no effect. A 9-pounder, at their advanced post within 600 yards of us, without breast-work or embrasure, is allowed to exist, and to plague us...
> 18th: The Commander-in-Chief [Abercromby] is likewise hurt and surprised that the effect of the artillery [against the Vigie] has not been greater. Those about him are equally disconcerted. When it is determined that a post cannot be assaulted, but must be reduced by cannon, a certain time is required; that time, according to circumstances must be greater or less. In a country so mountainous and difficult as this, it must be long.

Moore recommended the use of large calibre cannon and howitzers, believing that the extra labour involved in moving these weapons would be well rewarded. Heavier guns were required for siege work and the existence of powerful fortresses guarding the principal towns and harbours of the islands meant that attempts at their reduction were a regular feature of the West Indian campaigns. The military essentials of these sieges have been related in the campaign chapters but we will consider their human dimension. Siege work was brutal, dangerous and demoralising for the attacking force. The reliance on gun and spade was the same in the Caribbean as in Europe but the rocky terrain meant that the routine tasks of digging in, creating parallels and locating the batteries were especially challenging. As in Europe, the offensive army, usually the British, sometimes resorted to bombarding the fortress into submission.

The best eyewitness accounts of a siege are of the attack on Fort Desaix on Martinique in February 1809. Captain Thomas Henry Browne of the 23rd methodically details the preparations in his journal. The entries are mundane, but that was the nature of siege work.

> February 7th; Erection of batteries continued in very adverse weather. The French made a sortie against one of our advanced trenches, and carried away some of their tools...8th; Works continued. The picquets and covering parties were severely engaged today. We christened our advanced battery Fort Edward, and in this work several men were killed and wounded by the accidental explosion of a shell...9th; Incessant rains which render all progress in the batteries exceedingly tedious. Fluxes and fevers begin to show themselves...

Similar entries, detailing the exhausting work, continue up until the 20th when the British batteries opened fire.

James St Clair was determined to gain revenge for the loss of his brother William, killed earlier in the campaign, and he enjoyed pummelling the French defenders.

> ...the signal gun was fired by me, and I saw the ball speeding its whizzing course across the plain below us, skimming beautifully close over the parapet-slope into the fort...At night the flight of shells to one common centre, visible as they whirled through the air from their burning fuses, was a most beautiful sight.

Sailor James Scott visited the fort after its capitulation and made a more sober assessment of the effects of the bombardment; '...I left the scene of desolation and murderous havoc fully impressed with the extent of horrors entailed by a state of warfare'.

The best accounts by the besieged are French, notably Rochambeau's of the fall of Fort Royal in 1794 and Villaret's of Fort Desaix in 1809. We have nothing so evocative from the British side, although there are fragments of information revealing the misery of Prescott's 58-day defence of Fort Matilda at Basseterre on Guadeloupe in late 1794. The general, in his later dispatch, depicts the increasing desperation of the small garrison as the works crumbled under enemy fire and their own artillery decayed and malfunctioned. Bartholomew James describes the intolerable heat, the shortage of water, the desertions, the sickness and the incessant danger.

No part of the garrison was safe; the barracks of all descriptions were tumbling on our heads; hot shot was flying in all directions; killed and wounded men were lying in all parts of the works, and the whole garrison was a scene of distress and devastation.[10]

The subsequent rescue of Prescott's garrison by embarkation onto the ships of Jervis's fleet is a pertinent reminder of the central part played by the Royal Navy in the Caribbean. This is the subject of another book, but it must be acknowledged here that admirals often rescued generals, either by spiriting away defeated British forces from under the noses of the French, as at Fort Matilda, or in supporting the offensive campaigns not only by transferring and landing soldiers, but also by bombarding enemy defences and troops from the sea. Sailors also left their ships to join the fighting on land. For Grey's first expedition in 1794, numbers of seamen were exercised and trained in the use of small arms and pikes. They were formed into companies commanded by lieutenants of the navy with the rank of captain on shore. They did sterling work. Although there were inter-service rivalries, the sailors were generally acknowledged by the soldiers to be valuable additions to the ranks. William Bentinck saw them in action on Martinique in 1809.

The Sailors had been brought ashore to man the guns and do occasional hand to hand fighting, which they addressed greatly, not troubling to load their muskets when once discharged, but laying about the French with the stock, a tree bough, or their fists, as chance or inclination might dictate.

They were, Bentinck tells us, intolerant of the soldiers of the West India Regiments, whom they berated for being cowardly and lazy. Some black soldiers were 'whacked' by the seamen and others, who had thrown away their ammunition, were shot.[11]

Eighteenth-century war had been brutal enough but the Revolutionary and Napoleonic Wars introduced the concept of 'total war', where the object was to annihilate the enemy and where civilian populations were involved and persecuted in a manner not previously seen. Insurgency warfare, as seen in the Iberian Peninsula and the West Indies, was characterised by ruthlessness on both sides. The campaigns in the Caribbean were littered with well-documented atrocities; black slaves slaughtered white planters who reciprocated in kind; French Royalists and Republicans gave each other no quarter and regular British and French forces were guilty of excesses against each other and also against native insurgent forces and civilians, be they white, black or mulatto.

British troops were mindful of the consequences of capture by the enemy. On Guadeloupe, where they faced the army of Victor Hugues, reports of the massacre of the sick and wives of the 43rd Regiment in the hospital at Point-à-Pitre in the summer of 1794 were widely known. Captain William Stewart, fighting on the island, was reluctant to leave the wounded behind; 'Our feelings suffered an additional horror in this cruel necessity by having before our eyes an enemy who, from their savage natures, we could little expect would give quarter to our officers and soldiers...' In Saint Domingue, the greatest fear of Thomas Phipps Howard and his men was of getting lost and falling into the clutches of the brigands, '...who gave no Quarter to their Prisoners & would therefore have immediately put us to some cruel Death...' The suicide of Lieutenant Baskerville, abandoned in Fort Tiburon, and at the mercy of Rigaud's men, was understandable.

The British were no innocents in this fiendish war. Geggus states that there is substantial evidence of British atrocities in Saint Domingue, Toussaint complaining of '*cruautés atroces and inouis*'. Black captives were drowned at sea in batches, held in chains, branded and beheaded. Neither side were inclined to take prisoners in action. These were systemic cruelties, but there are also anecdotes of the dehumanising effect of the conflict on the ordinary British soldier. A horrified James McGrigor watched an infantryman on Grenada place his loaded musket to the head of a French prisoner and discharge the contents. On St Vincent, David Stewart of the Black Watch describes a similar incident:

> This day [8 June, 1796] occurred an instance of the power of example and habit in exciting ferocity. In the month of August 1795, I enlisted a lad of seventeen years of age. A few days afterwards one of the soldiers was cut in the head and face in some horse-play with his companions, in consequence of which his face and the front of his body were covered with blood. When the recruit saw him in this state, he turned pale and trembled, saying he was much frightened, as he had never seen a man's blood before. In the assault of the redoubts, as I leaped out of the second to proceed to the third, I found this lad, with his foot on the body of a French soldier, and his bayonet thrust through from ear to ear, attempting to twist off his head. I touched him on the shoulder, and desired him to let the body alone. 'Oh, the Brigand', says he, 'I must take off his head'.

The soldier only desisted and rejoined the attack when Stewart pointed out that his victim was dead and that he would be better fighting the living enemy.[12]

Antagonism between opposing British and French officers and rank and file was not ubiquitous and there are examples of empathy and fraternisation. Following the capture of St Lucia in 1803, the troops of both armies intermingled in friendly fashion. French memoirs contain instances of goodwill towards their British adversaries. Jean-Baptiste Lemonnier-Delafosse criticises the callous behaviour of a senior British naval officer in Saint Domingue but he is quick to point out that '*tous les Anglais ne professaient point, même alors, un telle animosité contre nous*'. Alexandre Moreau de Jonnès found that he had more in common with his British captors than he expected, '...I found in my enemies most well-affected friends'.[13]

The lot of prisoners of war was uneven. We have more information pertaining to the fate of French prisoners than British. Many of the captured French ended up in the notorious prison hulks either off the south coast of England or in the West Indies. It is debatable which were the worst. Lemonnier-Delafosse was held in a British floating prison off Jamaica in 1803.

> The English hulks and all the miseries that we experienced there are too well known to recall the details; but that which we did not know yet, and that which is difficult to believe of a nation which claims to be civilised, was the refinement of cruelties invented at Jamaica, that is to say in the harbour of Port-Royal. There, these prisons resembled those of England, but they had in addition vigilant guards in the water. Attracted by the filth of the boats, we saw every day circling in the harbour numerous groups of sharks.

It is likely that the British soldiers cooped up in prison hulks off Point-à-Pitre in 1794 suffered just as the French. Hugues had promised that Graham's captured force would be allowed to return to England, but instead they languished in the ships for more than a year, most dying of fever. Lemonnier-Delafosse eventually escaped and there are also instances of British officers fleeing their captors. Brigadier General Benedict Arnold, held by Hugues on a prison ship at Point-à-Pitre, was threatened with the guillotine. He slipped away in the night, letting himself over the side with a rope and making for the British fleet in a small canoe.

British soldiers who fell into the hands of men such as Hugues and Fédon could expect little mercy and the British reciprocated against those they identified as disloyal or insurgent elements. The near extermination of the Carib people has been recounted. On Grenada, James McGrigor witnessed the policy of repression.

> All the jails were now crowded with such of the rebels as had been made prisoners. Among them were most of the French proprietors who were taken with their arms in their hands. Having often before sworn allegiance to the British crown, there was no excuse for them. Again, some of these gentlemen were said to have been accessory to the murder in cold blood of Governor Home, and several of his council, some time after they had been treacherously made prisoners. In one day, about twenty of the French proprietors were executed on a large gibbet in the market place of St George's, leaving wives and families.

Little sympathy was shown to 'rebels' captured in action. In his diary entry for 2 July 1796, John Moore details his efforts to suppress the insurgents on St Lucia.

> As I passed through Souffrière four men were brought in who had been taken in a boat coming from St Vincent; there had been eight of them, four had escaped. I ordered the four prisoners to be shot.[14]

The profound impact of disease and the wider role of the medical services will be addressed in the next chapter, but we will briefly consider here the experience of wounding and the means of evacuating casualties from the field. Wounds were often the result of a direct hit from artillery, usually catastrophic and fatal, or musketry. In the West Indies it was not unusual for men to be injured by splinters of stones and rocks. Infections such as tetanus commonly intervened. Captain Lasalle de Louisenthal was wounded on St Lucia in 1796.

> I was easily recognisable, I wore a sash over my shirt; the enemy thus spotted me easily. I was wounded for the second time. I had received a first wound to the left thigh at the time of the attack against the first small fort. I received the second to the right thigh two inches below my side. This second shot made me roll over a good twenty metres and I would have hurtled down the slope if a chasseur had not caught me by my sash which had hooked on to some bushes. I was not able to stand. My men laid me down next to the troops. I was bleeding a lot. They tried to stop the haemorrhage. As there was no doctor they took me, according to orders, to the Ferrand plantation. I was immediately operated on there. This was not very easy, even for this country where one is used to difficulties.

It was normal to use nearby buildings, often on a plantation, as makeshift field hospitals.

Thomas Henry Browne was wounded in the arm at the storming of Fort Desaix in 1809, the musket ball carrying away a small artery, dividing a nerve and breaking the bone. After some treatment in the nearby general hospital he was eventually carried on an improvised stretcher of Indian corn straw to a small plantation hut where he was well attended by the local slaves under the direction of the French plantation owner's wife. He was most alarmed by the tarantula hanging over his sick bed.

> My Surgeon then broke to me his opinion, that it would probably be necessary for me to have the arm amputated. I told him, that if the necessity really existed, of course I had nothing to say, and was sure that

I should bear it with much greater patience, than I did the pain I was
then suffering. At the same time, I represented to him, how very anxious
I was to preserve the limb as I was just beginning to learn the Flute.

The intrepid Browne kept his arm, the wound responding to local treatment with
charcoal.

These accounts are by officers who received special attention. As on most
of the battlefields of the Napoleonic Wars, doctors were in short supply and
ordinary soldiers needed luck to survive. Bartholomew James comments that
at the failed attack on Point-à-Pitre on Guadeloupe in July 1794 there were at
least 300 wounded soldiers and sailors re-embarked, many of whom had lost
limbs, and that because of the want of surgeons most had not been dressed since
they had received their injuries. David Stewart confirms that few men could
expect medical treatment on the same day as their wounding; he expresses the
odd opinion that this was not harmful. Where doctors were available, they often
operated on the front line. James McGrigor recalls that whilst he was attending
the wounded under a tree during the attack on Port Royal in May 1796, two of
his patients were killed close to him. The doctor was covered with blood and
brains and he struggled to convince another regimental surgeon that he had not
been hit himself.

General orders usually stipulated that the men should not leave the ranks to
assist their injured comrades, this duty instead being delegated to non-
combatants such as musicians and drummers. A temporary truce was sometimes
declared at the end of the action to allow both sides to collect their casualties.
After initial treatment, it was common for the wounded to be moved elsewhere
on the island or be evacuated by sea. Lasalle de Louisenthal was transported
the five miles to headquarters on St Vincent on a stretcher borne by eight
chasseurs. They moved at a steady pace to minimise his pain and he was
sustained with goblets of punch. The troops carrying Prevost's wounded after
the fall of Roseau took four days to complete the difficult escape to Rupert's
Bay. On Grenada, William Dyott saw wounded officers and men evacuated on
litters on the shoulders of the black inhabitants; 'The sight of them (many having
been most dreadfully wounded) was shocking'. According to McGrigor, the
worst cases were moved on to Barbados.[15]

One incentive to fight, to run the risk of wounding, was prize money. Cooper
Willyams, writing in 1794, stresses its importance; 'If no booty, no prize money,
be the reward of successful heroism, after the dreadful fatigues, diseases and
dangers of war. Where then will be the spur to noble actions?' The furore which
followed the extraction and distribution of prize money during the Grey Jervis
expedition has been alluded to. Dundas gave Abercromby and Christian a
detailed explanation of their entitlement and the system was made fairer and
more efficient by the introduction of the 1805 Prize Act. Officers still harboured

hopes of a fortune; Jonathan Leach admitting that he and his comrades had 'golden dreams' of prize money as they first approached Barbados and George Pinckard joking that he might return home as wealthy as a 'Eastern Nabob'. The doctor knew that his chances of acquiring quick riches were slim and this was even more the case for the rank and file, who were only ever likely to receive modest amounts, which were often paid out slowly over many years. Expectations were usually disappointed as the impressive hauls were dissipated in the transfer to Europe and tortuous litigation.[16]

As for all wars, the morale of the British soldier in the Revolutionary and Napoleonic West Indies varied according to his level of training, the quality of leadership and the immediacy of the campaign. We can make some generalisations about efforts to boost morale and the mindset of the troops. The alien and frightening nature of the West Indian campaigns for European soldiers was well understood by good senior officers and men such as Grey and Abercromby missed no opportunity to lift the spirits of their charges. Grey praised his troops in general orders, emphasising their fighting abilities and the inferior quality of their mostly irregular opponents. He passed on the approbation of the King and promised them free postage home. Abercromby reminded his men that they should disregard the 'shouts of savages' and that they possessed 'infinite advantages over the enemy'. Success, he told them, was certain. These statements hit home and there are instances of high morale among soldiers and sailors. Bartholomew James saw an army and navy in 1794 which had complete confidence in its commanders; '...in short, the cause we were employed in created an emulation not to be surpassed and a true loyal joy not to be equalled'. Fifteen years later on Martinique, Thomas Henry Browne insists that the troops were impatient to get into action. An excellent speech by Beckwith was received with loud and enthusiastic cheers from the ranks. Some soldiers chose to remain in the Caribbean, spurning opportunities to return home. David Stewart informs us that in 1796 many men of the 79th in Martinique refused a transfer to the 42nd which was about to embark for England, suggesting that regimental loyalties persisted and that there was not universal demoralisation.

These anecdotes of good morale are greatly outnumbered by eyewitness testimonies of disillusionment. The reluctance of recruits to be sent to the region has been discussed and, in general, morale fell away in the course of campaigns, even Grey's keen and experienced force eventually becoming demotivated. Fortescue compares British West Indian service with the French experience in 1796, when the young Napoleon struggled to lead his men over the bridge of Arcola: 'There is a limit to human endurance and what is pardoned to Bonaparte's French in Italy must not be too harshly judged in the British soldier who was subjected to a far harder trial in the West Indies'. There were two overriding factors in the genesis of low morale. Firstly, there was the lack of official recognition for dangerous Caribbean service. Archibald Campbell, on Grenada in 1795, expresses a widely held opinion.

> The species of war in this island is such that a man may easily lose credit by the least *misfortune* but cannot gain any degree of honour in beating what may be termed a despicable enemy...

The second factor was the constant and overwhelming threat of debility and death from disease.[17]

Chapter 11

A Great Mortality: Disease

Men began to get sick and die before they reached the West Indies. Despite attempts to root out the most debilitated and vulnerable recruits, many soldiers who boarded ships in England or Ireland were unfit for Caribbean service. General John Whyte's force, collected at Cork in the autumn of 1795, suffered 500 deaths from disease before the planned departure for Saint Domingue. Once they arrived at their destination, the chances of an early death from obscure and little understood disease spiralled alarmingly. Soldiers saw their comrades perish and their regiments melt away in the tropical heat.

The available medical data is most accurate for individual units and a few examples illustrate that the fear of West Indian service was fully justified. After the capture of Port au Prince in Saint Domingue in the summer of 1794, it was reported that the troops newly arrived from Europe were dying of fever in 'incredible numbers'. The 41st Regiment lost 318 men in three months, 44% of its strength, and the 23rd 319 men, 48% of its number. In their first year in the colony, both regiments buried more than three-quarters of their men and many of the demoralised survivors deserted or were discharged. Particular regiments might be spared for a period, but eventually they too were overwhelmed. The 22nd, stationed at the Môle, avoided serious losses until September but then lost 60% of its men in eight weeks. Cavalry regiments did not escape; the 29th Light Dragoons lost two-thirds of its troops in six months. Overall annual death rates in Saint Domingue for the period 1794–1798 were in the region of 50–75%.

The regimental returns are likely to reflect the reality of cheap death in West Indian service, but it is problematic to calculate with any confidence the total number of deaths between 1793 and 1815. Historians have made what can be regarded as well informed guesses, but their estimates are confounded by disparate time periods and variable inclusion of deaths among sailors and the West India Regiments. Fortescue's figures are widely quoted – he asserted that there were 80,000 casualties of which 40,000 were deaths – but these numbers pertain only to the earlier part of the wars up to 1798. He later extended his calculation up until early 1799, now including navy losses, and concluded that the British had lost 100,000 men, half of them dead and the remainder permanently unfit for service. Michael Duffy also focuses on the early campaigns, deriving a figure of 44,000 deaths among white non-commissioned officers and men in the Caribbean and en route to the region between 1793 and 1801. There were perhaps 1,500 officer deaths. Roger Buckley extends his calculations to the entire period up until 1815 and gives the total number of casualties among white troops in British service as 352,000, of whom 70,000 perished. To these figures can be added the estimated 72,000 casualties and 5,000 deaths suffered by the West India Regiments. The term 'casualty' describes all episodes of sickness, wounding, reported missing and death. Less than 10% of all events were directly related to fighting, disease being the British army's greatest enemy. More than half of the fatalities occurred in the first six years of the war when the greatest burden of the campaigning fell upon European as opposed to West Indian troops. The relentless loss of lives was such that the garrison in the Windward and Leeward Islands had to be completely replaced every six years.

Whatever the caveats regarding the precise figures, this was clearly a human disaster. Death was not, however, entirely random. Army doctors were quick to discern that some soldiers were more at risk than others. Assistant Inspector of Hospitals for Saint Domingue Hector McLean tells us that younger men, those aged between 25 and 30 years, were more prone to 'rapid, serious and violent fevers' than their older comrades and women. William Fergusson, another experienced army doctor, noted that ordinary soldiers in Saint Domingue were more likely to become sick than their officers. Within the rank and file there were further distinctions to be made. McLean bemoans the fact that British soldiers fell ill more easily than their European enemy. 'The French possess other advantages. Their constitutions seem better calculated for warm climates than ours.' Most significantly, it was obvious that the native soldiers of the West India Regiments were much more resistant to the dangerous local diseases than their white counterparts. Mortality rates among black soldiers were only 25–50% of those of European soldiers. The causes of death were also different, black troops most likely to succumb to chest infections, dysentery and smallpox.[1]

It was the two mosquito-borne diseases, yellow fever and malaria, which cut swathes through the British and other European forces in the region. Yellow fever is caused by a virus which is carried from person to person by the mosquito. The virus attacks the liver causing a deep jaundice which gives the disease its modern name. Because of liver failure there is a tendency to bleed and the vomiting of dark blood (now often described as 'coffee grounds') accounts for the contemporary term 'black vomit'. In advanced disease there can be torrential bleeding – from the mouth, nose, rectum and any open skin lesions – and death often ensues in six or seven days. The onset of the disorder could be insidious and in the absence of jaundice or vomiting the diagnosis might not be obvious. Robert Jackson, an army doctor in the West Indies and one of the greatest experts on the local fevers, describes the possible early symptoms.

> In some instances the yellow fever began in the morning, though the evening, upon the whole, was the more usual time of its attack. The first symptoms were languor, debility and headache, together with an affection of the stomach peculiarly disagreeable. The last often preceded the others, and was in some measure characteristic; but it is impossible to give a clear idea of it in words: − anxiety, nausea, and certain unusual feelings were so strangely combined that any description which I might attempt to give of this complicated sensation would hardly be intelligible.

The nature of the illness became clear when the more characteristic symptoms and signs appeared. In describing a case, Jackson tells us that, '...on the morning of the fourth [day] he became a deep orange colour and vomited black matter in great quantity. I then suspected that this complaint, to which I had not paid particular attention, was actually the disease known by the name of yellow fever...'

Some survivors have left accounts of their struggle against the disease. George Pinckard contracted the malady in Demerara.

> I know not from which I suffered most, the excruciating pain, the insatiable thirst or the unappeasable restlessness; for all were equally insupportable, and either of them might have sufficed to exhaust the strongest frame. Combining their tortures they created a degree of irritation amounting almost to phrenzy.

Pinckard's morale cannot have been improved by the regimental officers who peered at him through the mosquito net. 'Ah poor doctor! We shall never see him again!' He gradually recovered, as did Harry Ross-Lewin who was hospitalised in Saint Domingue for 36 days. He heard the medical officers expressing the opinion that he would only live a few hours and this 'had the good effect of rousing me a little'.

Some sufferers became desperate, confused and even delirious. Thomas Phipps Howard saw men who 'were absolutely drowned in their own Blood, bursting from them at every Pore'. Some, he says, died 'raving mad' whilst others irrationally plotted their escape or were simply despondent. Death was present in 'every form an unlimited imagination could invent'. William Fergusson noted that, in his experience, patients often retained their self-control and awareness. All agreed that yellow fever could snatch people with shocking speed.

> Lieutenant Wright, one of my [Fergusson's] early patients at Port au Prince, St. Domingo, on the fourth day of the fever rose from his bed in perfect possession of his senses, dressed himself correctly, and went into the market-place accompanied by myself, where he spent some time purchasing fruits and other things, returned to his barrack-room where he shortly expired in a torrent of black vomit. Lieutenant Mackay, of the quarter-master-general's department, Cape St. Nicholas Mole, on the day of his death, was up and dressed on the sofa, with books and papers before him at ten in the morning, passing jokes of comparison between his own dingy complexion, made so by the disease, and that of his mulatto nurse; at two he expired in the same way as Lieutenant Wright.

In epidemics of the eighteenth and nineteenth centuries, the mortality rate from yellow fever was around 70% and although we have no precise disease related statistics for the British army in the West Indies, this is probably close to the truth.[2]

The second great mosquito-transmitted killer was malaria, much more widespread at the time of the Napoleonic Wars than it is today. Malaria affected troops in Europe but the tropical form of the disease was potentially more virulent. It was characterised by an intermittent fever and rigors, often occurring on the first and third day ('malignant tertian fever') and it had a propensity to relapse and cause prolonged debility. Army doctors referred to the disease as 'intermittent' or 'remittent' fever and the soldiers called it 'ague'. It was understood at the time that malaria blighted different parts of the world.

> ...there is much similarity among the diseases of warm climates: and the remittent fever appears to be the disorder which prevails in all of them. That disease, as described on the coast of Africa, and on the banks of the Ganges, would seem to be nearly the same as in Jamaica.

It was also appreciated that there were different subtypes of the disorder with different periodicities of fever; Jackson refers to tertian, quartan and quotidian forms.

Severe and fatal cases of malaria would often have been difficult to distinguish from yellow fever. Indeed, many soldiers who died from disease may have had multiple infections. We can be most confident of a diagnosis of malaria where soldiers describe an illness with intermittent fever, rigors, profound fatigue and a tendency to relapse. John Moore very likely had malaria on St Lucia, being 'seized with the fever' and so weakened that he could not work properly for a month. He was then well for three weeks before suffering a relapse; 'I believe I was very near dying'. He never recovered his full strength whilst in the Caribbean and was forced to return home the following year. Major General Hugh Carmichael was equally afflicted in Guadeloupe in 1810, complaining that many of his fellow officers were confined to bed with fever and that he was 'actively indisposed' and struggling to keep up his correspondence. Thomas St Clair gives one of the best accounts of a paroxysm of fever due to 'ague'.

> My fingers by degrees turned as white as snow, my nails a perfect blue; and, whilst occupied with breakfast, my teeth knocked so hard together that I really thought that they would have fallen out. I was now recommended to return to bed, when the fit soon came upon me with such violence that my trembling made the whole house shake on its foundation. Thus I continued until four o'clock in the afternoon, when the cold fit began to change to a burning fever; and in like manner as my shivering fit had made me consume gallons of hot water, Madeira and sugar, to warm me, I was now obliged to drink cold lemonade to cool my burning palate'.

St Clair's symptoms persisted for several months before resolving. He was, like many others, later to suffer a relapse which necessitated his evacuation from Demerara to Barbados.[3]

The West Indian garrison was affected by a large number of other diseases, some familiar to soldiers who had campaigned in Europe and some more tropical in nature. Typhus stalked overcrowded Napoleonic armies and civilian populations; it has been said that the history of the disease is 'the history of human misery'. It is caused by rickettsia, microorganisms somewhere between bacteria and viruses and is most commonly passed from person to person by the human body louse. Symptoms include fever, headache, the appearance of small haemorrhages in the skin (petechiae) and gangrene of the extremities. Typhus was relatively rare in the West Indies but it was very likely a significant cause of death among the troops first arriving from Europe. McLean refers to 'ship's fever' in the troops reaching Saint Domingue from Ireland and McGrigor, whose opinion is not to be discounted and who believed the term 'typhus' to be overly used, described the new soldiers in the colony as being 'overwhelmed' with the disease. He says that 'a great mortality' followed.

The disease which caused the most deaths in the Peninsular War was dysentery, and this affliction and related diarrheal disorders were prevalent in the Caribbean. Like typhus, the disorder tended to break out in unhealthy cramped conditions and was especially dangerous to men already debilitated by fever. McGrigor contracted the 'loathsome complaint' on Grenada and suffered greatly in suffocating quarters. He was fortunate to be treated with kindness by his fellow officers and he gradually recovered. Dysentery remained a problem throughout the period, Thomas Henry Browne noting in his journal in June 1809 on Martinique that the number of cases was increasing.

Whilst considering diseases not unique to the tropics we should also mention scurvy, the well-known affliction of the navy caused by a deficiency of vitamin C. The realisation towards the end of the eighteenth century that the disease could be prevented by the inclusion of lemon or lime juice in the diet was one of the great medical advances of the era. William Richardson confirms that the disorder had not been eradicated from the fleet returning from the West Indies in 1797, many of the sailors becoming ill with the deficiency.

Venereal disease – gonorrhoea and syphilis – must have been common. It is described in contemporary medical accounts of the West Indies but it is almost absent from soldiers' memoirs. Mentions of mental disease are also sparse, their inevitable presence in the garrison often having to be inferred from oblique allusions. In medical circles the psychoneuroses of the Napoleonic Wars were usually referred to using the catch-all term 'nostalgia'. Army Physician Benjamin Moseley confirms that the disorder afflicted soldiers in the Caribbean.

> Nostalgia – that longing after home, exerts its painful influence in the remotest regions, and magnifies to danger, the most trivial indisposition of either body or mind, when both are already half subdued by the heat and dread of climate.

George Pinckard describes army officers suffering from depression and there are a number of suicides documented in the mortality statistics. More bizarre derangements of mental state were variably defined as madness, insanity and imbecility.

The environment of the islands took its toll on the men. Sunstroke, leg ulcers and insect bites were all commonplace. The routine excessive consumption of alcohol must have caused great harm and some have claimed that it was a bigger killer than yellow fever and malaria. Major General Hugh Carmichael, a veteran of 15 years in the West Indies, believed the primary cause of morbidity and mortality to be the 'corrosive and insidious Effect of Rum'. There were multiple deleterious consequences of drinking the local rum and other alcoholic beverages; men fell down dead at the side of the road from dehydration when consuming spirits instead of water, they demised from liver disease and they probably also suffered lead poisoning. Lead entered rum from vessels used in the manufacturing process and this was the likely cause of 'dry bellyache' which was endemic among the British battalions in the region.[4]

We have listed a number of diseases which threatened the soldier on Caribbean service but we might also have included various anaemias, lung complaints and rheumatic disorders. The doctors accompanying the various expeditions between 1793 and 1815 had a daunting task. It was the responsibility of the Medical Board in London to provide an adequate number of medical officers for West Indian service. The members of the Board were subject to much criticism in the course of the wars but it was not easy to recruit sufficient army doctors for such an unpopular destination. There were good intentions on the part of the Government and Abercromby's first expedition to the region arguably had better medical arrangements than any previous force leaving British soil. The Portsmouth part of the army was accompanied by a staff of four physicians, six staff surgeons, four apothecaries, 30 hospital mates and nine purveyors whilst with the Saint Domingue contingent there were seven physicians, twelve staff surgeons, two apothecaries and 70 hospital mates. These medical staff – that part of the department later to be described by Wellington as the 'medical gentlemen' – were in addition to the regimental surgeons and assistant surgeons, the number of which had been augmented. Hospital equipment – cots, bedding, marquees and innumerable other items – was supplied on a massive scale and medicines such as Peruvian bark, opium and ipecacuanha were packed into barrels, bales and drums. As we have seen, the expedition's officers departed with the advice of a specially convened medical committee ringing in their ears.

These preparations were well-meaning but not all believed that the quality of medical provision matched the quantity. Colin Chisholm, an inspector general of the ordnance medical department in the West Indies, was scathing.

> The medical staff of Sir Ralph Abercromby's army was principally composed of young men who had little or no practice, and who were totally unacquainted with the climate, and its diseases...

There were, he says, a smaller number of regimental surgeons who had served before in the region and who had some experience of local conditions but they were unable to agree with the more senior medical staff regarding the nature of the prevailing fevers.

Whatever the competence of the army's doctors, and this was very variable, they were just as vulnerable to infections as their soldier patients. It has been estimated that a quarter of serving British medical officers died during the Revolutionary and Napoleonic Wars, mostly from disease. Of the 11 physicians who accompanied Abercromby to the West Indies, six died in the short campaign and only one, Nathaniel Bancroft, was still serving in 1800. We have no precise figures for the medical department's casualties for the totality of the Caribbean campaigns but the desperate state of affairs is revealed in contemporary medical reports. Inspector General of Hospitals Thomas Young struggled to obtain enough hospital mates (the most junior of the medical staff) to attend the hospitals on St Lucia in 1795, '...from the dreadful sickness and mortality that prevails there...it is with difficulty I can get any to go there – the C.O's are constantly asking for assistance: within the last twenty-four hours hospital mates Hall, Currie, Culpepper and McCauley are reported to be dead'. The surviving medical men were crushed by the burden of work. An apothecary in Saint Domingue in 1796 complained that the sick 'were in want of medical help' and that, in addition to his normal duties pertaining to the delivery of medicines, he was in medical charge of a hospital and the 56th and 67th Regiments.

We have fleeting glimpses of these doctors in soldiers' memoirs. Most of the references are complimentary. Thomas Phipps Howard applauds his regimental surgeon.

> We were here infinitely Obliged to the Humanity of Dr. [Alexander] Baillie, our Surgeon, who tho' ill himself & suffering every Deprivation with the rest of the Army, exerted himself in the relief of the Unfortunate Men by bleeding and other Remedies...

In similar vein, Lieutenant Henry Sherwood, struck down with yellow fever on Martinique in 1800, expressed his gratitude to his regimental surgeon who removed him to his own quarters and treated him with great kindness. 'He gave up his own bed for me for I had no bed of my own having always used a hammock.' Andrew Bryson had a more mixed experience; his regimental surgeon, Robert Salmon, was competent but the assistant surgeon, Samuel Cathcart, was a drunkard who 'could not keep from tumbling over the beds' when he entered the hospital.

Even the most sober medical officers had little real understanding of the diseases which affected their patients. The wars pre-dated by a full century the emergence of the science of microbiology with its insights into micro-organisms and the role of vectors such as mosquitoes. Most doctors believed that the majority of diseases were caused by 'miasma' or 'miasmata', invisible poisons in the air exuded from rotting animal and vegetable material, the soil and standing water. This theory was popular in the West Indies and was propagated by influential medical men including Robert Jackson.

> ...the physicians of every age do not entertain a doubt that fevers of the intermittent and remitting kind owe their origin to exhalations from swampy and moist grounds. Daily experience still proves it: and there are few men whose observations are so circumscribed, as not to know, that it is in the neighbourhood of swamps, and near the banks of fresh water rivers, that those disorders chiefly prevail.

Jackson's colleague, Colin Chisholm, held similar views, attributing the genesis of fevers to 'various combinations of gaseous productions of animal and vegetable substances in a putrescent state'. These intelligent men thought that the cause of the bewildering array of fevers that afflicted the army was to be found in 'the spoil of dunghills and the putrid thaw'. The soldiers were not inhaling pure air but 'a nauseous mass of all obscene, corrupt offensive things...' There were discordant voices. Indeed much of the medical debate was bad-tempered although there was no repeat of the duel fought in Jamaica in 1750 where the physicians John Williams and Parker Bennet slew each other following a dispute regarding the nature of yellow fever. Some army doctors proposed the 'contagion theory' where disease was somehow passed from person to person. Among the 'contagionists' was Thomas Dickson Reide, Surgeon to the 1st Foot Regiment who warned of the dangers of rejecting the new theory in his treatise on the diseases of the army published in 1793.

An opinion has lately gone forth into the world, that fevers are not contagious in warm climates; an opinion which, if believed, will be of the most dangerous consequences, not only to individuals but to Nature at large; for if a fever or dysentery break out among troops in barracks or on board His Majesty's ships, the idea of them not being contagious will throw inexperienced practitioners off their guard and a dreadful mortality will ensue.

The more astute army medical officers strained to better understand the fevers of the region and Chisholm performed experiments on Martinique in 1809. 'The air which was emitted from the bottom of the pool by stirring with a stick, deflagrated upon the approach of a torch, and appeared to be hydrogene in combination with carbonic gas.' He also performed post-mortems. Jackson admitted that he had no understanding of the nature of the 'effluvia' which were supposed to cause disease and Hector McLean conceded that fevers were the result of 'unknown powers'. It was tempting to fill this hiatus with fanciful theories, Jackson surprisingly invoking the full moon as a factor in some types of fever.[6]

This ignorance did not prevent the doctors of the West Indian army making cogent suggestions for the prevention of disease. Jackson and others advocated numerous reforms which, if they had been fully instituted, would undoubtedly have reduced the mortality among the troops. Some of these initiatives have been previously discussed and they will be only briefly recapitulated here. Jackson stressed the importance of relatively simple changes to the soldiers' lifestyle and accoutrements. They should eat in messes and their diets should be closely monitored by their officers, who were to impose penalties for 'transgressions'. Daily exercise, Jackson believed, was essential but it was 'an object very little attended to in the British Army'. He proposed changes to the kit for West Indian service whilst admitting that it was a difficult task to persuade the men to set aside a uniform which 'adds so much to the brilliancy of appearance'.

The timing of arrival in the Caribbean, the nature of the transfer from home, and the location of camps were all subjects which featured prominently in contemporary medical texts. Benjamin Moseley emphasises that an army must arrive in the region and commence active operations in the coolest months of December to March. Hector McLean, whose writings focus on Saint Domingue, advocates a period of 'seasoning' in the warm but healthy climate of Gibraltar before departing for the Tropics. Like Jackson, he stresses the importance of discipline, exercise and assiduous personal hygiene. All agree that the worst ravages of disease could be avoided if it were possible to station troops in the hills and mountains. Physician William Fergusson admits that this outpouring of well-intentioned advice was invariably not heeded.

> In the West Indies, I found medical opinion equally at a discount. The convenience of the Engineer, the whim of the Quarter-Master-General, or General commanding, and the profit of the contractor, seemed alone ever to be consulted. There was not a station in the command where the health of the troops seemed ever to have been thought of, or a health opinion called for.[7]

The sick troops benefitted little from the treatments they received. The misunderstanding of the nature of disease led to a reliance on 'antiphlogistic' regimens in which patients were purged, made to vomit, bled, doused with cold water and subjected to other indignities only likely to render them more miserable and shorten their lives. The following account of the management of fever cases in the West Indies in 1801 was written by a hospital mate.

> The men on admission were conducted to a wash house containing warm and cold baths. They were instantly bled to the quantity from 16 to 20 ounces. They were, on revival from fainting, which generally occurred, plunged into a warm bath in numbers of four to six together and confined in by blankets fastened over the machine till about suffocated. From here they were dashed into cold baths and confined until appearing lifeless. Immediately after, a strong emetic was administered, they were carried to bed, and a dose of 8 grains of calomel and 6 grains of James's powder given as a purge, which occasioned a train of distressing symptoms for the relief of which they were bled again and blistered from head to foot. They were bled a fourth and fifth time in the space of thirty hours, and usually lost 60 to 70 ounces of blood.

Most of the drugs were useless or harmful. A notable exception was Peruvian bark, the cinchona from which quinine was later to be extracted. Quinine remains an important drug in the treatment of malaria. Its efficacy in the West Indian campaigns very likely depended on its quality and the amount administered. George Pinckard relates an episode where he purchased the drug from a local doctor; 'His bark, he assured us, was 'of the best', for he had plenty of the 'Cort Peruv. *optimum*...'[8]

The hospitals were broadly of two types, regimental and general. The smaller regimental facilities were not much employed in the early years of the conflict. Robert Jackson was a great supporter of the regimental hospital system and when he arrived in Saint Domingue in 1796 he made efforts to extend its use. He was convinced that sick men would be better treated by their own regimental surgeons and that there would be less opportunity for malingering. The Medical Board was lukewarm in its support but Jackson made a success of the enterprise, changing the supply system so that the sick were fed with fresh food and there was an annual saving of £80,000. He had unequivocal support from at least some of the army's officers, Henry Clinton writing to his brother describing the doctor in glowing terms. There are relatively few allusions to regimental hospitals in soldiers' accounts; Andrew Bryson was variably admitted to general and regimental hospitals during his illness.

Despite Jackson's initiative, the major provision for sick men remained the large static 'garrison' or 'general' hospitals. These were opened throughout the wars on the islands held by the British. In 1796, there were eleven general hospitals with a total of 83 medical staff officers. The largest was on Martinique where there were 16 medical officers and the other sizeable institutions were on Barbados, St Lucia, Grenada and St Vincent. Scattered over 600 miles, these hospitals were administered by four assistant inspectors who were also expected to help out on the wards as physicians or surgeons.

We have only occasional glimpses of the routine of the general hospitals in the diaries and journals of the wars. Andrew Bryson informs us that when he was admitted to the hospital on Martinique he was put into a room of 24 beds, all of which were full. He survived his stay but not all were so fortunate; 'About 10 O Clock 2 men in the next beds died, which shocked me Very much, as one of them was in a Brain fever and was obliged to be tyed'. Bryson was informed by the surgeon that 'one man is as Good as another the moment they enter the Gates of the Hospital' but this was not true. Officers received preferential or at least separate treatment. When Captain Thomas Henry Browne was wounded on Martinique in 1809 he was first admitted to the general hospital converted from the house of a sugar plantation. He occupied a small room with four fellow officers, the men lying on Indian corn and dried plantation leaves and covered by blankets. When an officer of the 4th West India Regiment was admitted with a wound there was no space for another bed and Browne shared his.

The general hospitals were under constant strain and it was difficult for the medical staff to maintain high standards. Some buildings were of wholly unsuitable construction and inappropriately sited. The following extract relates to the naval hospital on Antigua in 1809 but it could equally apply to one the army's general hospitals. The institution was apparently well placed in an elevated position but the sanitation arrangements were primitive.

> The necessary [toilet] is situated to the westward of the hospital, and not above fourteen paces distant from it. Here, everything execrementitious has been, and is presently deposited, and allowed to rot immediately under the walls of the hospital...When the wind blows from the westward, or during the existence of calms, the hospital is completely charged with stench and pestilential exhalation. Here is an evident and fertile source of injury to those sent to this hospital for the cure of disease...

In Port au Prince, the packed wards of the general hospital were hot and stinking and the motionless patients afflicted by a 'low, muttering, grim, melancholy'. To add to this nightmarish scene, men delirious with yellow fever were liable to leap out of the windows. The eighty patients on each ward were the responsibility of a single doctor.

Soldiers feared the hospitals even more than disease itself. Bryson believed the hospital on Martinique to be 'loathsome' and most of his comrades would have agreed with him. In Demerara in 1796, George Pinckard tried to persuade a sick grenadier to attend the general hospital.

> He instantly expressed great alarm, and said, '*I am not ill: if you take me to the hospital, I shall catch the fever and die*.' – On my stating the impropriety of his remaining among the well men, and not using the proper means of recovery, he replied '*I am not sick, and only want an appetite to be quite well*', and when I urged him further to go into the hospital, he answered with quickness, '*Indeed I am not bad, and if I was, I would rather stab myself at once, than go where so many are dying every day of yellow fever*'.

Some attempts were made to compensate for the lack of suitable hospital buildings. Pinckard describes temporary hospital accommodation being brought ashore at Carlisle Bay in 1797. The wooden frames were reassembled by the Corps of Artificers and local workmen. Other strategies to cope with the overspill of sick soldiers included the employment of hospital ships, tents and convalescent facilities. Clinton approvingly notes that Jackson moved more than 200 debilitated men to a convalescent hospital in Jamaica. Often these measures have the air of desperation. Thomas Phipps Howard says that the mortality in Saint Domingue was at such a level that 'any Stable or Barn that would contain a quantity of Beds was obliged to be converted in [to] a Sick House'. At the height of the epidemics of yellow fever and malaria, the general hospitals were overwhelmed and many sick were housed in the regimental hospitals or outside the hospital system. A return for the Windward and Leeward Islands for the period April to October 1796 reveals that there were a total of 14,902 soldiers 'sick in hospital' and 10,058 'sick in quarters'. In the unhealthiest months the figures for the two are almost equal.[9]

The sick soldier in hospital needed not only a competent army doctor but also good quality nursing care. Unfortunately, these duties usually ended up in the hands of a few 'hospital orderlies' or 'assistants', non-combatants from the regiments. There were probably some good orderlies but, judging from soldiers' accounts, most appear to have been dredged from the army's disaffected elements. They treated their patients with disdain and fought over their belongings when they died. The sick were often left to cope as best they could. Harry Ross-Lewin was admitted to a general hospital in Saint Domingue in 1796.

The number of the hospital assistants was now reduced to the ratio of one to a hundred patients; when at least ten times as many were necessary; the consequences of this alteration to the sick were deplorable – the poor fellows, being unable to fan away the flies themselves, and having no proper attendance, died with their mouths full of them, and frequently, as their heads were shaved, they were covered with such swarms that the skin was completely hid.

One of the few initiatives taken to tackle this deficiency took place on Grenada at the end of 1795. The so-called 'Royal Hospital Corps' was established with the object that orderlies would be formally supplied to the hospitals from this organisation rather than haphazardly from the regiments. It was well organised with a command structure and a hundred men to do the ward duties but it only survived six months, probably decimated by infectious disease. William Fergusson gives an account of a similar body but he places it in Saint Domingue. It failed to solve the problem of low-quality orderlies.

Had they a man amongst them whom they were tired of flogging, and who could neither be induced to die or to desert, he was the elect for the hospital corps, or at best he might be a simpleton, not fit to stand sentry in a position of trust, or so awkward in the ranks that he could not be trusted with ball-cartridge. In short, such a collection of incorrigible and incapable villains I believe never was brought together; and it was a true relief to the army when their drunkenness and the yellow fever killed them off.

There are also references to a hospital corps on Martinique in 1797 so it may be that the idea was resurrected on other islands but we must assume that the outcome was much the same.

Sick soldiers sought sympathetic nursing wherever they could. Captain Lasalle de Louisenthal, suffering from yellow fever on Martinique in 1796, was fortunate to be cared for by the young wife of the regimental surgeon. 'Day and night, she sat next to my bed, calming me, giving me courage, and, gradually, things improved.' No doubt other army women made similar contributions but most sick men turned to the locals. Doctors and soldiers testify that these women were often superb nurses and that they saved many European lives. On no other subject related to the West Indian campaigns is there such unanimity in the eyewitness accounts. William Fergusson, whose writing is often sceptical, is unstinting in his praise.

> In the colonies, the colonial women of every class, whether blacks, mulattoes, or mustees [of mixed ancestry], make the best sick nurses in the world. Nothing can exceed their vigilance and tenderness. They also delight in the office far beyond European women of any class...

This opinion was based on personal experience, the doctor having contracted yellow fever whilst in residence at Port au Prince.

> I had no sooner taken possession of the sick quarter assigned to me, than two respectable-looking females of that class [local women], of matronly age, came to pay me a visit. They told me, for my comfort, that nine others had died in the very corner of the room where I was then lying – that the English doctors had killed them all, they killed every one, and certainly would me, if I took their physic, which I was never to do, but when any was left for me, to send for them; that they knew many herbs, and could prepare from them drinks (ptisans) of sovereign virtue. This to me, myself a mediciner, was very amusing and when my servant, in the course of the afternoon, brought in some new-baked bread, I, with his help, prepared a set of bread pills, and then sent to my new friends, to say that the English doctors had been with me and left their medicines. They came immediately. The pills were produced, which they crumbled down between their fingers, smelled them well, and bit, but very cautiously, with their teeth, and then declaring that they were the identical poison that had destroyed so many people, threw them with great indignation out of the window. They soon discovered who I was,

but so far from resenting the trick I had played upon them, they were unwearied in kindness, and I was much beholden to their Creole kitchen for many comforts during a long and difficult convalescence.

It is likely that by intercepting the army doctors' remedies the nurses did more good than harm. Others testify equally strongly to the crucial role played by such women. Thomas Phipps Howard was tended by local nurses on two occasions and was impressed that they demanded neither fee nor reward. Their comportment, he believed, would have made them 'an Honour to the most Civilised Society'. Norbert Landsheit, also in Saint Domingue, attributed his gradual recovery from fever to a black nurse, who looked after him with extreme kindness. 'She carried me about in her arms like an infant – she watched beside my bed day and night, and brought me through.' French soldiers fighting in the colony relate near-identical experiences. Sergeant-Major Philippe Beaudoin describes a young mulatto woman who assured him that his only hope of recovery from illness was to entrust his case to her. She was as good as her word. Unsurprisingly, such close liaisons led to romantic attachments. When Beaudoin was evacuated from Môle St Nicolas he tried to smuggle his Sophie on board dressed as a man and was devastated when she was discovered and sent back.[10]

When a soldier died there was a need to sort out his affairs and inform his family. The latter unpleasant duty generally fell to a senior officer of the regiment. Lieutenant Edward Teasdale's letters home from Jamaica stop in September 1808; the final letter in the file in the archive of the National Army Museum is in the hand of Major Robert Frederick, addressed to the soldier's mother and dated 19 November 1808.

> ... most truly do I console with you Madame on the loss of this admirable young man but it must be a great consolation to you to know that in the Circle in which he moved he was most highly respected and most deservedly beloved. His remains were interred with military honours, he was regretted by all, but by those who knew him his loss was most severely felt.

Another National Army Museum file details the arrangements which followed the death of Major George Tinling of the 38th Regiment on Martinique in 1797. He had been attached to the Royal Hospital Corps and, like Edward Teasdale, he very likely died of yellow fever. The responsibility for the disposal of his belongings was given to James Thornton of the 17th Dragoons, also seconded to the hospital corps. Thornton wrote to the dead officer's family from St Pierre.

> I should be glad to know what furniture and effects were in his house, as the keys were left in charge of the Woman whom he lived in the house

with: when I went into the room I saw two trunks and a small box, his sword and sash, the Books of the Royal Hospital Corps, the pattern of a scarlet coat, a quantity of shoes and boots, a Bed, Bedstead and Coverlid, with some Tables and Chairs, the latter articles the Woman of the house claimed. There is also a fine Parrot and Cage.

Similar letters must have been written innumerable times and funerals became part of the routine of the West Indian garrison. Henry Ross-Lewin describes the burial arrangements in Saint Domingue in 1797.

... the officer of the guard had orders to attend all internments, and see that three shovelfuls of quicklime were thrown into each grave. As the hospital-carts, each carrying three bodies, arrived almost without intermission during the day, this was both a sad and wearisome duty.

During the French campaigns in the colony the mortality was so great that the living and the dead became intermingled. Historian Antoine Métral claims that as it was necessary to remove the dying from the hospitals before they had actually expired it was not uncommon for soldiers to be thrown into graves still alive.

...in the bottom of the graves, they heard on several occasions, plaintive cries, muffled and pathetic. It was even said that some soldiers escaped from the piles of dead, reappearing among the living...

British graves were mostly respected; the alleged desecration of General Thomas Dundas's Guadeloupe grave by Victor Hugues, if it occurred, was exceptional. When Thomas Henry Browne walked through the churchyards of Barbados in December 1808 he found them already full of the resting places of British officers of all ranks who had fallen victim to disease. The battle honours 'Martinique' and 'Guadeloupe' emblazoned on regimental colours revive fading memories of the Caribbean campaigns of the Revolutionary and Napoleonic Wars. Perhaps the truest memorials of the British soldier who lived and fought in the West Indies are these inscribed gravestones, many still standing today.[11]

Notes

Chapter 1

1. Houlding, J.A., *Fit for Service*, pp. 3–4, 395; Buckley, R.N., *The British Army in the West Indies*, pp. 49–50, 56; Brumwell, S.B., *Redcoats. The British Soldier and War in the Americas 1755–1763*, pp. 69, 72.

2. Knight, R., *Britain against Napoleon*, pp. 77, 439–40; Duffy, M., *Soldiers, Sugar and Seapower*, pp. 195–6, 295; Houlding, pp. 12–13, 322; Mackesy, P., *British Victory in Egypt 1801*, p. 3; Steppler, G.A., *The British Army on the Eve of War*, p. 4.

3. Steppler, pp. 5–15; Mackesy, pp. 28–9, 35–7; Houlding, pp. 99–1, 115; Gates, D., *The British Light Infantry Arm c. 1790–1815*, pp. 49–50.

4. Houlding, pp. 13, 117, 125–6, 132; Buckley, *The British Army in the West Indies*, pp. 92–7; Duffy, *Soldiers, Sugar and Seapower*, pp. 170–1; Buckley, R.N., *Slaves in Redcoats*, p. 3; Coss, E.J., *All For The King's Shilling*, pp. 50–85; Haythornthwaite, P.J., *The Armies of Wellington*, p. 47; Durey, M., *Whites Slaves: Irish Rebel Prisoners and the British Army in the West Indies 1799–1804*, pp. 296–312.

5. Chartrand, R., *British Forces in the West Indies 1793–1815*, p. 3; Duffy, M., *The Caribbean Campaigns of the British Army 1793–1801*, pp. 23, 28; Buckley, *The British Army in the West Indies*, pp. 85–8; Bamford, A., *Sickness, Suffering and the Sword*, pp. 41–2; *Facts Relative to the Conduct of the War in the West Indies*, p. 65; Fortescue, J.W., *A History of the British Army*, Vol. IV (1), pp. 446–91; Duffy, *Soldiers, Sugar and Seapower*, pp. 144, 153–4, 231–2; Geggus, D., *Slavery, War and Revolution*, pp. 225, 275; Moore, J., *The Diary of Sir John Moore*, Vol. I, pp. 203–13; Gates, pp. 42–3.

6. Fortescue, Vol. IV (2), p. 896, Vol. VII, p. 1; Bamford, pp. 42–3; Buckley, *The British Army in the West Indies*, pp. 108–16; Howard, T.P., *The Haitian Journal of Lieutenant Howard*, pp. xl–l; Knight, pp. 78, 440; Chartrand, pp. 9–24; Haythornthwaite, p. 146; Duffy, *Soldiers, Sugar and Seapower*, pp. 175–6, 229–30, 281–9, 244; Lasalle de Louisenthal, *Adventures de guerre aux Antilles*, pp. 12–20, 26, 46; Landsheit, N., *The Hussar*, Vol. I, pp. 52–6.

7. Buckley, *Slaves in Redcoats*, pp. 5–6; Geggus, pp. 130, 317–8; Chartrand, pp. 16–17; Gates, pp. 68–9; Ellis, A.B., *The History of the First West India Regiment*, p. 55.

8. Buckley, *Slaves in Redcoats*, pp. 12–21, 33–8; Ellis, pp. 71–2; Nugent, M., *Lady Nugent's Journal of her residence in Jamaica*, p. xxiv; Geggus, p. 315; Duffy, *Soldiers, Sugar and Seapower*, p. 363.

9. Buckley, *Slaves in Redcoats*, pp. 24–36, 54–7, 65–6, 70, 79, 83–94, 113–18; Chartrand, pp. 4, 18; MacArthur, R., *The British Army Establishment during the Napoleonic Wars*, pp. 158, 164; Ellis, pp. 59, 72, 82, 92; Geggus, pp. 316–7; Pinckard, G., *Notes on the West Indies*, Vol. I, pp. 382–3; Moore, Vol. I, p. 240; Dyott, W., *Dyott's Diary 1781–1845*, Vol. I, p. 94; Browne, T.H., *The Napoleonic War Journal of Captain Thomas Henry Browne*, pp. 94–5.

10. Chartrand, pp. 35–42; Nugent, pp. xxvii–xxviii; Carmichael, NAM 1988–06–30; Buckley, *Slaves in Redcoats*, p. 7; Geggus, p. 110; Balcarres, *Lives of the Lindsays*, Vol.III, pp. 79, 92; Ellis, p. 79.

11. Chartrand, pp. 10–13; Geggus, pp. 116, 165–7, 174, 185, 217, 221; Howard, pp. 68, 133; Dyott, Vol. I, p. 114.

Chapter 2

1. Lynn, J.A., *The Bayonets of the Republic*, pp. 43–8, 60–1; Elting, J.R., *Swords around a Throne*, pp. 29–34; Chartrand, R., *Napoleon's Overseas Army*, pp. 8–11, 23–4; Poyen, H., *Les Guerres des Antilles de 1793 à 1815*, pp. 39, 46, 206, 230, 298, 339–40, 353, 378; Boyer-Peyreleau, E.E., *Les Antilles Françaises particulièrement la Guadeloupe*, pp. 227–8, 239, 246; Arvers, P., *Historique de 82e regiment d'infanterie de ligne*, pp. 77–95.
2. Chartrand, pp. 6–10, 20–33, 41; Poyen, pp. 46, 345, 357–8.
3. Duffy, M., *Soldiers, Sugar and Seapower*, pp. 119–20; Poyen, pp. 143, 144, 152; Chartrand, pp. 8–9; Willyams, C., *An Account of the Campaign in the West Indies in the year 1794*, appendix, p. 2; Ross-Lewin, H., *With the Thirty-Second in the Peninsula and Other Campaigns*, p. 23; Moore, J., *The Diary of Sir John Moore*, Vol. I, p. 205.
4. Chartrand, pp. 12–13, 16–17; Geggus, D., *Slavery, War and Revolution*, pp. 116, 131–2, 287–8, 318; Rainsford, M., *An Historical Account of the Black Empire of Hayti*, pp. 217–8, 255, 283; Ros, M., *Night of Fire*, pp. 38–40, 56, 95–7; Chalmers, C., *Remarks on the Late War in St Domingo*, pp. 61–5; Howard, T.P., *The Haitian Journal of Lieutenant Howard*, pp. 134–5; Lemonnier-Delafosse, M., *Seconde Campagne de Saint Domingue*, pp. 34–5.
5. Ros, pp. 105–6; Geggus, pp. 120, 124, 196, 264, 289, 330.
6. Schofield, V., *The Highland Furies*, pp. 193–4; Moreau de Jonnès, A., *Adventures in Wars of the Republic and Consulate*, pp. 120, 140–3.
7. Balcarres, *Lives of the Lindsays*, Vol. III, pp. 3–6; Fortescue, J.W., *A History of the British Army*, Vol. IV (1), pp. 459–60; Robinson, C., *The Fighting Maroons of Jamaica*, pp. 66–8; Dallas, R.C., *The History of the Maroons*, Vol. I, pp. 35–43.
8. Dyott, W., *Dyott's Diary 1781–1845*, Vol. I, pp. 104, 119, 124; Moore, Vol. I, pp. 234–5.
9. Chartrand, p. 38; *The London Gazette*, June 1804, 15712, p. 759; Duffy, pp. 278–89, 322–5; *Bulletins of the Campaign 1797*, pp. 49–50.

Chapter 3

1. Buckley, R.N., *The British Army in the West Indies*, p. 5; Duffy, M., *Soldiers, Sugar and Seapower*, pp. 5–27; Brumwell, S.B., *Redcoats. The British Soldier and War in the Americas 1755–1763*, pp. 31–2, 309; Duffy, M., *The Caribbean Campaigns of the British Army 1793–1801*, pp. 23–4; James, W.M., *The Naval History of Great Britain*, Vol. I, p. 112; Geggus, D., *Slavery, War and Revolution*, pp. 1–2, 34–64, 86–7; Fortescue, J. W., *A History of the British Army*, Vol. IV (1), pp. 75–9; Ros, M., *Night of Fire*, pp. 2, 5–8, 27–8, 43–7; Gasper, D.B., *A Turbulent Time*, pp. 78–84.
2. *Bulletins of the Campaign 1793*, pp. 30–42; Laurence, K.O., *Tobago in Wartime 1793–1815*, pp. 7–8; Fortescue, Vol. IV (1) p. 134; Duffy, *Soldiers, Sugar and Seapower*, pp. 31–5; Poyen, H., *Les Guerres des Antilles de 1793 à 1815*, pp. 18–19; James, Vol. I, pp. 114–15.
3. *Bulletins of the Campaign 1793*, pp. 95–8; Duffy, *Soldiers, Sugar and Seapower*, pp. 35–7; James, Vol. I, pp. 115–16; Poyen, pp. 21–8; Ellis, A.B., *The History of the First West India Regiment*, pp. 39–40; Fortescue, Vol. IV (1), pp. 134–5.
4. Fortescue, Vol. IV (1), pp. 327–9; Ros, pp. 12–13; Rainsford, M., *An Historical Account of the Black Empire of Hayti*, pp. 169–71; Geggus, pp. 65–8, 78–9, 101–4, 228–9; McLean, H., *An Enquiry into the Nature and Causes of the Great Mortality*, pp. 9–13, 215–23.
5. *Bulletins of the Campaign 1793*, pp. 224–39; Rainsford, pp. 172–4; Geggus, pp. 65, 105–8; James, Vol. I, pp. 116–17; Fortescue, Vol. IV (1), pp. 330–2.
6. Geggus, pp. 109–11; Duffy, *Soldiers, Sugar and Seapower*, pp. 97–8; Fortescue, Vol. IV (1), pp. 332–4; James, Vol. I, p. 118.
7. Geggus, pp. 111–13; Fortescue, Vol. IV (1), p. 334; Duffy, *Soldiers, Sugar and Seapower*, p. 98.

8. Geggus, pp. 112–13; *Bulletins of the Campaign 1794*, pp. 92–4, 112–15; Rainsford, pp. 175–9; James, Vol. I, pp. 225–6; Fortescue, Vol. IV (1), pp. 334–7.

9. Rainsford, pp. 182–3; Geggus, p. 113; Fortescue, Vol. IV (1), pp. 337–8.

10. Rainsford, pp. 179–82; Geggus, pp. 113–14; Fortescue, Vol. IV (1), p. 338.

11. *Bulletins of the Campaign 1794*, pp. 266–80; Duffy, *Soldiers, Sugar and Seapower*, pp. 101–4; Rainsford, pp. 184–90; Fortescue, Vol. IV (1), pp. 339–41; Geggus, p. 114; James, Vol. I, pp. 226–7.

12. Geggus, pp. 116–18; Fortescue, Vol. IV (1), pp. 342–3.

13. Geggus, pp. 118–24; Duffy, *Soldiers, Sugar and Seapower*, pp. 103–4; Fortescue, Vol. IV (1), pp. 340–1.

14. *Bulletins of the Campaign 1794*, p. 375; Geggus, pp. 128–9; Fortescue, Vol. IV (1), pp. 344–5; Rainsford, pp. 194–5.

15. Geggus, pp. 129–32, 151,

16. Fortescue, Vol. IV (1), pp. 345–6 Rainsford, p. 193; Geggus, p. 152.

17. Rainsford, pp. 195–6; Fortescue, Vol. IV (1), pp. 346–7; James, Vol. I, p. 227; Geggus, pp. 153–4.

18. Geggus, pp. 154–5; Fortescue, Vol. IV (1), pp. 347–9.

Chapter 4

1. Duffy, M., *Soldiers, Sugar and Seapower*, pp. 41–58; Nelson, P.D., *Sir Charles Grey, First Earl Grey*, pp. 136–40; Fortescue, J.W., *A History of the British Army*, Vol. IV (1), pp. 350–3.

2. Fortescue, Vol. IV (1), pp. 351–2; Duffy, pp. 59–61; Nelson, p. 141; Willyams, C., *An Account of the Campaign in the West Indies in the Year 1794*, pp. 9–10.

3. *Bulletins of the Campaign 1794*, pp. 97–8; Duffy, pp. 67–72; Poyen, H., *Les Guerres des Antilles de 1793 à 1815*, pp. 31, 39–40; Nelson, pp. 142–3; Pearse, H.W., *History of the East Surrey Regiment*, p. 275, Ellis, A.B., *The History of the First West India Regiment*, p. 41; Fortescue, Vol. IV (1), pp. 353–4; Willyams, pp. 16–17; James, W.M., *The Naval History of Great Britain*, Vol. I, p. 216.

4. *Bulletins of the Campaign 1794*, pp. 99–101; Duffy, pp. 73–6; Pearse, p. 281; James, *The Naval History of Great Britain*, Vol. I, pp. 216–17; Willyams, pp. 26–8; Fortescue, Vol. IV (1), pp. 354–6; Poyen, p. 32; James, B., *Journal of Rear-Admiral Bartholomew James 1752–1828*, pp. 229–30.

5. *Bulletins of the Campaign 1794*, p. 101; Duffy, p. 75; Fortescue, Vol. IV (1), p. 356; *Cumloden Papers*, p. 4.

6. *Bulletins of the Campaign 1794*, pp. 98–103; Fortescue, Vol. IV (1), pp. 356–9; Poyen, pp. 33–4; Duffy, pp. 74–5; Willyams, pp. 33–40.

7. *Bulletins of the Campaign 1794*, p. 103; Fortescue, Vol. IV (1), p. 359; Duffy, p. 77; Willyams, pp. 41–2; Poyen, pp. 34–5.

8. *Bulletins of the Campaign 1794*, pp. 103–5; Fortescue, Vol. IV (1), pp. 359–60; Duffy, pp. 77–80; James, *Journal of Rear-Admiral Bartholomew James*, pp. 232–3; Willyams, pp. 49–51; Poyen, p. 35.

9. Duffy, pp. 80–8; *Bulletins of the Campaigns 1794*, pp. 104–18; Fortescue, Vol. IV (1), pp. 360–2; Willyams, pp. 52–70; James, *Journal of Rear-Admiral Bartholomew James*, pp. 237–40; Poyen, pp. 35–54; Pearse, pp. 285–6; James, *The Naval History of Great Britain*, Vol. I, pp. 217–20.

10. Fortescue, Vol. IV (1), p. 362; *Bulletins of the Campaign 1794*, pp. 106–8, 125; Duffy, p. 88.

11. *Bulletins of the Campaign 1794*, pp. 172–4; Poyen, pp. 58–9; Duffy, pp. 89–91; Willyams, p. 80; Abercromby, NAM 2001-01-611; Nelson, p. 148.

12. Ellis, p. 42; *Bulletins of the Campaign 1794*, p. 181; Duffy, pp. 93–4; Fortescue, Vol. IV

(1), p. 363; Nelson, p. 149; James, *The Naval History of Great Britain*, Vol. I, p. 221.

13. *Bulletins of the Campaign 1794*, pp. 182–3; Fortescue, Vol. IV (1), p. 364; Willyams, p. 88; Duffy, p. 94.

14. *Bulletins of the Campaign 1794*, pp. 188–90; Poyen, pp. 66–8; Duffy, pp. 94–5; Fortescue, Vol. IV (1), p. 365.

15. *Bulletins of the Campaign 1794*, p. 191; Nelson, p. 150; Duffy, pp. 97–100, 114; Fortescue, Vol. IV (1), pp. 365–8.

16. Poyen, pp. 73–5; *Bulletins of the Campaign 1794*, pp. 316–22; Duffy, pp. 115–16; James, *The Naval History of Great Britain*, Vol. I, pp. 222–3.

17. Nelson, pp. 160–1; Fortescue, Vol. IV (1), pp. 370–1; Duffy, pp. 119–20; *Bulletins of the Campaign 1794*, p. 325.

18. *Bulletins of the Campaign 1794*, pp. 317, 331–3, 339–41; Nelson, p. 161; Fortescue, Vol. IV (1), pp. 371–2; Duffy, pp. 121–2; *Cumloden Papers*, pp. 11–13; Poyen, pp. 76–8; James, *The Naval History of Great Britain*, Vol. I, pp. 223–4.

19. *Bulletins of the Campaign 1794*, pp. 333–42; Duffy, pp. 122–6; Fortescue, Vol. IV (1), pp. 373–4; Poyen, pp. 78–9; *Cumloden Papers*, pp. 14–15; Pearse, p. 291; James, *Journal of Rear-Admiral Bartholomew James*, pp. 244–5; Nelson, pp. 162–3.

20. Fortescue, Vol. IV (1), pp. 374–8; Nelson, pp. 163–6; Duffy, pp. 129–31; Poyen, p. 81; James, *Journal of Rear-Admiral Bartholomew James*, p. 246, Willyams, p. 133.

21. Poyen, pp. 81–2; James, *The Naval History of Great Britain*, Vol. I, p. 224; Duffy, p. 131; Fortescue, Vol. IV (1), pp. 379–80; Willyams, p. 134.

22. Poyen, pp. 82–3; Fortescue, Vol. IV (1), pp. 380–1; Nelson, p. 166; Duffy, pp. 131–2; Willyams, pp. 136–8; *Bulletins of the Campaign 1794*, pp. 382–3.

23. *Bulletins of the Campaign 1795*, pp. 31–7; Duffy, pp. 132–3; Poyen, pp. 85–6; Fortescue, Vol. IV (1), pp. 381–2; James, *Journal of Rear-Admiral Bartholomew James*, pp. 250–66; James, *The Naval History of Great Britain*, Vol. I, p. 225; Nelson, p. 167.

24. Nelson, pp. 168–9; Willyams, pp. 58–9; Fortescue, Vol. IV (1), pp. 383–5; Duffy, pp. 134–5.

Chapter 5
1. Duffy, M., *Soldiers, Sugar and Seapower*, pp. 136–41; Fortescue, J.W., *A History of the British Army*, Vol. IV (1), pp. 424–5.

2. Poyen, H., *Les Guerres des Antilles de 1793 à 1815*, pp. 88–90; Fortescue, Vol. IV (1), pp. 425–7; Duffy, pp. 141–2.

3. Turnbull, G., *A Narrative of the Revolt and Insurrection of the French Inhabitants in the Island of Grenada*, pp. 9–70; Fortescue, Vol. IV (1), pp. 425–30; Duffy, pp. 142–3.

4. Turnbull, pp. 71–80; *Bulletins of the Campaign 1795*, p. 88; *A Collection of State Papers Relative to the War against France*, appendix, p. 61; Fortescue, Vol. IV (1), pp. 427–30.

5. Moreau de Jonnès, A., *Adventures in the Wars of the Republic and Consulate*, pp. 120–1, 140–3; Duffy, p. 142; *Bulletins of the Campaign 1795*, p. 89; Fortescue, Vol. IV (1), pp. 429–30.

6. Fortescue, Vol. IV (1), pp. 430–3; Duffy, pp. 139, 144–5.

7. *Bulletins of the Campaign 1795*, pp. 89–90, 97–9, 101–2; Ellis, A.B., *The History of the First West India Regiment*, pp. 46–7; Poyen, pp. 90–1; Fortescue, Vol. IV (1), pp. 434–6.

8. *Bulletins of the Campaign 1795*, pp. 109–10, 116; Poyen, pp. 92–3; Duffy, p. 145; Fortescue, Vol. IV (1), pp. 436–7; Ellis, pp. 47–8.

9. Everard, H., *History of Thomas Farrington's Regiment*, p. 20; Turnbull, pp. 92–101; *A Collection of State Papers Relative to the War against France*, appendix, p. 63; *Bulletins of the Campaign 1795*, p. 96; Fortescue, Vol. IV (1), pp. 437–8.

10. Everard, pp. 201–5; Turnbull, pp. 111–20, 131–3, 152–9; Poyen, p. 97; *Bulletins of the Campaign 1796*, pp. 3–7; Fortescue, Vol. IV (1), pp. 438–40.

11. *Bulletins of the Campaign 1796*, p. 60; Fortescue, Vol. IV (1), pp. 440–1; Duffy, p. 153.
12. *A Collection of State Papers Relative to the War against France*, appendix, pp. 61–6; *Bulletins of the Campaign 1795*, pp. 100–1; Poyen, p. 95; Fortescue, Vol. IV (1), pp. 441–2.
13. Coke, T., *A History of the West Indies*, Vol. II, pp. 218–23; Ellis, pp. 49–52; *Bulletins of the Campaign 1795*, pp. 111–12; Fortescue, Vol. IV (1), p. 442.
14. Coke, Vol. II, pp. 224–7; Fortescue, Vol. IV (1), pp. 443–4; Ellis, p. 52.
15. Ellis, p. 52; Fortescue, Vol. IV (1), p. 444; Coke, Vol. II, p. 228.
16. Coke, Vol.II, pp. 229–32; Ellis, pp. 52–3; Fortescue, Vol. IV (1), pp. 445–6.
17. *Bulletins of the Campaign 1795*, pp. 156–60; *A Collection of State Papers Relative to the War against France*, appendix, p. 70; Ellis, pp. 53–4; Duffy, p. 153; Fortescue, Vol. IV (1), p. 446.
18. *Bulletins of the Campaign 1796*, pp. 35–9; *A Collection of Papers Relative to the War against France*, appendix, pp. 74–6; Fortescue, Vol. IV (1), pp. 447–8.
19. *Bulletins of the Campaign 1796*, pp. 36, 59–60; *A Collection of Papers Relative to the War against France*, appendix, pp. 75–6, 78; Fortescue, Vol. IV (1), pp. 448–9.
20. *Bulletins of the Campaign 1795*, pp. 110–11; Poyen, p. 99; Fortescue, Vol. IV (1), pp. 449–50; Duffy, p. 146.
21. Fortescue, Vol. IV (1), pp. 450–4; Duffy, p. 147; Poyen, pp. 101–3.
22. Balcarres, *Lives of the Lindsays*, Vol. III, pp. 24–44; Robinson, C., *The Fighting Maroons of Jamaica*, pp. 83–6; Geggus, D., *Slavery, War and Revolution*, p. 88; Duffy, pp. 149–51; Fortescue, Vol. IV (1), pp. 461–3.
23. Balcarres, Vol. III, pp. 45–78; Robinson, pp. 87–104; Duffy, pp. 150–1; Fortescue, Vol. IV (1), pp. 463–4; Dallas, R.C. *A History of the Maroons*, Vol. I, pp. 231–2.
24. Balcarres, Vol. III, pp. 88–144; *Bulletins of the Campaign 1796*, pp. 57–9; Robinson, pp. 104–54; Dallas, Vol. I, p. 235; Duffy, pp. 242–4, 259–60; Fortescue, Vol. IV (1), pp. 464–5; *A Collection of Papers Relative to the War against France*, appendix, pp. 76–81.
25. Fortescue, Vol. IV (1), pp. 457–9, 466; Geggus, pp. 154–6; Duffy, pp. 147–9.
26. Geggus, pp. 164–5; Fortescue, Vol. IV (1), pp. 466–7.
27. Geggus, pp. 176–7; Duffy, p. 241; Fortescue, Vol. IV (1), pp. 467–8.
28. Duffy, pp. 241–7; Geggus, pp. 184–6; Fortescue, Vol. IV (1), pp. 468–71.
29. *Bulletins of the Campaign 1796*, pp. 78–9; Spencer, G., *Private Papers of George, second Earl Spencer*, Vol. I, pp. 283–4; Fortescue, Vol. IV (1), pp. 471–2; Duffy, pp. 245–8; Geggus, pp. 193–6; James, W.M., *The Naval History of Great Britain*, Vol. I, p. 370.
30. Robinson, pp. 22–3; Duffy, pp. 248–50; Geggus, p. 198; Fortescue, Vol. IV (1), pp. 472–3; Rainsford, M., *An Historical Account of the Black Empire of Hayti*, p. 202; James, Vol. I, p. 370.
31. *Bulletins of the Campaign 1796*, pp. 319–24; Duffy, pp. 250–2; Geggus, pp. 198–204; Fortescue, Vol. IV (1), pp. 474–6.

Chapter 6

1. Geggus, D., *Slavery, War and Revolution*, pp. 188–9; Duffy, M., *Soldiers, Sugar and Seapower*, pp. 163–6, 199–219; Fortescue, J.W., *A History of the British Army*, Vol. IV (1), pp. 477–85; Moore, J., *The Diary of Sir John Moore*, Vol. I, p. 208; Mackesy, P., *British Victory in Egypt 1801*, pp. 6–12, 30–6, 239–41; Clinton, NAM 1999–08–100; Stewart, D., *Sketches of the Character, Manners and Present State of the Highlanders of Scotland*, pp. 410–12, 428; Richardson, W., *A Mariner of England*, pp. 123–8; *Facts Relative to the Conduct of the War in the West Indies*, pp. 144–5; Dillon, W.H., *A Narrative of my Professional Adventures (1790– 1839)*, p. 209; Dyott, W., *Dyott's Diary 1781– 1845*, Vol. I, pp. 82–4; Howard, T.P., *The Haitian Journal of Lieutenant Howard York Hussars 1796– 1798*, pp. 139–6; Knight, R., *Britain Against Napoleon*, p. 74.

2. *A Collection of State Papers Relative to the War against France*, appendix, pp. 78–81; Dyott, Vol. I, pp. 102–4; Poyen, H., *Les Guerres des Antilles de 1793 à 1815*, pp. 96–8; Fortescue, Vol. IV (1), pp. 483–4.

3. Duffy, pp. 220–1; James, W.M., *The Naval History of Great Britain*, Vol. I, p. 367; *Bulletins of the Campaign 1796*, pp. 91–7, 107–9; Pinckard, G., *Notes on the West Indies*, Vol. II, pp. 165–6.

4. Duffy pp. 223–5; *Bulletins of the Campaign 1796*, pp. 97–9; Fortescue, Vol. IV (1), pp. 486–7; Moore, Vol. I, pp. 197–200; Dillon, Vol. I, p. 231; Poyen, pp. 128, 132; Clinton, NAM 1999–08–100; Ellis, A.B., *The History of the First West India Regiment*, p. 60.

5. Moore, Vol. I, pp. 200–5; *Bulletins of the Campaign 1796*, pp. 97–100; Poyen, p. 130; Duffy, pp. 225–6; Fortescue, Vol. IV (1), pp. 487–9.

6. *Bulletins of the Campaign 1796*, pp. 100–3, 106–7; Moore, Vol. I, pp. 207–8; Duffy, pp. 226–8; Fortescue, Vol. I, 489–90; Poyen, p. 131; Lasalle de Louisenthal, *Aventures de guerre aux Antilles*, pp. 20–2.

7. *Bulletins of the Campaign 1796*, p. 126; Duffy, pp. 229–30; Fortescue, Vol. IV (1), pp. 490–1; Clinton, NAM 1999–08–100; Poyen, pp. 132–4.

8. *Bulletins of the Campaign 1796*, pp. 126–7; Poyen, pp. 136–7; Duffy, pp. 230–2; Moore, Vol. I, p. 213; Fortescue, Vol. IV (1), p. 491; Richardson, pp. 130–1; Dillon, Vol. I, pp. 233–4; Lasalle de Louisenthal, p. 24.

9. *Bulletins of the Campaign 1796*, pp. 127–35; Duffy, pp. 233–6; Poyen, pp. 139–42; Fortescue, Vol. IV (1), pp. 491–2; Gasper, D.B., *A Turbulent Time*, p. 111; Moore, Vol. I, pp. 215–21; Dillon, Vol. I, p. 238.

10. *Bulletins of the Campaign 1796*, pp. 174–81; *Bulletins of the Campaign 1797*, pp. 10–13; Duffy, pp. 237–8, 256–63; Taylor, C., *The Black Carib Wars*, pp. 139–41; Fortescue, Vol. IV (1), pp. 493, 544; Schofield, V., *The Highland Furies*, pp. 191–4; Moreau de Jonnès, A., *Adventures in Wars of the Republic and Consulate*, p. 169; James, Vol. I, pp. 369–70.

11. *Bulletins of the Campaign 1796*, pp. 181–9; *Bulletins of the Campaign 1797,* pp. 9–10; Fortescue, Vol. IV (1), pp. 494–5; Dyott, Vol. I, pp. 112–17; Duffy, pp. 238–9; James, Vol. I, pp. 369–70; Lasalle de Louisenthal, pp. 34–5.

12. Duffy, pp. 240, 266–74; Fortescue, Vol. I, pp. 495–6, 537–9.

13. *Bulletins of the Campaign 1797*, pp. 44–57; Duffy, pp. 274–83; Fortescue, Vol. IV (1), pp. 539–40; Brisbane, T.M., *Reminiscences of General Sir Thomas Makdougall Brisbane*, pp. 16–17; Wainwright, NAM 2007–10–15; Lasalle de Louisenthal, pp. 48–54.

14. *Bulletins of the Campaign 1797*, pp. 74–8; Duffy, pp. 283–91; Fortescue, Vol. IV (1), pp. 541–3; Brisbane, p. 17; Schofield, pp. 195–6; Moore, Vol. I, p. 252.

15. Geggus, pp. 208–9, 211, 215, 221; Fortescue, Vol. IV (1), pp. 545–7.

16. Geggus, pp. 221–3; Fortescue, Vol. IV (1), pp. 547–8.

17. *Bulletins of the Campaign 1797*, pp. 108–10; Chalmers, C., *Remarks on the Late War in St. Domingo*, pp. 59–60; Rainsford, M., *An Historical Account of the Black Empire of Hayti*,p. 205; Geggus, p. 223; Fortescue, Vol. IV (1), pp. 548–9.

18. *Bulletins of the Campaign 1797*, pp. 89–96, 110–11; Chalmers, pp. 55–63; Howard, pp. 91–5; Geggus, pp. 224–5; Fortescue, Vol. IV (1), p. 549.

19. Duffy, pp. 303–4; Geggus, pp. 225–6; Fortescue, Vol. IV (1), pp. 549–52.

20. Geggus, pp. 374–8; Fortescue, Vol. IV (1), pp. 553–5.

21. Geggus, pp. 376–7; Duffy, pp. 305–7; Fortescue, Vol. IV (1), pp. 555–6.

22. Geggus, p. 378; Duffy, p. 307; Fortescue, Vol. IV (1), pp. 556–7.

23. Geggus, pp. 378–87; Fortescue, Vol. IV (1), pp. 559–65; Duffy, pp. 308–10; *Cumloden Papers*, pp. 21–2; Howard, pp. 147–56; Chalmers, pp. 77–81.

24. Duffy, pp. 311–12, 314–18, 320–5; Poyen, pp. 202, 208–9; Buckley, R.N., *The British Army in the West Indies*, p. 258; Dillon, Vol. I, pp. 398–400.

25. Muir, R., *Britain and the Defeat of Napoleon 1807–1815*, pp. 3–4; Buckley, p. 259; Knight, pp. 215–16; Poyen, p. 261; Duffy, p. 325.

Chapter 7

1. Knight, R., *Britain Against Napoleon*, pp. 238, 259–60, 285; Buckley, R.N., *The British Army in the West Indies*, pp. 85–8, 259–62; Duffy, M., *Soldiers, Sugar and Seapower*, p. 389; Fortescue, J.W., *A History of the British Army*, Vol. V, pp. 181–2.
2. Poyen, H., *Les Guerres des Antilles de 1793 à 1815*, pp. 226–43, 260; Fortescue, Vol. V, pp. 176–80, Vol. VII, p. 6; Buckley, pp. 260–1; Lemonnier-Delafosse, M., *Seconde Campagne de Saint Domingue*, pp. 265–8.
3. *Sketches and Recollections of the West Indies by a Resident*, pp. 105–14; Buckley, R.N., *Slaves in Redcoats*, pp. 76–8; Fortescue, Vol. V, pp. 180–1.
4. Knight, pp. 217–20; Buckley, *The British Army in the West Indies*, pp. 261–2; Fortescue, Vol. V, pp. 175, 181–2.
5. *The London Gazette*, July 26 1803, 15605, pp. 917–19, August 15 1803, 15610, pp. 1021–2; Poyen, pp. 268–9; Fortescue, Vol. V, pp. 182–3; Pakenham E., *Pakenham Letters 1800 to 1815*, p. 31; Lasalle de Louisenthal, *Aventures de guerre aux Antilles*, pp. 74–5.
6. *The London Gazette*, August 15 1803, 15610, pp. 1017–21; Poyen, pp. 268–9; Fortescue, Vol. V, pp. 183–4.
7. *The London Gazette*, November 26 1803, 15649, pp. 1655–63; Fortescue, Vol. V, pp. 184–6.
8. *The London Gazette*, June 19 1804, 15712, pp. 753–61; Fortescue, Vol. V, pp. 187–91.
9. Fortescue, Vol. V, pp. 191–2.
10. *Sketches and Recollections of the West Indies by a Resident*, pp. 158–86; *The London Gazette*, 4 May 1804, 15804, pp. 601–3; Ellis, A.B., *The History of the First West India Regiment*, pp. 73–82 Poyen, pp. 278–82; Moreau de Jonnès, A., *Adventures in Wars of the Republic and Consulate*, pp. 291–6; Fortescue, Vol. V, pp. 245–8
11. Fortescue, Vol. V, pp. 249, 255–8; Poyen, pp. 283–92.
12. *The London Gazette*, February 9 1808, 16116, pp. 193–5; Fortescue, Vol. VII, pp. 2–9; Ellis, p. 84; Lunt, J.D., *Scarlet Lancer*, pp. 23–6.
13. *The London Gazette*, April 13 1809, 16245, pp. 481–90; Fortescue, Vol. VII, pp. 11–17; Poyen, pp. 338–67; Ellis, pp. 88–92; Campbell, N., *Napoleon at Fontainebleau and Elba*, pp. 14–16; Browne, T.H. *The Napoleonic War Journal of Thomas Henry Browne*, pp., 100–7; St Clair, *A Soldier's Recollections of the West Indies and America*, Vol. II, pp. 236–46, Graves, D.E., *Dragon Rampant*, pp. 82–3; Scott, J., *Recollections of a Naval Life*, Vol. II, pp. 129–55; Bentinck, R., *The Very Thing*, pp. 30–1.
14. *The London Gazette*, May 30 1809, 16262, pp. 779–8; Fortescue, Vol. VII, pp. 17–18; Poyen, pp. 381–4.
15. *Bulletins of the Campaign 1810*, pp. 37–75; Fortescue, Vol. VII, pp. 19–25; Ellis, pp. 93–7.
16. Hall, C.D., *British Strategy in the Napoleonic War 1803–15*, pp. 185–6; Muir, R., *Britain and the Defeat of Napoleon 1807–1815*, pp. 309, 326; Fortescue, Vol. VII, p. 25; Poyen, pp. 413–14; Buckley, *The British Army in the West Indies*, pp. 267–8.
17. *The London Gazette*, July 25 1815, 1513, pp. 1515–16; Leith, J., *Memoirs of the late Lieutenant-General Sir James Leith GCB*, pp. 147–8; Poyen, pp. 417–22.
18. Leith, pp. 148–58, appendix, pp. 8–14; Haggard, D., *The Last Fight for Napoleon*; Ellis, pp. 110–12; Poyen, pp. 433–48; Anderson, J., *Recollections of a Peninsular Veteran*, pp. 93–5.
19. Muir, pp. 370–3; Duffy, p. 389; Gasper, D.B., *A Turbulent Time*, p. 92; Buckley, *The British Army in the West Indies*, p. 268.

Chapter 8

1. Knight, R., *Britain Against Napoleon*, pp. 77−8; Duffy, M., *Soldiers, Sugar and Seapower*, pp. 173−4; Buckley, R.N., *The British Army in the West Indies*, pp. 59−61; Moore, J., *The Diary of Sir John Moore*, Vol. I, p. 193; McLean, H., *An Enquiry into the Nature and Causes of the Great Mortality*, pp. viii−x; Haythornthwaite, P.J., *The Armies of Wellington*, p. 215; Bryson, A., *Andrew Bryson's Ordeal*, pp. 83−4; Durey, M., *White Slaves*, p. 307; Dillon, W.H., *A Narrative of my Professional Adventures (1790− 1839)*, Vol. I, pp. 200−1; Pinckard, G., *Notes on the West Indies*, Vol. I, pp. 15−17, 79−80; Thoumine, R.H., *Scientific Soldier*, p. 53; Muir, R., *Wellington. The Path to Victory 1769− 1814*, p. 29; Leach, J., *Rough Sketches of the Life of an Old Soldier*, p. 5; Sherwood, NAM 1999−09−41; St Clair, *A Soldier's Recollections of the West Indies and America*, Vol. I, pp. 46−7; Pakenham, E., *Pakenham Letters 1800 to 1815*, p. 17; Teasdale, NAM 2011−08−34.

2. Howard, T.P., *The Haitian Journal of Lieutenant Howard*, p. 8; Pinckard, Vol. I, pp. 33−9, 62−4, 83; Dyott, W., *Dyott's Diary 1781− 1845*, Vol. I, p. 82; Moore, Vol. I, p. 193; Surtees, W., *Twenty-Five Years in the Rifle Brigade*, pp. 323−5; *Facts Relative to the Conduct of the War in the West Indies*, p. 155; McGrigor, J.,*The Autobiography and Services of Sir James McGrigor Bart*, pp. 48−9; Everard, H., *History of Thomas Farrington's Regiment*, pp. 183−9; Schofield, V., *The Highland Furies*, p. 189; Landsheit, N., *The Hussar*, Vol. I, pp. 49−50; Duffy, M., *The Caribbean Campaigns of the British Army 1793− 1801*, p. 30.

3. Knight, pp. 176−90; Fortescue, J.W., *A History of the British Army*, Vol. IV (2), pp. 882−4; Duffy, *Soldiers, Sugar and Seapower*, pp. 184−5; Condon, M.E., *Living Conditions on Board Troopships*, p. 19; Brownrigg, B., *The Life and Letters of Sir John Moore*, pp. 55−6; Pinckard, Vol. I, pp. 52−3, 142−4; Bryson, p. 78; Landsheit, Vol. I, pp. 87−8.

4. Condon, pp. 14−15; Duffy, *Soldiers, Sugar and Seapower*, pp. 353−4; Pinckard, Vol. I, pp. 98−100, Vol. II, pp. 152−6; Surtees, pp. 325−6; McGrigor, p. 54; Landsheit, Vol. I, pp. 87−8; Richardson, W., *A Mariner of England*, p. 197; Lloyd, C., *Medicine and the Navy 1200− 1900*, Vol. III, p. 72.

5. Moseley, B., *A Treatise on Tropical Diseases*, pp. 16−17; St Clair, Vol. I, pp. 59−61; Bryson, p. 70.

6. Condon, pp. 15−18; *Facts Relative to the Conduct of the War in the West Indies*, p. 183; Bryson, pp. 70−1; Powell, NAM 1976−07−45; Dyott, Vol. I, pp. 84−90; Ross-Lewin, H., *With the Thirty-Second in the Peninsula*, p. 15; Howard, p. 20; Pinckard, Vol. I, pp. 106−7.

7. Condon, pp. 16−17; Pinckard, Vol. I, p. 116.

8. Clinton, NAM 1999−08−100; Aytoun, J., *Redcoats in the Caribbean*, p. 5; Howard, p. 17; Willyams, C., *An Account of the Campaign in the West Indies in the Year 1794*, pp. 4−5; Browne, T.H., *The Napoleonic War Journal of Captain Thomas Henry Browne*, pp. 89−90.

9. Knight, pp. 189−90; Brisbane, T.M., *Reminiscences of General Sir Thomas Makdougall Brisbane*, pp. 13−14; Powell, NAM 1976−07−45; Bryson, pp. 79−80; Howard, p. 19; Pinckard, Vol. I, pp. 193−5.

10. Surtees, pp. 327−8; St Clair, Vol. I, pp. 83−4; Howard, pp. 18−21; Aytoun, p. 5; Nichol, NAM 1977−12−29; Dyott, Vol. I, pp. 87−9; Pinckard, Vol. I, pp. 206−8; Willyams, pp. 6−7; Browne, pp. 89−91; Bryson, pp. 73−4.

11. Clinton, NAM 1999−08−100; Aytoun, p. 5; James, B., *Journal of Rear-Admiral Bartholomew James 1752− 1828*, pp. 227−8; Dyott, Vol. I, p. 85; Pinckard, Vol. I, pp. 192, 436−7; Buckley, *The British Army in the West Indies*, p. 30.

12. Howard, pp. 28−30; Willyams, p. 29; Bryson, pp. 81−2; Dyott, Vol. I, pp. 90−1; St Clair, Vol. I, pp. 88−9; *Cumloden Papers*, p. 413; Moore, Vol. I, pp. 208−9; Buckley, *The British Army in the West Indies*, p. 29.

13. Chisholm, C., *An Essay on the Malignant Pestilential Fever*, pp. 69−74; Howard, pp. 37, 58−60, 67, 119−20; Sherwood, NAM 1999−09−41; Dyott, Vol. I, p. 114; St Clair, Vol. I, pp.

235–6; Fergusson, W., *Notes and Recollections of a Professional Life*, p. 232; Richardson, pp. 149–50; Buckley, *The British Army in the West Indies*, pp. 33–6; Bryson, p. 82; Leach, p. 10; Browne, pp. 92, 105; Pinckard, Vol. II, p. 233; Moseley, p. 29.

14. Pinckard, Vol. I, pp. 181–2; Anderson, J., *Recollections of a Peninsular Veteran*, pp. 87–8; Leach, pp. 10–11; Bryson, p. 80; St Clair, Vol. I, pp. 90–1; Surtees, p. 329; Browne, pp. 92–3.

15. Pinckard, Vol. I, pp. 229–32, 283, 367, Vol. II, pp. 201–8, 216–17; Dyott, Vol. I, pp. 93–4; Ross-Lewin, pp. 20–1, 34–5; St Clair, Vol. I, pp. 189–97, 203, 221–4, 249; Aytoun, pp. 21–2, 28–9, 35; Leach, pp. 19–20; Willyams, pp. 12–14; Rainsford, M., *An Historical Account of the Black Empire of Hayti*, p. 102; Moore, Vol. I, pp. 224, 257.

Chapter 9

1. *Sketches and Recollections of the West Indies by a Resident*, pp. 39–40; Buckley, R.N., *The British Army in the West Indies*, pp. 325–56; Aytoun, J., *Redcoats in the Caribbean*, p. 7; Dyott, W., *Dyott's Diary 1781–1845*, Vol. I, p. 107.

2. Aytoun, pp. 8–10; Houlding, J.A., *Fit for Service*, pp. 160–1.

3. Buckley, *The British Army in the West Indies*, pp. 104, 210–12, 216–26, 227–37; Nelson, P.D., *Sir Charles Grey, First Earl Grey*, p. 144; Moore, J., *The Diary of Sir John Moore*, Vol. I, pp. 236–7; Dyott, Vol. I, p. 105; Nugent, M., *Lady Nugent's Journal*, p. 231; Willyams, C., *An Account of the Campaign in the West Indies in the Year 1794*, p. 28, appendix, pp. 24, 36; Métral, A., *Histoire de L'Expédition des Français a Saint-Domingue*, p. 115; *Cumloden Papers*, pp. 5, 20–1; Howard, T.P., *The Haitian Journal of Lieutenant Howard*, pp. 20, 119; St Clair, *A Soldier's Recollections of the West Indies and America*, Vol. I, pp. 102–3; Myatt, F., *Peninsular General*, p. 35; Bryson, A., *Andrew Bryson's Ordeal*, pp. 93, 99, 102; Lasalle de Louisenthal, *Aventures de guerre aux Antilles*, pp. 52, 54; James, C., *A Collection of the Charges, Opinions and Sentences of General Courts Martial*, pp. 559–679; Aytoun, pp. 11, 15–16, 18, 25–6; Richardson, W., *A Mariner of England*, pp. 186–7.

4. Geggus, D., *Slavery, War and Revolution*, p. 280; Buckley, *The British Army in the West Indies*, p. 64; Sherwood, NAM 1999–09–41; Pakenham, E., *Pakenham Letters 1800 to 1815*, p. 26; Aytoun, p. 24; Schofield, V., *The Highland Furies*, p. 195.

5. *Facts Relative to the Conduct of the War in the West Indies*, pp. 179–92; Chartrand, R., *British Forces in the West Indies 1793–1815*, pp. 8–9; McLean, H., *An Enquiry into the Nature and Causes of the Great Mortality*, pp. 268–70; Stewart, D., *Sketches of the Character, Manners and Present State of the Highlanders of Scotland*, pp. 408–9; Nelson, p. 168; Fortescue, J.W., *A History of the British Army*, Vol. IV (2), pp. 899–901; Aytoun, p. 1; Browne, T.H., *The Napoleonic War Journal of Captain Thomas Henry Browne*, p. 99.

6. Haythornthwaite, P.J., *The Armies of Wellington*, pp. 61–3; Pinckard, G., *Notes on the West Indies*, Vol. I, pp. 253–4, 301, Vol. II, pp. 100–3, Vol. III, pp. 62–3, 449; *Facts Relative to the Conduct of the War in the West Indies*, pp. 175–91; Aytoun, pp. 6–7, 12, 36; St Clair, Vol. I, pp. 109–11, 127, 345; Dyott, Vol. I, pp. 92, 119–20; Sherwood, NAM 1999–09–41; Beaudoin, P., *Carnet d'Étapes*, pp. 55, 65; Jane, C.W.E., *Shirley Heights*, pp. 24, 51; Smith, V.T.C., *Fire and Brimstone*, pp. 56–8; Leach, J., *Rough Sketches of the Life of an Old Soldier*, p. 12; Willyams, pp. 58, 143–4; Schofield, p. 196; Howard, *The Haitian Journal of Lieutenant Howard*, pp. 10, 114; Ross-Lewin, H., *With the Thirty-Second in the Peninsula*, p. 23; Landsheit, N., *The Hussar*, Vol. I, pp. 62–3; Howard, M.R., *Red Jackets and Red Noses*; Buckley, R.N., *Slaves in Redcoats*, pp. 100–4; Fergusson, W., *Notes and Recollections of a Professional Life*, p. 85; McLean, p. 257.

7. Jane, p. 23; Smith, p. 33; Buckley, *The British Army in the West Indies*, pp. 78–9, 327–8; Dyott, Vol. I, pp. 96–7; *Facts Relative to the Conduct of the War in the West Indies*, pp. 186–7; Nugent, NAM 1968–07–183–02; Pinckard, Vol. III, pp. 61–2; Nugent, *Lady Nugent's*

Journal, p. xxvi; Geggus, p. 193; Buckley, *Slaves in Redcoats*, p. 110; Reide, T.D., *A View of the Diseases of the Army*, pp. 178–9; Fergusson, p. 49; Tulloch, A.M., *Statistical Report*, p. 4; Schofield, pp. 194–5.
8. St Clair, Vol. I, pp. 373–4, Vol. II, pp. 235–6; Browne, p. 101; Howard, *The Haitian Journal of Lieutenant Howard*, pp. 86, 95–6; Willyams, appendix, p. 25; Dyott, Vol. I, pp. 106–13, 120; Moore, Vol. I, p. 206; Fergusson, p. 52; Sherwood, NAM 1999–09–41; Stewart, p. 427; McGrigor, J., *The Autobiography and Services of Sir James McGrigor Bart*, pp. 54, 66; Jane, pp. 25–6; Smith, pp. 33, 52; Pinckard, Vol. I, pp. 240, 249, Vol. II, pp. 231, 252–3; Scott, J., *Recollections of a Naval Life*, Vol. II, pp. 102–3; Landsheit, Vol. I, pp. 67–9; Geggus, p. 175.
9. Buckley, *The British Army in the West Indies*, pp. 146–6, 342–3; *Facts Relative to the Conduct of the War in the West Indies*, p. 195; Willyams, appendix, p. 8; Nugent, *Lady Nugent's Journal*, pp. 32, 184, 192–3; Smith, pp. 38, 42; Aytoun, pp. 28, 35; Howard, *The Haitian Journal of Lieutenant Howard*, pp. 101, 170–1; Wainwright, NAM 2007–10–15; Pinckard, Vol. II, p. 472; St Clair, Vol. I, pp. 112–14; Myatt, F., *Peninsular General*, p. 40; Dillon, W.H., *A Narrative of my Professional Adventures (1790–1839)*, Vol. I, p. 407.
10. Landsheit, Vol. I, pp. 57–8; Bryson, pp. 84–5; *Facts Relative to the Conduct of the War in the West Indies*, p. 193; Geggus, p. 7; Browne, pp. 91, 95; Nugent, *Lady Nugent's Journal*, pp. 37, 196, 210; Pinckard, Vol. I, pp. 284–5, 331, Vol. III, p. 131; Willyams, p. 94; Howard, *The Haitian Journal of Lieutenant Howard*, p. 63; Leach, p. 18; Fortescue, Vol. IV (1), p. 325; Pakenham, pp. 27–8; Teasdale, NAM 2011–08–34; Abercromby, NAM 2001–01–611.

Chapter 10
1. Duffy, M., *The Caribbean Campaigns of the British Army*, pp. 26–9; Buckley, R. N., *The British Army in the West Indies*, pp. 11–12, 23; Brumwell, S.B., *Redcoats. The British Soldier and War in the Americas 1755–1763*, pp. 138–41, 196–203; Nelson, P.D., *Sir Charles Grey, First Earl Grey*, p. 159; Geggus, D., *Slavery, War and Revolution*, pp. 156, 277, 281; Ellis, A.B., *The History of the First West India Regiment*, p. 112; Howard, T.P., *The Haitian Journal of Lieutenant Howard*, pp. 79–80; Stewart, D., *Sketches of the Character, Manners and Present State of the Highlanders of Scotland*, p. 416; Moore, J., *The Diary of Sir John Moore*, Vol. I, p. 235; Abercromby, NAM 2001–10–611.
2. Duffy, M., *Soldiers, Sugar and Seapower*, pp. 67–9, 290–1; Nelson, pp. 144–6; Howard, p. 98; Geggus, p. 181; Carmichael, NAM 1988–06–30; Poyen, H., *Les Guerres des Antilles de 1793 à 1815*, p. 121; Clinton, NAM 1999–08–100; Balcarres, *Lives of the Lindsays*, Vol. III, p. 46; Moore, Vol. I, pp. 226, 231; Knight, R., *Britain Against Napoleon*, pp. 131–4, 292, Buckley, pp. 82–3; Jane, C.W.E., *Shirley Heights*, p. 34.
3. Browne, T.H., *The Napoleonic War Journal of Captain Thomas Henry Browne*, p. 98; Willyams, C., *An Account of the Campaign in the West Indies in the Year 1794*, appendix, p. 35; Duffy, *Soldiers, Sugar and Seapower*, pp. 93–4, 220, 280; Pinckard, G., *Notes on the West Indies*, Vol. II, pp. 161–7; Wainwright, NAM 2007–10–15; Southey, T., *Chronological History of the West Indies*, Vol. III, p. 461; Moore, Vol. I, pp. 198–9.
4. Haythornthwaite, P.J., *The Armies of Wellington*, p. 197; Fortescue, J.W., *A History of the British Army*, Vol. IV (1), pp. 358, 442, 225, Vol. V, p. 189; Stewart, p. 425; Carmichael, NAM 1988–06–30; Geggus, pp. 240, 276; Aytoun, J., *Redcoats in the Caribbean*, p. 16; Moore, Vol. I, pp. 204, 216; Willyams, appendix, p. 7; *Cumloden Papers*, p. 4; Dyott, W., *Dyott's Diary 1781–1845*, Vol. I, pp. 99, 121; Howard, p. 39.
5. Willyams, appendix, pp. 6–7, 21; Duffy, *Soldiers, Sugar and Seapower*, pp. 223, 248; Howard, pp. 37, 62, 76, 97, 112; Geggus, p. 193; Balcarres, Vol. III, pp. 40, 138; Landsheit, N., *The Hussar*, Vol. I, p. 61; Chalmers, C., *Remarks on the Late War in St. Domingo*, pp. 38–41; Stewart, pp. 409–10.

6. Browne, pp. 97–8; Willyams, appendix, pp. 16–17;Nelson, pp. 43, 45, 143, 150, 160; Duffy, *Soldiers, Sugar and Seapower*, pp. 65, 223, 231; Moore, Vol. I, p. 200; Buckley, R.N., *Slaves in Redcoats*, p. 84; Gates, D., *The British Light Infantry Arm c. 1790–1815*, pp. 53–4, 69–70; Fortescue, Vol. IV (1), pp. 464, 487; Verner,W., *History and Campaigns of the Rifle Brigade*, Vol. II, pp. 7–8

7. Howard, p. 54; Moore, Vol. I, pp. 202–3, 216–18; Bentinck, R., *The Very Thing*, p. 28; Brisbane, T.M., *Reminiscences of General Sir Thomas Makdougall Brisbane*, pp. 15–16; *Cumloden Papers*, pp. 4, 19–20; McGrigor, J, *The Autobiography and Services of Sir James McGrigor Bart*, pp. 61–2; Willyams, pp. 88–91.

8. Brumwell, pp. 246–7; Muir, R., *Tactics and the Experience of Battle in the Age of Napoleon*, pp. 86–8; Moore, Vol. I, p. 24; Willyams, appendix, p. 7; Browne, p. 98; Everard, H., *History of Thomas Farrington's Regiment*, pp. 195, 200–1; Dyott, Vol. I, p. 111; Ross-Lewin, H., *With the Thirty-Second in the Peninsula*, pp. 23–5; *Sketches and Recollections of the West Indies by a Resident*, pp. 87–9; Nugent, NAM 1968–07–183–2.

9. Fortescue, Vol. IV (1), pp. 381, 443, Vol. V, pp. 18–19; Duffy, *Soldiers, Sugar and Seapower*, p. 286; Poyen, p. 343.

10. St Clair, *A Soldier's Recollections of the West Indies and America*, Vol. II, pp. 237–46; Turnbull, G., *A Narrative of the Revolt and Insurrection*, p. 158; Balcarres, p. 73; Howard, p. 54; Moore, Vol. I, pp. 208–13; Buckley, *The British Army in the West Indies*, pp. 72–5; Browne, pp. 101–8; Scott, J, *Recollections of a Naval Life*, Vol. II, pp. 152–4; Ellis, pp. 43–4; James, B., *Journal of Rear-Admiral Bartholomew James 1752–1828*, pp. 250–66.

11. Willyams, p. 10; *Cumloden Papers*, pp. 6–7, 20; Richardson, W., *A Mariner of England*, pp. 130–1; James, pp. 234–5, 237; Bentinck, p. 29.

12. Duffy, *Soldiers, Sugar and Seapower*, p. 120; *Cumloden Papers*, p. 15; Howard, p. 65; Geggus, pp. 282–3; McGrigor, pp. 63–4; Stewart, p. 421.

13. Fortescue, Vol. V, p. 183; Lemonnier-Delafosse, M., *Seconde Campagne de Saint Domingue*, pp. 57–8; Moreau de Jonnès, A., *Adventures in Wars of the Republic and Consulate*, p. 163.

14. Poyen, p. 367; Lemonnier-Delafosse, pp. 95–8; Willyams, p. 127, appendix, p. 62; Nelson, p. 166; Turnbull, p. 75; McGrigor, pp. 66–7; Moore, Vol. I, pp. 226–8.

15. Willyams, pp. 80, 121; James, pp. 246, 260; Lasalle de Louisenthal, *Aventures de guerre aux Antilles*, pp. 22–4, 35; Brisbane, p. 17; Browne, pp. 98, 102–6; Stewart, p. 422; McGrigor, pp. 60–4; Dyott, Vol. I, p. 104.

16. Willyams, p. 104; Duffy, *Soldiers, Sugar and Seapower*, pp. 197, 340; Leach, J., *Rough Sketches of the Life of an Old Soldier*, p. 8; Pinckard, Vol. II, pp. 194–5; Knight, p. 399.

17. Nelson, pp. 143, 161–3; Duffy, *Soldiers, Sugar and Seapower*, pp. 120, 223; James, pp. 228–31; Browne, pp. 95–7; Stewart, p. 420; Fortescue, Vol. IV (1) p. 455; Everard, pp. 205–6.

Chapter 11

1. Buckley, R.N., *The Destruction of the British Army in the West Indies 1793–1815*; Duffy, M., *Soldiers, Sugar and Seapower*, pp. 326–34; Geggus, D., *Slavery, War and Revolution*, pp. 354–7; Fortescue, J.W., *A History of the British Army*, Vol. IV (1), pp. 496, 565; McLean, H., *An Enquiry into the Nature and Causes of the Great Mortality*, pp. 13–15, 37–8; Fergusson, W., *Notes and Recollections of a Professional Life*, pp. 150–1.

2. Howard, M.R., *Wellington's Doctors*, pp. 160–1; Jackson, R., *A Treatise on the Fevers of Jamaica*, pp. 253–63; Bancroft, E.N., *An Essay on the Disease called Yellow Fever*, pp. 2–15; McLean, pp. 105–10, 165–70; Fergusson, pp. 146–7; Pinckard, G., *Notes on the West Indies*, Vol. III, pp. 138–46; Ross-Lewin, H., *With the Thirty-Second in the Peninsula*, pp. 32–3.

3. Howard, *Wellington's Doctors*, p. 161; Jackson, pp. 14–18; Reide, T.D., *A View of the*

Diseases of the Army, p. 218; Moore, J., *The Diary of Sir John Moore*, Vol. I, pp. 240–1; Carmichael, NAM 1988–06–30; St Clair, *A Soldier's Recollections of the West Indies and America*, Vol. I, pp. 354–8, 371–2.

4. Howard, *Wellington's Doctors*, pp. 155–90; Chisholm, C., *An Essay on the Malignant Pestilential Fever*, pp. 313–15; McGrigor, J., *The Autobiography and Services of Sir James McGrigor Bart*, pp. 53, 64–6; Bancroft, p. 533; Browne, T.H., *The Napoleonic War Journal of Captain Thomas Henry Browne*, p. 110; Reide, pp. 282–3, 358; Moseley, B., *A Treatise on Tropical Diseases*, pp. 131–2, 171–2, 531–2; Pinckard, Vol. III, pp. 18–19; Nugent, M., *Lady Nugent's Journal*, pp. 232–3; Cantlie, N., *A History of the Army Medical Department*, Vol. I, pp. 243, 255; Buckley, *The Destruction of the British Army*; Howard, M.R., *Red Jackets and Red Noses*.

5. Cantlie, Vol. I, pp. 239–46; Chisholm, pp. xix–xx, 242–3; Ackroyd, M., *Advancing with the Army*, pp. 46–7; Howard, T.P., *The Haitian Journal of Lieutenant Howard*, pp. 83–4; Sherwood, NAM 1999–09–41; Bryson, A., *Andrew Bryson's Ordeal*, pp. 86, 95–6.

6. Howard, *Wellington's Doctors*, pp. 182–3; Jackson, pp. 77–8, 90–1, 133; Chisholm, pp. 183, 258–62, 279; Moseley, pp. 126–7; Reide, pp. 188–9; Veitch, J., *A Letter to the Commissioners*, pp. 10–11; McLean, pp. 63–4.

7. Jackson, pp. 399–411; Moseley, pp. 8–9, 82–3; McLean, pp. 40, 201, 206–7; Fergusson, pp. 67–8.

8. Howard, *Wellington's Doctors*, pp. 162–6; Jackson, p. 226; Pinckard, Vol. I, pp. 390–1.

9. Howard, *Wellington's Doctors*, pp. 91–121; Cantlie, Vol. I, pp. 213, 244–8; Clinton, NAM 1999–08–100; Bryson, pp. 86, 101; Browne, pp. 105–6; Veitch, pp. 153–4; Geggus, pp. 277, 364; Pinckard, Vol. I, pp. 383–5, Vol. II, p. 141, Vol. III, pp. 113–14; Howard, *The Haitian Journal of Lieutenant Howard*, p. 49.

10. Howard, *Wellington's Doctors*, pp. 93–7; Ross-Lewin, pp. 30–1; Cantlie, Vol. I, pp. 245, 247; Fergusson, pp. 62–4; Tinling, NAM 1994–09–129; Lasalle de Louisenthal, *Aventures de guerre aux Antilles*, pp. 27–8; Howard, *The Haitian Journal of Lieutenant Howard*, p. 105; Landsheit, N., *The Hussar*, Vol. I, pp. 79–80; Beaudoin, P., *Carnet d'Étapes*, pp. 66–72.

11. Teasdale, NAM 2011–08–4; Tinling, NAM, 1994–09–129; Ross-Lewin, p. 30; Métral, A., *Histoire de L'Expédition des Français a Saint-Domingue*, p. 120; James, B., *Journal of Rear-Admiral Bartholomew James 1752–1828*, p. 261; Browne, p. 94.

Bibliography

Manuscripts

National Army Museum (NAM), London;

1968–07–183–2: Miscellaneous correspondence relating to the West Indies, 1802, associated with Major General Sir George Nugent.

1973–05–4: A Sketch of the Military Service of Lieutenant Colonel William Stewart of the 3rd Foot containing an account of his service in the West Indies 1796–1802.

1976–07–45: Diary of Captain T Powell 14th Regiment of Foot March 1793 – March 1796.

1977–12–29: Memoirs of Colour Sergeant William Nichol 8th (The King's) Regiment of Foot written in 1822 and covering the years 1790–1809.

1977–12–43: Commander-in-Chief's orderly book 24 February – 24 July 1797.

1988–06–30: Letter book of Major General Hugh Carmichael 1810–1811.

1993–10–23: Manuscript order book of Captain Murray's Light Infantry Company 31st Regiment 1796 including orders for the attack on St Lucia.

1994–09–129: Letters and a statement of account relating to Major George Tinling 38th Regiment of Foot and his death in 1797 on Martinique while serving in the Army Hospital Corps.

1999–08–100: Letters from Lieutenant Henry Clinton describing Abercromby's operations in the West Indies 1796.

1999–09–41: Diary of Lieutenant Henry Sherwood, 1777–1849, 53rd Regiment covering his service in the West Indies 1798–1802.

2001–01–611: Letter 27 April 1794 from Johnston Abercromby to his wife describing the capture of West Indian islands in the expedition led by General Sir Charles Grey.

2007–10–15: Biographical diary of Ensign David Wainwright, 2nd (Queen's Royal) Regiment of Foot 1787–1802.

2011–08–34: Letters and papers relating to Lieutenant Edward Teasdale 54th (West Norfolk) Regiment of Foot 1806–1809 to his death from yellow fever in 1808.

Primary Printed Sources

A Collection of State Papers Relative to the War against France, London, 1796.

Anderson, Lt Col J., *Recollections of a Peninsular Veteran*, London, 1913.

Aytoun, J., (ed. Lewis A.S.), *Redcoats in the Caribbean*, Blackburn, 1984.

Balcarres, Earl of, (ed. Lindsay, Lord), *Lives of the Lindsays or a Memoir of the Houses of Crawford and Balcarres*, Vol. III, London, 1849.

Bancroft, E.N., *An Essay on the Disease called Yellow Fever*, London, 1811.

Beaudoin, Sergent-Major P., *Carnet d'Étapes. Souvenirs de guerre et de captivité lors de l'Expédition de Saint-Domingue*, Paris, 2000.

Bell, J., *An Enquiry into the Causes which produce and the Means of Preventing Diseases among British Officers Soldiers and Others in the West Indies*, London, 1791.

Bentinck, R., (ed. Crook, J.), *The Very Thing. The Memoirs of Drummer Richard Bentinck Royal Welch Fusiliers 1807–1823*, London, 2011.

Brisbane, Gen Sir T.M., *Reminiscences of General Sir Thomas Makdougall Brisbane*, Edinburgh, 1860.

Browne, Capt T.H., (ed. Buckley, R.N.), *The Napoleonic War Journal of Captain Thomas Henry Browne*, London, 1987.

Bryson, A., (ed. Durey, M.), *Andrew Bryson's Ordeal. An Epilogue to the 1798 Rebellion*, Cork, 1998.

Bulletins of the Campaign, London, 1793–1810.

Campbell, N., *Napoleon at Fontainebleau and Elba, being a Journal of Occurrences in 1814–1815*, London, 1869.

Castlereagh, Viscount, *Correspondence, Despatches and other Papers of Viscount Castlereagh*, 12 Vols., London, 1848–1853.

Chalmers, Col C., *Remarks on the Late War in St. Domingo*, London, 1803.

Chisholm, C., *An Essay on the Malignant Pestilential Fever introduced into the West Indian Islands*, 2 Vols., London, 1801.

Coke, T., *A History of the West Indies*, 3 Vols., Liverpool, 1811.

Cumloden Papers, Edinburgh, 1871.

Dillon, Sir W.H., (ed. Lewis, M.A.), *A Narrative of my Professional Adventures (1790–1839)*, Vol. I, London, 1953.

Dyott, W., (ed. Jeffery, R.W.), *Dyott's Diary 1781–1845*, Vol. I, London, 1907.

Facts Relative to the Conduct of the War in the West Indies Collected from the Speech of The Right Hon. Henry Dundas, London, 1796.

Fergusson, W., *Notes and Recollections of a Professional Life*, London, 1846.

Fernyhough, T., *Military Memoirs of Four Brothers*, Staplehurst, 2002.

Gilbert, C.N.P., *Histoire Médicale de L'Armée Française a Saint-Domingue*, Paris, 1803.

Gillespie, L., *Observations on the Diseases which Prevailed on Board a Part of His Majesty's Squadron on the Leeward Islands Station from 1794 to 1796*, London, 1800.

Guilmot, Officier de Santé, *Journal et Voyage à Saint-Domingue (1802)*, Paris, 1997.

Hay, J., *A Narrative of the Insurrection in the Island of Grenada which took place in 1795*, London, 1823.

Howard, Lt T.P., (ed. Buckley, R.N.), *The Haitian Journal of Lieutenant Howard York Hussars 1796–1798*, Knoxville, 1985.

Hunter, J., *Observations on the Diseases of the Army in Jamaica*, London, 1788.

Jackson, R., *A Treatise on the Fevers of Jamaica*, London, 1791.

Jackson, R., *Sketch of the History and Cure of Febrile Diseases most particularly as they appear in the West Indies among the Soldiers of the British Army*, 2 Vols., London, 1817.

James, B., (ed. Laughton, J.K.), *Journal of Rear-Admiral Bartholomew James 1752–1828*, London, 1896.

James, C., *A Collection of the Charges, Opinions and Sentences of General Courts Martial published from the year 1795 to the present time*, London, 1820.

Landsheit, N., (ed. Gleig, G.R.), *The Hussar*, 2 Vols., London, 1837.

Lasalle de Louisenthal, Capitaine, *Aventures de guerre aux Antilles (Saint-Lucie, la Martinique, Trinidad) (1769–1805)*, 1980.

Leach, Lt Col J., *Rough Sketches of the Life of an Old Soldier*, London, 1831.

Leith, Sir J., *Memoirs of the late Lieutenant-General Sir James Leith GCB*, London, 1818.

Lemonnier-Delafosse, M., *Seconde Campagne de Saint Domingue*, Havre, 1846.

Lempriere, W., *Practical Observations of the Diseases of the Army in Jamaica as they occurred between the years 1792 and 1797*, 2 Vols., London, 1799.

McGrigor, Sir J., *The Autobiography and Services of Sir James McGrigor Bart*, London, 1861.

McLean, H., *An Enquiry into the Nature and Causes of the Great Mortality among the Troops at St. Domingo*, London, 1797.

Métral, A., *Histoire de L'Expédition des Français a Saint-Domingue sous le Consulat de Napoléon Bonaparte (1802–1803)*, Paris, 1985.

Moore, Sir J., (ed. Maurice, J.F.), *The Diary of Sir John Moore*, 2 Vols., London, 1904.

Moreau de Jonnès, A., *Adventures in Wars of the Republic and Consulate*, London, 1920.

Moreau de Jonnès, A., *Essai sur l'Hygiène Militaire des Antilles*, Paris, 1816.

Moseley, B., *A Treatise on Tropical Diseases on Military Operations and on the Climate of the West Indies*, London, 1792.

Napoleon, *Correspondence de Napoléon 1er*, 32 Vols., Paris, 1858–1870.

Nugent, Lady M., (ed. Wright, P.), *Lady Nugent's Journal of her residence in Jamaica from 1801 to 1805*, Kingston, 1966.

Pakenham, E., *Pakenham Letters 1800 to 1815*, London, 1914.

Parsons, G.S., *I Sailed with Nelson*, Maidstone, 1973.

Picton, Lt Gen Sir T., (ed. Robinson, H.B.), *Memoirs of Lieutenant-General Sir Thomas Picton*, 2 Vols., London, 1836.

Pinckard, G., *Notes on the West Indies*, 3 Vols., London, 1806.

Pym, W., *Observations on the Bulam Fever which has of late years prevailed in the West Indies*, London, 1815.

Rainsford, M., *An Historical Account of the Black Empire of Hayti*, London, 1805.

Reece, R., *Medical Guide for Tropical Climates*, London, 1814.

Regulations to be observed by Troops embarked in transports For Service Abroad particularly by those designed for the West Indies, London, 1795.

Reide, T.D., *A View of the Diseases of the Army in Great Britain, America, the West Indies*, London, 1793.

Richardson, W., (ed. Childers, S.), *A Mariner of England*, London, 1908.

Roberts, R., (ed. Crook, J.), *Incidents in the Life of an Old Fusilier. The Recollections of Sergeant Richard Roberts of the 23rd Foot*, Huntingdon.

Ross-Lewin, H., (ed. Wardell, J.), *With the Thirty-Second in the Peninsula and Other Campaigns*, Dublin, 1904.

St Clair, Lt Col, *A Soldier's Recollections of the West Indies and America with a narrative of the Expedition to the Island of Walcheren*, 2 Vols., London 1834.

Scott, J., *Recollections of a Naval Life*, Vol. II, London, 1834.

Sketches and Recollections of the West Indies by a Resident, London, 1828.

Spencer, G. Second Earl, (ed. Corbett, L. M.), *Private Papers of George, second Earl Spencer First Lord of the Admiralty 1794– 1801*, Vol. I, London, 1913.

Standing Orders and Regulations for the Army in Ireland, Dublin, 1794.

Stewart, Col D., *Sketches of the Character, Manners and Present State of the Highlanders of Scotland with details of the Military Service of Highland Regiments*, Vol. I, Edinburgh, 1822.

Surtees, W., *Twenty-Five Years in the Rifle Brigade by the late Quartermaster William Surtees*, London, 1973.

The London Gazette, 1794–1815.

Tulloch, Capt A.M., *Statistical Report of the Sickness, Mortality and Invaliding among the Troops in the West Indies*, London, 1838.

Turnbull, G., *A Narrative of the Revolt and Insurrection of the French inhabitants in the Island of Grenada*, Edinburgh, 1795.

Veitch, J., *A Letter to the Commissioners for Transports and Sick and Wounded Seamen on the non-contagious nature of Yellow Fever*, London, 1818.

Willyams, Rev C., *An Account of the Campaign in the West Indies in the Year 1794*, London, 1796.

Secondary Printed Sources
Ackroyd, M., Brocklis, L., Moss, M., Retford, K. and Stevenson, J., *Advancing with the Army. Medicine, the Professions and Social Mobility in the British Isles 1790– 1850*, Oxford, 2006.

Arvers, P. *Historique du 82e regiment d'infanterie de ligne et du 7e regiment d'infanterie légère 1684–1876*, Paris, 1876.

Bamford, A., *Sickness, Suffering, and the Sword. The British Regiment on Campaign 1808–1815*, Norman, 2013.

Blanco, R.L., *Wellington's Surgeon General: Sir James McGrigor*, Durham, 1974.

Boyer-Peyreleau, Col E.E., *Les Antilles Françaises particulièrement la Guadeloupe*, 3 Vols., Paris, 1826.

Brownrigg, B., *The Life and Letters of Sir John Moore*, Oxford, 1923.

Brumwell, S.B., *Redcoats. The British Soldier and War in the Americas 1755–1763*, Cambridge, 2002.

Buckley, R.N., *The Destruction of the British Army in the West Indies 1793–1815: A Medical History*, Journal of the Society for Army Historical Research (1978), Vol. 56, pp. 79–92.

Buckley, R.N., *Slaves in Redcoats. The British West India Regiments 1795–1815*, New Haven, 1979.

Buckley, R.N., *The British Army in the West Indies. Society and Military in the Revolutionary Age*, Gainesville, 1988.

Burnham, R. and McGuigan, R., *The British Army against Napoleon*, Barnsley, 2010.

Cantlie, Lt Gen Sir N., *A History of the Army Medical Department*, Vol. I, Edinburgh, 1974.

Cary, A.D.L., *Regimental Records of the Royal Welch Fusiliers*, London, 1921.

Chartrand, R., *British Forces in the West Indies 1793–1815*, Oxford, 1996.

Chartrand, R., *Napoleon's Overseas Army*, London, 1989.

Condon, M.E., *Living Conditions on Board Troopships during the War against Revolutionary France 1793–1802*, Journal of the Society for Army Historical Research (1971), Vol. 49, pp. 14–19.

Coss, E.J., *All For The King's Shilling. The British Soldier under Wellington 1808–1814*, Norman, 2010.

Devas, R.P., *The Island of Grenada (1650–1950)*, Grenada, 1964.

Dallas, R.C., *The History of the Maroons*, 2 Vols., London, 1803.

Duffy, M., *Soldiers, Sugar and Seapower. The British Expeditions to the West Indies and the War against Revolutionary France*, Oxford, 1987.

Duffy, M., *The Caribbean Campaigns of the British Army 1793–1801*, in Guy, A.J., *The Road to Waterloo*, London, 1990.

Durey, M., *White Slaves: Irish Rebel Prisoners and the British Army in the West Indies 1799–1804*, Journal of the Society for Army Historical Research (2002), Vol. 80, pp. 296–312.

Edwards, B., *The History Civil and Commercial of the British Colonies in the West Indies*, 5 Vols., London, 1819.

Ellis, A.B., *The History of the First West India Regiment*, 2010.

Elting, J. R., *Swords around a Throne. Napoleon's Grande Armée*, London, 1988.

Everard, Maj H., *History of Thomas Farrington's Regiment subsequently designated the 29th (Worcestershire) Foot 1694 to 1891*, Worcester, 1891.

Forrest, A., *Soldiers of the French Revolution*, Durham, 1990.

Fortescue, Hon. J.W., *A History of the British Army*, Vols. IV, V, VII, London, 1915.

Fraser, L.M., *History of Trinidad*, London, 1971.

Fuller, Col J.F.C., *British Light Infantry in the Eighteenth Century*, London, 1925.

Gasper, D.B. and Geggus, P.G., *A Turbulent Time. The French Revolution and the Greater Caribbean*, Bloomington, 1997.

Gates, D., *The British Light infantry Arm c. 1790–1815*, London, 1987.

Geggus, D., *Slavery, War, and Revolution: The British Occupation of Saint Domingue 1793–1798*, Oxford, 1982.

Geggus, D., *Yellow Fever in the 1790s: The British Army in Occupied Saint Domingue*, Medical History (1979), Vol. 23, pp. 38–58.

Glover, R., *Peninsular Preparation. The Reform of the British Army 1795–1809*, Cambridge, 1963.

Graves, D.E., *Dragon Rampant. The Royal Welch Fusiliers at War 1793–1815*, London, 2010.

Griffith, P., *The Art of War in Revolutionary France 1789–1802*, London, 1998.

Haggard, D., *The Last Fight for Napoleon*, Journal of the Society for Army Historical Research (1935), Vol. 14, pp. 231–2.

Hall, C.D., *British Strategy in the Napoleonic War 1803–15*, Manchester, 1999.

Haythornthwaite, P.J., *The Armies of Wellington*, London, 1994.

Houlding, J.A., *Fit for Service. The Training of the British Army 1715–1795*, Oxford, 1981.

Howard, M.R., *Medical Aspects of Sir John Moore's Corunna Campaign 1808–1809*, Journal of the Royal Society of Medicine (1991), Vol. 84, pp. 299–302.

Howard, M. R., *Red Jackets and Red Noses. Alcohol and the British Napoleonic Soldier*, Journal of the Royal Society of Medicine (2000), Vol. 93, pp. 38–41.

Howard, M.R., *Walcheren 1809. The Scandalous Destruction of a British Army*, Barnsley, 2012.

Howard, M.R., *Wellington's Doctors. The British Army Medical Services in the Napoleonic Wars*, Staplehurst, 2002.

Ingram, K.E., *Manuscript Sources for the History of the West Indies*, Barbados, 2000.

James, W.M., *The Naval History of Great Britain during the French Revolutionary and Napoleonic Wars*, Vol. I, London, 2003.

Jane, C.W.E., *Shirley Heights. The Story of the Redcoats in Antigua*, Antigua, 1982.

Knight, R., *Britain Against Napoleon. The Organisation of Victory 1793–1815*, London, 2013.

Kup, A.P., *Alexander Lindsay 6th Earl of Balcarres, Lieutenant Governor of Jamaica 1794–1801*, Bulletin of the John Rylands Library (1975), Vol. 57, pp. 327–365.

Laurence, K.O., *Tobago in Wartime 1793–1815*, Kingston, 1995.

Lloyd, C. and Coulter, J.S., *Medicine and the Navy 1200–1900*, Vol. III, Edinburgh, 1961.

Lunt, J.D., *Scarlet Lancer*, London, 1964.

Lynn, J.A., *The Bayonets of the Republic*, Urbana, 1984.

MacArthur, R., *The British Army Establishment during the Napoleonic Wars Part I – Background and Infantry*, Journal of the Society for Army Historical Research (2009), Vol. 87, pp. 150–172.

Mackesy, P., *British Victory in Egypt 1801*, London, 1995.

Muir, R., *Britain and the Defeat of Napoleon 1807–1815*, New Haven, 1996.

Muir, R., *Tactics and the Experience of Battle in the Age of Napoleon*, New Haven, 1998.

Muir, R., *Wellington. The Path to Victory 1769–1814*, New Haven, 2013.

Myatt, F., *Peninsular General. Thomas Picton 1758–1815*, Newton Abbot, 1980.

Nelson, P.D., *Sir Charles Grey, First Earl Grey. Royal Soldier, Family Patriarch*, Madison, 1996.

Oman, Carola, *Sir John Moore*, London, 1953.

Ott, T., *The Haitian Revolution 1789–1804*, Knoxville, 1973.

Pearse, Col H.W., *History of the East Surrey Regiment*, London, 1916.

Poyen, H., *Les Guerres des Antilles de 1793 à 1815*, Paris, 1896.

Robinson, C., *The Fighting Maroons of Jamaica*, Jamaica, 1969.

Ros, M., *Night of Fire. The Black Napoleon and the Fight for Haiti*, New York, 1994.

Saintoyant, J.F., *La Colonisation Française pendant la Période Napoléonienne 1799–1815*, Paris, 1931.

Sandeau, J., *Une catastrophie épidémiologique: la fièvre jaune à Saint-Domingue (1802–1803)*, Nantes, 2009.

Schofield, K., *The Highland Furies. The Black Watch 1739–1899*, London, 2012.

Smith, V.T.C., *Fire and Brimstone. The Story of the Brimstone Hill Fortress, St Kitts, West Indies, 1690–1853*, St Kitts, 1992.

Southey, Capt T., *Chronological History of the West Indies*, Vol. III, London, 1827.

Spring, M.H., *With Zeal and With Bayonets Only. The British Army on Campaign in North America 1775–1783*, Norman, 2010.

Steppler, G.A., *The British Army on the Eve of War*, in Guy, A.J., *The Road to Waterloo*, London, 1990.

Taylor, C., *The Black Carib Wars*, Oxford, 2012.

The New Cambridge Modern History, Vol. IX, War and Peace in an Age of Upheaval (ed. Crawley, C.W.), Cambridge, 1975.

Thoumine, R.H., *Scientific Soldier. A Life of General Le Marchant 1766–1812*, London, 1968.

Verner, Col W., *History and Campaigns of the Rifle Brigade*, 2 Vols., London, 1919.

Index

Colonial troops in British Service:
European, 8–18, 109; *Bouillé's
Uhlans Britanniques*, 9–10, 16;
*Hompesch's Hussars/Light
Infantry*, 9–10, 88, 106; *La Tours
Royal Étranger*, 9; *Lowenstein's
Chasseurs/Legion*, 9–10, 97,
105–6, 108 ; *Royal Foreign
Artillery*, 9; *York Hussars*, 9, 142;
York Light Infantry Volunteers, 9,
120, 127, 131; *Royal York Rangers*,
122, 131–5; *Royal West India
Rangers*, 135; *York Chasseurs*, 135
West Indian, 15–16, 41*; Dessource's
Volunteers/Légion,* 15, 22, 35, 111,
113; *Dillon's Regiment*, 15, 36;
Jean Kina's Corps, 15–16, 39;
*Légion Britannique de Saint
Domingue*, 15–16, 41; *Légion de la
Grand Anse (Montalembert's)*, 15,
88; *Légion d'York*, 15; *Prince
Edward's Black Chasseurs*, 110
Colonial troops in French service,
20–1; *Bataillon Antilles*, 67, 100
Colonists, relationship with British
army, 57–8, 78, 80, 123
Colville, Captain Charles, 15
Colville, Lieutenant George, 52
Coote, Lieutenant Colonel Eyre, 50,
125
Cornwallis, Lord, 114
Corruption, 16
Courts-martial, 160–1
Craddock, Lieutenant Colonel, 49
Crossing the line ceremony, 149–50
Curaçao, 95; capture of 1800, 113;
failed naval attack on 1804, 123
Cuyler, Major General Cornelius,
31–3, 109

Dallas, Robert, 24, 83
Danish troops in West Indies, 26

Demerara, 181
Denmark, 26, 126
Depestre, Julien, 111
Desaix, Fort, 127
Desertion, 160–1, 179
Dessource, Claude Bruno, 15
Dieudonné, Pierre, 85–7
Dillon, Midshipman William, 93,
100, 102, 138, 175
Disease, 199–205; mortality from,
42, 65–6, 199–200, 202; yellow
fever, 42, 200–3; attempts to
prevent, 145–6, 207–8;
seasickness, 144–5; alcohol as
cause of, 167–8, 204; tetanus, 195;
malaria, 202; dysentery, 203–4;
heatstroke, 204; mental disorders,
204; scurvy, 204; contemporary
views on, 206–7; treatment of,
208–9
Dogs, Spanish, 84
Dominica, 181; repelled invasion of
1795, 79–80; mutiny of 8th West
India Regiment, 116–17; failed
French attack on 1805, 123–5
Douglas, Major General Robert, 135
Drummond, Lieutenant Colonel
James, 58–9, 63, 101
Duckworth, Commodore John, 88,
123
Duffy, Michael, 42
Dundas, Colonel David, 4
Dundas, Colonel Francis, 60
Dundas, Major General Thomas, 47,
49, 58, 160, 214
Dundas, Secretary of State Henry, 7;
views on West Indies, 30, 35, 44,
70, 86, 106, 114
Durey, Michael, 5, 200
Durham, Admiral Sir Charles, 135
Dutch troops in West Indies, 26, 122,
133